Spenser and Virgil

The Manchester Spenser

The Manchester Spenser is a monograph and text series devoted to historical and textual approaches to Edmund Spenser – to his life, times, places, works and contemporaries.

A growing body of work in Spenser and Renaissance studies, fresh with confidence and curiosity and based on solid historical research, is being written in response to a general sense that our ability to interpret texts is becoming limited without the excavation of further knowledge. So the importance of research in nearby disciplines is quickly being recognised, and interest renewed: history, archaeology, religious or theological history, book history, translation, lexicography, commentary and glossary – these require treatment for and by students of Spenser.

The Manchester Spenser, to feed, foster and build on these refreshed attitudes, aims to publish reference tools, critical, historical, biographical and archaeological monographs on or related to Spenser, from several disciplines, and to publish editions of primary sources and classroom texts of a more wide-ranging scope.

The Manchester Spenser consists of work with stamina, high standards of scholarship and research, adroit handling of evidence, rigour of argument, exposition and documentation.

The series will encourage and assist research into, and develop the readership of, one of the richest and most complex writers of the early modern period.

General Editor J.B. Lethbridge
Editorial Board Helen Cooper, Thomas Herron, Carol V. Kaske, James C. Nohrnberg & Brian Vickers

Also available

Literary Ralegh and visual Ralegh   Christopher M. Armitage (ed.)

A Concordance to the Rhymes of The Faerie Queene—Richard Danson Brown & J. B. Lethbridge

A Supplement of the Faery Queene: By Ralph Knevet   Christopher Burlinson & Andrew Zurcher (eds)

Monsters and the poetic imagination in Edmund Spenser's The Faerie Queene: *'Most ugly shapes and horrible aspects'*   Maik Goth

Celebrating Mutabilitie: Essays on Edmund Spenser's Mutabilitie Cantos
Jane Grogan (ed.)

Castles and Colonists: An archaeology of Elizabethan Ireland   Eric Klingelhofer

Shakespeare and Spenser: Attractive opposites   J.B. Lethbridge (ed.)

A Fig for Fortune: By Anthony Copley   Susannah Monta Brietz

Renaissance erotic romance: Philhellene Protestantism,
Renaissance translation and English literary politics   Victor Skretkowicz

God's only daughter: Spenser's Una as the invisible Church—Kathryn Walls

Spenser and Virgil

The pastoral poems

SYRITHE PUGH

Manchester University Press

Copyright © Syrithe Pugh 2016

The right of Syrithe Pugh to be identified as the author of this work has been asserted by her in accordance with the Copyright, Designs and Patents Act 1988.

Published by Manchester University Press
Altrincham Street, Manchester M1 7JA, UK
www.manchesteruniversitypress.co.uk

British Library Cataloguing-in-Publication Data is available

ISBN 978 1 5261 0117 4 hardback
ISBN 978 1 5261 1988 9 paperback

First published by Manchester University Press in hardback 2016

This edition published 2020

The publisher has no responsibility for the persistence or accuracy of URLs for any external or third-party internet websites referred to in this book, and does not guarantee that any content on such websites is, or will remain, accurate or appropriate.

Typeset by Koinonia, Manchester

A few pages for my Onic,
who always greets his mother with a smile

Contents

Acknowledgements	*page* ix
Introduction	1
1 Intertextuality and allegory in Virgil's *Eclogues*	41
2 Virgilian negotiations in *The Shepheardes Calender*	82
3 Virgilian structure in *The Shepheardes Calender*	159
4 Reshaping the Virgilian *cursus*: pastoral vocation in 'Astrophel'	182
5 Reimagining the pastoral muse in 'Colin Clouts Come Home Againe'	222
Bibliography	302
Index of works and passages	318
General index	328

Acknowledgements

The seeds of the idea that I should one day have to write a book about Spenser and Virgil were first planted by the judicious critical remarks of Richard McCabe and Heather James on my first book, *Spenser and Ovid*. After lying dormant for several years, they were coaxed towards the light by Julian Lethbridge, that good gardener, to whom I am grateful not only for his tireless support and encouragement in this project but also (as all Spenserians are) for creating in the Manchester Spenser Series an environment so conducive to the flourishing of Spenser studies generally.

Portions of my argument have been delivered orally as conference papers, at two events hosted by the Herbert Grierson Centre at the University of Aberdeen (a workshop on Satire in 2014, and an interdisciplinary symposium *Reviving the Dead: Classical and Renaissance Intertextuality* in May 2015) and at the conference of the International Spenser Society held in June 2015 in Dublin. My thanks to the participants and organizers of these events, where I benefited enormously from the stimulating conversation and generous encouragement of friends both old and new: they are too numerous to name, but I want to mention particularly James Nohrnberg, Andrew Laird, Lynn Enterline, Stephen Hinds, Philip Hardie, Jane Grogan, Jean Brink, Susanne Wofford, Sarah Van Der Laan, David Adkins, Linda Gregerson, Richard Danson Brown, Paul Hecht and Clare Carroll. I am also indebted to Lynn Enterline, James Nohrnberg, David Adkins and Tim Markey for allowing me to see unpublished work, to Samantha Newington for conversations about Theocritus, to Philip Hardie for generously going through large portions of the manuscript and saving me from many infelicities, and to the anonymous reader for the press for helpful comments on the whole. (I am of course entirely to blame for whatever remains unregenerate in the text.)

The staff at Manchester University Press has been very accommodating, particularly about length (in a book about little books, too). I should also like to thank the staff of the university library and of the Kilau coffee shop in Aberdeen, who have fuelled the whole process with books and tea. Last but not least, I am profoundly grateful to my family for their unending patience and support.

Introduction

Fundamental to this book is the claim that Spenser's poetry is filled with imitation of and allusion to the poems of Virgil, and that this is an important part of how it constructs its meaning – it is intended to be perceived and interpreted. But this is not quite what Spenser's contemporaries and those who lived soon after him meant when they compared him to Virgil, as they often did. They were responding chiefly to one, relatively simple and obvious, fact about his published work: that it resembled Virgil's by beginning with pastoral and by including an epic praising his ruler, Queen Elizabeth.[1] In pointing this out their chief aim was not to provoke the kind of detailed intertextual study this book attempts, but to assign to Spenser the same kind of monumental status at the pinnacle of English vernacular literature which Virgil had enjoyed in relation to Roman literature since classical times, and still enjoyed in the Renaissance – to claim for him a literary authority analogous to and closely implicated in the political authority of the Queen and the hierarchical structure of the society she ruled over, reflecting the time-honoured perception of Virgil's relation to Augustus and imperial Rome. When Spenser and Virgil are mentioned in the same breath by modern critics, as they frequently are, it is almost always in response to the same underlying similarity in their careers – the progression from pastoral to epic – and with a similar concern either to indicate or to scrutinize his position of cultural authority and its relation to Elizabeth's authority as

---

1 *The Shepheardes Calender* was Spenser's first published work as sole author, but he had earlier provided anonymous translations from Petrarch and Du Bellay for Van der Noodt's *Theatre for Worldlings*, which he would later rework and own in the *Complaints* volume. For early comparisons of Spenser to Virgil, see R. M. Cummings, *Spenser: The Critical Heritage* (London: Routledge & Kegan Paul, 1971), *s.v.* 'Virgil'.

monarch.² These ideas are indeed an important part of the process of interpretation which Spenser wants to elicit from his reader, though they are only its beginning. We need to examine them more closely before we embark on our sustained and detailed reading.

Virgil owed his canonical status to the authorizing institutions of his own society, becoming an instant classic, doubtless not only because of his popularity or because of admiration for his poetic skill (though these are also well attested) but also because his works were perceived to foster a set of social values and beliefs beneficial to the state and its newly imperial regime.³ The *Eclogues* and *Georgics* were the subjects of lectures as early as 26 BCE; the *Aeneid* joined them when it was published (in its allegedly unfinished state) after his death in 19 BCE, and Quintilian recommends them as school-texts in the *Institutes*.⁴ His continuing canonical status in sixteenth-century England can also be measured by his role in pedagogy, with the *Eclogues*, *Georgics* and *Aeneid* forming part of the normal grammar-school curriculum.⁵

---

2 For modern considerations of Spenser's 'Virgilian career', see Richard Helgerson, 'The New Poet Presents Himself: Spenser and the Idea of a Literary Career', *PMLA* 93 (1978), 893–911, and *Self-Crowned Laureates: Jonson, Spenser, Milton* (Berkeley: University of California Press, 1983); Richard Neuse, 'Milton and Spenser: The Virgilian Triad Revisited', *ELH* 45 (1978), 606–39; David Lee Miller, 'Authorship, Anonymity, and *The Shepheardes Calender*', *MLQ* (1979), 219–36; Louis Adrian Montrose, '"The Perfecte Paterne of a Poete": The Poetics of Courtship in *The Shepheardes Calender*', *Texas Studies in Literature and Language* 21 (1979), 34–67; Patrick Cheney, *Spenser's Famous Flight: A Renaissance Idea of a Literary Career* (Toronto: University of Toronto Press, 1997), and 'Spenser's Pastorals', in Andrew Hadfield (ed.), *The Cambridge Companion to Spenser* (Cambridge: Cambridge University Press, 2001), pp. 79–105; Michael L. Donnelly, 'The Life of Vergil and the Aspirations of the "New Poet"', *Spenser Studies* 17 (2003), 1–35; David Scott Wilson-Okamura, 'Problems in the Virgilian Career', *Spenser Studies* 26 (2011), 1–30, and *Spenser's International Style* (Cambridge: Cambridge University Press, 2013), pp. 20–4.
3 On Virgil's reception in antiquity, see R. J. Tarrant, 'Aspects of Virgil's Reception in Antiquity', in Charles Martindale (ed.), *Cambridge Companion to Virgil* (Cambridge: Cambridge University Press, 1997), pp. 56–72; R. F. Thomas, *Virgil and the Augustan Reception* (Cambridge: Cambridge University Press, 2001).
4 Quintilian, *Institutes* 1.8.5 and 12.11.26. For Virgil as school text in Rome, see N. M. Horsfall, 'Virgil's Impact at Rome: The Non-literary Evidence', in N. M. Horsfall (ed.), *A Companion to the Study of Virgil* (Leiden: Brill, 1995), pp. 249–56; Stanley F. Bonner, *Education in Ancient Rome: From the Elder Cato to the Younger Pliny* (Abingdon: Routledge, 2012), pp. 213–14. Jean-Michel Hulls, 'Recasting the Master: Further Faces of Virgil in Imperial Rome', *Proceedings of the Virgil Society* 27 (2011), 156–84, explores how Statius plays with Virgil's monumental cultural status with particular reference to his use in pedagogy.
5 The *Georgics* were not always included. See T. W. Baldwin, *William Shakespere's Small Latine and Lesse Greeke*, 2 vols (Urbana: University of Illinois Press, 1944), I.305–6, on Virgil in curricula under Edward VI, the time at which Baldwin sees the curriculum as attaining its definitive form; Margaret Tudeau-Clayton, *Jonson, Shakespeare and Early*

The curricula of English grammar schools centred on the study of Roman authors because their prime purpose was to impart to schoolboys fluency in the Latin language (in which legal and official state business was still principally conducted), and rhetorical skill, as preparation for careers in the legal or ecclesiastical professions or in government service. Lessons revolved around the practices of 'double translation' (translating passages out of and then back into Latin) and imitation, so that rhetorical and poetic skills were acquired along with understanding of Latin, and schoolboys were taught to imitate and emulate their Roman literary models. Virgil was particularly attractive to such a project, however, because he was considered a shining example of moral as well as of linguistic and stylistic 'purity': as Tudeau-Clayton observes, he was treated both 'as formal model (a *norma loquendi*) and ... as moral guide (a *norma vivendi*)'.[6] The virtuous example offered by the hero of the *Aeneid* (read in the fifth form as the culminating achievement of the pupil's acquisition of Latin) consists centrally in his decision to reject *amor* (his love for Dido) in favour of *Roma* (his duty to the destiny of the state he will found in Italy), obeying the gods' command. The same turn from *Amor* to *Roma* can be charted in the progress of Virgil across his works, which were studied in the order they were written. The *Eclogues*, in keeping with the Greek bucolic tradition Virgil inherited, are largely concerned with love, and associated with youthful play. The didactic *Georgics* proclaim their practical social usefulness, while the *Aeneid* both celebrates and serves the Roman state and its emperor Augustus, whose rule is presented as Rome's divinely ordained destiny. There was, as Lynn Enterline puts it, a clear 'resonance between humanist admiration for Vergil's theme of civic duty and the school's announced goal of fashioning a gentleman for the good of the realm'.[7] The shape of Virgil's career itself reflects a process of growth towards this ideal.

The epic's explicit foregrounding of this theme was of chief importance, but the earlier works provided an induction peculiarly amenable to humanist pedagogy, with its emphasis on delightful learning. The

---

Modern Virgil (Cambridge: Cambridge University Press, 1998), pp. 44–77, on the ideological motivations of study of Virgil in the grammar schools. A recent study of the use of Virgil in Tudor grammar schools argues that Virgil composed with self-conscious awareness of contemporary use of his poems as school texts, and thematized it in a 'pedagogical subplot', to which humanist educators responded (Andrew Wallace, *The Poetics of Pedagogy in Renaissance England* (Oxford: Oxford University Press, 2010), p. 122).

6 Tudeau-Clayton, *Jonson, Shakespeare and Early Modern Virgil*, p. 47.
7 Lynn Enterline, *Shakespeare's Schoolroom: Rhetoric, Discipline, Emotion* (Philadelphia: University of Pennsylvania Press, 2011), p. 77.

Eclogues, usually the first Latin texts studied by schoolboys after the basics of grammar had been taught (sometimes in connection with the moralizing neo-Latin eclogues of Baptista Mantuan), were appropriate not only because their brevity made them relatively easy but also because their self-proclaimed playfulness and their theme of love made them 'fun'. In a chapter on 'What order shulde be in lernynge, and which autours shulde be fyrste redde' in the *The Book named the Gouernour* (1531) – a work which shares the assumptions and goals of the public schools – Elyot recommends Homer above all others, for his 'discipline of armes', his 'instructions for polytike gouernaunce' and his 'laude of noble princis': epic, with its public themes, is the principal *desideratum* of the Tudor boy's education.[8] But 'for as moche as the sayd warkes be very longe' (not to mention in Greek – a rarer commodity in the sixteenth century, and taught only after Latin in those grammar schools where it was taught at all, as it was in the school Spenser attended), he recommends Virgil as respite, treating the three works in order. 'No warke soo nyghe approcheth to the commune dalyance & maners of chyldren' as the *Eclogues*, '& the praty controuersies of the simple shepeherdes therin conteyned, wonderfully reioyceth the chylde that hereth it wel declared, as I know by mine own experience.'[9] The *Georgics* are advocated for their appeal to those (presumably slightly older) boys interested in husbandry, horse-breeding or astronomy.[10] Finally the *Aeneid* will teach the boy to 'abhorre tyrany, fraude, & auarice' and to admire 'noble princis and capitaynes' for 'aduauncing the publyke weales of theyr countryes', and will 'minister to hym audacytie, valiaunt courage and polycie, to take and susteyne noble enterprises.'[11] As the boy progresses from the *Eclogues*, through the *Georgics* to the *Aeneid*, youthful delight in play gives way gradually to interest in practical skills and finally to admiration and emulation of the virtues of great men, with increasing mastery of his own desires and dedication to the 'publyke weale'.

Elyot is describing the education of a future 'gouernour', at the top of the social hierarchy, but the grammar schools similarly served a social

---

8 Thomas Elyot, *The boke named the Gouernour* ([London]: Thomas Berthelet, 1537), Dvv.
9 Elyot, *Gouernor*, Dviv.
10 The *Georgics* would already furnish more political lessons, too: earlier in the treatise, Elyot has used the bees of the fourth *Georgic* to illustrate the necessity of monarchy, a commonplace of Renaissance discourse. (*Gouernor*, Aviiv to Aviiir). Baldwin remarks 'Probably no Elizabethan schoolboy ever escaped those bees' (*William Shakespere's Small Latine and Lesse Greeke*, 1.331).
11 Elyot, *Gouernor*, Dviiv.

elite: even if many of the boys who attended grammar schools came from poor backgrounds (and there was often generous provision for such students), they were nevertheless being prepared to take up high positions in society. Those who went on, as Spenser did, to attend one of the universities – where they continued to study Virgil – acquired the coveted status of 'gentleman' regardless of their background. It was the eloquence acquired through their study of Virgil that fitted them to take up these positions: as Tudeau-Clayton argues,

> As paradigmatic example of a normative, 'proper Language', constituting at once a form of property and power, Virgil may ... be described as a figure of the 'Father tongue', the Language used by the few with education, property, wealth and power, whose use of these discourses served to underwrite their difference and power.[12]

What Tudeau-Clayton calls the 'Father tongue' here is not merely Latin but the set of 'formal and moral discourses' embodied by Virgil as a school text, 'which served doubly to reproduce the hierarchy between high and low born, gentleman and commoner'.[13] This social hierarchy was also inscribed within Virgil's texts, along with the ideal of civic duty. Virgil's three works treated three social groupings in ascending social order, from the lowly herdsmen of the *Eclogues*, to the farmers of the *Georgics*, to the kings of the *Aeneid*, and they were often adduced in the Renaissance in relation to the division of style into low, middle and high. Central to the rhetorical skills Tudor schoolboys were expected to acquire from their study of his texts was the principle of decorum, a knowledge of what style and kind of language is appropriate, not only on specific occasions or for specific purposes but also in relation to persons of different rank. In *The Art of English Poesy* – a work which teaches how to obtain a high social position as much, and almost as explicitly, as it teaches poetic eloquence – Elyot's nephew George Puttenham insists that

> to have the style decent and comely, it behooveth the maker or poet to follow the nature of his subject; that is, if his matter be high and lofty, that the style be so too; if mean, the style also be mean; if base, the style humble and base accordingly.

High subjects, he explains, are 'divine things' and 'noble gests and great fortunes of princes'; mean matters 'concern mean men', by which he means 'the civiler and better sort' such as 'lawyers, gentlemen, and merchants';

---

12 Tudeau-Clayton, *Jonson, Shakespeare and Early Modern Virgil*, p. 37.
13 Tudeau-Clayton, *Jonson, Shakespeare and Early Modern Virgil*, p. 10.

while 'base and low matters be the doings of the common artificer, servingman, yeoman, groom, husbandman, day-laborer, sailor, shepherd, swineherd, and such like of homely calling, degree, and bringing up'. These three social 'degrees' 'require to be set forth ... every one in his degree and decency', so that 'all eclogues and pastoral poems' should be 'in the low and base style'.[14] Virgil's three works serendipitously align with this tripartite division of styles and of social degree. Even Virgil's apparent deviations can serve to illustrate Puttenham's rule: he notes the 'somewhat swelling style' of the fourth eclogue approvingly as suitable to its subject, heralding 'the birth of Marcellus, heir apparent to the Emperor Augustus'. So strong is the connection between 'decent' style, social degree and the art of prince-pleasing for Puttenham that he imagines he has 'read ... somewhere' that Octavian, believing the eclogue to have written 'to the honor of Pollio, a citizen of Rome and of no great nobility', 'misliked' its 'swelling style' as 'nothing decent nor proportionable to Pollio's fortunes and calling'.[15] There is no known source for this story; it seems to have been generated in Puttenham's subconscious by the 'Father tongue' he had learned at school, with its minute and obsessive attention to distinctions of social rank.

Commenting on John Brinsley's recommendations for successive imitation of Virgil's three works in his pedagogical handbook *Ludus Literarius* (1612), Tudeau-Clayton describes it as 'an ideal, hierarchically organised career through the school which retraces the "career" of Virgil from *humilis* (the "lowest kind"), through *medius* ("something a loftier") to *grandiloquus* ("the stateliest kind"), a career assiduously followed by Spenser, amongst others'.[16] In fact, Spenser does not follow this career as 'assiduously' as he himself leads his readers to expect, but the basic point is useful: in his allusions to and variations on the Virgilian career, Spenser is evoking the process of linguistic, literary and ideological induction he and his educated male readers have gone through in grammar school, and with it the values and attitude to authority internalized by such products of the system as Puttenham.[17]

---

14 *The Art of English Poesy by George Puttenham: A Critical Edition*, ed. Frank Whigham and Wayne A. Rebhorn (Ithaca: Cornell University Press, 2007), pp. 234, 237 (Book 3, chapters 5–6).
15 Puttenham, *Art of English Poesy*, p. 235.
16 Tudeau-Clayton, *Jonson, Shakespeare and Early Modern Virgil*, p. 54.
17 For Enterline, the authors of Elizabethan epyllia provide examples of schoolboys not so successfully inculcated (her main focus being on gender roles); Tudeau-Clayton analogously finds in Shakespeare a reaction against and sceptical critique of the values inscribed in Virgil as a school text, exemplifying what she calls 'the Protestant turn' in Elizabethan and Jacobean thought towards a questioning of authority. My analysis of

I say that Spenser 'alludes to' and produces 'variations on' the Virgilian career, because, as critics have often pointed out, Spenser's career does not map neatly on to it. The progression from eclogue book in *The Shepheardes Calender* to dynastic epic in *The Faerie Queene* is recognizably Virgilian, and as we shall see Spenser is at pains to point this out to his reader. But there is no work which corresponds clearly to Virgil's middle stage, the *Georgics* – an omission which some try to explain by arguing that 'georgic poetry' is replaced in Spenser's career by another genre, such as epithalamion,[18] others by arguing that 'georgic' is 'infolded' into Spenser's pastoral or epic poems.[19] Moreover, Spenser doesn't *restrict* himself to Virgilian genres. There is nothing Virgilian about the *Amoretti and Epithalamium* volume of 1595 or the *Fowre Hymnes* of 1596.[20] The *Complaints* volume of 1591 is a more ambiguous case.[21] Innovative and difficult to define, it is perhaps best described as a collection of experiments adapting medieval complaint poetry to Tudor times, but it includes Spenser's only direct translation of a Virgil poem in *Virgils Gnat*. The *Culex* was included in Renaissance editions of Virgil, as one of a number of poems then usually described as his juvenilia, though their authorship had already been cast in doubt: modern scholars reject these works and refer to them collectively as the *Appendix Virgiliana*. Containing within itself a rehearsal in miniature of the familiar triadic Virgilian career, it is at once a complaint poem, a beast fable, and an epyllion – all genres represented in other poems in the volume. By including his translation here, Spenser thus finds in 'Virgil' other possible generic alignments which turn aside from the relentless upward trajectory traced by the three more canonical works.[22] I shall have more to say about the poem and

Spenser in relation to Virgil could be said to reflect Tudeau-Clayton's 'Protestant turn', and involves Spenser's response to the Elizabethan vogue for epyllion.
18 Neuse, 'Virgilian Triad'.
19 Jane Tylus, 'Spenser, Virgil, and the Politics of Poetic Labour', *ELH* 55 (1988), 53–77; Anthony Low, *The Georgic Revolution* (Princeton: Princeton University Press, 1985), ch. 2.
20 On the supplementation of Virgil and the Virgilian genres with other models and genres in Spenser's career, see Cheney, *Famous Flight*, pp. 507; Syrithe Pugh, *Spenser and Ovid* (Aldershot: Ashgate, 2005), pp. 1–2, 58–69; Rebecca Helfer, *Spenser's Ruins and the Art of Recollection* (Toronto: University of Toronto Press, 2012), pp. 14–25.
21 On the *Complaints* volume as complicating the idea of Spenser's Virgilian career, see Richard Rambuss, *Spenser's Secret Career* (Cambridge: Cambridge University Press, 1993), p. 64, and Katherine A. Craik, 'Spenser's *Complaints* and the New Poet', *Huntington Library Quarterly* 64 (2001), 63–79; Helgerson, *Self-Crowned Laureates*, pp. 82–9, sees it as a simple interruption.
22 On the rehearsal of the triad of genres within the *Culex*, see G. Most, 'The Virgilian *Culex*', in Michael Whitby, Philip Hardie and Mary Whitby (eds), *Homo Viator: Classical Essays for John Bramble* (Bristol: Bristol Classical Press, 1987), pp. 199–209, at 208–9.

the volume below. Finally, and most significantly for my purposes, where Virgil never writes another explicitly pastoral poem after the end of the *Eclogues*, Spenser returns to pastoral *after* 'ascending' to epic, when he publishes a second pastoral volume, *Colin Clouts Come Home Againe*, in 1595.[23] This is the most marked and pointed deviation from the Virgilian path, because it is conducted in terms of recognizably Virgilian genres, throwing the Virgilian career into reverse.[24] It is in terms of these two genres – pastoral and epic – that Spenser provokes his reader to reflect on the relation between his career and Virgil's. Both of Spenser's pastoral volumes are much more deeply and intricately involved with the model of Virgil's eclogue book than has previously been recognized, and we must study their intertextual engagement with Virgilian pastoral with care and sustained concentration if we are to understand them properly. What is fundamentally at stake in this engagement is Spenser's conception of his role as a poet in relation to society and to political power – a role he conceives and articulates in relation to and contradistinction from Virgil, and the political ends mapped out in the Virgilian career.

Spenser alludes to Virgil's career and invites us to compare it to his own with a series of clear signposts. Firstly, the mysterious editor E.K. (whose contributions may well have been written by Spenser himself), in *The Shepheardes Calender*'s prefatory epistle to Gabriel Harvey, draws attention to pastoral as a Virgilian career-opening for the New Poete,

> following the example of the best and most aunceint Poetes, which deuised this kind of wryting, being both so base for the matter, and homely for the manner, at the first to trye theyr habilities: and as young birdes, that be newly crept out of the nest, by little first to proue theyr tender wyngs, before they make a greater flyght ... So flew Virgile, as not yet well feeling his winges.[25]

On Spenser's response to the *Appendix Virgiliana* in *Virgils Gnat* and in the imitation of the *Ciris* in Book III of *The Faerie Queene*, see Colin Burrow's deeply suggestive paper, 'English Renaissance Readers and the *Appendix Vergiliana*', *Proceedings of the Virgil Society* 26 (2008), 1–16. Burrow emphasizes that the poems of the *Appendix* 'did something to straddle the perceived divide between epic and satire in this period', 'because they could not be fitted within a clear career structure or hierarchy of genres', and goes so far as to suggest that the *Complaints* volume represents an attempt 'to invent satirical and metamorphic juvenilia for Spenser: it is, as it were, an *Appendix Spenseriana*', constructed as an equivalent to the Virgilian appendix.

23 Cheney, 'Spenser's Pastorals', pp. 82, 97–100. Throughout, I shall use italics for *Colin Clouts Come Home Againe* as the title of the 1595 pastoral volume, and refer to the eclogue of that name as 'Colin Clouts Come Home Againe'.

24 The movement is repeated with the pastoral episode near the end of the 1596 *Faerie Queene*.

25 E.K., 'Epistle to Harvey', in Richard McCabe (ed.), *Edmund Spenser: The Shorter Poems*

The passage clearly hints at future epic. E.K. gives this only as one possible explanation for Spenser's choice of pastoral; a few lines earlier he has offered a quite different one, arguing that 'by the basenesse of the name' (Colin Clout, Spenser's pastoral persona) 'he chose rather to vnfold great matter of argument couertly, then professing it'. This does not detract from, but rather adds another dimension to, the analogy between Spenser and Virgil, however. His opening gloss on the *Januarye* eclogue explains 'Colin Cloute' as a name 'Vnder which ... this Poete secretly shadoweth himself, as sometime did Virgil vnder the name of Tityrus', and Puttenham uses similar terms to associate such Virgilian indirection with political caution:

> the poet devised the eclogue ... in rude speeches to insinuate and glance at greater matters, and such as perchance had not been safe to have been disclosed in any other sort, which may be perceived by the *Eclogues* of Vergil, in which are treated by figure matters of greater importance than the loves of Titirus and Corydon.[26]

The anonymously published *Calender* flaunts its political sensitivity and the risk of censorship and punishment its author runs (primarily in its opposition to the Queen's planned marriage to the Duc d'Alençon, veiled beneath a cautious allegory). In doing so, as we shall see below, he is drawing on an important aspect of Virgil's *Eclogues*, which is in tension with the ideological work performed by Virgil's developmental career and the uses to which it is put in Tudor pedagogy. The significance of the Virgilian career is already being complicated in this early signpost, but still it is a signpost, inviting us to consider the parallel between the poets.

A second prominent signpost occurs in the *October* eclogue, as Piers advises Cuddie (another persona of 'the authour selfe', as E.K. suggests in his gloss on 'Cuddie' at *October* 1),

> Abandon then the base and viler clowne,
> Lyft vp thy selfe out of the lowly dust:
> And sing of bloody Mars, of wars, of giusts.
> Turne thee to those, that weld the awful crowne.
> (*October* 37–40)

Cuddie recognizes this as a Virgilian programme, responding with a description of the 'three severall workes' of 'the Romish Tityrus' (the *Eclogues*, the *Georgics* and the *Aeneid*), but rejects it as impossible

---

(Harmondsworth: Penguin, 1999), p. 29. All quotations from the shorter poems will be from this edition.
26 Puttenham, *The Art of English Poesy*, pp. 127–8.

because of the corruption of the age, which, unlike Virgil's Rome, affords neither examples of virtue and heroism as subject matter for the poet nor a benign system of patronage to support him. Much is made in the *Calender* of Colin's similar inability or reluctance to proceed to epic, but Spenser himself will do just this, when he publishes the first instalment of *The Faerie Queene* in 1590. This too opens with a signpost emphasizing the parallel with Virgil's career:

> Lo I the man, whose Muse whilome did maske,
> As time her taught, in lowly Shepheards weeds,
> Am now enforst a far vnfitter taske,
> For trumpets sterne to chaunge mine Oaten reeds,
> And sing of Knights and Ladies gentle deeds ...
> (*The Faerie Queene* I.Proem.1)[27]

This imitates the lines which open the *Aeneid* in sixteenth-century editions:

> Ille ego qui quondam gracili modulatus avena
> carmen et egressus silvis vicina coegi
> ut quamvis avido parerent arva colono,
> gratum opus agricolis, at nunc horrentia Martis
> arma virumque cano ...

['I am he who once played my song on a slender oaten reed, and leaving the woods made the neighbouring fields fruitful for the eager settler, a work welcome to farmers, but now of bristling arms and the man I sing ...']

The lines are rejected by most commentators today, and do not appear in modern editions of the *Aeneid*, but would have been recognized by Spenser's contemporaries as the clear model underlying the opening of his epic, a reflection on the progress of his own career and its generic 'ascent' conspicuously recalling both Virgil's career and one of Virgil's distinctive passages of reflection upon it.[28]

This disputed *sphragis* (or personal 'signature') at the beginning of the *Aeneid* is one of several forward and backward glances by which Virgil links his three works and charts the progress of his career as a poet. These links are foregrounded so deliberately, at crucial moments in the three works, that one recent critic sees Virgil as inviting the reader to regard

---

27 Spenser, *The Faerie Queene*, ed. A. Hamilton (London: Longman, 1977). All subsequent quotations will be taken from this edition. Hamilton also prints the dubious opening lines of the *Aeneid*. (Translations from Latin will be my own throughout.)

28 Against the Virgilian authorship of the lines, see for instance Roland G. Austin, '*Ille ego qui quondam* ...', *Classical Quarterly* 18 (1968), 107–15; and for a defence of them, Peter Allan Hansen, '*Ille ego qui quondam* ... Once Again', *Classical Quarterly* 22 (1972), 139–49.

his entire *opus* as a single, unified whole, which she calls 'the Book of Virgil'. Virgil's progress through them creates a sense of a 'linear or teleological impulse', 'in which the three texts are united in the striving for the generic and political climax of the *Aeneid*'.[29] Firstly, the *Eclogues* contain several references to the possibility of composing heroic epic, which we could call anticipations or *recusatios* ('refusals' to compose epic, at least for now), depending on our perspective. The *recusatio* is a typical gesture of Callimachean poetics (developed in the Greek poetry of Callimachus and his colleagues and followers in third-century BCE Alexandria), with its aesthetic objections to heroic composition: these aesthetic ideals were dear to the loose circle of 'neoteric' Roman poets including Catullus in the mid-first century BCE, from which Virgil emerged, and the gesture is familiar from examples in poets like Propertius and Horace, who really meant it, and never did write epic.[30] But in Virgil (who of course would), these passages have more of an air of putting it off for now, even of pointedly anticipating it – especially, of course, when read with retrospective awareness of his later work.[31]

Eclogue 4 – which opens by announcing that it will stretch the bounds of pastoral (figured in the *humiles myricae*, 'humble tamarisks') to please a consul, with that decorous adjustment of style in deference to social rank which so impressed Puttenham – ends with one of these passages, as the poet anticipates a time when he will praise the mature deeds of the boy whose birth he now prophesies, in a song clearly intended to be understood as heroic epic which will outvie Orpheus, Linus and Pan. At the beginning of Eclogue 6 (so that the two passages frame the climactic Eclogue 5),[32] a proem in the voice of Tityrus reports that, after first playing with pastoral, he was preparing to sing of kings and battles (*reges et proelia*, 6.3), when

> Cynthius aurem
> vellit et admonuit 'pastorem, Tityre, pinguis
> pascere oportet ovis, deductum dicere carmen.'
>
> (*Eclogues* 6.3–5)

---

29 Elena Theodorakopoulos, 'Closure: The Book of Virgil', in Charles Martindale (ed.), *The Cambridge Companion to Virgil* (Cambridge: Cambridge University Press, 1997), pp. 155–65, at p. 156.
30 On the Callimachean principles of the neoterics and their uses of *recusatio*, see D. O. Ross, *Backgrounds to Augustan Poetry* (Cambridge: Cambridge University Press, 1975); Wendell Clausen, 'Callimachus and Roman Poetry', *Greek, Roman, and Byzantine Studies* 5 (1964), 181–96.
31 R. F. Thomas, 'From *recusatio* to Commitment', *Papers of the Liverpool Latin Seminar* 5 (1985), 61–71.
32 See Chapter 3 on the concentric structure of Virgil's eclogue-book.

['Apollo tweaked my ear and cautioned me "It befits a shepherd, Tityrus, to feed his sheep fat, but to sing a fine-spun song".]

The passage is closely modelled on a *recusatio* of epic from Callimachus' *Aetia*:

For, when I first placed a writing-tablet on my knees, Lycian Apollo said to me, 'Poet, feed your burnt offering to be as fat as possible, but your Muse, my friend, keep her slender.'[33]

It is on one level a clear statement of Virgil's Callimachean aesthetic ideals. *Deductum* is a polysemous word in Latin, but its meaning in relation to spinning (desirably) fine thread is clearly uppermost here, and it is used frequently by neoteric poets and those influenced by them as an equivalent to Callimachus' *leptos* ('husked'), to describe the aesthetic ideal of elegance and refinement. But Virgil's changes are also significant. Firstly, Callimachus' sacrificial victim becomes Tityrus' sheep, which must be fattened up simply because this is what shepherds do with their flocks – a witty adaptation to the pastoral subject matter of his book, but one which also throws emphasis on Tityrus' lowly social position, so different from Callimachus', who as librarian at Alexandria was also a priest of the Muses. Secondly, Apollo's tweaking Tityrus' ear has a decidedly comical effect. In the Callimachus passage, Apollo is a figure of inspiration, and his familiar address to the poet as 'friend' – though distinctive in its tone of intimacy where we might have expected religious awe – is a mark of honour, suggesting Callimachus' exceptional skill. But here Apollo becomes like a stern schoolmaster reproving Tityrus, the elderly shepherd of Eclogue 1 now presented as like a naughty schoolboy in need of discipline – perhaps because he is attempting, prematurely and presumptuously, something only his master is capable of.[34] (Apollo with his lyre is closely associated with epic poetry, and the epic anticipated at the end of Eclogue 4 was

---

33 Quoted and translated in Wendell Clausen (ed.), *A Commentary on Virgil Eclogues* (Oxford: Clarendon, 1994), p. 174. Spenser would not have known this fragment, which was not published until the twentieth century, though he could have known the similarly programmatic statement, rejecting the muddy river of heroic epic in favour of the pure springs of refined poetry, in Callimachus' *Hymn to Apollo* (ll. 105–12). Callimachus' *Hymns* were printed in the original Greek in Paris in 1549, and together with Latin translation, in the second edition of Stephanus, *Poetae Principes Heroici Carminis et alii nonnulli* (Geneva, 1577), and in *Callimachi Cyrenaei hymni, epigrammata et fragmenta, quae extant, et separatim, Moschi Syracusii, et Bionis Smyrnaei idyllia* (Antwerp: Plantin, 1584). He would certainly have known the neoteric *recusatios* of Catullus, Propertius, Horace and Ovid – some of which are invoked by way of comparison to this passage in the Plantin edition.

34 On the comic schoolroom overtones, see Eleanor Windsor Leach, *Vergil's Eclogues: Landscapes of Experience* (Ithaca: Cornell University Press, 1974), p. 251.

to outdo Linus even assisted by his father Apollo.) Later in Eclogue 6 we have the scene of Virgil's friend and contemporary Gallus, a neoteric and elegiac poet, led up on to Mount Helicon, where he is honoured by the Muses and Apollo's son Linus in a reworking of Hesiod's initiation at the beginning of the *Theogony*, and instructed to compose an etiological poem on the origins of the Grynean grove – a work in the middle range, higher than pastoral but lower than heroic epic, and still acceptably Callimachean.[35] Gallus here functions as a proxy for Virgil, and the passage anticipates Virgil's own progression to the *Georgics*, modelled most obviously on Hesiod's didactic *Works and Days*.

The eighth eclogue, after announcing its subject as the emphatically *Pastorum Musam Damonis et Alphesiboei* ('the pastoral muse of Damon and Alphesiboeus', 8.1), pauses for a moment before relaying their songs, to ask his patron whether the day will ever come when he will be allowed to tell of his deeds and spread his fame; again this is a clear reference to a possible future epic celebrating Octavian.[36] At the end of the book, 10.70–2, Virgil addresses the Muses:

> Haec sat erit, divae, vestrum cecinisse poetam,
> dum sedet et gracili fiscellam texit hibisco,
> Pierides ...

['This will be enough, divine Muses, for your poet to have sung, while he sits and weaves a basket of slender hibiscus.']

As Servius points out, the basket stands for the eclogue-book itself. Virgil is announcing that he has sung enough pastoral poetry, and he closes with the injunction *surgamus; solet esse gravis cantantibus umbra* ('let us arise: the shade is wont to be oppressive to singers', 10.75). *Umbra*, shade, is a figure which recurs frequently throughout the book and has come to stand metonymically for Virgil's pastoral poetry; *surgamus* seems to indicate an intention to 'rise' to 'higher' genres or poems, leaving *humilis* pastoral behind.

The second half of the *Georgics* is framed by forward and backward glances. Book 3 opens with an anticipation of heroic epic:

---

35 On etiological poetry as a Callimachean genre, see Richard Hunter, 'The Aetiology of Callimachus' *Aitia*', in Marco Fantuzzi and Richard Hunter, *Tradition and Innovation in Hellenistic Poetry* (Cambridge: Cambridge University Press, 2004), pp. 42–88, and Ross, *Backgrounds to Augustan Poetry*, pp. 18–38.
36 Servius identifies Octavian as the addressee, though Servius Danielis adds that some think the poem is addressed to Pollio. Modern commentators are divided: for a review of the evidence (and a decision in favour of Octavian), see Clausen (ed.), *Eclogues*, pp. 233–7.

> temptanda via est, qua me quoque possim
> tollere humo victorque virum volitare per ora.
>
> (*Georgics* 3.8–9)

['I must try the path by which I may lift myself from the ground and fly as a victor on the lips of men.']

Echoing Ennius, he refers clearly to the fame accruing to the poet of heroic epic. In a remarkable allegorical ekphrasis, he figures this poem (which will eventually take shape as the *Aeneid*) as a temple to Octavian which he will build on the banks of the Mincius, elaborately decorated with representations of Octavian's military triumphs. But inextricably bound up with this projected celebration of his patron is his own triumph as a poet, as he imagines himself *victor ... Tyrio conspectus in ostro* ('a victor, conspicuous in Tyrian purple', 3.17), urging on a hundred four-horse chariots and awarding the prizes in chariot-races (*cursibus*, 20) in which all Greece shall come together for him. Virgil's progress from lowly pastoral towards the high style of heroic epic is here paralleled with a civic career ascending towards the highest honour available in contemporary Rome, the right to hold a military triumph. Virgil is paralleled with Octavian himself, the general's vanquishing of foreign nations with Virgil's empire over Greek literary traditions. This image of the triumphal car is elided with the grand, festive public display of the chariot race (like those presided over by Achilles in *Iliad* 23 and by Aeneas in *Aeneid* 5): such a race, *cursus* (literally 'running'; thence 'race' and 'race-track'), is the root meaning of *cursus* as 'career', capturing the fundamental competitiveness of the Roman *cursus honorum* and of the idea of the literary *cursus* here being invented by Virgil.[37]

In the *sphragis* which ends Book 4 (4.561–2), Virgil reflects that he has sung about farming while Octavian conducts his wars by the Euphrates,

> victorque volentis
> per populos dat iura viamque adfectat Olympo.

['and as victor gives laws to the willing peoples, and tries the path to Olympus'.]

---

[37] On the racing connotations of *cursus*, see Philip Hardie and Helen Moore (eds), *Classical Literary Careers and Their Reception* (Cambridge: Cambridge University Press, 2010), p. 3; on similar connotations in the English 'career', see Patrick Cheney, 'Introduction: "Jog On, Jog On": European Career Paths', in Patrick Cheney and Frederick A. De Armas (eds), *European Literary Careers: The Author from Antiquity to the Renaissance* (Toronto: University of Toronto Press, 2002), pp. 3–23, at p. 8; on the image of the chariot in relation to literary careers, see Philip Hardie, *The Epic Successors of Virgil: A Study in the Dynamics of a Tradition* (Cambridge: Cambridge University Press, 1993), pp. 100–1.

The first impression is one of contrast, but echoes of 3.8–9 remind us that Virgil's own, analogous, triumphant flight, predicted there, is still ahead of him, and will come. He closes with a backward glance to the *Eclogues* (4.563–6):

> illo Vergilium me tempore dulcis alebat
> Parthenope, studiis florentem ignobilis oti,
> carmina qui lusi pastorum audaxque iuventa,
> Tityre, te patulae cecini sub tegmine fagi.

['In those days sweet Parthenope nourished me, Virgil, flourishing in the pursuits of ignoble idleness – I who played with the songs of shepherds, and, reckless in my youthfulness, sang of you, Tityrus, beneath the cover of the spreading beech.']

The final line repeats almost exactly the opening line of the *Eclogues*, *Tityre, tu patulae recubans sub tegmine fagi* ('You, Tityrus, reclining beneath the cover of the spreading beech', *Ecl.* 1.1). In the *Georgics* passage, it is impossible to know whether *patulae sub tegmine fagi*, 'beneath the cover of the spreading beech', refers to Tityrus or to the speaker Virgil. The *otium* of the herdsmen of pastoral poetry (e.g. Tityrus' *otia* at *Ecl.* 1.6) is identified with his own early studies or pursuits (the composition of the *Eclogues*), and disparaged as *ignobilis*, and as a form of 'play' suited to 'youth'. The hierarchy of the genres from pastoral to heroic epic is mapped on to the hierarchy of nobility and social rank (as in Eclogue 4, where the *humilis myrices* of pastoral were not 'worthy of a consul', and in Eclogue 6, where it did not 'befit a shepherd' to sing heroic song), and on to the process of ageing as an increase in dignity and worth (as in the schoolroom overtones of the opening of Eclogue 6). Looking back from here to the *surgamus* of Eclogue 10, the 'rising' of the singer from his prone position in the shade (cp. Tityrus *recubans* at *Ecl.* 1.1) appears as the beginning of the upward movement which will continue in the flight of fame anticipated in *Georgics* 3, the flight which will 'lift' the poet 'from the ground' (*tollere humo, Geo.* 3.9), to a position analogous with the emperor's. *Humus*, 'ground or earth', is the root of *humilis*, 'base' or 'humble' in a social sense; the poet's upward movement is identified with the Roman *cursus honorum*, the progress through positions of increasing civic responsibility and dignity, through which the Roman youth, engaged in a virtuous life of *negotium* ('business', the opposite of *otium*, 'idleness'), hopes to ascend the social hierarchy as he matures.

In other words, the ideological implications of Virgil's progress from pastoral to epic which we saw exploited in humanist pedagogy – the connections between the generic or stylistic hierarchy, the hierarchy of ethical values, and the social hierarchy – are already clearly and deliberately inscribed in Virgil's texts, in the passages where he reflects on his own career and the relation between his successive poems. Spenser's nods towards the Virgilian *cursus* respond directly to these implications. E.K.'s epistle recalls the association of pastoral with youth from *Georgics* 4.565 and the opening of Eclogue 6, and epic as a famous flight from *Georgics* 3; Piers' advice in *October* recalls the link between the poet's physical arising and his ascent in social rank, mirroring the ascending rank of his subjects – his 'Lyft vp thy selfe out of the *lowly dust*' capturing the connection of *humus* and *humilis*; the *Faerie Queene* proem recalls the progress from the playfulness of youth (masking 'as time her taught') to the onerous duties of maturity. Even E.K.'s alternative description of pastoral as a 'couert' means of conveying arguments 'such as perchance,' in Puttenham's formulation of the same idea, 'had not been safe to have been disclosed in any other form', is connected to the *audax* of *Georgics* 4.565, on which Servius Danielis comments:

> quidam 'audax' propterea dictum volunt, quod in duabus eclogis, quae sunt in bucolicis, occulte invectus sit in Augustum propter agros.
>
> ['Some would have it that he said "audax" because in two eclogues in the *Bucolics* he covertly attacks Augustus because of the farms.']

The two eclogues he has in mind are 1 and 9, which include daring criticism of Octavian's land confiscations; as Servius points out (and as I shall discuss in Chapter 1), other eclogues can also be read as referring 'couertly' (*latenter* or *occulte*) to the same topical issue under the veil of allegory. Looking back from here to the end of Eclogue 10 once more, the shade that is wont to be oppressive and harmful to singers could suggest the danger of political disapproval courted by such audacious political critique. But the Latin *audax* has pejorative overtones, connoting not just boldness but culpable presumption, and in the closing *sphragis* of the *Georgics* Virgil seems to be putting the audacity of the *Eclogues* behind him, along with youth, irresponsible play and lowly social status. His self-reflexive passages associate generic ascent with an embracing of Rome's hierarchical structure, and his successive works – at least on the surface – appear to move ever closer towards whole-hearted support for Augustus, and away from the deeply ambivalent political stance of the *Eclogues*.

In his acutely self-conscious mapping of his own poetic progress in these passages, Virgil is not only creating the influential paradigm of the Virgilian career but also, as Joseph Farrell argues, creating the very idea of a literary career, on the model of the Roman civic career, the *cursus honorum*.[38] Archaic and classical Greek poets always specialized in one genre – or rather, composition in one metre, the basis for categorizing poetry throughout the classical period – the choice of metre being seen as reflecting the poet's peculiar personality. For instance, an iambic poet would be characterized as aggressive by nature, since iambics were the metre used for satire and invective. When poetry became professionalized in third-century Alexandria, developing and exercising one's skill across a range of metres, or types of poetry, became the norm, but there was no sense of order or progression through them: the aim was to achieve a perfect refinement within each. It was not until Virgil – responding to hints in the early Roman epicist Ennius, whom we saw him echoing in the Proem to *Georgics* 3 – mapped his progress from pastoral to epic on to the *cursus honorum* that the idea of an ordered progress through an ascending hierarchy of poetic kinds was born.

Before Virgil, the place of pastoral and its relation to heroic epic was very different. I shall argue that Spenser recognizes and responds critically to the ways in which Virgil develops, changes and even flouts aspects of the Hellenistic poetic tradition from which his eclogue-book emerges; we must consider this Hellenistic tradition more closely before we go on. As we turn to look at it, we should for now set the term 'pastoral' aside, as a post-classical term, in favour of the classical designation 'bucolic song', which does not mean exactly the same thing. By the late sixteenth century, Puttenham and Sidney could list 'pastoral' among a range of poetic genres, and the term is useful for talking about Renaissance poems about shepherds, which followed Virgil and imitated him. But Virgil's contemporaries had no exact equivalent for this term. In the *Eclogues*, Virgil's chief model is very obviously Theocritus of Syracuse (as he indicates explicitly when he refers to 'Syracusan verse' at the beginning of Eclogue 6), who in the third century BCE had created in his *Idylls* the kind of poetry which classical commentators call 'bucolic'. This is not a genre, but merely a particular strain of *epos* (which by this time had evolved from its original meaning, 'word', to refer to narrative poetry in dactylic hexameters), distinctively developed by Theocritus in differentiation from the heroic *epos* of Homer.[39]

---

38 Joseph Farrell, 'Greek Lives and Roman Careers in the Classical Vita Tradition', in Patrick Cheney and Frederick A. De Armas (eds), *European Literary Careers: The Author from Antiquity to the Renaissance* (Toronto: University of Toronto Press, 2002), pp. 24–46.

39 John Van Sickle, 'Epic and Bucolic (Theocritus, Id. VII; Virgil, Ecl. 1)', *Quaderni Urbinati di cultura classica* 19 (1975), 45–72, and 'Theocritus and the Development of the Conception of Bucolic Genre', *Ramus* 5 (1976), 18–44. The insistence by some modern classicists on the use of the term 'bucolic' rather than 'pastoral' when discussing

Virgil's eclogue-book seems to have been titled *Bucolica*, the title it would bear in the earliest commentary (that of Servius), and Minturno's *De Poeta* (1559) recognizes the generic framework within which Virgil is working, when he treats *Bucolici* as one of three subdivisions of hexameter poetry (the lowest – *infimi* – with *Heroici* as the highest, or *summi*).[40] 'Bucolic' comes from the Greek word *boukolos* ('cowherd'); in Theocritus it is used frequently and only to describe the songs of herdsmen (see *Idylls* 1.20, 5.44, 5.60, 7.36, 7.49). Though Theocritus' *Idylls* also contain elaborate praise poems to powerful patrons (idylls 16 and 17), realistic urban 'mimes' (like Idyll 15's depiction of two gossipy Alexandrian housewives attending a civic ceremony), and brief mythological epics of the type which have come to be called 'epyllia' (such as idylls 13 and 24), almost half of the *Idylls* – what are now referred to as his bucolic poems – are peopled by herdsmen in rustic settings, engaging in song contests or talking about their loves and their flocks. It is these poems which are most heavily alluded to and imitated in Virgil's eclogue book.

In these poems, Theocritus employs Homer's metre, traditionally associated with grand and heroic subject matter, to focus on the humdrum and everyday, eschewing grand heroic themes, and concerning himself with humble characters and ordinary situations.[41] The commonplace vicissitudes of love replace the Iliadic theme of warfare. Both the continuity and the contrast with heroic *epos* are emphasized by artful imitation of and allusion to Homer. A comic effect is created when herdsmen analogize themselves with or echo the words of heroic or tragic mythical figures (as when the goatherd of Idyll 3 compares himself to Hippomenes and Endymion), and Theocritus' ingenuity is displayed when heroic passages are imitated in a humbler context (as when Homer's ekphrasis of the Shield of Achilles from *Iliad* 18 becomes the model for Theocritus' ekphrasis

---

Theocritus and Virgil is a useful corrective to the tendency to regard this poetry as a genre wholly distinct from heroic *epos* – a tendency instigated by Virgil's reflections on his own career. But it is motivated partly by a desire to separate Renaissance pastoral poetry from classical bucolic, on the theory that Renaissance pastoralists were themselves oblivious to this ancient continuity of the different strains of *epos*. (See Ernst A. Schmidt, 'Arcadia: Modern Occident and Classical Antiquity', in Katherina Volk (ed.), *Oxford Readings in Classical Studies: Vergil's Eclogues* (Oxford: Oxford University Press, 2008), pp. 16–47.) I shall soon revert to the term 'pastoral', and treat it normally as interchangeable with 'bucolic', since I shall be arguing that Spenser at least was fully aware of that continuity, and used his pastoral poems to engage with and to reverse the hierarchical generic divisions originating in the structure of the 'Book of Virgil'.

40 See Nicholas Halperin, *Before Pastoral: Theocritus and the Ancient Tradition of Bucolic Poetry* (New Haven: Yale University Press, 1983), p. 257.

41 Marco Fantuzzi, 'Theocritus and the Bucolic Genre', in Marco Fantuzzi and Richard Hunter, *Tradition and Innovation in Hellenistic Poetry* (Cambridge: Cambridge University Press, 2004), pp. 133–90.

of the carved wooden cup offered as a reward for song in Idyll 1).[42] The places where Homer abates the sternness of his style to treat lowly characters and humble or domestic matters (especially the second half of the *Odyssey*, with its extended treatment of the 'noble swineherd' Eumaios) are frequently alluded to. Bucolic emerges as a strain of *epos* treating the humble and the everyday, with a degree of comic detachment rather than high pathos, to be read with an appreciation both of its contrast with and its intimate relation to the heroic *epos* of Homer, and with the apparent purpose (as in the herdsmen's songs in the 'pastoral' idylls) of recreation and amusement.

In all this, Theocritus was following the precepts of art associated with his friend and colleague at the library of Alexandria, Callimachus, who denounced bombastic attempts to emulate the heroic verse of the supreme poet Homer, and promoted instead the aesthetic ideal of refinement, elegance, slightness – *leptotes*. We glanced above at two of Callimachus' programmatic statements about this aesthetic ideal, from the *Aetia* and the *Hymn to Apollo*. Simichidas, the goatherd of Idyll 7 who has been read since classical times as representing Theocritus himself, makes the same point at lines 47–8, criticizing ranters who try to compete with Homer, before inviting his companion to join with him in singing 'bucolic songs'. This preference for slightness also underlies the popularity among Callimachus' followers of 'epyllia' – *brief* epics, to be numbered in (at most) hundreds, not thousands, of lines. Such Callimachean 'epyllia', as in Theocritus' Idylls 13 and 24, achieve a tempering of Homeric *epos* analogous to the effect of Theocritus' bucolic poems, tending to focus on the domestic and everyday details of their grand mythological subjects, and on lowly characters (often females and servants) peripheral to the heroic action, often to comical effect.[43] Idyll 13 is even referred to as a bucolic poem in one ancient source, and the later Hellenistic poets Bion and Moschus, who identify themselves as bucolic poets and followers of Theocritus, are fond of writing brief mythological epyllia (often about Eros or Aphrodite).[44] Halperin probably goes too far when he argues that 'bucolic' as a category in classical thought embraced non-pastoral and mythological hexameter poems,[45] but, nevertheless, we can see bucolic

---

42 Halperin, *Before Pastoral*, pp. 176–80.
43 Richard Hunter, 'Epic in a Minor Key', in Marco Fantuzzi and Richard Hunter, *Tradition and Innovation in Hellenistic Poetry* (Cambridge:Cambridge University Press, 2004), pp. 201–10; and Marco Fantuzzi, 'The Style of Hellenistic Epic', in Marco Fantuzzi and Richard Hunter, *Tradition and Innovation in Hellenistic Poetry* (Cambridge: Cambridge University Press, 2004), pp. 255–66.
44 For the identification of Idyll 13 as bucolic, see Halperin, *Before Pastoral*, pp. 126–7.
45 Fantuzzi, 'Theocritus and the Bucolic Genre', p. 137.

and epyllion as complementary, reflecting the same aesthetic ideal and set of concerns played out through a reworking and tempering of heroic *epos*.

The herdsmen-singers of Theocritus' bucolic idylls provide him 'with a figure which could serve as the type of the Alexandrian poet who lavishes in a leisurely and playful fashion ... a high degree of refinement upon a humble or even pedestrian craft'.[46] The humble subject matter of Callimachean poetry is thus emphatically not intended as a marker or admission of poetic inferiority: the Callimachean poet 'wears his "humility" with pride', as Farrell puts it,[47] and associates the opposite – emulation of Homer's heroic *epos* – with vulgarity, the filth dragged along by the great river in Callimachus' *Hymn to Apollo*.[48] Virgil's *Eclogues* are also highly refined and artful: indeed one of their chief differences from Theocritus' bucolics is their avoidance of what is often seen as Theocritus' deliberately rustic use of dialect and moments of comic realism about his herdsmen's earthy lives. The Virgilian idea that bucolic poetry is the product of youth and of lowly social status, and a form of play, also chimes with Callimachean poetics: Callimachus and his followers often compare themselves to children, to highlight the playful and recreative aims of their poetry, their eschewal of vulgar self-importance, and tend to prefer ordinary people as their subjects.[49] Virgil's *Eclogues* are in many respects recognizably a product of the Callimacheanism of the neoterics.[50] But as we have seen, there are also hints in the *Eclogues*, which will be developed as Virgil's career progresses, suggesting the inferiority of bucolic to heroic *epos*, and the desirability of ascending from the one to the other, in a highly non-Callimachean way. The enormously influential commentary of Servius, from the late fourth century, would lay great emphasis on the differences between Virgil's three works, stressing in particular (and even exaggerating) their reliance on different models, moving from Theocritus in the *Eclogues* to Hesiod in the *Georgics*, and Homer in the *Aeneid* (like the ranters decried in Idyll 7).[51] In doing so he paves the way for the sixteenth-century categorization of pastoral as a distinct genre. But before

---

46 Halperin, *Before Pastoral*, pp. 243–4.
47 Farrell, 'Greek Lives and Roman Careers', p. 33.
48 See note 33 above.
49 On Callimachus' self-presentation as a child, see Hunter, 'The Aetiology of Callimachus' *Aitia*', p. 50.
50 On the application of Callimachean ideas to the reading of Virgil in the sixteenth century, particularly in France, see the doctoral dissertation (in progress at the University of Toronto) by David Adkins, 'Spenser's Humanist Virgil: The Recovery of Alexandrian Poetics in Sixteenth-Century Poetry and Philology'; I am grateful to him for letting me see his opening chapter.
51 See particularly Servius' preface to the *Georgics*.

Virgil bucolic and heroic were merely intimately related strains of the single genre of *epos*: indeed, all of Virgil's three works are composed throughout in dactylic hexameters, and would thus have been seen in his own time as exercises in a single genre.

A poem attributed to one of Theocritus' late Hellenistic followers, Moschus, to which both Virgil and Spenser respond, lays out with particular clarity the equally high status of bucolic and heroic *epos*. The *Lament for Bion*, composed in the second century BCE, identifies its subject as a bucolic poet (indeed as a cowherd), a singer of Doric song (Theocritus' bucolic idylls are mostly composed in Doric Greek) and 'a Theocritus'. Addressing a river of Smyrna, birthplace of Bion and allegedly also of Homer, the poet cries (70–84):

> τοῦτό τοι ὦ ποταμῶν λιγυρώτατε δεύτερον ἄλγος,
> τοῦτο, Μέλη, νέον ἄλγος. ἀπώλετο πρᾶν τοι Ὅμηρος,
> τῆνο τὸ Καλλιόπας γλυκερὸν στόμα, καί σε λέγοντι
> μύρασθαι καλὸν υἷα πολυκλαύτοισι ῥεέθροις,
> πᾶσαν δ' ἔπλησας φωνᾶς ἅλα· νῦν πάλιν ἄλλον
> υἱέα δακρύεις, καινῷ δ' ἐπὶ πένθεϊ τάκῃ.
> ἀμφότεροι παγαῖς πεφιλημένοι, ὃς μὲν ἔπινε
> Παγασίδος κράνας, ὃ δ' ἔχεν πόμα τᾶς Ἀρεθοίσας.
> χὠ μὲν Τυνδαρέοιο καλὰν ἄεισε θύγατρα
> καὶ Θέτιδος μέγαν υἷα καὶ Ἀτρείδαν Μενέλαον·
> τῆνος δ' οὐ πολέμους, οὐ δάκρυα, Πᾶνα δ' ἔμελπε,
> καὶ βούτας ἐλίγαινε καὶ ἀείδων ἐνόμευε,
> καὶ σύριγγας ἔτευχε καὶ ἀδέα πόρτιν ἄμελγε,
> καὶ παίδων ἐδίδασκε φιλήματα, καὶ τὸν Ἔρωτα
> ἔτρεφεν ἐν κόλποισι καὶ ἤρεθε τὰν Ἀφροδίταν.

['O tunefullest of rivers, this makes thee a second grief; this, good Meles, comes to thee a new woe. One melodious mouthpiece of Calliope is long dead, and that is Homer; that lovely son of thine was mourned, 'tis said, of thy tearful flood, and all the sea was filled with the voice of thy lamentation: and lo! now thou weepest for another son, and a new sorrow melteth thee away. Both were beloved of a water-spring, for the one drank at Pegasus' fountain and the other got him drink of Arethusa; and the one sang of the lovely daughter of Tyndareus, and the great son of Thetis, and of Atreid Menelaus; but this other's singing was neither of wars nor tears but of Pan; as a herdsman he chanted and kept his cattle with a song; he both fashioned the pipes and milked the gentle kine; he taught the lore of kisses, he made a fosterling of Love, he roused and stirred the passion of Aphrodite.'][52]

---

52 *The Greek Bucolic Poets*, tr. J. M. Edmonds (Cambridge, MA: Harvard University Press,

There ensues a catalogue of other Greek poets to whom Bion, like Homer, is superior. What distinguishes the two equally worthy strains of *epos* here is their themes – Bion's love contrasted with Homer's warfare. This brings out a significant development within bucolic since Theocritus, which was important to both Virgil and Spenser. As observed above, love was already an important theme, conspicuously replacing Iliadic warfare, in Theocritus. But in common with other Callimachean poetry, Theocritus tends to treat love as a pathology and a source of suffering. In Idyll 1, for instance, the exact events which have led to Daphnis' death are left unclear, but what is clear is that it is caused ultimately by Aphrodite. The goatherd of Idyll 3, spurned by Amaryllis, plans to commit suicide. The song of the love-sick Cyclops in Idyll 11 is introduced as demonstrating to Theocritus' addressee, a physician-friend, that song can be a therapy for the disease of love. In Idyll 7, the songs exchanged by Simichidas and Lycidas share the theme of epicurean release from the pains of love. In the poems of Bion, by contrast, romantic love is often treated sympathetically and sentimentally – one example being Bion's *Lament for Adonis*, a pathos-filled account of Aphrodite's mourning, to which the *Lament for Bion* frequently alludes. Bion's positive celebration of faithful and passionate romantic attachment was to exert a strong influence on the Roman elegists, who often echo his poems.[53]

Theocritus' treatment of love as a pathology is followed by Virgil, not only in his *Eclogues* (where eclogues 2, 8 and 10 draw heavily on Idylls 1, 3 and 11 particularly, and like them associate love with madness and death), but also in that turn from *Amor* to *Roma* we have traced across his career and within the plot of the *Aeneid*. This aspect of Theocritean and Virgilian bucolic is useful to Spenser in his first pastoral volume, because of the *Calender*'s chief polemical purpose as a warning to the Queen against her planned marriage. Moreover, according to the commentary tradition, Virgil used his imitations of Theocritean love-suffering in the *Eclogues* as an allegorical veil for political criticism – so that, for instance, Corydon's rebuke to his 'cruel' Alexis (imitating the goatherd of Idyll 3) can be interpreted *crudelis Caesar, qui non flecteris meis scriptis et non das ereptos agros* ('cruel Caesar, who are not softened by my writings and

---

1912). All translations of Bion, Moschus and pseudo-Moschus will be taken from this edition.
53 On the influence of Bion, see J. D. Reed (ed.), *Bion of Smyrna: The Fragments and the Adonis* (Cambridge: Cambridge University Press, 1997), pp. 57–64; on his positive treatment of love and its influence on the Roman elegists, see Fantuzzi, 'Theocritus and the Bucolic Genre'.

do not give back the seized lands').⁵⁴ This too is important to Spenser's imitation of Virgil in the *Calender*. But if the negative presentation of love is used in the *Eclogues* in the service of political critique, in Virgil's later works love as a destructive madness is increasingly aligned with the forces of disorder which oppose Augustus' rule and the cosmic harmony it reflects. For Spenser, by contrast, once the *Calender* and its immediate polemical purpose is behind him, the Virgilian (and Theocritean) attitude to love is deeply antipathetic. Recognizing Virgil's persistent anti-eroticism as inextricably bound up with his growing dependence on and complicity with imperial power, Spenser seeks to distance himself from both, taking issue with Virgil, and frequently looking back to the poems of Bion and Moschus, with their high valuation of love.⁵⁵ Even as he follows the Virgilian trajectory to heroic epic, he adapts the form to place a positive eros on at least as high a level as political praise – announcing his intention to do so already in the Proem to Book I, with its (Ariostan) addition of 'Ladies' and 'faithfull loues' to the 'Knights' and 'Fierce warres' of the *Aeneid* opening. Redcrosse's abandonment of Una in canto ii is programmatic, replaying Aeneas' defining act of *pietas* – his desertion of Dido in Book IV – as a wholly culpable breach of faith which combines and allegorically identifies amatory infidelity with impiety, the soul's turning away from truth and from God.⁵⁶ Book III in particular is concerned with distinguishing false love from true: in the Garden of Adonis, the celebration of procreative love as sustaining creation in accordance with God's will conspicuously replaces the political prophecies of Virgil's underworld as the visionary heart of his epic.⁵⁷ The description of the Garden is prefaced with an imitation of Moschus' epyllion 'Love the Runaway'. In 1595, Spenser publishes (as

---

54 Servius, *ad Eclogues* 2.6. The interrelated topics of Theocritean imitation and allegory in Virgil's *Eclogues* are the subject of Chapter 1 below.
55 The poems by Bion and Moschus were available in several editions, both in Greek and with Latin translations. On the textual and editing history, see Reed (ed.), *Bion of Smyrna*, pp. 64–87. Merritt Y. Hughes, 'Spenser and the Greek Pastoral Triad', *Studies in Philology* 20.2 (1923), 184–215, and T. P. Harrison, Jr, 'Spenser, Ronsard, and Bion', *MLN* 49 (1934), 139–45, regard Spenser as knowing the Greek poems only through translations by the Pléiade; Michael O'Connell, '*Astrophel*: Spenser's Double Elegy', *SEL* 11 (1971), 27–35, argues for more direct knowledge of the texts.
56 Spenser does this in part by responding to hints of counter-Augustan scepticism within Virgil's text itself, for the voice of dissent does not disappear from Virgil after the *Eclogues*, but merely becomes more subterranean and less open. See Pugh, 'Reinventing the Wheel: Spenser's "Virgilian Career"', in Paul Hecht and Julian Lethbridge (eds), *Spenser in the Moment* (Teaneck, NJ: Fairleigh Dickinson University Press, 2015), pp. 1–31.
57 See Pugh, *Spenser and Ovid*, ch. 4.

well as his second pastoral volume) the *Amoretti and Epithalamium*, an anti-Petrarchan sonnet sequence celebrating the consummation of love in Protestant companionate marriage; again, procreative married love is presented as a reflection of the love between humanity and God, a part and expression of Christian faith.[58] The fourth of the *Anacreontea* which come between the sonnet sequence and the concluding *Epithalamium* imitates a poem ascribed to Theocritus in early editions, and still referred to as [Theocritus] 19, though now usually ascribed to Bion, as well as *Anacreontica* 33 (which may imitate it).[59] *Colin Clouts Come Home Againe*, which in the same year pointedly reverses Virgil's upward trajectory from pastoral to epic, engages in a profound and sustained critique of Virgil's tenth eclogue, with its rejection of love and of pastoral. Bion and Moschus are again in the background of this volume (with particular prominence in 'Astrophel'), as Spenser creates a new pastoral centred on the celebration of love, and a role for himself as a supremely authoritative poet-prophet founded on his amatory and Christian teachings as Love's 'Priest'.

The role of love in *Colin Clouts Come Home Againe* is central to the way in which the volume critiques, and indeed overturns, the ethical, social and generic hierarchies implicit in the idea of the Virgilian *cursus*. In a pastoral locale newly imagined as a space outside Cynthia's realm, beyond her control and the corruptive influence of her perniciously hierarchical court, Spenser constructs for himself and for the community of his readers an alternative to the 'Father tongue' absorbed through Virgil in the Tudor grammar schools. A *vita contemplativa* of poetry, virtue and religion, symbolized by and best expressed in shepherds' song, is preferred before the *vita activa* of service to a corrupt court and government, and its reflection in both courtly Petrarchan poetry and panegyrical epic. But this turn in Spenser's career to contemplative pastoral is not, as it is so often presented, a 'withdrawal ... from direct engagement with the historical world'.[60] Anti-court satire is central to 'Colin Clouts Come Home Againe'.

---

58 Reed Way Dasenbrock, 'The Petrarchan Context of Spenser's Amoretti', *PMLA*, 100 (1985), 38–50; J. L. Klein, '"Let us love, dear love, lyke as we ought": Protestant Marriage and the Revision of Petrarchan Loving in Spenser's *Amoretti*', *Spenser Studies* 10 (1992), 109–38; Anne Lake Prescott, 'The Thirsty Deer and the Lord of Life: Some Contexts for Amoretti 67–70', *Spenser Studies* 6 (1985), 33–76.
59 The poem has also been attributed to Moschus; see A. S. F. Gow (ed.), *Theocritus*, 2 vols (Cambridge: Cambridge University Press, 1950), Vol. 2, p. 362.
60 David Lee Miller, 'Spenser's Vocation, Spenser's Career', *ELH* 50 (1983), 197–231, at 216; for similar statements see Helgerson, *Self-Crowned Laureates*, p. 97; David Lee Miller, 'Abandoning the Quest', *ELH* 46 (1979), 174; John D. Bernard, *Ceremonies of Innocence: Pastoralism in the Poetry of Edmund Spenser* (Cambridge: Cambridge University Press,

The pastoral episode in the final book of *The Faerie Queene* (including another of the epic's visionary climaxes in the vision of the dancing Graces summoned to Mount Acidale by Colin's piping) likewise forms part of that book's dark reflections on contemporary politics: the disruption of the vision by Calidore, emissary of the court, prefigures both the destruction of the pastoral community by brigands, which Calidore fails to prevent, and the breaking off the poem itself under attack from the Blatant Beast, operating through the 'mightie Pere' Burghley. This is a pastoral which contemplates politics, its detachment from the centre of power representing neither defeatism nor transcendence of worldly affairs, but independence, to be used precisely for political ends – in the service of his community, though not of his Queen and her government.

It is worth briefly comparing this return to pastoral with the lingering traces and backward glances through which pastoral resurfaces in Virgil's later works, after he has ostensibly abandoned it at the end of the *Eclogues*. The second, Iliadic half of the *Aeneid* (like Book VI of *The Faerie Queene*) contains a pastoral episode, as Aeneas visits the kingdom of Evander, an Arcadian living in exile on the site where Rome will one day arise. The final line of the poem, the flight of Turnus' soul *sub umbra* ('beneath the shades') as he dies at Aeneas' hand takes the receptive reader back to both sides of the dynamic of the first eclogue, with its sheltering pastoral *umbra* enjoyed by Tityrus, its evening shadows closing in at the end, and the flight of Meliboeus from his homeland.[61] Elena Theodorakopoulos suggests that such moments encourage a 'circular' reading of the 'Book of Virgil', pulling against the 'linear and teleological impulse' of the Virgilian *cursus*, figuring at once 'the poet's resistance to epic and empire' and 'his resistance to his own paradigmatic career-progress':

> In this circular enclosure the world of the *Eclogues* with its small-scale songs of love and exile becomes part of the 'private voice' of the *Aeneid*, which in the midst of empire and ideology may take us back to an Italian landscape which is not yet part of the public world of epic.[62]

But this 'private voice' of pastoral in the *Aeneid* is defined by nostalgia and regret, not by the potency of a possible alternative to the imperial future.[63]

1989), p. 163.
61 See Michael Putnam, 'Some Virgilian Unities', in Philip Hardie and Helen Moore (eds), *Classical Literary Careers and Their Reception* (Cambridge: Cambridge University Press, 2010), pp. 17–38.
62 Theodorakopoulos, 'Closure: The Book of Virgil', p. 157.
63 Cp. Adam Parry, 'The Two Voices of Virgil's Aeneid', *Arion: A Journal of Humanities and the Classics* 2 (1963), 66–80.

Like the Arcadia of the tenth eclogue – pointedly revised and reimagined in the allegorized Ireland of Spenser's 'Colin Clouts Come Home Againe' – they figure pastoral as a space of retreat and imaginative escape from politics, not of engagement and social change. They may express pity for the helpless victims of imperial power, but do not extend any hope of independence or freedom from it.

This is not how pastoral is imagined earlier in the *Eclogues*, where Virgil engages in contemporary politics and attempts to negotiate actively with Octavian, precisely by raising – and keeping open – the question of how the 'Book of Virgil' will unfold. At this stage, when the poet has not yet embarked on his literary *cursus honorum*, and hints at the desirability of such an 'ascent' are still only a riddling and discordant note in the book's Callimachean poetics, pastoral is a space where the lowly may bargain with political power. Demonstrating his ability to compose persuasive Caesarean propaganda in eclogues 4 and 5, Virgil holds out the possibility of future epic praise, but at the same time (particularly in 1 and 9, the eclogues explicitly addressing the land-confiscations) shows that he is capable of exposing and publically condemning injustice where he finds it. One of the song fragments recited in Eclogue 9 – an anticipation of future epic like those in Eclogues 4 and 8 – makes clear the negotiation involved(9.27–9):

> 'Vare, tuum nomen, superet modo Mantua nobis,
> Mantua vae miserae nimium vicina Cremonae,
> cantantes sublime ferent ad sidera cycni.'

['Varus, if only Mantua remains to us (Mantua, alas, too near wretched Cremona), singing swans shall bear your name on high to the stars.']

The song, we are told, is *necdum perfecta* ('not yet finished'). In fact, we have just heard that its author Menalcas' petition to Octavian to revoke the confiscation of the Mantuan farmlands has been refused. Thus it is clear this projected epic will never be completed: Varus, having failed to meet Menalcas' condition, will be denied the proffered immortality, and Menalcas will not pursue a 'Virgilian career' leading from pastoral to epic. But the pastoral negotiations of the *Eclogues* are predicated on the abandonment of pastoral. For all his hints in eclogues 8 and 9 at the quasi-magical power of song to inflict damage on enemies (hints expanded by a near-contemporary in the *Dirae*, another poem in the *Appendix Virgiliana*), Virgil shows little faith that this power will not evaporate unless hitched to Octavian's triumphal car (as in *Georgics* 3). The eclogue-book finally offers no secure alternative prospect between, on the one hand, the deifying praise of Tityrus in Eclogue 1 and of the projected epics of eclogues 4 and 8, and, on the other, being cast into the outer darkness and falling silent with the exiled Meliboeus and Moeris of eclogues 1 and 9. The best that the 'Book of Virgil' can offer, meanwhile, is the 'private voice' of regret, and subterranean undercurrents of scepticism with regard to its own surface ideology. The negotiating strategy of the *Eclogues* is fundamental to the *Calender*, but already here Spenser shows disquiet about the traces of dependency adhering to this model of pastoral. In his later pastorals he seeks to ground the political engagement of the *Eclogues* in a surer authority which escapes such dependence on political power.

One sign of the increased confidence and authority of Spenser's later pastoral poems is their sheer length. At 985 lines, 'Colin Clouts Come Home Againe' far exceeds the longest of Virgil's eclogues and any in the *Calender*, approximating rather to the length of a single book of the *Aeneid*. In fact, it rather resembles a brief epic, or 'epyllion'.[64] 'Astrophel', though much shorter at 342 lines (including the 'Lay of Clorinda'), is still much longer than eclogues tend to be, and in subject matter and treatment more clearly resembles epyllion as we know it in Spenser's contemporaries. Its narrative of love and death is conspicuously modelled on the myth of Adonis, as told in Bion's *Lament for Adonis* and Ovid's *Metamorphoses*, and already taken as the subject for Shakespeare's erotic epyllion *Venus and Adonis*. First of the poems by other hands included in the volume is Lodowick Bryskett's 'The Mourning Muse of Thestylis', which is clearly a minor epic in form.[65] The two Spenserian poems blend epyllion with pastoral, creating a distinctive twist on both genres. The 1590s saw a vogue for epyllion, a form used by Lodge, Nashe, Shakespeare, Marlowe and others for erotic mythological narratives, based on tales taken from Ovid (principally the *Metamorphoses*, but often also drawing on his *Heroides*). It is worth considering Spenser's late pastorals in relation to this vogue and the tradition it springs from – a tradition with connections to pastoral, and particularly to the hierarchy of genres constructed by Virgil's career.

The minor epic is in origin a Callimachean form, one of the artfully diminutive versions of *epos* favoured by Alexandrian poets including

---

64 The suggestion may seem less odd if we consider its inclusion of Colin's mock-epic voyage. As we shall see in Chapter 5, the lay of Bregog and Mulla also engages with epic intertexts in both the *Aeneid* and the *Metamorphoses*, in a way which, like the erotic epyllia of his contemporaries, responds to Ovid's subversive treatment of Virgil.
65 Bryskett's poem is less Ovidian and more heroic in colouring than the erotic epyllia of the 1590s (with frequent echoes of the *Aeneid*), and based largely on Bernardo Tasso's 'Seva nella morte del S. Luigi Gonzaga', from his *Rime* printed in 1560. See W. P. Mustard, 'Lodowick Bryskett and Bernardo Tasso', *AJP* 35 (1914), 192–9.

Theocritus in some of his non-bucolic idylls, by the late Hellenistic bucolic poets Bion and Moschus, and by the Roman neoterics. Virgil's fourth and sixth eclogues evoke and engage with epyllia by the neoterics, Catullus and Calvus.[66] Ovid's *Metamorphoses*, which the 1590s epyllia mined for their subjects, can be seen as an assemblage of neoteric epyllia offered as a challenge and alternative to the grand unity and teleological design of Virgilian epic. The story taken as the subject for Lodge's *Scylla and Glaucus*, which began the Elizabethan vogue in 1589, is an epyllion-like episode with which Ovid pointedly interrupts his retelling of Aeneas' wanderings in Books 13 to 15 of the *Metamorphoses*, diverting attention from the forward progress of the Virgilian hero on to a fantastical myth of love and magic.[67] Lynn Enterline has recently argued that the popularity of the form in the 1590s grew out of the humanist pedagogical practice of Tudor grammar schools and the Inns of Court – a pedagogy consciously structured on the generic progression of the Virgilian career – but reacted specifically against its ideals. These poets 'happily displaced the *Aeneid*'s plot of epic masculinity; and in so doing, they called into question the institutional and pedagogical *telos* of civic duty that gave Virgil's imperial epic pride of place'.[68] The epyllion poets of the 1590s used the form to position themselves on the margins of society, and to adopt an irreverent and critical perspective on it, particularly distancing themselves from the public duties of the male subject by sympathetic identification with their heroines.[69] Their heroines frequently voice lengthy complaints against their fates, but they expend their rhetoric in vain – necessarily, because the endings of their mythological narratives are already written, and cannot be changed. Thus, as Enterline observes, the authors of these epyllia raise serious questions about the efficacy of rhetoric, so attacking a basic principle of the Tudor pedagogy which used linguistic and rhetorical training to induct boys into a *vita activa* in the service of the

---

66 On Callimachean epyllion, see Fantuzzi, 'Epic in a Minor Key'; on neoteric epyllia, see Ross, *Backgrounds to Augustan Poetry*, with connections to Eclogue 6 at pp. 37–8.
67 Like Spenser and the Elizabethan epyllion-poets, Ovid engages deliberately and playfully with the idea of the Virgilian career, and the ideological connotations it had already acquired. See Joseph Farrell, 'Ovid's Virgilian Career', *Materiali e discussioni per l'analisi dei testi classici* 52 (2004), 41–55.
68 Lynn Enterline, 'Drama, Pedagogy, and the Female Complaint: or, What's Troy Got to Do with It?', forthcoming in Elizabeth Dutton and James McBain (eds), *Swiss Papers in English Language and Literature*, vol. 31 (Tübingen: Gunter Narr Verlag). (I am grateful to Prof. Enterline for allowing me to see this paper in advance of its publication.)
69 See Georgia Brown, *Redefining Elizabethan Literature* (Cambridge: Cambridge University Press, 2004), pp. 102–77, on these poets' 'self-marginalization', their peculiar 'self-confidence grounded on fragility' (p. 109).

commonwealth, but simultaneously, by identifying with these heroines, presenting themselves as fatally disempowered in an oppressive social system.[70] Spenser's epyllia take a similarly critical attitude to the model of social utility as dutiful service to established political authority, institutionalized in Tudor pedagogy and reflected in Virgil's career, but unlike the Elizabethan erotic epyllia they propose an empowered – and socially useful – role for the poet.

Across his career Spenser shows an interest in epyllia which is not limited to the Ovidian sources favoured by his contemporaries. He imitates Bion 13 in the *March* eclogue,[71] and two classical epyllia in Book III of *The Faerie Queene* (Moschus' 'Love the Runaway' in canto vi, and the pseudo-Virgilian *Ciris*, a poem from the *Appendix Virgiliana*, in canto ii). Many of *The Faerie Queene*'s episodes are epyllion-like – unsurprisingly, since the poem formally draws on Ariostan romance and its classical model in Ovid's *Metamorphoses*, which as noted above can be seen as a compilation of neoteric epyllia – and the deeply Ovidian *Mutabilitie Cantos* are in themselves a brief epic, which also contains a briefer (and more recognizable) epyllion in the Faunus episode.[72] The fourth of the 'Anacreontics' which come between the *Amoretti* and the *Epithalamium* may imitate the late Hellenistic epyllion wrongly ascribed to Theocritus as Idyll 19. But none of these is a quite free-standing poem. The only poem by Spenser which is normally mentioned in discussions of 1590s epyllia is *Muiopotmos*, the obviously Ovidian brief epic (closely related to Ovid's Arachne in the *Metamorphoses*) in the *Complaints* volume of 1591. In fact there are three, interrelated epyllia in this volume, in which Spenser tries out variations on the form, exploring its potential as a side-path which leads away from the Virgilian *cursus* and its implied values, while seeking ways to avoid the disempowerment involved in the anti-Virgilian and Ovidian stance of his contemporaries. In the first of the three, Spenser finds epyllion – the genre which for his contemporaries marked a pointed resistance to the Virgilian *cursus*, and which indeed had its origins in Callimachean objections to the heroic epic to which that *cursus* leads –

---

70 Enterline, 'Drama, Pedagogy, and the Female Complaint'.
71 I follow the numbering used in A. S. F. Gow, *Bucolici Graeci* (Oxford: Clarendon Press, 1952).
72 This kind of binary form is typical of neoteric epyllion, which often contains one narrative nested within another, as for instance in Catullus 64. This is one of the epyllion-like features of Ovid's Scylla and Galatea digression, where Galatea relates her tale to Scylla within Ovid's telling of Scylla's. If we think of 'Colin Clouts Come Home Againe' as related to epyllion, we might also reflect that it too contains another epyllion-like song in the lay of Bregog and Mulla.

within Virgil himself, in his translation of the pseudo-Virgilian *Culex*. The other two epyllia in the volume spring from this translation, developing elements of its narrative in two different directions – in the partly Virgilian *Mother Hubberds Tale* which immediately follows it, and in the Ovidian *Muiopotmos* (another tragicomic tale of the death of an insect) at the end of the volume. Accepting the (already disputed) Virgilian authorship of the *Culex* meant that poets of Spenser's generation were free to see Virgil as capable of taking up a similar kind of critical perspective on the telos of heroic epic exemplified in Ovidian narrative – and moreover as doing so in a way intimately connected to his use of allegory for political critique which the commentary tradition saw in his pastoral poetry.

The *Culex* is framed as a pastoral. It is the tale of a gnat (*culex*) who stings a sleeping shepherd in order to awaken him to his danger from a serpent, but is thoughtlessly killed by a slap from the shepherd's hand. The gnat's shade visits the shepherd to complain of the injustice, relating his gloomy descent into the Underworld, and begging the shepherd to grant him burial. The figure of the gnat combines the lengthy complaint of a victim, familiar from the heroines of Tudor Ovidian epyllia, with a comically exaggerated form of the baseness and meanness of the lowly shepherds of pastoral, and of the style and self-presentation of the pastoral poet who figures himself in them. As shepherds are to kings (and to the *barbari miles* they send to confiscate those shepherds' farms), so the gnat is to the shepherd – an unimportant, nigh-invisible, and almost entirely powerless victim. But the gnat, and the poet, do not adhere to the decorum of the base and mean style, and the comedy of the poem springs also from its mock-heroic aspects. The combat with the serpent is told in heroic style, particularly recalling the sea-serpent of *Aeneid* 2, and the gnat's descent to the Underworld recalls *Aeneid* 6, though concentrating on the plights of its female denizens (like Virgil's model for Aeneas' katabasis in *Odyssey* 11, and in a way reminiscent of Ovid's approach to Greek myth and the stuff of epic). The poem offers us a parodic and humorous perspective on the grandest and most solemn themes of Virgilian epic.[73] The sonnet to Leicester prefacing Spenser's translation, explicitly presenting the poem as a 'riddle rare' about a 'wrong' he has suffered at the hands of this 'great Lord' but does not dare to express openly, brings out the way in which the poem pulls against the drive to praise the ruler or patron characteristic of the *Aeneid*, drawing attention at once to pastoral's ability to expose and criticize injustice on the part of

---

73 The distinctive blend of epic and pastoral in the *Culex* is echoed in *The Faerie Queene* in the simile comparing Redcrosse to a shepherd brushing off gnats (I.i.23), a hint that the epic heroism of Redcrosse's battle with Errour is not all that it seems.

the powerful, and to the oppressive conditions of censorship which make it impossible to do so openly. At the same time, the gnat's heroic self-sacrifice, ultimately recognized by the penitent shepherd, demonstrates that the humble pastoral poet does indeed serve the public good.

This theme is developed further in *Mother Hubberds Tale*, the next poem in the volume. This is a vastly extended Aesopian beast-fable, with mock-epic elements and intermittent pastoral colouring.[74] The Ape and the Fox begin their nefarious career by impersonating shepherds, while preying on the flocks entrusted to their care, recalling the foxes and wolves who allegorize bad pastors in *The Shepheardes Calender* and Mantuan's eclogues. The transition is therefore unsurprising when, following the advice of a lazy and ignorant curate in the next stage of their career, they obtain a benefice, which they similarly abuse. From here they move on to the court, where their braggadocio and self-serving dishonesty are perfect qualifications, and ensure their success for a time. The lengthy satire of corrupt and foolish courtiers (with a passage on the ideal courtier acting like a foil to emphasize the general corruption) strongly anticipates the anti-court satire of 'Colin Clouts Come Home Againe'. Finally they acquire rule of the kingdom, stealing the royal insignia of the sleeping lion and impersonating her to exercise outright tyranny. The poem draws on the medieval tradition of estates satire, cataloguing abuses at all levels of society, but with more radical implications, as it shows the same vicious and self-serving impulses motivating the lowest vagabond and the highest in the realm. The theft of the royal insignia by both the Fox and the Ape satirizes the abuses carried out by the powerful statesman Burghley in the name of the 'sluggish' Queen, who (culpably) does not see or prevent his crimes.[75] But even more radically, the image of the Ape as a usurper, both foolish and evil, with no true authority, and himself dependent on and used by the Burghley-like Fox, raises the possibility of viewing the monarch herself as an impostor, both manipulated by and complicit with her evil adviser.

Their rake's progress is also a parody of the social and generic ascent of the Virgilian *cursus*, of the Roman *cursus honorum* it mimics and of the Tudor boy's progress through humanist education into a career of public service. Its ending strikingly recalls the climax of the *Culex*, but replays it

---

74 On beast fable and its use for political satire, see Annabel Patterson, *Fables of Power: Aesopian Writing and Political History* (Durham, NC, and London: Duke University Press, 1991), and Blair Worden, *The Sound of Virtue: Philip Sidney's* Arcadia *and Elizabethan Politics* (New Haven: Yale University Press, 1996), pp. 63–5, 265–80.
75 On Burghley as the satirical target of the *Tale*, see Worden, *Sound of Virtue*, pp. 265–80.

in a more openly epic key. Just as the gnat awakens the shepherd, alerting him to his danger, saving his life, and bringing about the slaying of the serpent, so here Mercury, a *deus ex machina* sent by Jove, intervenes to awaken the sleeping lion (the true monarch), bringing about the restoration of justice with the punishment of the malefactors and redress of the wrongs inflicted on society by their abuse of power. Mercury's flight is conspicuously modelled on his embassy in *Aeneid* 4 as messenger of Virgil's Jove. But he is also recognizably a figure of the poet himself, who in this poem is alerting the public and the Queen to the injustices being perpetrated in her name by Lord Burghley, while she lets her justice sleep. If the humble gnat is one persona of the poet, with his stinging but salvific pastoral poetry and his plaint against injustice, the god Mercury, conduit of divine truth and saviour of the nation, is another. Jove is tempted simply to use his thunderbolt to get rid of the usurpers, but (1239–42)

> rather chose with scornfull shame
> Him to auenge, and blot his brutish name
> Vnto the world, that neuer after anie
> Should of his race be voyd of infamie.

It is Spenser's poem itself which 'blots' the 'brutish name' of the main satirical target, Lord Burghley, whom contemporaries recognized as underlying the Fox of the *Tale*; despite its presentation as mere pastime for an 'idle stound' (26), 'base' of 'stile' and 'matter meane' (44), the poem is the instrument of divine justice. Like the heroines in the erotic epyllia of Spenser's contemporaries, the speakers of these poems are marginalized and disempowered figures, a frail gnat, and the lower-class female Mother Hubberd, whose 'bad ... tongue' (1388) is made the vehicle and cover for Spenser's daring political satire. They are figures who stand outside the powerful hegemonies of Tudor society and resist its structuring ideology, even as the poems resist strict generic classification, and the volume in which they appear resists the expectations of the Virgilian literary *cursus*. But at the same time they co-opt the prophetic and authoritative voice of Virgilian epic in the service of oppositional ends.

But the generic in-between world of Spenser's 1591 epyllia cannot offer a real escape from the pressures of the Virgilian *cursus* and its implied values. 'Virgils Gnat' presents itself fundamentally as an amusing trifle, as humble and unimportant as the gnat itself, whose comedy depends on an acceptance of the Virgilian hierarchy of genres and values, and the triumph of justice at the end of *Mother Hubberds Tale* is parasitic on the structures of authority delineated in the *Aeneid*. The poems' evasive strategies do not grant the poet security from retribution: the indirections of *prosopopoeia* ('impersonating a character' – a rhetorical term, a grammar-school exercise and the alternative title of *Mother Hubberds Tale*), by which Spenser seeks (unconvincingly) to distance himself from Mother Hubberd's 'bad ... tongue', did not fool the authorities. The volume was recalled, Spenser finally falling victim to the censorship feared so openly in the *Calender*, and figured in such punished speakers as Bonfont and Faunus in *The Faerie Queene*.[76] It is only in the 1595 volume that Spenser fully achieves his radical rejection of the Virgilian *cursus* and its implied hierarchies, by turning them simply upside-down, making the lowest rung of Virgil's generic ladder into the home for a politically independent poetic authority.

If *Mother Hubberds Tale* drew its figure of divinely inspired utterance from the *Aeneid*'s Mercury, 'Colin Clouts Come Home Againe' looks instead to the evocations, threaded through the *Eclogues*, of Orpheus, the legendary poet with divine parentage and the supernatural power to animate the landscape with his song. Sometimes in the *Eclogues* the aspiration to Orphic song is connected with the notion of ascent to 'higher' genres, as when the *recusatio* at the end of Eclogue 4 anticipates a heroic epic better than Orpheus could sing, or when, in the initiation scene of Eclogue 6, the pipes with which Gallus will ascend to Hesiodic poetry are credited with Orpheus' power to draw trees down the mountainside. But elsewhere in the *Eclogues* such Orphic potency seems to be already achieved within pastoral itself: the song of Silenus which forms the bulk of Eclogue 6 moves wild animals and stiff oaks more than ever Orpheus delighted Rhodope and Ismarus; the pastoral muse of Damon and Alphesiboeus in Eclogue 8 entrances lynx and heifer and makes rivers change their course; in Menalcas' hymn in Eclogue 5, a landscape rhetorically animated through personification (or *prosopopoeia*) cries out to proclaim Daphnis a god. Yet such suggestions of the quasi-magical power of song are hedged about, in the *Eclogues*, with darker notes of scepticism. Moeris in Eclogue 9 declares that, in the face of political oppression, poets are in reality as helplessly vulnerable, and songs as powerless, as doves attacked by eagles, and, for the despairing lover of Damon's song in Eclogue 8, the notion that the humble shepherd Tityrus might be an Orpheus in the woods constitutes a flagrant and absurd reversal of the natural order.

Indeed, in the Aristaeus episode at the end of the *Georgics*, Orpheus despairing over his lost Eurydice (in what is effectively an epyllion set

---

76 For evidence that the *Complaints* volume was called in, see Richard S. Peterson, 'Laurel Crown and Ape's Tail: New Light on Spenser's Career from Sir Thomas Gresham', *Spenser Studies* 12 (1998), 1–35.

into Virgil's didactic work) becomes emblematic precisely of the futility of amatory poetry. The depiction of Orpheus here is fraught with reminiscences of the despairing lovers of the *Eclogues*, particularly Gallus in the tenth, and just as Virgil closes the fourth *Georgic* with a disparaging (though nostalgic)[77] glance backward at pastoral as the songs of ignoble idleness, so the outcome of this narrative, with Orpheus' death and Aristaeus' successful restoration of his bees, implies a rejection of Orphic song and an embrace of the Augustan values of *labor* and *pietas* in its place.[78] In fact, Virgil seems to have invented the story of Orpheus' failure. In all earlier accounts – including the *Lament for Bion*, ll. 122–5 – the myth appears to end with Eurydice's return to the upper world.[79] Virgil's version, which quickly became canonical, seems devised precisely in order to promote the values embodied in Aristaeus – values of practicality, piety, statesmanship and public duty (for Aristaeus' bees are an elaborate metaphor for the orderly society) – over the passionate love for an individual, nostalgic attachment to the past, and poetry itself conceived as an inspired Platonic *furor poeticus* which Orpheus represents.[80] After his second loss of Eurydice Orpheus is presented as living entirely in the past, and does not use his powers in the service of any public good. The lessons which Aeneas will have to learn in the *Aeneid*, to relinquish his emotional attachment to the past – including his lost wife Creusa, in a scene in Book

---

[77] On the 'tantalizing sense of ambivalent nostalgia' in the closing *sphragis*, see Gale, 'Poetry and the Backward Glance' (349).

[78] See G. B. Miles, *Virgil's Georgics: A New Interpretation* (Berkeley: University of California Press, 1980), pp. 272–81; Gian Bagio Conte, *The Poetry of Pathos: Studies in Virgilian Epic*, ed. S. J. Harrison (Oxford: Oxford University Press, 2007), ch. 4, 'Aristaeus, Orpheus, and the *Georgics*: Once Again' (pp. 123–49).

[79] See Charles Segal, *Orpheus: The Myth of the Poet* (Baltimore: Johns Hopkins University Press, 1989), pp. 1–10; M. O. Lee, *Virgil as Orpheus: A Study of the Georgics* (Albany: State University of New York Press, 1996), pp. 1–13; Monica R. Gale, 'Poetry and the Backward Glance in Virgil's *Georgics* and *Aeneid*', *TAPA* 133 (2003), 323–52, at 333–4. The earliest reference outside Virgil to the failure of Orpheus' attempt to recover Eurydice is in the mythographer Conon (*Diegeseis* 45.2), who was probably writing around the same time as Virgil.

[80] In the *Phaedrus* (245a), Plato contrasts such inspired poetry with poetry produced by mere laborious craftsmanship; such pedestrian *labor* is of course reflected in the character of Virgil's Aristaeus, and in both the subject matter and the didactic utility of Virgil's *Georgics* as a whole. Virgil comes closest to presenting *himself* as inspired with an Orphic or Platonic *furor* at *Georgics* 3.291–3, where desire drags him through steep wastes of sweet Parnassus, unmarked by the wheel-tracks of any previous chariot. The passage is preceded by his description of the destructive *furor* of sexual passion among cattle and horses, and strongly recalls it: he particularly resembles the inflamed mares, led by desire over mountains and through rivers (3.269–70), so that, in retrospect, the image of the mares 'pregnant with the wind' (3.275) and issuing a slimy discharge reads like a parodic version (a deflation, in fact) of the *afflatus* of poetic inspiration.

2 which alludes heavily to the Orpheus episode of the fourth *Georgic* – and to dedicate himself to his people's future, amount to a change from imitating Orpheus to imitating Aristaeus, a process which culminates in Anchises' closing advice to his son in Book 6, that Romans must leave art to the Greeks and concentrate instead on war and government.[81] The triumph of Aristaeus over Orpheus at the end of the *Georgics* represents the subordination of the *vita contemplativa* to the *vita activa*.[82] In the *Eclogues* such a subordination was lamented as violence perpetrated by barbarous and impious soldiers against innocent poet-herdsmen, by eagles against helpless doves, but the subsequent works – at least on the surface – advocate it in increasingly positive terms. As Virgil advances towards his own poetic triumph by celebrating Augustus, fantasies of Orphic supernatural abilities which would render the poet independently powerful are put aside in favour of complicity with political power.[83]

The pseudo-Virgilian *Culex* repeats the *Georgics*' version of the Orpheus myth, whereby Eurydice is lost a second time. But curiously, Spenser's translation of this poem in *Virgils Gnat* is the only place in all his works where Spenser makes any mention of the supposed failure. E.K.'s gloss to *October* 28, where Piers compares Cuddie's power to entrance his audience with song to Orpheus' taming of Cerberus with 'His musicks might' (30), states unambiguously that Orpheus 'by his excellent skil in Musick and Poetry ... recouered his wife Eurydice from hell', provocatively ignoring altogether the more canonical Virgilian version (influentially taken up by Ovid, and by Spenser's day by far the better known). Spenser's other allusions to the myth follow suit: in *The Ruines of Time*, the Muses are said to have sent Eurydice 'back againe to life' for Orpheus' sake; and at *Faerie Queene* IV.x.58 we are likewise told that '*Orpheus* did recoure / His Leman from the Stygian Princes boure'. The *Epithalamion* likens its own triumphant wedding song to Orpheus', made 'for his owne bride' (16), an allusion which makes far more sense in the context of the happy ending to which Spenser elsewhere subscribes. Editors and commentators have noted locally that Spenser 'may refer to the less

---

81 The relation of the loss of Creusa to the Orpheus epyllion relies in part on the fact that Aeneas' wife is given the name Eurydice in the *Cypria*, as reported by Pausanias 10.26.1.
82 G. B. Conte, *The Rhetoric of Imitation: Genre and Poetic Memory in Virgil and Other Latin Poets*, tr. Charles Segal (Ithaca: Cornell University Press, 1986), pp. 133–40.
83 Again, this is at least what is happening on the surface: as with his other works, there are notes of ambivalence in the *Georgics* too. See for instance Christine Perkell, *The Poet's Truth: A Study of the Poet in Virgil's* Georgics (Berkeley: University of California Press, 1989); S. Kyriakidis, 'Georgics 4.559–566: The Vergilian Sphragis', *Kleos* 6 (2000), 535–47; Gale, 'Poetry and the Backward Glance'.

common version of the story in which Orpheus recovered Eurydice' (Hamilton's gloss to *FQ* IV.x.58.4–5), or speculated that the omission of the tragic ending imports a sinister subtext pulling against the speaker's optimism (McCabe's gloss to *Epithalamion* 16, and headnote to *Amoretti and Epithalamion*, p. 669).[84] What has not been considered is the possibility that Spenser is pointedly and deliberately rejecting Virgil's innovation and looking back beyond him to the earlier state of the myth, before the forward momentum of the Virgilian *cursus* had recast Orpheus as a failure. The values of passionate wedded love and Platonic *furor poeticus* which Virgil rejects in the person of the defeated Orpheus of the *Georgics*, choosing instead political commitment to the emperor, are precisely the values which Spenser embraces: the argument to *October*, where an Orphic Cuddie explicitly rejects the Virgilian *cursus* on political grounds, presents him as 'the perfecte paterne of a Poete' inspired with 'a certaine *enthousiasmos* and celestiall inspiration'; in 'Colin Clouts Come Home Againe', Colin displays his divine inspiration in a hymn to procreative love.

'Colin Clouts Come Home Againe' amplifies the Orphic subcurrent of the *Eclogues*, as the divinely inspired Colin entrances, sustains and revives his community through his songs' aesthetic beauty, political insight and religious teachings, and rhetorically animates the landscape through *prosopopoeia* in the lay of Bregog and Mulla. But he pointedly removes the intermittent tendency of the *Eclogues* to associate Orphic aspiration with ascent to 'higher' genres. The animate Irish landscape of the lay of Bregog and Mulla reworks the landscape of Sicily as personified in the nymphs and monsters of an interrelated group of texts in ancient bucolic and epic, texts in which Theocritus, Virgil and Ovid had already staged confrontations and negotiations between the poetic kinds and their implicit values. Entering into this negotiation, Spenser produces in the lay a new myth in which pastoral trumps epic, as it does in the poem as a whole, in the volume as a whole and in what we might call the 'Book of Spenser'. And as pastoral trumps epic, so pastoral's traditional subject matter of love trumps epic's *reges et proelia*, kings and battles. But this is not the love condemned by Virgil as destructive madness or *furor*; rather

---

84 Joseph Loewenstein, 'Echo's Ring: Orpheus and Spenser's Career', *ELR* 16 (1986), 287–302, builds heavily on the assumption that allusion to Orpheus and Eurydice means allusion to Orpheus' tragic failure. Loewenstein valuably emphasizes, however, that Spenser foregrounds the 'heterodoxy' of his career in relation to the Virgilian paradigm (300). I am not sure whether, by referring to *cursus Vergiliani* ('Virgilian careers') in the plural (pp. 298 and 299), he means to imply that such departures from Virgil's career path are also in a sense Virgilian, as intended to be read in relation to Virgil.

it is love conceived as the basis at once of faithful marriage, of friendship and of equitable social relations in a truly civilized society. It is in keeping with the other episode in the Orpheus myth to which Spenser alludes in *The Faerie Queene* (IV.ii.1) – the account, taken from the *Argonautica* of Apollonius of Rhodes (contemporary and friend of Callimachus and Theocritus), of how Orpheus resolved the strife between the Argonauts by taking 'His siluer Harpe in hand' (*FQ* IV.ii.1.9) and singing a creation hymn: 'Such Musicke is wise words with time concented, / To moderate stiffe minds, disposd to striue' (IV.ii.2.5–6). (The passage strongly recalls E.K.'s lengthy gloss on the power of music at *October* 28.) In the egalitarian community of the 'shepheards nation', bound by ties of friendly love, Spenser offers an alternative to the corrupt ethos of worldly ambition and competitiveness which dominates the perniciously hierarchical court and kingdom of 'Cynthia' or Elizabeth – that competitive urge to power inscribed in the very notion of the *cursus* as a 'race' to the top, in Virgil's literary *cursus* as in the civic *cursus honorum*. The shepherd Colin is indeed 'an Orpheus in the woods' of pastoral, and the volume shows us that the pastoral setting, as reimagined by Spenser, is precisely Orpheus' natural home. It is here, in the eclogues of *Colin Clouts Come Home Againe*, that the figure of Colin as a poet-prophet – a figure which was to exert a strong influence on Milton – fully emerges. But in fact it was always implicit in Spenser's pastorals, as we can see from the Orphic depiction of the divinely inspired Cuddie, *alter ego* of Colin and of Spenser. The professions of humility, and the idea of pastoral as a mere youthful preparation for future heroic epic, 'by little first to proue theyr tender wyngs, before they make a greater flyght', peddled by E.K.'s invocation of the Virgilian *cursus* in the epistle to Harvey, were always a ruse. Indeed, as E.K. there lists his examples of such pastoralists, the first in his list, preceding 'So flew Virgile, as not yet well feeling his winges', points to the underlying reality of Spenser's investment in the genre: 'So flew Theocritus, as you may perceiue he was all ready full fledged.' Before the invention of the Virgilian career, when bucolic *epos* was an equally worthy form of poetry, and the poet's authority had not yet been hitched so decisively to the triumphal chariot of the emperor, Theocritus and his Hellenistic followers showed that bucolic song was an appropriate exercise for the 'full fledged' poet. The shape of the 'Book of Spenser' is intended precisely to restore that status, to undo the Virgilian career and all that it implies.

Chapter 1 makes a case for taking seriously the allegorical mode of reading Virgil's *Eclogues* prominent in the commentary tradition from Servius to the Renaissance, by way of an examination of his method of imitation. Virgil's politicization of bucolic is not just a matter of alternating contemporary political themes with Theocritean amatory ones, but rather reworks Theocritean love as political allegory. As the relations of Virgil's herdsmen to political power (as its protegés or as its victims) are modelled on the amatory plights of Theocritus' herdsmen, so their connection to the more obviously Theocritean lovers of the amatory eclogues, based on the same idylls, constructs a pattern of analogy – even of allegorical equivalence – between love and politics across the book. The Theocritean wooing-song becomes a figure for the poet's attempt to negotiate a bargain with political power, and the dynamics and possible outcomes of that attempted transaction are figured in an array of reworkings of the pastoral wooing-gift of lambs or fruit, figuring both the political contract binding society generally, and the role the poet himself might play as future propagandist or satirist.

Chapter 2 examines how *The Shepheardes Calender* seeks to replicate the Virgilian dynamic of bargaining with power in its opposition to the D'Alençon match, in a way which both deepens the gloom of the original and heightens the confidence of the poet in his own power to influence public opinion through his poetic skill. Colin's love for Rosalind reflects and develops the intimate relation between love and political complaint in Virgil's eclogue-book. His reluctance to ascend to higher genres is a response to Elizabeth's perceived betrayal of her true spouse, England, and draws on Virgilian *recusatios* to drive a bargain, balancing the offer of praise if she calls off the planned Catholic marriage with the threat of satire if she does not. Colin's public songs in *Aprill* and *Nouember* rework Virgil's Caesarean eclogues 4 and 5, but from the bitterly ironic perspective of the ninth eclogue, remembering the hopes Elizabeth's Protestant subjects placed in her reign at her coronation twenty years earlier, but mourning them as disappointed and unfulfilled. Virgil's recurrent motif of the pastoral gift, with its connotations of political contract and poetic negotiation, threads through the amatory and the openly political themes of the *Calender*, but what is at stake is now no less than the physical and spiritual death of the nation.

In Chapter 3 I look beyond the four eclogues – *Januarye*, *June*, *Aprill* and *Nouember* – which were my focus in the previous chapter, to consider the structure of the *Calender* as a whole. Drawing attention to striking patterns which have not previously been noticed, I argue that the structure of the work represents an orderly and significant development of the concentric ring-structure of Virgil's eclogue book, focused on the displacement of Caesarean praise by an amplification of topical satire as defining Colin's public role. A surprising pattern of line numbers also emerges, by which Colin's contributions and the politically contentious topic of love are consistently associated with the unlucky number 13, and *June* and *October* are singled out as sharing the line-total 120. This number, as the product of Virgil's ten eclogues and Spenser's twelve, underlines the fact that these are the two eclogues in which Spenser directly addresses the question of his relation to Virgil, and the reasons for his divergence from his model; the chapter ends with a reading of *October*'s reflections on the Virgilian *cursus*.

Chapters 4 and 5 analyse the volume in which Spenser returns to pastoral in 1595, *Colin Clouts Come Home Againe*, focusing respectively on the two eclogues by Spenser which comprise most of its bulk, but considering them in the context of the whole. Both poems engage particularly with Virgil's tenth and final eclogue, in which he bids farewell to pastoral, and together they work to reject the values which motivate that farewell, and to place a new version of pastoral, reconceived as prophetic, at the top of the generic hierarchy, above epic's tales of kings. The failure of Gallus' poetic vocation as depicted in Virgil's sixth and tenth eclogues, leading to Virgil's investiture as the Muses' poet, is the model for Spenser's treatments of Sidney and of Ralegh in his two poems, Virgil's critique of Gallus' elegiac love-frenzy becoming the basis for Spenser's rejection both of Petrarchism and of the values of the court. The lament for Sidney (Chapter 4) blames his loss on the court's privileging of a frivolously conceived *vita activa* and foolish undervaluing of poetry, and conspicuously replaces expected claims for the immortality of Sidney's verse with echoes of Spenser's earlier poems, to imply that Spenser's own dedication to the *vita contemplativa* and championing of procreative love consoles the community and compensates for the nation's loss. In 'Colin Clouts Come Home Againe' (Chapter 5), Ralegh's Petrarchan love is presented as an unhealthy state of dependency arising from the corrupt patronage system of a perniciously hierarchical court; it is rejected in favour of a vision of mutual love and equitable social relations following the ethical, political and religious teachings of a prophetic Colin. In the lay of Bregog and Mulla, Spenser reimagines Virgil's pastoral muse, the virginal Arethusa, in conjunction with her epic intertexts in Virgil and Ovid, to elevate pastoral and its amatory subject matter above epic and the contaminating influence of courtly values. Virgil's Arcadia, a space of retreat from politics, is replaced by an Ireland transformed, in Spenser's originary mythopoeic imagination, into an allegorical space of independence from Cynthia's political power. This landscape, animated by Colin's Orphic powers, recreates pastoral as a fitter channel than Virgilian epic for truly prophetic poetry, while the 'shepheards nation' whose dialogue structures both the poem and the co-authored volume figures the Republic of Letters as a meritocratic space of friendly exchange, uncontrolled by political allegiances. Spenser's 1595 return to pastoral represents a pointed and meaningful break both with the Virgilian career path and with the ideological role it played in Tudor society; it can only be properly understood in relation to the *cursus* it reshapes.

1

Intertextuality and allegory in Virgil's Eclogues

Servius and political allegory

Virgil's chief innovation in pastoral, it has long been recognized, is his introduction of contemporary political realities. Theocritus' *Idylls* are varied in subject matter, sometimes set in a bustling city, sometimes speaking of or addressing contemporary rulers, sometimes miniaturizing heroic epic, but the group of idylls recognized in antiquity as 'bucolic songs' deal with herdsmen concerned mainly with singing and with love, in a world apparently sealed off from the events of history.[1] The first, violent intrusion of the world of politics into the lives of Virgil's herdsmen comes at the very opening of his book, as the dialogue between Tityrus and Meliboeus in Eclogue 1 confronts us with the distress caused by Octavian's policy of confiscating farmlands in the regions around Cremona and Mantua, to reward the troops who had won the Battle of Philippi for him. These land-confiscations will also be the explicit subject of Eclogue 9. The issue was intensely topical, and politically sensitive: we know from classical historians that public protest against the injustice of the policy constituted a real threat to the regime.[2] Four centuries later, this topic looms large in Servius' commentary on the *Eclogues*.[3]

---

1 This is not to say that Virgil was unaware of, or indeed uninfluenced by, the explicit political concerns of some of Theocritus' non-bucolic idylls. For instance, Tityrus' promise of regular sacrifice to the godlike youth he has met in Rome seems to be modelled on Theocritus 17.126–7, praising Ptolemy for building temples and offering sacrifice to his own mother and father.
2 The chief classical authority for the history of the civil war period, Appian, describes how 'Not only the cities that had been designated for the army, but almost the whole of Italy, rose' in protest against Octavian's land-confiscations, 'fearing like treatment' (Appian, *The Civil Wars*, tr. Horace White (Cambridge, MA: Harvard University Press, 1913), 5.27).
3 The commentary of Servius exists in two forms. The shorter form was printed and reprinted in most early editions of Virgil, while the longer form, an expanded

He assumes an autobiographical underpinning, relating an elaborate story of the confiscation and subsequent restoration of Virgil's own estate, and notes supposed references to it not only in the two eclogues which treat the confiscations directly, but *per allegoriam* in what might seem to us the unlikeliest places.[4] Indeed, though Servius' proem stresses the contrast between Virgil's allegorical complexity and Theocritus 'who is everywhere simple', he tells us in a gloss on Eclogue 3 that veiled references to the confiscations are the only allegories he will permit. Servius' commentary exerted a profound influence on readings of Virgil to Spenser's day and beyond.[5]

This theme in Virgil's *Eclogues*, then, is what licenses the practice of using pastoral to comment on contemporary affairs in Petrarch and Mantuan, a practice which by the late sixteenth century had become an expectation, and fundamental to the theory of pastoral.[6] Though Virgil devotes a lot of time in the *Eclogues* to Theocritean themes of love and mythology, Sidney's encapsulation of the genre

---

version referred to today as Servius Danielis, or 'D Servius', was first printed by Pierre Daniel in 1600. I am concerned here with the shorter text, which would have been known to Spenser and his contemporaries. I use the edition of Georg Thilo and Hermann Hagen, *Servii Grammatici qui feruntur in Vergilii carmina commentarii*, 3 vols (Leipzig, 1878–87).

4 Servius derives the biography from Donatus' *Vita*; see also Quintilian, *Institutes* 8.6.46–7. On the evidence, or lack of it, for the biographical claim, see Horsfall, *A Companion to the Study of Virgil* (Leiden: Brill, 1995), pp. 12–13; Richard Jenkyns condemns Servius' allegorical method generally as 'nonsense, but extremely influential' (Richard Jenkyns, *The Legacy of Rome: A New Appraisal* (Oxford: Oxford University Press, 1992), p. 155).

5 See Peter K. Marshall, *Servius and Commentary on Virgil*, Center for Medieval & Renaissance Studies, Occasional Papers 5 (Asheville, NC: Pegasus, 1997); Annabel Patterson, *Pastoral and Ideology: Virgil to Valéry* (Oxford: Clarendon Press, 1988), pp. 9–42. On the allegorizing tendencies of the commentaries more generally, see David Scott Wilson-Okamura, *Virgil in the Renaissance* (Cambridge: Cambridge University Press, 2010), 47–76. Chaudhuri also provides a good overview, while making no effort to conceal her disdain for such allegorical reading, which she calls a 'common malady' (Sukanta Chaudhuri, *Renaissance Pastoral and Its English Developments* (Oxford: Clarendon Press, 1989), pp. 9–22; quotation at p. 16).

6 Again, Chaudhuri offers a helpful but deeply disparaging overview of this trait in European Renaissance pastoral (pp. 24–57): the allegorical or allusive impetus for her marks the 'atrophy of pastoral', whose true purpose is to convey 'a coherent picture of shepherds' lives' (18) and the 'intrinsic beauty' (57) of an 'idealized poetic world like Theocritus' Cos or Sicily' (52). See also W. W. Greg, *Pastoral Poetry and Pastoral Drama* (London: Bullen, 1906). Thomas G. Rosenmeyer, too, describes the allegorizing tendency of Renaissance pastoral as 'foreign to the original pastoral impulse' as he conceives it (*The Green Cabinet: Theocritus and the European Pastoral Lyric* (1969; repr. London: Bristol Classical Press, 2004), pp. 267–80; quotation at 273). For a thorough and less pejorative account, see Helen Cooper, *Pastoral: Medieval into Renaissance* (Ipswich: D. S. Brewer, 1977), pp. 36–46, 108–11.

> which sometimes out of Meliboeus' mouth can show the misery of people under hard lords and ravening soldiers, and again, by Tityrus, what blessedness is derived to them that lie lowest from the goodness of them that sit highest[7]

focuses on the competing political perspectives offered by pastoral, summed up in the situation of Virgil's first eclogue. Puttenham emphasizes that

> the poet devised the eclogue ... not of purpose to counterfeit or represent the rustic manner of loves and communication: but under the veil of homely persons and in rude speeches to insinuate and glance at greater matters, and such as perchance had not been safe to have been disclosed in any other sort, which may be perceived by the Eclogues of Vergil, in which are treated by figure matters of greater importance than the loves of Titirus and Corydon.[8]

What Puttenham seems to see as the triviality of the light, Theocritean theme of love is merely a ruse by which the poet takes occasion to glance at greater matters. As modern readers, it is natural to us to separate these themes of love and politics. All recognize that eclogues 1 and 9 are political, and most agree that eclogues 4 and 5 are strongly linked to contemporary political figures, but other poems, like Eclogue 2, deal with love, and are normally seen today as unconnected to these political concerns. The love poetry merely supplements the political poetry, or the other way round – at any rate, they stand apart. What Puttenham has in mind, though, is something different: he is thinking of Servian allegory. The loves of Corydon *represent* graver matters. Underlying this remark is, in particular, Servius' commentary on Eclogue 2, where Corydon is seen as representing Virgil, and Alexis either a beautiful slave-boy gifted to him by Octavian or by Pollio (the poem thus becoming a tribute showing his gratitude for the gift), or even as Octavian himself, so that Corydon's wooing becomes a plea for political favour – specifically, it appears in Servius' glosses to lines 6 and 73, a request that Octavian should return his confiscated lands.

When such readings are presented starkly as allegories it is easy for us to dismiss them as far-fetched and unVirgilian, and this is how Servius' allegorizing strain has tended to be received by twentieth- and twenty-first-century classicists. But there are two things I

---

7 Sidney, *Apology for Poetry*, 2nd ed., ed. R. W. Maslen (Manchester: Manchester University Press, 1989), p. 97.
8 Puttenham, *The Art of English Poesy*, I. 18, pp. 127–8.

want to note here. The first is simple and obvious. It is that Spenser would have been taught the *Eclogues*, at an early age, with the aid of the Servian commentary, and would have known and very likely accepted such allegories, like his contemporary Puttenham. The second is more complex, but equally important. Virgil's *Eclogues* are an intricate web of imitations from Theocritus, woven in the neoteric style then popular in Rome, to delight an audience familiar with the Greek originals by the ingenious and playful ways in which he reworks and recombines his materials. These allusions not only connect Virgil to Theocritus but also frequently connect separate Virgilian eclogues to each other, as different reworkings of a single idyll. To a reader who recognizes the allusions and appreciates the game, Virgil's treatments of love and of politics are so closely interwoven as to make at least analogies (if not allegories) hard to avoid. Spenser surely was such a reader. He would have been taught Greek both at the Merchant Taylors' School and later at Cambridge. E.K.'s notes (very likely written by Spenser himself) refer to Theocritus frequently and quote him in Greek, and several scholars have argued in recent years that Spenser knew Homer in the original. Even if we are sceptical about the extent of Spenser's Greek, Theocritus' pastoral idylls were readily available in Latin translation.[9] Spenser's own intertwining of the amatory and the political in *The Shepheardes Calender* is deeply influenced by his appreciation of the games Virgil plays with Theocritus in the *Eclogues*, and to understand his own reworking of Virgilian pastoral we have to bear Theocritus in mind too. So by way of preparation for an examination of how Spenser handles Virgil in *The Shepheardes Calender*, the following is an exploration of how Theocritean allusion contributes to meaning and to the interconnection of the amatory and political themes, in the Virgilian eclogues which seem to have been most important to Spenser. It will aim in part to encourage greater openness to Servian allegoresis, enabling us to see it not as reductive but as a shorthand expression, or intermittent glimpses, of a rich and complex mode of reading.

Rewriting Theocritus: love and politics

I have said that Virgil's first eclogue would have come as a shock to contemporary readers because it deals with contemporary politics,

---

9 Eobanus Hessus and Joachim Camerarius, *Theocriti Syracusani Eidyllia triginta sex ... Latino carmine reddita* (Basel, 1531).

Intertextuality and allegory

subject matter alien to Theocritean pastoral.[10] The shock is inflicted on the reader through a very concrete and specific twist on Theocritus in the opening lines, which sets up an analogy between the themes of love and politics from the start (1.1–5).

> Tityre, tu patulae recubans sub tegmine fagi
> silvestrem tenui musam meditaris avena:
> nos patriae fines et dulcia linquimus arva;
> nos patriam fugimus: tu, Tityre, lentus in umbra
> formosam resonare doces Amaryllida silvas.

['You, Tityrus, reclining beneath the cover of the spreading beech, meditate the woodland Muse on your slender oaten reed; we are leaving behind the boundaries of our native land and the sweet fields. We are fleeing our country; you, Tityrus, at ease in the shade, teach the woods to echo "Beautiful Amaryllis".']

The lines allude to the opening of Theocritus' third idyll (1–7):

> Κωμάσδω ποτὶ τὰν Ἀμαρυλλίδα, ταὶ δέ μοι αἶγες
> βόσκονται κατ' ὄρος, καὶ ὁ Τίτυρος αὐτὰς ἐλαύνει.
> Τίτυρ' ἐμὶν τὸ καλὸν πεφιλαμένε, βόσκε τὰς αἶγας,
> καὶ ποτὶ τὰν κράναν ἄγε Τίτυρε, καὶ τὸν ἐνόρχαν
> τὸν Λιβυκὸν κνάκωνα φυλάσσεο, μή τι κορύψῃ.
> Ὦ χαρίεσσ' Ἀμαρυλλί, τί μ' οὐκέτι τοῦτο κατ' ἄντρον
> παρκύπτοισα καλεῖς τὸν ἐρωτύλον; ἦ ῥά με μισεῖς …

['I go to serenade Amaryllis, and my goats graze on the hill, and Tityrus herds them. Tityrus, sweet friend, graze the goats and take them to the spring; and mind the he-goat, the tawny Libyan, lest he butt thee. Charming Amaryllis, why no more dost thou peep out of thy cave and call me in – me, thy sweetheart? Dost hate me?'][11]

This is the first of only two occasions where 'Tityrus' is mentioned in the *Idylls*. (In the other, Idyll 7, he is again a minor character, imagined as singing to Lycidas. This idyll is also significant here, and we shall

---

10 I see Virgil as positing an ideal reader who would recognize his Theocritean allusions and adaptations, though the common run of readers would probably not have done so: Theocritus does not seem to have been widely read in Virgil's Rome. In a way, Virgil was more likely to find such ideal readers in the sixteenth century, when Theocritus was held in high esteem largely as a result of Virgil's canonical status, raising classical bucolic poetry in general to prominence, and Virgilian commentaries noting many of his Theocritean allusions (such as that by Eobanus Hessus, first printed in 1527) were available.
11 A. S. F. Gow (ed. and tr.), *Theocritus*, 2 vols (Cambridge: Cambridge University Press, 1950).

come back to it.)[12] Virgil's eclogues often name some particular Theocritean shepherd in the opening line.[13] Here the allusion is especially marked by the repetition of *Tityre* in both passages, and of course by the song that Virgil's Tityrus is singing: *formosam ... Amaryllida* (which would be the Latin title of the song of Theocritus' goatherd, since poems were commonly referred to by their opening words in classical Rome). And Virgil underlines the fact that he is echoing Theocritus here in the image of the echoing woods: throughout the *Eclogues* this image is used as a self-referential 'marker' highlighting imitation of earlier poetry.[14] These same opening lines of Theocritus' idyll will be translated closely in Eclogue 9, ll. 23–5, as a remembered fragment of a song by Menalcas.[15]

But there is a twist. In Theocritus, 'beautiful Amaryllis' is the despairing song of the unnamed goatherd to his stony-hearted beloved, which makes up the rest of Idyll 3. In Virgil, not only is the song transferred to Tityrus himself, but it is transformed, implicitly, into a song of happy mutual love. Tityrus' content as he lies at ease in the shade contrasts not only with Meliboeus' fate, as he flees his homeland, but also with the misery of Theocritus' goatherd, who plans to climb to the top of a cliff and throw himself off (3.25–6). We learn a little later that Amaryllis is indeed Tityrus' faithful lover, in a passage which suggests the purpose and significance of Virgil's allusion (1.27–39):

> Tityrus:
> Libertas, quae sera tamen respexit inertem,
> candidior postquam tondenti barba cadebat,
> respexit tamen et longo post tempore venit,
> postquam nos Amaryllis habet, Galatea reliquit.
> namque fatebor enim – dum me Galatea tenebat,
> nec spes libertatis erat nec cura peculi.
> quamvis multa meis exiret victima saeptis
> pinguis et ingratae premeretur caseus urbi,
> non umquam gravis aere domum mihi dextra redibat.

---

12 Antonio Mancinelli, in *P. Virgilii Maronis Opera ... cum ... commentariis Servii, Donati, Probi, Mancinelli* (Venice, 1544) and Petrus Ramus, in *P. Virgilii Maronis Bucolica, P. Rami, professoris regii praelectionibus exposita* (Paris, 1572) note that Virgil has taken the name from these idylls.
13 Clausen, *Eclogues*, p. 34.
14 This is an example of what Stephen Hinds calls 'reflexive annotation'; see Stephen Hinds, *Allusion and Intertext: Dynamics of Appropriation in Roman Poetry* (Cambridge: Cambridge University Press, 1998), pp. 1–16.
15 As noted by Eobanus Hessus, *In P. Vergilii Maronis Bucolica* (Strasbourg, 1540), *ad* 9.23.

Meliboeus:
Mirabar quid maesta deos, Amarylli, vocares,
cui pendere sua patereris in arbore poma.
Tityrus hinc aberat. ipsae te, Tityre, pinus,
ipsi te fontes, ipsa haec arbusta vocabant.

['*Tityrus*: Liberty, who looked upon me in my idleness, though late – when the clippings of my beard had begun to fall white as it was cut. Yet she looked upon me, and came after a long time, after Amaryllis possessed me and Galatea left me. For indeed, I will confess, while Galatea ruled me, there was no hope of liberty, nor attention to savings. Though many a victim left my enclosures and many a fat cheese was pressed for the ungrateful town, my right hand never returned home heavy with coins. *Meliboeus*: I used to wonder why, so sorrowful, you called on the gods, Amaryllis, and for whom you allowed the apples to hang on their trees. Tityrus was away from here. The very pines, Tityrus, the very springs, these very orchards were calling you.']

It is as if, as Hubbard notes, 'the subordinate Tityrus of Theocritus ... supplants the goatherd to become the lover of Amaryllis himself', succeeding where the goatherd failed.[16]

This little passage of biography, which seems so casual, is itself deeply suggestive. Tityrus links his two loves, Galatea and her successor Amaryllis, to the two phases of his life, his servitude and his manumission (or release from slavery). On the literal level there is an implied chain of cause and effect. Loving Galatea, it would seem, necessitated spending all his money on presents for her, so that he could not save up to purchase his freedom; the inference that Galatea was an unresponsive mistress who could be wooed only with endless gifts is supported, as we shall see, by her significant name. When he switched his affections on to Amaryllis, such expenditure was no longer necessary – as Meliboeus' reply makes clear, she returned his love – so that Tityrus was able to save to buy himself out of slavery. So, although his present happiness contrasts with the speaker of Idyll 3, we are invited to imagine an earlier period of Tityrus' life when their situations were not so different. Now, Theocritus' third idyll bears a strong similarity to Idyll 11, the song of the lovesick Cyclops to the disdainful nymph Galatea; it has even been described as a rewriting of Idyll 11 'with an almost carbon-copy effect'.[17] Like

---

16 Thomas K. Hubbard, *The Pipes of Pan: Intertextuality and Literary Filiation in the Pastoral Tradition from Theocritus to Milton* (Ann Arbor: University of Michigan Press, 1998), p. 50.
17 Kathryn Gutzwiller, *Theocritus' Pastoral Analogies: The Formation of a Genre*

the goatherd of Idyll 3, the Cyclops of Idyll 11 offers a catalogue of gifts to his unmoved beloved. By using Galatea's name in an eclogue which began with an allusion to Idyll 3, Virgil pointedly evokes its partner idyll. Where he transforms Theocritus' stony Amaryllis into an undemanding and responsive mistress, he also brings in her icy Theocritean double unchanged. As Tityrus progresses from irksome slavery to security on his farm, he passes simultaneously from the position of the despairing lovers of idylls 3 and 11 to comfortable mutual love.

The close connection between these movements implies analogy between them at the very least. Once again, Servius puts it starkly as an allegory, in his gloss on line 29: 'for Galatea is Mantua, Amaryllis Rome'. At first glance this looks absurd and reductive. But modern commentators agree that there is a need to appeal to something other than the literal level to explain what is going on here, for something rather odd is going on.[18] The nature of Tityrus' reprieve and present happiness is ambiguous. According to his account he goes to Rome to purchase his freedom from slavery, but the response of the godlike youth he meets there makes no mention of this, and is addressed instead to the question of the land confiscations: *'pascite, ut ante, boves, pueri; submittite tauros'* ('"Pasture your cattle as before, lads; rear your bulls"', 1.45), where 'as before' seems even to emphasize that Tityrus' slave-status has not changed.[19] This restoration of land explains the anomaly which has puzzled Meliboeus from the start of the eclogue, the fact that Tityrus is reclining at ease while his fellow shepherds trudge into exile – an exile which is the general

---

(Madison: University of Wisconsin Press, 1991), p. 115. See also Francis Cairns, *Generic Composition in Greek and Latin Poetry* (Edinburgh: Edinburgh University Press, 1972), pp. 145–7.

18 That such oddness on the literal level is a signal that the reader should turn to allegorical interpretation is the explicit position of Francis Bacon, another of Spenser's contemporaries, in the *De sapientia veterum* (1609): 'There is another Argument (and that no small one neither) to prooue that these Fables containe certaine hidden and inuolued meanings, seeing some of them are obserued to be so absurd and foolish in the very relation, that they shew, and as it were proclaime a parable afar off' (trans. Arthur Gorges, in *The wisdome of the ancients written in Latine by the Right Honourable Sir Francis Bacon ... done into English by Sir Arthur Gorges, Knight* (London, 1619), sig. a8v). My thanks to Julian Lethbridge for drawing my attention to this.

19 In fact Tityrus seems to remain a slave. The suggestion that his dependence on his patron Octavian, with the resulting necessity of tributes of lambs and praise-poetry, is servile, undignified and un-Roman from a Republican perspective is picked up, as we shall see later, by the pseudo-Virgilian *Dirae*, a pastoral work which Spenser would probably have known as Virgil's.

fate, and not Meliboeus' alone, as his repeated *nos* in lines 3–4 and again at line 64 makes clear. The importance of the line as marking the crucial difference between their situations is underlined by the rueful sarcasm with which Meliboeus echoes it later on: *insere nunc, Meliboee, piros, pone ordine vites* (1.73). But if we are dealing here simply with a successful appeal against the confiscations, why then does Tityrus talk about slavery? Clausen's answer is that Virgil deliberately confuses the public and private meanings of the *Libertas* invoked in line 27. Far from merely evoking the manumission of a slave, *libertas* was a term carrying a strong political charge in the late republic, and had been used as a slogan in the civil war period both by Octavian and by his recently defeated enemy Sextus Pompeius.[20] It strikes Servius, too, as having wider implications than mere manumission, concerning the liberty of the citizen and its infringement under Octavian's rule (*ad loc.*):

> et aliter dicit servus, libertatem cupio, aliter ingenuus: ille enim carere vult servitute, hic habere liberam vitam, pro suo scilicet arbitrio agere: sicut nunc Vergilius sub persona Tityri dicit se amore libertatis Romam venire compulsum, et item latenter carpit tempora, quibus libertas non nisi in urbe Roma erat.

> ['A slave says "I desire freedom" in one sense, and a free-born man says it in another; for the former wants to be free of his servitude, the latter to have a free life, that is to act according to his own will; just as now Virgil under the persona of Tityrus says he is driven to come to Rome by his love of liberty, and also covertly criticizes the times, in which there was no liberty except in the city of Rome.']

The implication, of course, is that the victims of the confiscations are being treated like slaves; and the original audience would have been equally alert to the political connotations of slavery, a commonplace figure for subjection to a tyrant in contemporary discourse.[21]

Tityrus' personal history begins to feel just a little like a simile – or an allegory, we might say. Libertas, Amaryllis, and the godlike youth he encounters in Rome all smile on Tityrus' suit with the same

---

20 See Ronald Syme, *The Roman Revolution* (Oxford: Oxford University Press, 1963 [1939]), p. 155.
21 See the Ciceronian examples gathered by Clausen, *Eclogues*, p. 31, n. 10. If Tityrus has not been manumitted, we might also wonder what has become of the *peculi* (1.32) saved up to purchase his manumission. Those coins whose weight was felt so tangibly at line 35 are not mentioned again. Might we infer that Tityrus has had to part with them to purchase his current security? Is Octavian using the threat of the land-confiscations to run a protection racket?

gesture. Personal liberty, fulfilled desire and political protection are brought together in a single image, while memories of the less fortunate love-suit addressed to Galatea (as to the beloveds of Idylls 3 and 11) become analogous to the political situation of Meliboeus and those like him, who have failed to achieve a similar restoration of their lands.[22] The linkage between love and slavery here is conventional in the *servitium amoris* trope of Roman amatory elegy; Virgil's expansion of the trope, via the conventional political connotations of slavery and *Libertas* as a slogan, to include the relation of subject and ruler can also be seen echoed in later elegy, for instance in Ovid's casting of Augustus as an elegiac *dura puella* in his exile elegies.[23] In Eclogue 1, then, a narrative which remains contradictory and puzzling when interpreted literally makes more sense when we focus on the bigger political issues it shadowily evokes. It is really not so very far from here to the sense that Galatea and Amaryllis have a figurative as well as a literal import, as reflected in Servius' allegory, perhaps suggesting that Tityrus' late love for Amaryllis symbolizes conversion to Octavian's cause.[24]

Meliboeus' response to Tityrus' tale is an idyllic description of the ease Tityrus will continue to enjoy on the lands which will remain his (1.51–8):

> fortunate senex, hic inter flumina nota
> et fontis sacros frigus captabis opacum;
> hinc tibi, quae semper, vicino ab limite saepes
> Hyblaeis apibus florem depasta salicti
> saepe levi somnum suadebit inire susurro;
> hinc alta sub rupe canet frondator ad auras,

---

[22] When Lycidas recites his direct translation of Idyll 3, lines 3–5 in Eclogue 9, lines 23–5, he introduces it as a song he overheard Moeris singing recently on his way to woo 'our Amaryllis'. Moeris, thus identified with the lovelorn goatherd of Idyll 3, is a victim of the land-confiscations like Meliboeus. Later in Eclogue 9 (lines 39–43), he will recite what is effectively a brief Latin version of Polyphemus' love-song to Galatea in Idyll 11. The ninth eclogue shows again that memories of the despairing love of Idylls 3 and 11 are intimately bound up with Virgil's thinking about the confiscations.

[23] Philip Hardie, *Ovid's Poetics of Illusion* (Cambridge: Cambridge University Press, 2002), p. 186; Niklas Holzberg, *Ovid: The Poet and His Work*, tr. G. M. Goshgarian (Ithaca: Cornell University Press, 2002), p. 177; Betty Rose Nagle, *The Poetics of Exile: Program and Polemic in the* Tristia *and* Epistulae ex Ponto *of Ovid* (Brussels: Latomus, 1980), pp. 43–68.

[24] Ludovico Vives, in the sixteenth century, would identify Amaryllis as either Rome or Octavian (*In publii Vergilii Maronis Bucolica interpretatio, potissimum allegorica* (Antwerp, 1543), A3v). See also Joy Connolly, 'Border Wars: Literature, Politics, and the Public', *TAPA* 135 (2005), 103–34 (at 119–20).

> nec tamen interea raucae, tua cura, palumbes
> nec gemere aeria cessabit turtur ab ulmo.

['Lucky old man! Here among familiar streams and sacred springs you will seek out the shady cool. Henceforward, as ever, from the neighbouring boundary, the hedge whose willow-flowers are grazed by Hyblaean bees will often invite you with its soft murmur to fall asleep. Henceforth under the high-reared cliff the woodman shall sing to the breezes; nor meanwhile will your hoarse beloved wood-pigeons, or the turtle-dove, cease to moan from the lofty elm.']

The passage has long been recognized as an imitation from another of Theocritus' idylls, number 7 (135–46):

> πολλαὶ δ' ἁμὶν ὕπερθε κατὰ κρατὸς δονέοντο
> αἴγειροι πτελέαι τε· τὸ δ' ἐγγύθεν ἱερὸν ὕδωρ
> Νυμφᾶν ἐξ ἄντροιο κατειβόμενον κελάρυζε.
> τοὶ δὲ ποτὶ σκιαραῖς οροδαμνίσιν αἰθαλίωνες
> τέττιγες λαλαγεῦντες ἔχον πόνον· ἁ δ' ὀλολυγὼν
> τηλόθεν ἐν πυκιναῖσι βάτων τρύζεσκεν ἀκάνθαις.
> ἄειδον κόρυδοι καὶ ἀκανθίδες, ἔστενε τρυγών,
> πωτῶντο ξουθαὶ περὶ πίδακας ἀμφὶ μέλισσαι.
> πάντ' ὦσδεν θέρεος μάλα πίονος, ὦσδε δ' ὀπώρας.
> ὄχναι μὲν πὰρ ποσσί, παρὰ πλευραῖσι δὲ μᾶλα
> δαψιλέως ἁμῖν ἐκυλίνδετο· τοὶ δ' ἐκέχυντο
> ὄρπακες βραβίλοισι καταβρίθοντες ἔραζε ...

['Many a poplar and elm murmured above our heads, and near at hand the sacred water from the cave of the Nymphs fell plashing. On the shady boughs the dusky cicadas were busy with their chatter, and the tree-frog far off cried in the dense thorn-brake. Larks and finches sang, the dove made moan, and bees flitted humming about the springs. Pears at our feet and apples at our side were rolling plentifully, and the branches hung down to the ground with burden of sloes.'][25]

The speaker here, Simichidas, together with his companions, has been on the road through the bulk of the idyll, a weary journey in the noonday heat – when even the lizard seeks shade – relieved by exchange of songs with the goatherd Lycidas, whom they have encountered on the way. Now they have arrived at last at the harvest festival to which they were bound, and as they lie down rejoicing, we get this, the fullest and most delightful *locus amoenus* in Theocritus. In Meliboeus' imitation the jouissance is steeped in irony, for its point is that he, and apparently all the shepherds of the region apart from

---

25 All translations of Theocritus are taken from Gow, *Theocritus*.

Tityrus, are excluded from such pastoral delight. Most specifically, the Theocritean context is the celebration of a successful harvest, and the idyll ends with a prayer for future harvests, while Meliboeus will end by reflecting bitterly that a barbarous soldier will reap the crops he has sown. But there is another significant aspect to consider here: the songs exchanged on the road in Idyll 7 are all about escaping from the torments of love into Epicurean detachment. Lycidas describes the celebration he will hold with song and music when his beloved, Ageanax, arrives safely at distant Mitylene, and Lycidas is free from the furnace of his love. Simichidas replies with a song advising his friend Aratus to abandon his painful love for the boy who scorns him and enjoy peace of mind. There is therefore an implied analogy between Meliboeus' sufferings and the torments of unrequited love, both in his exclusion from Simichidas' Epicurean contentment and in the contrast with a Tityrus whose happiness has been defined partly in a pointed contradistinction from the goatherd of Idyll 3. And indeed Meliboeus ends like that goatherd by swearing that he will sing no more: *carmina nulla canam* ('I shall sing no more songs', l. 77; cp. *Id.* 3.52). So again, the intertextual aspects of the eclogue suggest an almost allegorical equivalence between the political and amatory themes.

Virgil has already introduced an allusion to Idyll 7 into the evocation of the beginning of Idyll 3 in the opening lines of his eclogue. Tityrus' posture, recumbent under the trees, is modelled on the apostrophe to the legendary shepherd Comatas at the end of Lycidas' song:

> ὥς τοι ἐγὼν ἐνόμευον ἀν' ὤρεα τὰς καλὰς αἶγας
> φωνᾶς εἰσαΐων, τὺ δ' ὑπὸ δρυσὶν ἢ ὑπὸ πεύκαις
> ἁδὺ μελισδόμενος κατεκέκλισο θεῖε Κομᾶτα.
>
> (Idyll 7, 87–9)

['would thou hadst been numbered with the living in my day, that I might have herded thy fair goats upon the hills and listened to thy voice, while thou, divine Comatas, didst lie and make sweet music under the oaks or pines'.]

It is in fact ambiguous whether Lycidas has returned to speaking in his own voice here, or whether he is still recounting the song which will be sung to him at the celebration he has been imagining – a song sung by none other than Tityrus! So Tityrus' pastoral ease in Eclogue 1 reflects equally the Epicurean detachment from passion of Idyll 7, the fulfilment of love denied to the goatherd of Idyll 3, and the liberty of the citizen who enjoys the protection of a beneficent ruler.[26]

In Eclogue 2 we have a close imitation of Idyll 3, that same idyll alluded so prominently at the beginning of Eclogue 1. Idyll 11 is more often named as Virgil's model in the second eclogue, but in fact the resemblance to Idyll 3 is quite as strong, though with details added in from 11 (and indeed from other idylls). As we have seen, idylls 3 and 11 are in any case a closely related pair. Virgil's eclogue recounts the despairing song of the shepherd Corydon, whose hopeless love for Alexis, a slave-boy loved by his master in the city, has driven him away from his normal pursuits and his community to sing in solitude to the woods and mountains. His song begins (2.6–7) with an echo of the goatherd's song of Idyll 3.[27]

> 'O crudelis Alexi, nihil mea carmina curas?
> nil nostri miserere? mori me denique cogis?'

['O cruel Alexis, do you not care for my songs? Do you not pity me at all? Do you compel me, in short, to die?']

The name is changed, of course, but the adjective 'beautiful' replaced by *crudelis* here is only shifted to the opening of the eclogue itself, where *formosum ... Alexim* frames the first line.

In the song that ensues Corydon follows Idyll 3 closely in his catalogue of gifts. At lines 40–4 he offers Alexis a pair of white-spotted fauns which he has been keeping by allowing them to suckle the same ewe; Thestylis has been begging him to give them to her instead, he adds, and he has a good mind to do just that, since Alexis scorns his gifts. The lines are modelled on Idyll 3.34–6,[28]

> ἦ μάν τοι λευκὰν διδυματόκον αἶγα φυλάσσω,
> τάν με καὶ ἁ Μέρμνωνος ἐριθακὶς ἁ μελανόχρως
> αἰτεῖ, καὶ δωσῶ οἱ, ἐπεὶ τύ μοι ἐνδιαθρύπτῃ.

['Truly I keep for thee a white nanny-goat with two kids which Mermnon's swarthy serving-girl begs of me. And I will give it her since thou art so haughty with me.']

---

26 There is also a further possible implication suggested by this allusion to Idyll 7. The narrative that immediately precedes these lines in Tityrus' imagined song tells of how Comatas was unjustly imprisoned by a tyrannical ruler, but kept alive by bees who fed him honey. Bees are prominent in Meliboeus' imitation of Idyll 7, and called 'bees of Hybla' apparently in tribute to the Sicilian Theocritus. The reader may be invited to compare Comatas' imprisonment with the political oppression by Octavian which Tityrus – but only Tityrus – has managed to escape (or *partly* to escape: see n. 19 above).
27 As noted by Eobanus Hessus, *In P. Vergilii Maronis Bucolica*, ad 2.6.
28 Noted by Eobanus Hessus, *In P. Vergilii Maronis Bucolica*.

merely substituting the more exotic and aesthetically pleasing wild animals for the practical pastoral one, as more likely to please the city boy. He goes on to offer him garlands of flowers (45–50), like Theocritus' goatherd at 3.22–3. Finally he promises (2.51–2):

> ipse ego cana legam tenera lanugine mala
> castaneasque nuces, mea quas Amaryllis amabat ...

['I myself shall pluck tender quinces, white with down, and chestnuts, which my Amaryllis loved ...']

The lines recall Idyll 3.10–11 (which will be translated closely as one of the contributions of Menalcas to the song-contest of Eclogue 3). And here he inserts a little joke. These are what he used to offer his Amaryllis, and she loved them: are we invited to imagine that Corydon *was* the goatherd of Idyll 3, but has now moved on to love Alexis instead? Or merely that (like Tityrus in Eclogue 1) he was another of Amaryllis' lovers, who used the same gift as Theocritus' goatherd (and apparently with more success, in the context of that relationship, since Amaryllis loves rather than scorning the gifted fruit)? There is a similar suggestion earlier, at lines 14–15: *nonne fuit satius, tristes Amaryllidis iras atque superba pati fastidia?* ('Was it not better to suffer the bitter anger and the proud disdain of Amaryllis?') Again the implication is that he was Theocritus' goatherd, and that his present distress is merely a later and even worse episode in the same life.

So Corydon is aligned with the despairing lover of Idyll 3, to whom Tityrus in Eclogue 1 was contrasted. Eclogue 2's topic of misfortune in love is thus woven together with Eclogue 1's theme of political fortune and misfortune through a common Theocritean intertext. Another Theocritean allusion in the opening lines (2.8–9, 12–13), moreover, connects Corydon to Meliboeus, for he too imitates Idyll 7.

> nunc etiam pecudes umbras et frigora captant,
> nunc virides etiam occultant spineta lacertos ...
> at mecum raucis, tua dum vestigia lustro,
> sole sub ardenti resonant arbusta cicadis.

['Now even the cattle seek out the shade and the cool, now the thorny brakes hide even the green lizard ... But with me, as I track your footprints, the trees under the burning sun resound with the harsh sound of the cicadas.']

The lines echo Lycidas' first words when he encounters Simichidas:[29]

---

29 Noted by Eobanus Hessus, *In P. Vergilii Maronis Bucolica*, ad 2.9.

'Σιμιχίδα, πᾷ δὴ τὸ μεσαμέριον πόδας ἕλκεις,
ἀνίκα δὴ καὶ σαῦρος ἐν αἱμασιαῖσι καθεύδει ...
(Idyll 7.21–2)

['Whither now, Simichidas, art thou footing it in the noontide, when even the lizard sleeps in the wall and the tomb-crested larks fare not abroad?']

Like Simichidas, Corydon is abroad in the noonday sun, whose ardour in Virgil reflects Corydon's burning passion (*ardebat*, l. 1; *urit*, l. 68). But unlike Simichidas, the restless Corydon can look forward neither to Epicurean immunity from the pangs of love nor to the delightful ease in the *locus amoenus* which awaits Simichidas on his arrival. He is like Meliboeus in Eclogue 1, excluded from that same *locus amoenus* and instead condemned to continue in a harsher and sadder version of Simichidas' initial journeying. The political cause of Meliboeus' unhappiness is paralleled with the amatory cause of Corydon's.

Corydon's suit to Alexis is thus suggestively paralleled with Tityrus' combined amatory and political suits to Galatea, Amaryllis and Octavian. Against this background, the Servian allegory begins to sound less arbitrary, for instance in his gloss on *crudelis* in line 6:

vel allegorice crudelis Caesar, qui non flecteris meis scriptis et non das ereptos agros. (*ad* 2.6)

['or allegorically cruel Caesar, who are not softened by my writings and do not give back the seized lands.'][30]

From such a perspective, the carefully reared twin fauns Corydon offers so conditionally might remind us of the regular tribute of a lamb from his sheepfolds which Tityrus promises to sacrifice to Octavian in his gratitude (as well as the darker image of the twin kids which the less fortunate Meliboeus has just lost on the flinty rocks). His gift of fruit, meanwhile, as we have seen, is modelled on Theocritean lines which will be translated more closely at lines 70–1 of Eclogue 3:

Quod potui, puero silvestri ex arbore lecta
aurea mala decem misi; cras altera mittam.

['I have sent the boy what I could – ten golden apples picked from a tree in the woodland; tomorrow I shall send as many more.']

---

30 Servius' allegorical reading of Corydon's wooing was widely echoed; see for instance Paulus Manutius' glosses on 2.1 and 2.7 in *Opera P. Virgilii Maronis, Pauli Manutii annotationes brevissimae in margine adscriptae* (Antwerp, 1572), p. 3.

Servius' gloss there will preserve another allegory, which brings out the implication in the gloss on line 6's *crudelis* that the gifts which fail to 'soften' Alexis/Octavian might be read as the eclogues themselves:

> et volunt quidam hoc loco allegoriam esse ad Augustum de decem eclogis: quod superfluum est: quae enim necessitas hoc loco allegoriae? (ad 3.71)

> ['and some want there to be an allegory here about the ten eclogues for Augustus. But this is superfluous, for what necessity is there for allegory here?']

Although Servius himself rejects this allegory, thanks to him we know – and Servius' Renaissance readers knew – that some classical commentators had interpreted Eclogue 3's love-gifts as signifying the poet's 'gift' of poetic praise to the ruler.[31] The conditionality of Corydon's offer of the twin fauns at 2.40–4, though Servius does not make any political application here, seems to make this transaction into a political bargain. Like a lover bribing his beloved with gifts, the poet woos the *princeps*, promising to offer further gifts of poetic praise – perhaps celebrating him publicly as a god, as Tityrus does in Eclogue 1 – but only in return for patronage, or even perhaps on condition that he change his policies. One of the song-fragments recited in Eclogue 9 will spell out the transaction between poet and potentate in these terms, making praise for Varus explicitly contingent on the revocation of the policy of land-confiscations in Mantua (9.27–9).

> 'Vare, tuum nomen, superet modo Mantua nobis,
> Mantua vae miserae nimium vicina Cremonae,
> cantantes sublime ferent ad sidera cycni.'

> ['Varus, if only Mantua remains to us (Mantua, alas, too near wretched Cremona), singing swans shall bear your name on high to the stars.']

The song, we are told, is yet unfinished (*necdum perfecta*), and the implication is clearly that it shall remain so unless the policy is reversed and Mantua spared.

And what, meanwhile, will the poet do if the ruler fails to keep his side of the bargain? He will omit to lift Varus' name to the stars, as Eclogue 9 makes clear. Less explicitly but more threateningly, in Eclogue 2, he will give his gift to another instead, as Corydon

---

31 The idea that pastoral gifts in general could symbolize poems is widespread in Renaissance commentary. See for instance Ludovico Vives on the flowers offered by Corydon to Alexis at 2.46ff. (*flores ad pastoricium poema pertinent*), *In publii Vergilii Maronis Bucolica interpretatio*, A8r.

threatens to give the fauns to Thestylis. Servius' gloss on the end of Eclogue 2 explains the political implication. Corydon recognizes the hopelessness of his suit and tries to call himself back to his senses, in a passage (69-73) which imitates the end of Idyll 11:[32]

> a, Corydon, Corydon, quae te dementia cepit!
> semiputata tibi frondosa vitis in ulmo.
> quin tu aliquid saltem potius, quorum indiget usus,
> viminibus mollique paras detexere iunco?
> invenies alium, si te hic fastidit, Alexin.

['Ah, Corydon, Corydon! What madness has possessed you? Your vine is half-pruned on the leafy elm. Why do you not rather at least get ready to plait, out of osiers and the pliant rush, something your practical need requires? You will find another Alexis, if this one scorns you.']

Idyll 11 is altogether more sanguine than Idyll 3, introduced from the start as a demonstration of the therapeutic powers of song, with the implication that Polyphemus has recovered from the extremity of his passion by the end of the poem. In Corydon's case it is less clear that there has been any cure, but nevertheless the closing echo of Polyphemus adumbrates a possible relinquishing of passion. In another allegory reported by Servius, this is taken to mean a change of political allegiance. Servius glosses 'You will find another Alexis' with 'you will find another emperor, if Augustus spurns your petition for your lands' (*invenies alium imperatorem, si te Augustus te contemnit pro agris rogentem*). In the unsettled period of the second triumvirate when the *Eclogues* were composed, and Octavian's hold on power was far from certain, such a possibility would have real significance – both as a suggestion that Virgil himself might lend his considerable poetic powers to celebrating one of Octavian's enemies and as a suggestion to his reading public that they might change allegiance themselves.[33]

---

32 The imitation is noted by Eobanus Hessus, *ad loc.*
33 Powell sees Meliboeus' reference to bees of Hybla (in Sicily), which is strikingly anomalous in what otherwise appears to be an Italian setting, as a veiled hint of a similar transferral of political allegiance – a suggestion that the dispossessed Meliboeus intends to join Octavian's enemy Sextus Pompeius in Sicily, as did the majority of the victims of the land-confiscations and of those escaping the proscriptions (Anton Powell, *Virgil the Partisan: A Study in the Re-Integration of Classics* (Swansea: Classical Press of Wales, 2008), pp. 190–2).

Gifts and curses

Again Servius rejects the allegory he preserves for us here, but nevertheless adds, as though in its favour: 'Yet in truth a little later he says almost openly of Augustus Caesar "since fortune changes all things …"' (*illud vero paulo post paene aperte dicetur in Augustum Caesarem "quoniam Fors omnia versat"*, gloss to 2.73). He is referring here to Eclogue 9, the second of the eclogues explicitly on the topic of the land-confiscations, where Moeris mournfully explains to Lycidas that, driven into exile like Meliboeus in Eclogue 1, he is on his way first to deliver a gift of kids to the soldier who has thrown him off his farm (9.5–6).

> Nunc victi, tristes, quoniam fors omnia versat,
> hos illi (quod nec vertat bene!) mittimus haedos.

['Now defeated, sorrowful, since chance reverses all things, we are sending him these kids. May no good come of it to him!']

Modern translators and commentators tend to interpret *quoniam fors omnia versat* at line 5 as a rueful reflection on how his own fortune has changed,[34] but in his gloss to 2.73 Servius evidently takes it as a transparent reference to Moeris' hope for a future change in the fortunes of the new owner and of the ruler behind him. At 9.5 he expands: 'it is said severely against Augustus, whose felicity he says, like everything else, can change' (*aspere contra Augustum dictum est, cuius felicitatem, sicut omnia, dicit posse mutari*). And this is more clearly implied by the curse Moeris sends with the gift: *quod nec vertat bene* ('may no good come of it to him'), which Servius glosses:

> quae res in perniciem eius vertatur, id est ut malo omine hoc munus accipiat. tractum autem hoc est ab Hectore et Aiace: nam Hector dedit Aiaci gladium, quo se Aiax postea interemit; Hector vero balteum accepit ab Aiace, quo circa muros patriae tractus est postea.

['May this thing be turned to his ruin, that is may he receive this gift with an evil omen. This is drawn from Hector and Ajax: for Hector gave Ajax a sword, with which Ajax later killed himself; Hector truly accepted a baldric from Ajax, by which he was later dragged around the walls of his city.']

This ironic version of the exchange of gifts between Hector and Ajax at *Iliad* 7.299–305 is taken from Sophocles' *Ajax* 1031–4. It is striking

---

34 E.g. Robert Coleman, *Vergil: Eclogues* (Cambridge: Cambridge University Press, 1977), *ad loc.*

that Servius takes Moeris' ill-will so seriously as to compare it at such length to the deadly power-struggle in the higher genres. Moeris' kids recall Tityrus' promised tribute of a lamb, but where that offering was presented as a spontaneous effusion of gratitude and quasi-religious devotion, here tribute from lowly shepherds to the more powerful is reinterpreted in a darker light, as extorted by force and accompanied by resentment and a desire for revenge – however impotent – as bitter as the hatred between Troy and Greece. They also recall the twin kids, emblematic of Meliboeus' loss, dropped on the bare rock as he trudges into exile, and, especially, the twin fauns of Corydon's conditional offer to Alexis. Remembering that gifts can represent the poet's gift of pastoral praise to the ruler, we see here that the leverage the poet at least hopes he can command is not confined to merely withholding the gift by ceasing to sing, nor merely to bestowing it on a rival instead, but that the 'gift' itself may be designed to harm the recipient.

If Moeris' curse is simply read as a literal piece of superstition, it seems unlikely to have any real effect, though even that possibility is suggestively left open by the context. The last of the two songs in the preceding eclogue took the form of a magic spell, in which a shepherdess attempts to recall her lover from the city (modelled on Theocritus' Idyll 2). Part of her incantation is a vaunting claim for the power of 'spells', or 'songs' (the Latin word, *carmina*, is the same) (8.69–71):

> Carmina vel caelo possunt deducere lunam;
> caminibus Circe socios mutavit Vlixi;
> frigidus in pratis cantando rumpitur anguis.

['Songs can even drag down the moon from the sky; with songs Circe transformed Ulysses' companions; by singing the cold snake in the meadows is burst apart.']

At the end of the eclogue, there is some doubt over whether the spell has worked, or whether it is only the speaker's fancy that she hears her Daphnis approaching. The final refrain, however, suggests that it is true – that these *carmina*, unlike Corydon's *carmina* (2.6), have compelled the beloved to return from the city.[35] And the speaker

---

35 It is not without reason that I draw this connection with Eclogue 2. The first of Eclogue 8's two songs is, like Corydon's song, another close imitation of Idyll 3, so that Alphesiboeus' spell-song reads very much as a response to, a bettering of, the same ineffective wooing song by a despairing lover we found in the earlier eclogue. Meanwhile, the opening lines of Eclogue 2 include a reference to 'Thestylis' as

claims to have obtained her magic herbs from none other than Moeris, whom she describes as a master-sorcerer capable of amazing feats. We might therefore not be *entirely* dismissive of Moeris' power to curse in Eclogue 9. But more tangibly, his curse forms part of an eclogue – a potential gift of pastoral poetry – which is harshly critical of Octavian's policy, and part of an eclogue-book which includes a fair amount of such negative publicity mingled with its gift of public praise. The *carmina* which may have the force to compel the unwilling beloved in Eclogue 8, and the malediction of Moeris which bodes ill to the new owner (and, according to Servius, to Octavian) in Eclogue 9, are, we might infer, Virgil's *Eclogues* themselves, which may do harm to Octavian's public image, and thus endanger his rule, by associating him with tyranny, injustice and the impiety of civil war.[36]

There are a number of poems which Spenser would have accepted as Virgil's, though later scholarship has largely rejected the attribution. Among these is the *Dirae*, a pastoral poem explicitly on the topic of the land-confiscations, and replete with allusions to Virgil's *Eclogues*.[37] The whole poem is a curse, expanding on Moeris' hint in Eclogue 9, and provides an interesting gloss on all that we have been saying. The poet of the *Dirae* invites a friend, Battarus, to join him in cursing their farms, which have been taken by one Lycurgus and other soldiers, so that their new possessors will get no joy of them: the crops will fail; when the impious soldier cuts down the shady trees, the timber will be burned to ashes by lightning from Jove; the land will be consumed by the conflagration; and finally the sea will overwhelm all. This is followed by eighty hexameters now regarded as a separate poem by the same poet (Valerius Cato being the most widely accepted candidate), and given the title *Lydia*: they are a love poem in a pastoral setting where the speaker, dying of grief in his separation from his beloved, envies the woods and meadows where she remains.

---

preparing a dinner of herbs for the reapers: this is an allusion to Theocritus' second idyll, the model for Alphesiboeus' song, in which Theocritus' sorceress calls on Thestylis to mix her magic herbs. Meanwhile, one of the main changes which Eclogue 2 rings on Idylls 3 and 11 is the location of the beloved (Theocritus' Amaryllis is inside her cave, and Galatea in the sea): Virgil's substitution of the city seems clearly designed to evoke the situation of Idyll 2.

36 Badius Ascensius' commentary on Eclogue 8, in fact, interprets the incantation of the shepherdess in Alphesiboeus' song as an allegory for Virgil's appeal to Augustus for the restitution of his lost lands, and as offering an example of what can be achieved by *carmina* (both 'songs' and 'spells').

37 On the *Dirae* and its imitation of the *Eclogues*, see Brian W. Breed, 'The Pseudo-Vergilian *Dirae* and the Earliest Responses to Vergilian Pastoral', *Trends in Classics* 4 (2012), 3–28.

This division into two separate poems was not made until the late eighteenth century, however, and sixteenth-century readers would have encountered a single, long poem with no obvious break, under the heading 'Dirae'. The closing address to Lydia at the end of the curse reads, in any case, as a kind of segue into the ensuing love-song.[38]

The poem offers an interesting and explicit example of what the veiled threats detected by Servius may be taken to imply – a determination to use the power of song openly against a political enemy, and specifically Octavian. The *Dirae* has been dated to within a few years of the publication of the *Eclogues*, and thus provides an exceptional insight into how a contemporary read Virgil's inaugural work – and at the same time an oblique commentary on it, which would have influenced sixteenth-century readers who believed it to be by Virgil himself.[39] A close reading of the *Dirae*'s allusions to the *Eclogues* interestingly confirms much of what we have been arguing about the importance of the politically oppositional strains in Virgil's pastoral, about the validity of connecting its amatory and political themes in the manner of Servius, and about the power of song in the gift-exchange or bargain which pastoral attempts to negotiate with political power.

Given the subject matter of the *Dirae* proper (or the first half of the poem as it appears in early modern editions), it is not surprising that among its many echoes of the *Eclogues* are reminiscences of Meliboeus in Eclogue 1. We have execrations against *militis impia ... dextera* ('the soldier's impious right hand', l. 31), recalling Meliboeus' *impius ... miles* (*Ecl.* 1.70), and against *inimica pii semper Discordia civis* ('Discord, always the enemy of righteous citizens', l. 83), recalling Meliboeus' *en quo discordia cives / produxit miseros!* ('See where Discord has brought miserable citizens!', *Ecl.* 1.72); we

---

38 The early reader of the *Eclogues* who wrote the *Dirae* thus clearly associated the amatory and political complaints of Virgil's shepherds closely enough to combine them in a single poem.

39 For sixteenth-century readers like Spenser, it would also have resonated with the so-called romance of Virgil, first published in French at the beginning of the sixteenth century, and published in English in Holland (?1518) and then in London (?1550) with the title *This boke treateth of the lyfe of Virgil, and of his death, and many other marvayles that he did in his lyfe tyme by witchecrafte and nygromancy, through the develles of hell*. The opening chapters repeat the narrative familiar from Servius' commentaries on eclogues 1 and 9 of Virgil's trip to Rome to seek restitution of his confiscated farm, but here his petition is refused, and he uses magic to avenge himself on his enemies. See J. W. Spargo, *Virgil the Necromancer: Studies in Virgilian Legends* (Cambridge, MA: Harvard University Press, 1934), pp. 236–53, and Tudeau-Clayton, *Jonson, Shakespeare and Early Modern Virgil*, pp. 98–101.

have lingering descriptions of the speaker's last look at his lands, which he will be without for so long (86, 91–4), recalling Meliboeus' wistful question whether he shall ever, after long years, gaze again on his home (*Ecl.* 1.67–9); and like Meliboeus at *Ecl.* 1.74-8, the speaker addresses his goats, telling them that they shall never more graze on their familiar food (91–2). Nor is the echo of Moeris from Eclogue 9 surprising (*advena* at ll. 80–1 recalling *Ecl.* 9.2–3). What is perhaps more unexpected and revealing is the nature of the references to Virgil's Tityrus, which offer a distinctly sceptical gloss on the Caesarean strain in Virgil's *Eclogues*.

The adynata with which Tityrus expresses his devotion to Octavian at *Ecl.* 1.59–63 –

> Ante leves ergo pascentur in aethere cervi
> et freta destituent nudos in litore pisces,
> ante pererratis amborum finibus exsul
> aut Ararim Parthus bibet aut Germania Tigrim,
> quam nostro illius labatur pectore vultus

['Therefore, sooner shall sprightly deer graze in the upper air and the seas set down the defenceless fish on the shore, sooner shall the Parthian exile drink from the Arar or Germany from the Tigris, than his countenance shall fade in my heart.']

– are imitated twice, bookending the curse. The second passage expresses the speaker's devotion, not to a godlike ruler, but rather to the fond memory of what he is forced to leave behind (both his lands and his beloved Lydia) (98–101):

> dulcia amara prius fient et mollia dura,
> candida nigra oculi cernent et dextera laeva,
> migrabunt casus aliena in corpora rerum,
> quam tua de nostris emigret cura medullis.

['Sooner shall bitter things become sweet and hard things soft, the eyes see black as white and left as right, the fall of things depart into foreign bodies, than care for you will leave my inmost heart.']

The vow never to forget his love for what he has lost implies also that he shall never relinquish his fierce anger at those who have deprived him of them. And this is the thrust of the opening imitation of the same Virgilian passage (4–8):

> ante lupos rapient haedi, vituli ante leones,
> delphini fugient pisces, aquilae ante columbas
> et conversa retro rerum discordia gliscet –

Intertextuality and allegory

> multa prius fient quam non mea libera avena:
> montibus et silvis dicam tua facta, Lycurge.

['Sooner shall kids seize wolves and calves lions, sooner shall dolphins flee fish and eagles doves, and the discord of things increase, turned backwards – many things will come to pass sooner than that my oaten reed shall not be free: to the mountains and the woods shall I tell your deeds, Lycurgus.']

Tityrus' vow of loyalty has become this speaker's vow of unending hostility. The specific impossibilities he invokes, though, allude to other eclogues. The first item, the kids preying on wolves, is drawn from the beginning of the following passage on 'the world turned upside-down' in Damon's song in Eclogue 8 (52–6):

> Nunc et ovis ultro fugiat lupus; aurea durae
> mala ferant quercus, narcisso floreat alnus,
> pinguia corticibus sudent electra myricae,
> certent et cycnis ululae, sit Tityrus Orpheus,
> Orpheus in silvis, inter delphinas Arion.

['Now let the wolf voluntarily flee the sheep; let hard oaks bear golden apples, the alder blossom with narcissus, tamarisks exude rich amber from their bark, and owls contend with swans; let Tityrus be an Orpheus, an Orpheus in the woods, an Arion among the dolphins.']

(The mention of dolphins also connects the passages.) These lines in Eclogue 8 are closely followed by Damon's parting curse on the landscape, before he bids it farewell: *omnia vel medium fiat mare* ('Indeed, let all things become mid-ocean', 8.58), a wish which the *Dirae* develops at length at ll. 48–62. We recall that Damon's song is closely modelled on Idyll 3, one of the prominent intertexts of Eclogue 1 as well as the chief model of Eclogue 2, and thus its amatory despair, like Corydon's, partakes of Eclogue 1's pronounced blending of love and politics – hence the *Dirae*'s allusion to it in this context makes sense. It also suggests that very early readers of the *Eclogues* were sensitive to the close analogical relation between the themes of love and politics in the work, long before Servius relays these ideas in his allegories. The eagles fleeing the doves in the *Dirae*'s opening adynata, meanwhile, are clearly an allusion to Moeris' gloomy diagnosis on the power of song in Eclogue 9 (7–13):

> *Lycidas*:
> Certe equidem audieram ...
> omnia carminibus vestrum servasse Menalcan.

Moeris:
Audieras, et fama fuit; sed carmina tantum
nostra valent, Lycida, tela inter Martia, quantum
Chaonias dicunt aquila veniente columbas.

['*Lycidas*: Indeed, surely I had heard ... that your Menalcas had saved everything with his songs. *Moeris*: You had heard it, and so went the rumour. But our songs have as much power amid the weapons of war, Lycidas, as they say the Chaonian doves have when the eagle approaches.']

The suggestion of a reversal in the unequal power-relations symbolized by Moeris' doves and eagles is striking. Of course, it is here offered as an impossibility, yet another of the things which the *Dirae*'s adynata inherit from Tityrus' in Eclogue 1 is the suggestion that what they declare impossible is in fact possible. Tityrus' adynata ironically include images of exile painfully like the fate that awaits Meliboeus in reality, and here the last item in the speaker's adynaton – that universal chaos shall return – is precisely what his curse will strive with such confidence to effect. The impossibility of the other items thus appears less than unambiguous, and the idea of imperial eagles fleeing poetic doves takes on a certain reality. After all, the very basis of the *Dirae* is the belief that *carmina* – spells and curses as well as songs – do have the power to affect the world, whatever Moeris may have said to the contrary.[40]

The end and whole point of this Tityrean adynaton is *multa prius fient quam non mea libera avena* ('many things shall come to pass, sooner than that my oaten reed shall not be free', l. 7). Now the *avena* is what Tityrus is said to be playing on in the opening lines of Eclogue 1. Van Sickle has demonstrated that it is an unlikely and unprecedented musical instrument, and would have struck contemporary readers as distinctive and surprising, because the brittle reeds of oat, like the *stridens stipula* ('squeaking straw') mentioned in Eclogue 3 (l. 27), are capable of producing only a puny squeaking noise.[41] It is so familiar from later pastoral that its oddity no longer strikes us, but

---

40 Though here that power is to be used to destroy the landscape, rather than to 'save' it as Menalcas was rumoured to have done in Eclogue 9. See below on the speaker's active rejection of *otia*. The supposed supernatural efficacy of these *carmina* also recalls Alphesiboeus' song in Eclogue 8, which as we have seen itself casts doubt on the pessimism that follows at 9.11–13.
41 Van Sickle, 'Virgil *vs* Cicero, Lucretius, Theocritus, Plato, & Homer: Two Programmatic Plots in the First Bucolic', *Vergilius* 46 (2000), 21–58, at 41–2; see also Van Sickle, 'Virgil Bucolics 1.1–2 and Interpretive Tradition: A Latin (Roman) Program for a Greek Genre', *Classical Philology* 99 (2004), 336–53.

Van Sickle also suggests that perhaps 'in Latin literature and its heirs, every use of *avena* in metonymy for Pan-pipe pays implicit homage to Virgil'.[42] Given the topic and the density of the allusions to the *Eclogues* in the *Dirae*, and the immediate context of the imitation of Tityrus' adynaton, this surely qualifies as such a case – though let us say 'allusion' here rather than 'homage', since it is clearly part of a strategy of imitating Eclogue 1 which contributes to the poem's meaning. *Libera* meanwhile evokes the liberty Tityrus longed for, but, as we saw above, did not actually get, the grant made by the godlike youth merely granting him security in his old way of life rather than manumission from slavery (*ut ante*, 'as before', particularly marking the lack of change in his status). What he got instead of liberty was *otia*, the ease in which we find him singing Octavian's praises. The *avena* and its owner in the *Dirae* possess freedom (without ease), and he uses it to tell the truth about the impious Lycurgus' deeds to the mountains and woods (*montibus et silvis*). We should pause to note that this is a close echo of Eclogue 2, line 5, where the same phrase in the same line position describes Corydon's song of 'cruel Alexis', sung 'to the mountains and woods' (*montibus et silvis*). Like Servius' allegorical gloss on 2.6, *vel crudelis Caesar*, the *Dirae* apply Corydon's complaint to the perpetrators of the land-confiscations, again confirming that a contemporary reader saw the amatory and political suits of the *Eclogues* as intimately connected. The liberty, then, which this speaker claims, and which Tityrus lacked, is interpreted here as freedom of speech, the freedom to voice openly the criticisms which were veiled and indirect in the *Eclogues*. While he clings to it he will continue to use it to curse his oppressors:

> desint et silvis frondes et fontibus umor,
> nec desit nostris devotum carmen avenis.
>
> (*Dirae* 18–19)

['Let leaves fail the woods and water the springs, but let not the cursing song fail my oaten reeds.']

The implication is that Tityrus' use of song in Eclogue 1 to praise Octavian rather than to condemn him was the sign of his continued servitude, an example of how a citizen effectively enslaved by a tyrannical regime is *constrained* to speak.

The *otium* which Tityrus enjoyed in place of liberty, meanwhile, and which is denied to the speaker of the *Dirae*, seems also to be

---

42 Van Sickle, 'Two Programmatic Plots', 42 n. 88.

actively rejected by him. Lines 26 to 36 take as their subject the shady trees which were so important a feature of the opening description of Tityrus in Eclogue 1:

> ludimus et multum nostris cantata libellis,
> optima silvarum, formosis densa virectis,
> tondemus virides umbras, nec laeta comantis
> iactabis mollis ramos inflantibus auris
> (nec mihi saepe meum resonabit, Battare, carmen),
> militis impia cum succedet dextera ferro
> formosaeque cadent umbrae, formosior illis
> ipsa cades, veteris domini felicia ligna –
> nequiquam: nostris potius devota libellis
> ignibus aetheriis flagrabit. Iuppiter (ipse
> Iuppiter hanc aluit), cinis haec tibi fiat oportet.

['Best of woods, much sung of in our entertainments and little books, dense with beautiful greenery, we shall shear your green shades. Neither will you, joyous, toss your branches full of soft foliage as the breezes blow through them; nor will it often echo my song back to me, Battarus. When the impious right hand of the soldier shall fell it with the axe, and the beautiful shades shall fall, you, more beautiful than they, shall fall, oh fruitful timber of the old master – and to no purpose: rather, cursed by our little books, it will burn with heavenly fires. Jupiter himself made this wood grow – you must see to it, Jupiter, that it becomes ashes.']

Though it is the soldier's impious right hand which will fell the beautiful shady trees at l. 31, the speaker and his friend claim agency in this, as part of their curse, in *tondemus* at l. 28, and of course call down the lightning of Jupiter that will complete the destruction (itself recalling the lightning which struck the oaks and should have warned Meliboeus of the impending disaster at *Ecl.* 1.17). This is the essence of the curse's vengeance: what is unjustly taken from them, they will themselves destroy. And here it is identified with Tityrus' *otia*, as line 30's 'nor will it often re-echo my song to me', with its distinctive and unusual transitive use of *resonare*, recalls

> tu, Tityre, lentus in umbra
> formosam resonare doces Amaryllida silvas.
>
> (*Ecl.* 1.4–5)

['You, Tityrus, lounging in the shade, teach the woods to echo "Beautiful Amaryllis".']

The poet of the *Dirae* is actively rejecting and destroying the shady retreat which made it possible for Tityrus to continue his distinctive brand of song, praising his benefactor – the shady retreat which symbolized that beneficent protection, and which re-echoed, relayed and preserved the Caesarean strain of the *Eclogues* exemplified by Tityrus' praise. What emerges is the sense that Virgil's Tityrus represents citizens who, in supporting Octavian's unjust rule, have traded their republican liberty for the servile dependency of subjects, thinly veiled as idyllic pastoral ease, and entailing the obligation to utter nothing but praise of the regime. In rejecting this dependency by targeting specifically Tityrus' shady trees, the *Dirae* is responding to the negative associations of *umbra* with sloth and a culpable withdrawal from political engagement in the discourse of the late Republic.[43] Open criticism of injustice, from such a perspective, is not just a right of the free citizen, but his political duty.

The *Eclogues* themselves never directly address the issue of freedom of speech, though Virgil's awareness of the danger of speaking openly is of course implicit wherever we accept one of Servius' 'carping' allegories. The dangers of outspoken political critique will, of course, be a major theme in *The Shepheardes Calender*, addressed most explicitly in *September*, where Hobbinol warns the ruined and embittered Diggon (136–9):

> ... I see thou speakest to plaine:
> Better it were, a little to feyne,
> And cleanly couer, that cannot be cured.
> Such il, as is forced, mought nedes be endured.

Hobbinol's cautious position here is aligned with the Tityrus of Eclogue 1 when *September* ends with Hobbinol imitating Tityrus' closing offer of hospitality to Meliboeus (254–7):

> But if to my cotage thou wilt resort,
> So as I can, I wil thee comfort:
> There mayst thou ligge in a vetchy bed,
> Till fayrer Fortune shewe forth her head.

A generation schooled in Servius and not questioning the authorship of the *Dirae* would evidently have been well equipped to read pastoral as endurance of forced ill, and to look beneath the feigning

---

43 E.g. Cicero, *Pro L. Morena oratio* 30 and *Tusculan Disputations* 5.78; and see Peter L. Smith, '"Lentus in Umbra": A Symbolic Pattern in Vergil's *Eclogues*', *Phoenix* 19 (1965), 298–304, at 301–2.

surface of the *Eclogues* to decipher the political criticisms it covers. To sixteenth-century readers taking Virgil as the author of the *Dirae*, and especially to those among them who were alive to its allusions (which surely would have been hard to miss, given the familiarity of the *Eclogues* as among the first Latin poetry to be taught in grammar-school curricula), the poem must have weighed heavily in favour of privileging the Meliboean voice of the *Eclogues*, which shows 'the misery of the people under hard lords and ravening soldiers', over the Tityrean voice, which shows 'what blessedness is derived to them that lie lowest from the goodness of them that sit highest'. And not only this. Where Meliboeus' misery is helpless, and Moeris laments the dovelike powerlessness of song at the approach of the imperial eagle, the *Dirae* throws emphasis on the poet's real power to oppose and to harm a political enemy, which lies latent in the veiled threats spelled out in Servius' commentary four centuries later, and moreover imply that the poet has a moral and political duty not to abdicate this freedom and this power.

Apples for Augustus

In what we have covered so far, we have been concerned principally with Servius' allegories related to the land-confiscations, and the picture of the *Eclogues* which has emerged has therefore seemed strongly aligned with what has been called the 'pessimist' school of Virgil criticism, which emphasizes the aspects of Virgil's work which appear to criticize Octavian and to cast doubt on the 'new mythology' of his rule.[44] But it is vital that we remember at the same time that Virgil is also one of the chief architects of this 'new mythology', not least within the *Eclogues* themselves. The *Dirae* itself presents its open speech as a pointed contrast to Tityrus' deifying praise of Octavian, the opening chord of a panegyrical strain which will be counterpointed with the darker voice of complaint throughout Virgil's book. The commentaries from Servius on emphasized this panegyrical strain, alongside the more negative political readings. Even in the case of the land-confiscation theme, commentaries tend to stress Virgil's gratitude to Octavian for his supposed exemption.

---

44 Influential examples of 'pessimist' criticism of the *Eclogues* include Michael Putnam, *Virgil's Pastoral Art: Studies in the Eclogues* (Princeton: Princeton University Press, 1970), and A. J. Boyle, *The Chaonian Dove: Studies in the Eclogues, Georgics, and Aeneid of Virgil* (Leiden: Brill, 1986). I take the phrase 'new mythology' from Paul Zanker, *The Power of Images in the Age of Augustus* (Ann Arbor: University of Michigan Press, 1988).

More unambiguously, eclogues 4 and 5 mark a climax in the book, concluding its first half with a crescendo of what can only be called fervent Caesarean propaganda.

Eclogue 4 prophesies the return of the mythical Golden Age, marked by universal peace and plenty, with the imminent birth and growth to maturity of a boy. The boy and his parents are unidentified, and commentators ancient, Renaissance and modern have disagreed over possible candidates, but it is explicit that the child is to be born under the consulship of Pollio (i.e. in 41 BCE), and therefore under the second triumvirate, with Octavian presiding in Rome. The theme, as the commentaries point out, redounds to the praise of Octavian as well as to that of the miraculous child himself, 'for the felicity of the times pertains to the praise of the emperor', as Servius remarks at line 6. Indeed, *tuus iam regnat Apollo* ('your own Apollo now reigns', 4.10) is read by Servius as a flattering allegorical reference to Octavian, which participates in his iconographical and ideological programme to associate himself with divine authority: 'and it touches Augustus, whose statue was made with all the marks of Apollo'. The gloss was to be echoed by many later commentators. Some, like Paulus Manutius glossing 4.17, have no doubt that Octavian himself is the *puer*. The obvious objection is that Octavian is already a grown man, so that it would be a nonsense to prophesy his birth. Yet he is reported to have thought of himself as reborn at the appearance of the *sidus Iulium*, the comet whose appearance after Caesar's death was hailed by Octavian as Caesar's apotheosis.[45] It is the *puer* himself of whom it is said *pacatumque reget ... orbem* ('he will rule a pacified world', 4.17), which certainly could not be applied to a mere son of a consul like Pollio. It indicates at the very least that the prophesied Golden Age is explicitly monarchical, in line with the style of government which had been so controversially introduced by Julius Caesar and would be continued by Augustus, since 'In the Republic, only Roma, the Roman people, could be said to rule the world, not an individual

---

45 Pliny, *Natural History* 2.93–4: *admodum Faustus Divo Augusto iudicatus ab ipso .... namque his verbis in gaudium prodit is: '... eo sidere significari vulgus credidit Caesaris animam inter deorum inmortalium numina receptam ...' haec ille in publicum; interiore gaudio sibi illum natum seque in eo nasci interpretatus est. et, si verum fatemur, salutare id terris fuit* ('[This comet] was thought by the divine Augustus to be very auspicious for him ... for he expressed his joy in these words: "... the common people took the star to signify that Caesar's soul had been taken in among the immortal gods ..." This he said in public; but with inward joy he construed it as born for him, and himself as reborn in it. And, if we acknowledge the truth, it was advantageous to the country').

man'.[46] This monarchical age is presented as divinely ordained and unquestionably ideal, an end to sin itself and the proper culmination of human history. If Octavian's rule flouts republican tradition and notions of liberty and justice, the ecstatic vision teaches us, it is because it represents a divinely approved revolution of the ages, not to be judged by the merely human standards of a corrupt world which is now to be superseded by perfection.

In Eclogue 5, meanwhile, we have an exchange of songs between Mopsus and Menalcas on the theme of the death of Daphnis. Mopsus' song imitates Theocritus' first idyll (also on the death of the legendary shepherd), telling how all of nature mourns Daphnis, and ending with instructions for an epitaph to be carved on his tomb, boasting of his fame that reaches 'from here even to the stars' (*hinc usque ad sidera*, 5.43). Menalcas' reply goes beyond this, promising to raise Daphnis himself to the stars: *Daphnimque tuum tollemus ad astra*, 5.51). It tells of Daphnis on the threshold of Olympus, and of nature's rejoicing cry that he has become a god (*'deus, deus ille, Menalca!'*, 5.64), and promises to set up altars to him and to honour him with annual sacrifice, alongside Apollo, Bacchus and Ceres. The commentary tradition has again debated the identity of the supposed historical figure mourned as Daphnis, but the most popular and oft-named candidate is Julius Caesar, *qui in senatu a Cassio et Bruto viginti tribus vulneribus interemptus est* ('who was killed by Cassius and Brutus in the senate with twenty-three wounds').[47] An intertextual consideration again supports the identification, since Daphnis' mother, clasping his body and decrying the cruelty of the gods (5.22-3) strongly recalls the behaviour of Aphrodite, mother of Aeneas and thus claimed as the original 'mother' of the Julian line, as she appears in an earlier imitation of Theocritus' first Idyll, Bion's *Lament for Adonis*.[48] In reality, Julius Caesar had been officially declared a god when, in July 44 BCE, four months after his assassination and during the games

---

46 I. M. Le M. Du Quesnay, 'Vergil's Fourth Eclogue', *Papers of the Liverpool Latin Seminar* 1 (1976), 25–99, at 61.
47 Servius, gloss to 5.20. Servius also reports the views of those who think that Daphnis is not allegorized at all, but simply the legendary shepherd Daphnis, and of those who think he represents Quintilius Varus, who, he thinks, was related to Virgil. The life of Donatus claims that Daphnis represents a brother of Virgil's called Flaccus. Vives argues that Virgil is misinterpreting a Sybilline prophecy of the death and resurrection of Christ, misapplying it to Julius Caesar (*In publii Vergilii Maronis Bucolica interpretatio*, B7r).
48 Servius Danielis' addition to the line 20 gloss tells us: *sed si de Gaio Caesare dictum est, multi matrem Venerem accipiunt* ('But if it is said of Julius Caesar, many take "mother" as referring to Venus').

which Octavian was holding in his honour, a comet was spotted in the sky, and dubbed the *sidus Iulium*.[49] Octavian dedicated a temple to his adoptive father, and thereafter named himself *divi filius*, 'son of a god', on coins. The piece of evidence that Servius offers as the most unequivocal proof that Daphnis is Caesar – the claim in his gloss to line 29 that Caesar was the first to introduce the rites of Bacchus to Rome – is false, and this was already recognized in Vives' sixteenth-century commentary. But the eclogue's recurrent stellar imagery in combination with its theme of apotheosis must surely have recalled the *sidus Iulium* irresistibly to its original readers.[50]

Both these eclogues, then, strongly imply the superhuman status of Octavian, in keeping with his recently adopted title *divi filius*, and thus contribute to the association of his personal power with divine authority, by which he would seek (like Julius Caesar before him) to make his absolute monarchy acceptable to a Rome proud of its centuries of republican freedom. Tityrus' outburst in Eclogue 1, *deus nobis haec otia fecit* (1.6), is presented as intensely personal: he immediately adds *namque erit ille* mihi *semper deus* ('for he will always be a god *to me*', 1.7). Octavian was wary of permitting Romans to worship him as a god, for fear of offending republican sensibilities – ruler-worship smacked too much of the Hellenistic monarchies of the East, long denounced by republican Romans as tyrannies, and a major factor in the assassination of Julius Caesar had been his unabashed ambition to be worshipped as a god.[51] But nevertheless, Octavian allowed temples to be dedicated to him outside Italy, and at home would permit domestic sacrifice to the Genius Augusti.[52] Tityrus' *mihi* keeps the deification and promised sacrifice safely within the bounds of such private devotion, and its subjective status as an expression of individual feeling is reinforced by Tityrus' isolation in the eclogue,

---

49 In Ovid's version of this apotheosis in *Metamorphoses* 15, it is Caesar's 'mother' Venus who bears him to the stars.
50 Coleman observes 'it is incredible that anyone in the late 40s could have read a pastoral poem on this theme without thinking of Caesar ... Vergil intended readers to make just this association' (*Vergil: Eclogues*, p. 173). Ever wary of allegorical correspondences, modern classicists continue to debate the identification: for bibliography, see W. W. Briggs, Jr, 'A Bibliography of Virgil's *Eclogues* (1927–1977)', *Aufstieg und Niedergang der römischen Welt* II.31.2 (1981), 1265-357, at 1326-7, and V. A. Sirago, 'Cesare', in *Enciclopedia Virgiliana* 1 (1985), 756.
51 On which see Suetonius, *Divus Julius* 76, Cicero, *Second Philippic* 110 and Duncan Fishwick, *The Imperial Cult in the Latin West: Studies in the Ruler Cult of the Western Provinces of the Roman Empire*, Vol. I (Leiden: Brill, 1987), Part i, pp. 56–72.
52 See Fishwick, *Imperial Cult*, Vol. I, Part i, pp. 73–82, and Vol. 2, Part i (Brill, 1991), pp. 375–87.

as the apparently sole exception to the suffering which afflicts the rest of his community. In Eclogue 5, by contrast, the very woods and mountains proclaim *deus, deus ille, Menalca!* ('He is a god – a god, Menalcas!', 5.64), and the entire rural community, Menalcas promises, will celebrate feast-days and make vows in his honour, *ut Baccho Cererique* ('just as we do for Bacchus and Ceres', 5.79). These rites will be honoured, with a reminiscence of Tityrus' adynata of 1.59–63, as long as boars love the mountains and fish the rivers (5.76). To any reader, then, who identifies Daphnis as Julius Caesar, and who associates the *puer* of Eclogue 4 either with Octavian himself or with his reign, eclogues 4 and 5 constitute boldly hyperbolic and deifying praise of the new regime.[53]

Both eclogues shared a similar fate at the hands of Christian commentators suspicious of the Caesarean cult. Eclogue 4 was appropriated for Christian purposes at an early date, and Virgil was seen as a prophet who was himself unable fully to understand the vision granted him of the birth of Christ.[54] Eclogue 5, in turn, was later interpreted as treating of his death and resurrection, again unwittingly: Vives argues that Virgil was ignorant of the true subject of his own eclogue, misapplying a Sybilline prophecy to Caesar. Sannazaro's neo-Latin Christian epic, *De Partu Virginis*, appropriates and combines the eclogues in this way, where the shepherds of Bethlehem respond to angelic tidings of Christ's birth by reciting a close adaptation of the fourth eclogue (3.196–232), and the landscape re-echoes their song, proclaiming 'deus, deus ille, Menalca' (3.233–6) in lines lifted directly from Eclogue 5. The Christian interpretation of Eclogue 4 is preserved alongside political readings in the margins of most early printed editions, and thus the commentary tradition imbues both eclogues with overtones of a debate over the relation between imperial ideology and Christian belief.[55] On one hand, Eclogue 4 can still,

---

53 In the *Aeneid* Virgil would use both motifs – the return of the Golden Age and the *sidus Iulium* as a sign of Caesar's apotheosis – in ways explicitly linked to Augustus, furnishing strong support for such a reading of these eclogues. See Mary Frances Williams, 'The *Sidus Iulium*, the Divinity of Men, and the Golden Age in Virgil's *Aeneid*', *Leeds International Classical Studies* 2 (2003), 1–29. Servius refers to the *sidus Iulium* in his glosses on *Aeneid* 1.287 (Jove's prophecy of a Caesar whose fame shall be bounded by the stars, where Servius quotes *Ecl.* 9.47), on *Aen.* 6.790 (on the descendants of Julius entering heaven), and at 8.861 (on the star above Augustus' head on Aeneas' shield).

54 See Stephen Benko, 'Virgil's Fourth Eclogue in Christian Interpretation', *Aufstieg und Niedergang der römischen Welt* II.31.1 (1980), 646–705.

55 Admittedly Vives' Christian interpretation of Eclogue 5 was not likewise taken up by other commentators, but his commentary had considerable currency,

in almost Servian terms, redound to the credit of Augustus, since the coming of Christ occurred under his rule: Orosius' influential Christian schematization of world history argued that Augustus' reign was arranged by divine Providence, so that the *Pax Augusta* would make the world a safer place, in which the disciples could travel more freely and spread the word of God.[56] On the other hand, the competing identifications of the *puer* of Eclogue 4 and the Daphnis of Eclogue 5 could be seen as reflecting the hubris of mortal potentates demanding the worship due only to God.

But Eclogue 5's deification of 'Daphnis' did not have to wait for the accretion of Christian commentary to receive an ironic gloss, for its status is thrown sharply into question within Virgil's eclogue book itself. Eclogue 9, the darkest of all Virgil's eclogues, returns to the theme of the land-confiscations addressed in Eclogue 1, and clearly evokes one of its major Theocritean intertexts, Idyll 7.[57] But where Theocritus' Simichidas and Lycidas exchange their own songs to lighten their journey away from the city to a pastoral *locus amoenus*, the shepherds of Virgil's eclogue, Lycidas and the dispossessed Moeris, are travelling towards the city, and exchange remembered fragments of songs by the absent master-singer Menalcas. Lycidas has heard that Menalcas had successfully petitioned Rome to restore the confiscated lands to the Mantuan farmers, and is now surprised to learn from Moeris that this was merely a false rumour. Menalcas himself, we learn, has with Moeris narrowly escaped being killed. The failure of Menalcas' petition strikingly recalls and inverts the success of Tityrus' at the beginning of the book.

As they had done with Tityrus in Eclogue 1, the commentators identified Menalcas with Virgil himself, following Virgil's lead in Eclogue 5, where Menalcas claims authorship of eclogues 2 and 3 (5.86-7) and echoes Tityrus' words from Eclogue 1 (5.64, 76-7). Taken in the order they appear in the book, then, Eclogue 9 seems to represent an overturning of the good fortune celebrated in Eclogue 1, and even in fact to accord it the status of a mistake or false rumour. Ancient commentators avoided this implication in various ways. Probus argued that Eclogue 9 was composed earlier, before the show of favour described in Eclogue 1, but that the celebratory poem was

---

going through sixteen printings by the end of the 1570s. (See Wilson-Okamura, *Virgil in the Renaissance*, 'Appendix B: Virgil commentaries ranked by number of printings'.)
56 Orosius, *Seven Books of Histories Against the Pagans*, 6.1.
57 As noted by Eobanus Hessus, *In P. Vergilii Maronis Bucolica*, ad 9.1.

placed in the more prominent opening position for emphasis, with the earlier, discontented poem buried later in the book so as not to offend Octavian (*ne offenderet imperatorem*).[58] Servius instead constructs a narrative by which, after the official reprieve granted by Octavian in Rome and described in Eclogue 1, Virgil, on his return to Mantua, encountered violent resistance from the centurion Arrius who had taken over his farm (a temporary setback occasioning Eclogue 9, and allegorized at 3.94–7), and was successfully reinstated only after Octavian sent three men to help him in response to his renewed appeal. But such dodges apart, the overriding impression is certainly of a gloom descending to efface the serenity and gratitude voiced by Tityrus at the beginning of the book. This tendency is strengthened by Eclogue 9's ironic echoes of other earlier eclogues, most notably of Eclogue 5.

Lycidas reacts to the news of Menalcas' narrow escape from death with alarm: it would have left the countryside bereft (9.19–20).

> quis caneret Nymphas? quis humum florentibus herbis
> spargeret aut viridi fontis induceret umbra?

['Who would sing of the Nymphs? Who would strew the ground with flowering herbs, or cover the fountains with green shade?']

The lines echo Mopsus' lament for Daphnis in Eclogue 5, with its *Nymphae* (5.20), its reference to the flowers which have deserted the grief-stricken earth (5.38–9) and its instruction (5.40–1):

> spargite humum foliis, inducite fontis umbras,
> pastores (mandat fieri sibi talia Daphnis).

['Strew the ground with leaves, shepherds; draw shades over the fountains (Daphnis commands that such things be done for him).']

The echoes align Menalcas not only with Mopsus and the shepherds who observe the rites but also with Daphnis, whose presence preserved the now vanished flowers, with an implication counter to the Caesarean myth of eclogues 4 and 5: the beauty and fertility of nature now seem to depend not on the ruler but on the poet.

Lycidas then recites a fragment of one of Menalcas' songs, as another thing which the countryside would have lost. It is a translation of the opening lines of Theocritus' third idyll, the lines also alluded to in Meliboeus' speech at the beginning of Eclogue 1 (23–5):

---

58 Probus, in Thilo and Hagen (eds), *Grammatici qui feruntur in Vergilii carmina commentarii*, Vol. III, p. 328, ll. 9–19.

> 'Tityre, dum redeo (brevis est via) pasce capellas,
> et potum pastas age, Tityre, et inter agendum
> occursare capro (cornu ferit ille) caveto.'

['Tityrus, feed my nanny-goats until I return (the road is short), and drive them to water after they have fed, and as you drive them take care not to run into the billy-goat (he butts with his horn)'.]

Servius glosses with another biographical allegory –

> Theocritus' verses are translated word for word, but however it contains Virgil's affairs, for he allegorically commands them that they should mind his affairs and, however, that they mustn't dare to go against the orders of Arrius

– confirming the observation in his preface to the *Bucolica* that Virgil mixes in figurative meanings even where he follows Theocritus verbatim. This is the first of four fragments remembered, with difficulty, by the two shepherds, the first and third Theocritean and amatory, the second and fourth political and Roman. As we have just seen, Servius extends the political and Roman reference even to this direct translation of Theocritus. The second fragment, recited by Moeris, is the one we looked at earlier, in which Menalcas tries to strike a bargain with Varus over the land-confiscations, promising songs in his praise if only Mantua is spared. But we should note here that the terms of the promise, to extol Varus' name to the stars (*ad sidera*, 9.29), echo Menalcas' promise in Eclogue 5 (51–2):

> Daphnim tuum tollemus ad astra;
> Daphnim ad astra feremus

['I shall lift your Daphnis to the stars; I shall bear Daphnis to the stars.']

In the context of Eclogue 9 the bargain is broken, and the song, *necdum perfecta* ('not yet finished', 9.26), will presumably never be composed. It is as if Menalcas is unspeaking his Caesarean hymn.

For the third fragment, also offered by Moeris, we return to amatory subject matter, with a little encapsulation of the cyclops' love song to Galatea from Theocritus' Idyll 11, evoking Corydon's lament in Eclogue 2, which was largely modelled on the same idyll, and which Menalcas claimed in Eclogue 5 to have authored.[59] The

---

59 Though Servius has no gloss to this effect here, the connection with Eclogue 2, in the context of Eclogue 9's explicitly political concerns, could well have reminded readers of his allegorization of Corydon's unrequited love as a failed petition against the land confiscations (see p. 55 above).

fourth and last is again Roman and political, taking the *sidus Iulium* as its explicit subject (9.46–50).⁶⁰

> 'Daphni, quid antiquos signorum suspicis ortus?
> ecce Dionaei processit Caesaris astrum,
> astrum, quo segetes gauderent frugibus et quo
> duceret apricis in collibus uva colorem.
> insere, Daphni, piros; carpent tua poma nepotes.'

['Daphnis, why do you observe the rising of the old constellations? Lo, the star of Caesar, descendant of Venus, has gone forth – the star by whose means the fields may rejoice with crops and the grape-cluster take on colour on the sunny hills. Graft your pears, Daphnis; your grandchildren will harvest your fruit.']

Caesar's recent historical apotheosis is treated directly, and at the same time clearly paralleled with the apotheosis of Daphnis in Eclogue 5, the framing address to Daphnis making sure that we remember it here. The epithet *Dionaeus* ('descended from Venus') given to Caesar, designating him by reference to the 'mother' of his line, might also remind us of the mention of Daphnis' grieving mother at 5.22–3.⁶¹ As in the song to Varus, here too we seem to be encountering a kind of reworking of Menalcas' hymn to Daphnis, this one apparently removing the veil to describe literally what Eclogue 5 treated allegorically, revealing the praise for Caesar underlying the songs about 'Daphnis'. On the surface it seems to introduce a current of Caesarean praise into Eclogue 9, but the closing line disturbs this picture. As Servius notes, 'it looks back to that which he said bitterly above' (*nam illud respicit, quod supra invidiose ait*) – Meliboeus' ironic *insere nunc, Meliboee, piros, pone ordine vites* ('Graft your pears now, Meliboeus; plant your vines in rows', 1.73). Servius thinks that the confidence of the line here undoes the despair of Meliboeus' remark (*ac si diceret, nihil est quod possis timere*; 'as if he should say, there is nothing which you should fear'), but it is at least as likely to strike the reader the other way round. The failure of the petition against the land-confiscations which is the main subject of Eclogue 9 has, after all, confirmed the hopelessness of Meliboeus and others like him (including Moeris, to whom sixteenth-century editors attributed these lines). The earlier fragment addressing Varus promised to raise him to the stars, but

---

60 The manuscript tradition is divided on its attribution to Lycidas or Moeris, but sixteenth-century editions give the lines to Moeris, the option which lends itself most readily to the ironic reading I suggest below.
61 See Servius Danielis' gloss to 5.20, *multi matrem Venerem accipiunt*, and the connection with Bion argued above.

conspicuously held back from doing so as a result of the land-confiscations; here too we have a rhetorical stellification, and a closing reminder of the land-confiscations which undermines it. Put your faith in the protective beneficence of the Caesars, the fragment seems to say, and you will end up in the bitter despair of the exile, seeing the fruit of your labour reaped by your oppressor.[62]

Just as these literal fruit – the produce of agricultural labour – will be lost, so too, the eclogue suggests, the allegorical fruit of the poet's labour – the *aurea mala* of Eclogue 3 which Servius interpreted as the eclogues themselves – will likewise be lost. Moeris resists Lycidas' urging to continue his singing after this last fragment, and ends by lamenting his age, which has carried away his memory of so many songs and his very voice (9.53–4). The sparse fragments which the eclogue presents as all that can be salvaged from a supremely valuable poetic *corpus* are testimony to the wasted effort invested in offering poetic tributes such as eclogues 4 and 5 to ungrateful rulers, the futility of pastoral's attempt to strike a bargain with power.

Yet the eclogue ends with the hope of Menalcas' return, and with it a return of the power of song (*carmina tum melius, cum venerit ipse, canemus*, 9.67). This is not to be Virgil's final word, then. But the nature of these future songs is as yet undetermined. Will they resume the task of lifting the names of Varus and Caesar to the stars, of assimilating Octavian to the gods, of praising and exonerating the new regime with their gifts of golden apples?[63] Or will they be apples of discord, like Eclogue 9 itself, highlighting the injustice of that regime, stirring up dissent and indignation among the reading public? The question is left open. There is room – just conceivably – for an unconditional surrender to power, and a simple resumption of the panegyrical stance of eclogues 4 and 5 in the service of Octavian (or whoever succeeds him). But there is room too for the poet to turn his skill to avenging the disappointed hopes of the Republic, as the author of the *Dirae* is shortly to do. And there is also room for negotiations to recommence – for Octavian to demonstrate, by a change of policy, that Moeris is wrong about the futility of the pastoral bargain, wrong about the inefficacy of dovelike song. The answer will depend,

---

62 At the same time, the fertility supposedly guaranteed by Caesar's star recalls the fertility of the earth in the returned Golden Age of Eclogue 4, also apparently under the beneficent influence of the Caesarean dynasty, so that the passage arguably places a question mark over the promise of that eclogue too.
63 Will they, in short, take the form of the epic poems tentatively and conditionally promised at the end of Eclogue 4 and in the proem to Eclogue 8?

we are justified in understanding, on the actions of the ruler, on the interpretative and practical response to Virgil's book by its primary reader, in full consciousness of that ability to influence a wider readership, for good or ill, which gives the poet his bargaining power.

Conclusion

What has been dubbed the 'optimistic' school of Virgil criticism sees the panegyric of eclogues 4 and 5 and of Tityrus in Eclogue 1 as the dominant strain of the book, and strives to minimize the doubts cast on that panegyric by such aspects of the work as I have been exploring here.[64] There is ground for suspecting that a somewhat teleological impulse underlies such an approach, looking back at the *Eclogues* from the clearer (though still not wholly unambiguous) Augustanism of Virgil's later works, the *Georgics* and especially the *Aeneid*, regarded (however unconsciously) as not merely the end but the goal of Virgil's career. The *Aeneid* has always attracted more attention from commentators, and in the history of criticism ideas about and approaches to Virgil have normally arisen first in this context, before trickling down into readings of the earlier works.[65] Many scholars, however, dissatisfied by the apparent partiality of any reading which allows *either* strain to dominate over the other, have sought refuge in the notion of a 'suspension' or 'balance' of competing voices or political views in the *Eclogues*, an idea of the book as irreducibly 'multivocal', capable of seeing things from every perspective without offering judgement, and ultimately as transcending the petty squabbles of politics in their loftier concern with universal and eternal matters like Art, Death and Human Nature. Such notions have been particularly influential on students of Renaissance pastoral, who often (explicitly or implicitly) regard it as the defining characteristic of pastoral as a mode or genre.[66]

---

64 For an 'optimistic' reading of the *Eclogues*, see for example Brooks Otis, *Vergil: A Study in Civilized Poetry* (Oxford: Clarendon Press, 1963).
65 Katherina Volk (ed.), *Oxford Readings in Classical Studies: Vergil's Eclogues* (Oxford: Oxford University Press, 2008), p. 3.
66 Charles Segal ('*Tamen Cantabitis, Arcades*: Exile and Arcadia in Eclogues One and Nine', *Arion* 4 (1965), 237–66) finds 'a certain quality of suspension … between fundamental contraries of human life' in the *Eclogues*, which nevertheless ultimately 'affirms a hope and belief in order and beauty' (262). Segal's term 'suspension' was adopted, heavily emphasized, and popularized among students of English Renaissance literature by Paul Alpers, who argues in *What Is Pastoral?* (Chicago: University of Chicago Press, 1996) that Eclogue 1 'finally suspends the difference between the two speakers in the harmonies of verse' (169), 'a way of

With regard to Virgil, though the determination not to ignore or minimize either side of the competing political views given voice in the *Eclogues* is laudable, the idea of 'suspension' results in an image of Virgil as either sitting on the fence or perching there in order to take flight into the clouds, and this image does a disservice to the intensity and conviction with which *both* views are presented in their respective places, and also to the urgency of the task Virgil sets his reader – the task of negotiating between such starkly opposed positions. So irreconcilable are the views offered by Tityrus and Meliboeus in Eclogue 1, for instance, or by eclogues 5 and 9, that merely concluding that they offer different but equally valid perspectives seems like backing down in the face of a challenge. Even choosing a side and arguing for its rightful dominance – despite the danger of partiality – seems to rise to the occasion better than this. But the formulation of a recent contribution to the 'optimist' camp is altogether more equal to the task. Anton Powell offers strongly Augustan readings of the *Georgics* and the *Aeneid*, and indeed sees allegiance to Octavian as Virgil's intention from the beginning of his career. But he sees the *Eclogues* as only extending to Octavian a conditional offer of such allegiance, in an attempt to influence his political actions (crucially over the land-confiscations). The balance of political praise and critique in the *Eclogues* is to be understood as 'a delicate and integrated negotiation' with Octavian, offering masterly public relations services on certain conditions, but also carrying 'an implicit threat' to 'help the opposition' if those conditions are not met.[67] They propose a bargain, in short – a bargain fulfilled on Virgil's side, according to Powell, in his later work as apologist for the regime. It is the conditionality of the offer and the mutual negotiation of the imagined bargain which is such a crucial contribution to study of the *Eclogues*. Whether the bargaining ends so abruptly and finally in partisan commitment after that inaugural work is another ques-

bringing matters to a close without resolving issues' which he sees as characteristic of the whole book (173); even in Eclogue 9, he thinks, 'critical, ironic and affirmative elements are held in suspension' (171). Alpers then goes on to describe the 'sense of both sides being heard' and the suspension of 'disagreement' in Spenser's *Calender* (178). See also Alpers, *The Singer of the Eclogues* (Berkeley: University of California Press, 1979), pp. 65–105, for a fuller treatment of 'suspension' in Virgil. Cp. Gordon Williams, *Tradition and Originality in Roman Poetry* (Oxford: Clarendon Press, 1968), p. 329, on Virgil's political 'ambivalence' and reluctance 'to take sides' in the *Eclogues*, and Judith Haber's frequent recourse to the term 'suspension' in *Pastoral and the Poetics of Self-Contradiction: Theocritus to Marvell* (Cambridge: Cambridge University Press, 2006).

67 Powell, *Virgil the Partisan*, pp. 194–202, quotation at 195.

tion.⁶⁸ It will be clear too, from what goes before, that I do not share Powell's sense that Virgil is already, at the outset of his career, strongly inclined towards the role of apologist for Octavian, should circumstances (and Octavian's actions on his side of the bargain) permit. But the concept of the negotiation attempt seems (from the perspective of my own, more 'pessimistic', reading) to account very well for the relation between the divergent currents of praise and criticism in the work, while doing justice to its political involvement and insistent concern with the efficacy of song. And it answers perfectly to the way in which the *Eclogues* repeatedly figure the transactions between poet and ruler in the motif of gifts accompanied by the hope of some consequence or return – lambs sacrificed to a protecting deity, fauns offered conditionally to a reluctant beloved, kids sent with a curse, apples given as a wooing gift together with the promise of more, or the apples of the future confiscated by barbarous soldiers.⁶⁹ The attempt to set up a relationship of mutual obligation between poet and ruler, reflecting the wider political relationship of allegiance and obligation between the ruler and all citizens, is obliquely thematized in the *Eclogues* as a ritual of gift-exchange – taking its cue from the love-gifts of Theocritean pastoral courtship, but variously adapted to encompass the manifold possible abuses and failures of the ideal mutuality of the gift-exchange dynamic through the threat or fact of compulsion, natural or supernatural, or through the simple refusal to reciprocate. This theme, and this pattern of imagery, emerges as the eclogue book's figurative presentation of its own attempt to negotiate a bargain with political power.

With regard to Spenser, such political involvement and such a focus on the efficacy of song sits comfortably alongside the period's humanist emphasis on rhetorical persuasion as central to the functioning of society, and theories of poetry's social role like that articulated in Sidney's *Apology* – much more comfortably than the

---

68 Powell's rigorous historicizing perspective brings new evidence to bear on the *Aeneid*, in particular, which weighs heavily in the 'optimist' side of the scales, but the arguments of the 'pessimists' retain force. For pessimistic readings of the *Aeneid*, see for example Michael C. J. Putnam, *The Poetry of the Aeneid: Four Studies in Imaginative Unity and Design* (Cambridge, MA: Harvard University Press, 1965); Boyle, *The Chaonian Dove*; R. O. A. M. Lyne, *Further Voices in Virgil's Aeneid* (Oxford: Clarendon Press, 1992). Though there have been advocates (for example W. Ralph Johnson, *Darkness Visible: A Study of Vergil's Aeneid* (Berkeley: University of California Press, 1976)) of the view that the poem is 'polysemous' and 'unresolved', reminiscent of the 'suspension' theory of the *Eclogues*, Powell's concept of negotiation has not been applied to Virgil's epic.
69 Or even the savings of Tityrus offered as a bribe: see note 21 above.

indecision, neutrality or metaphysical aloofness implied by the idea of pastoral 'suspension' could do. These ideas are more substantially and self-consciously bodied forth in Spenser's pastoral poems than in any others of the period. As we have seen, persistent strains in the commentary tradition would have encouraged him to see Virgil as equally politically involved. Spenser's imitations of and allusions to Virgil in his pastoral works make it clear that he is fully alive to both views voiced in the *Eclogues* – the political praise and the political critique. In the *Shepheardes Calender*, however, it is made very clear that Spenser, as a reader of Virgil, did not think it possible simply to hold both, 'in suspension'. Colin Clout is continuously presented as forced to choose between the two modes of song, but neither for Colin nor for the reader is this simply a matter of choosing a side and striving to make it dominant over the other. Rather, the relationship between the two strains is worked out as part of poetry's negotiation with power, a bargain in which the temporal aspect of all bargains is crucial – the gap between promise and fulfilment, bringing with it obligation, contingency and conditionality. As in Virgil's *Eclogues*, the bargain is seen as one aspect of the relationship of mutual obligation binding the ruler and *all* subjects – a vision of the political system which makes it appear strongly contractual in nature. The alternative (and in Spenser's age more orthodox) view of monarchical authority as quasi-divine and not contingent on the fulfilment of any negotiated agreement emerges, like the deifying praise of Virgil's fourth and fifth eclogues (in their own time the more radical position), as part of the propaganda the poet can offer the ruler on his side of the poetic bargain. His negotiating power resides in his ability to influence his readership – the ruler's subjects – in their perception of the political system, their sense of the validity of the wider political bargain and of their own obligations. And as in Virgil's *Eclogues*, these bargains are thematized and figured through an insistent focus on the offering of gifts – the traditional pastoral gifts of flowers, fruit and lambs which derive ultimately from Theocritus' wooing-gifts and rewards for song, but permeated with the full political significance we have seen them acquire in Virgil.

2

Virgilian negotiations in *The Shepheardes Calender*

What would new readers have thought on opening *The Shepheardes Calender, Conteyning twelve Aeglogues proportionable to the twelve monethes* in 1579? The very title is a kind of riddle, alluding to the humble shepherds' almanac, yet also indicating that it belongs to the venerable genre of pastoral poetry.[1] It would have reminded its original readers startlingly of the editions of Virgil's *Eclogues*, and of his complete works, with which they had been familiar since their earliest schooldays, with its woodcut illustrations, and most of all its inclusion of extensive glosses and prefatory material ostensibly by another hand, the mysterious 'E.K.', a commentator who undertakes to assist the reader as best he can by virtue of his partial but not complete knowledge of the author's meaning. Such commentary would immediately have evoked the Virgilian commentary tradition.[2] At the same time, they may have been reminded of the games played with teasing and misleading commentary in the paratexts of humanist texts like

---

1 On the unique appearance of the volume, see Ruth Samson Luborsky, 'The Allusive Presentation of *The Shepheardes Calender*', *Spenser Studies* 1 (1980), 29–67.
2 On the commentary evoking Servius, see Richard McCabe, 'Annotating Anonymity, or Putting a Gloss on *The Shepheardes Calender*', in Joe Bray, Miriam Handley and Anne C. Henry (eds), *Ma(r)king the Text: The Presentation of Meaning on the Literary Page* (Aldershot: Ashgate, 2000), pp. 35–54; on the woodcuts in relation to sixteenth-century Virgil editions, see Ruth Samson Luborsky, 'The Illustrations to *The Shepheardes Calender*', *Spenser Studies* 2 (1981), 3–53, and 'The Illustrations to *The Shepheardes Calender*, II', *Spenser Studies* 9 (1988), 249–53; on the paratext in general, see Luborsky, 'Allusive Presentation', and Richard McCabe, '"Little booke: thy selfe present": The Politics of Presentation in The Shepheardes Calender', in Howard Erskine-Hill and Richard McCabe (eds), *Presenting Poetry* (Cambridge: Cambridge University Press, 1995), pp. 15–40. I agree with those critics who see 'E.K.' as Spenser himself: see Penny McCarthy, 'E.K. was Only the Postman', *N&Q* 47 (2000), 28–31; Louise Schleiner, 'Spenser's "E.K." as Edmund Kent (Kenned / of Kent): Kyth (Couth), Kissed, and Kunning-Conning', *ELR* 20 (1990), 374–407; and Louis Waldman, 'Spenser's Pseudonym "E.K." and Humanist Self-Naming', *Spenser Studies* 9 (1988), 21–31, who compares E.K.'s role to that of Servius.

More's *Utopia*, and of the elaborate smoke-screens of fictional editors behind which Gascoigne hides in the *Hundreth Sundrie Flowers* – the first in the context of radical political ideas, the second in the context of Gascoigne's much-advertised (and possibly fictional) tribulations with the censors.

Such connotations of heterodox and censurable ideas would have been buttressed by the anonymity of the publication. Though the elegant verse 'Goe little booke' and the prefatory epistle to Harvey explain this with reference to the modesty of the 'new poet', frequent references in both text and paratext to 'secret meaning' and the political necessity of cloaking it would have suggested another motivation.[3] The names which *do* appear on the title-page would, meanwhile, have strengthened this impression of political heterodoxy and suggested more precisely wherein it lay. Philip Sidney, the dedicatee, was currently out of favour as a result of his outspoken letter to the Queen counselling her against her planned marriage to the French Catholic Duc d'Alençon. Henry Singleton, the printer, had recently and narrowly escaped sharing the fate of John Stubbes, whose right hand had been publicly severed as punishment for authoring a tract in the same cause, *A Gaping Gulfe*, which Singleton had printed earlier in the same year. The work is thus aligned with the Protestant campaign to prevent a marriage which, it was feared, would damage England's sovereignty and lead to the undoing of the Reformation in England, a cause which scholars have found reflected throughout the *Calender*, accompanied by Protestant polemic on other issues. Altogether, the self-presentation of the work evokes Virgil's *Eclogues*, but in a way which throws emphasis on the subversive aspect of Virgilian pastoral, and associates the commentary tradition with the cautious revelation of dangerously heterodox political ideas.

As we shall see, the *Shepheardes Calender* is an extraordinarily sophisticated (and purposeful) imitation of Virgil's eclogue book. Responding to the intricate ways in which Virgil interweaves his amatory and political themes through intertextual play with Theocritus, and finding support in this for a Servian allegorical reading of Virgil, Spenser applies similar methods to Virgil in turn. Commixing imitation of and allusion to amatory and political eclogues (the Renaissance term is *contaminatio*), he exploits the

---

3 And was meant to: that the anonymity of the volume is intended to be significant, an aspect calling for interpretation, is suggested by the fact that Spenser never put his name to any of the subsequent editions appearing during his lifetime, even though he was publicly recognized as the author from an early date.

allegorical potential of the form, bringing the varieties of pastoral love-misery to bear on the political situation of 1579 – a move made easier for him, of course, by the gender of his ruler. He is clearly open to the darker aspects of the *Eclogues*, and when he imitates Virgil's Augustan voice (in *Aprill* and *Nouember*) it is even more hedged about with conditionality, irony and pessimism than in the Virgilian text. But, as in Virgil, what emerges most strongly is a sense of the poet's attempt to negotiate a bargain with political power, through the conditional promise of poetic praise, backed by the threat that, should Elizabeth not heed his warnings, he can deploy his poetic authority and persuasive power to blacken her name and shake the loyalty of her subjects. As in Virgil, so too in Spenser the dynamics of this bargain are worked out in large part through the recurring motif of the pastoral gift, in the various guises it assumes throughout the work: the wooing gifts of *Januarye* and *June*; the floral pledges of allegiance to the monarch, and religious offerings of sacrificial lambs, in *Aprill*; the funeral offerings to a mortal queen, and wistful memories of royal munificence, in *Nouember*. The status of the poem itself as a gift – whether like a Theocritean love-gift it expects a return, or whether like a Tityrean sacrifice it expresses unconditional devotion – defines the balance of power between poet and Queen, and draws in wider social relations to reflect on the nature of monarchical authority and its relation to the monarch's duty to her subjects. The ludic and as-yet-anonymous poet emerges as an arbiter of such fundamental political questions and shaper of public opinion on them, and therefore as both a valuable potential ally and a formidable potential opponent for the Queen to reckon with.

Januarye

Primed by the Virgilian self-presentation of the book, the contemporary reader would have approached *Januarye* with an expectation that it would imitate Virgil's first eclogue, and curious as to how it would adapt or diverge from its putative model. The first thing she would have seen was the woodcut, which resembles illustrations of the first eclogue in contemporary editions of Virgil. As Ruth Luborsky has shown, it recalls especially the illustrations to Sebastian Brant's remarkable edition of 1531. In Brant's illustration, the background shows Rome in one corner and a smaller market town in the other, while in the foreground Tityrus sits beneath his shady tree and Meliboeus stands before him. The background of the *Januarye* woodcut also has in one corner a city, recalling sixteenth-century woodcut depictions of Rome, and in the other a more rustic dwelling. Its foreground contains a leafless tree, an image which will be picked up in Colin's address to 'You naked trees, whose shady leaues are lost' at l. 31: it at once alludes to the beech which shelters Tityrus and marks the absence of such protecting shade. The lone figure in the composition stands under it, in the position of Brant's Tityrus but the posture of his Meliboeus, with his bagpipe broken at his feet.[4]

The woodcut thus draws attention immediately to a striking difference between this eclogue and Virgil's. Where Virgil's is a dialogue between the contented Tityrus, expressing his devotion to the godlike ruler who protects him, and the forlorn Meliboeus, complaining of the policies of the same ruler to which he has fallen victim, Spenser's will be a monologue, expressing only one point of view. That his song is a complaint aligns him, as does his posture in the illustration, with Meliboeus.[5] Meliboeus points out early on that his flock share his sorry state (12–13):

> en, ipse capellas
> Protinus aeger ago; hanc etiam vix, Tityre, duco.

['See, I myself, sick at heart, am driving my goats onwards; and this one, Tityrus, I can barely lead.']

Colin's are in like plight (5–6):

> So faynt they woxe, and feeble in the folde,
> That now vnnethes their feete could them vphold

and their weakness is also compared to their owner's (43–8). This, it would appear, is to be a gloomy reworking of Virgil.

The cause of Colin's downcast state, however, differs strikingly from Meliboeus', for, as the *Argument* informs us, it is caused by '*his vnfortunate loue*'. Meanwhile, E.K.'s first gloss, on 'Colin Cloute', answers our expectation that the opening of the book would present us with a figure both representing the author and modelled on Tityrus: 'vnder which name this Poete secretly shadoweth himself, as sometime did

---

4 Annabel Patterson, *Pastoral and Ideology: Virgil to Valéry* (Oxford: Clarendon Press, 1988), pp. 123–4.
5 See for instance Anthony M. Esolen, 'The Disingenuous Poet Laureate: Spenser's Adoption of Chaucer,' *Studies in Philology* 87 (1990), 285–311, at 297; McCabe, '"Little booke: thy selfe present"', 39–40, and 'Authorial Self-Presentation', in McCabe (ed.), *The Oxford Handbook of Edmund Spenser* (Oxford: Oxford University Press, 2010), pp. 462–82, at 465; Philip Hardie, 'Ovid and Virgil at the North Pole: Marvell's "A Letter to Doctor Ingelo"', in Jennifer Ingleheart (ed.), *Two Thousand Years of Solitude: Exile After Ovid* (Oxford: Oxford University Press, 2011), pp. 135–51, at 148.

Virgil vnder the name of Tityrus', setting up a tension with all the indications of Colin's resemblance to Meliboeus. In fact, in the history of his love which Colin recounts at ll. 49-54, Spenser combines and reworks Tityrus' amatory and political experiences which we saw paralleled in Virgil's first eclogue. Like Tityrus making the journey to Rome, Colin tells us he has visited 'the neighbour town' (49-54).

> A thousand sithes I curse that carefull hower,
> Wherein I longd the neighbour towne to see:
> And eke tenne thousand sithes I blesse the stoure,
> Wherein I sawe so fayre a sight, as shee.
> Yet all for naught: such sight hath bred my bane.
> Ah God, that loue should breede both ioy and payne.

But where Tityrus ascribes his good fortune to the sight he had there of the young god, Colin in contrast ascribes his misfortune to his sight of Rosalind. The sixteenth-century reader accustomed to Servian allegory would expect a gloss identifying the historical figure behind this name, and E.K. teasingly acknowledges the legitimacy of the question while frustratingly withholding the information:

> Rosalinde) is also a feigned name, which being wel ordered, wil bewraye the very name of hys loue and mistresse, whom by that name he coloureth ... And this generally hath bene a common custome of counterfeicting the names of secret Personages.

Paul McLane argues that Rosalind signifies the *rosa linda* or 'beautiful rose', and thus the Tudor rose, Elizabeth.[6] It is a convincing solution to E.K.'s riddle,[7] and would confirm the expectation set up by the Virgilian intertext. Tityrus' meeting with the young god had been glossed as Virgil's meeting with Octavian throughout the history of Virgil commentary; the reader familiar with the famous identification would be primed to expect Colin to meet his Queen as a result of his similar trip to town.

The effect on Colin's psyche is of course markedly opposite to the effect on Tityrus of his interview with Octavian, and plunges him

---

6 Paul McLane, *Spenser's* Shepheardes Calender: *A Study in Elizabethan Allegory* (Notre Dame: University of Notre Dame Press, 1961), pp. 27-46, etymology of 'Rosalind' at p. 32.

7 Though it has gained wide currency, some critics still demur from the identification of Rosalind with Elizabeth: see for instance Andrew Hadfield, 'Spenser's Rosalind', *MLR* 104 (2009), 935-46; Lynn Staley Johnson, *The Shepheardes Calender: An Introduction* (Philadelphia: Pennsylvania State University Press, 1990); Helfer, *Spenser's Ruins and the Art of Recollection*; Willy Maley, *Salvaging Spenser: Colonialism, Culture and Identity* (New York: St Martin's, 1997), pp. 28-9.

into a despair which makes him resemble instead Tityrus' foil, Meliboeus. Colin's malaise has often been described as Petrarchan, and this is undeniably appropriate: here and elsewhere in the *Calender* Colin's songs imitate details from Petrarch's *Rime sparse*, many of them already conventional in the tradition of love poetry written in imitation of Petrarch.[8] Such Petrarchan posturing also readily lent itself, in an England ruled by the still unmarried Queen, to veiled but decodable political complaint.[9] But by turning too quickly to Petrarch we are in danger of missing the ingenious play with Virgil. In Virgil's first eclogue, as we have seen, Tityrus' amatory suits to Galatea and Amaryllis were paralleled with his political suit to Octavian, and the happy outcome of the latter appeared as a repetition of Tityrus' happy relationship with Amaryllis, and in contrast to his earlier relationship with an implicitly scornful Galatea.[10] The gender of Spenser's queen makes it possible for him to collapse these figures into one, with Rosalind filling the place both of the love object and of the young god in the city. But instead of resembling the Amaryllis who returns Tityrus' love, Rosalind recalls what is implied of Tityrus' first love, Galatea, scorning all the gifts he can offer. And here we should recall that Tityrus' experience with the godlike youth in Rome was not the only visit to a city he referred to. While he belonged to Galatea, he tells Meliboeus, he never managed to bring money home, however many cheeses he pressed 'for the ungrateful city' (*ingratae urbi*). This city is presumably Mantua, and it is ungrateful because it will not reward him with a high price for his cheese, but this meanness only exacerbates the problem caused by the demanding mistress: we are reminded of Servius' claim that Galatea is an allegory for Mantua. Colin's trip to the 'neighbour towne', then, collapses Tityrus' successful journey to Rome into his earlier trips to market in the 'ungrateful city', and his encounter with the young god into his earlier amatory misery when he was enthralled to Galatea, *nec spes*

---

8 E.g. David Shore, 'Colin and Rosalind: Love and Poetry in the Shepheardes Calender', *Studies in Philology* 73 (1976), 176–88, and *Spenser and the Poetics of Pastoral: A Study in the World of Colin Clout* (Montreal: McGill-Queen's University Press, 1985), pp. 68–104; S. F. Walker, 'Poetry Is/Is Not a Cure for Love: The Conflict of Theocritean and Petrarchan Topoi in *The Shepheardes Calender*', *Studies in Philology* (1979); Louis Adrian Montrose, '"The perfecte paterne of a Poete"'.
9 A. F. Marotti, '"Love Is Not Love": Elizabethan Sonnet Sequences and the Social Order', *ELH* 49 (1982), 396–428; Ann Rosalind Jones and Peter Stallybrass, 'The Politics of *Astrophil and Stella*', *SEL* 24.1 (1984), 53–68.
10 Vives' allegorical gloss on Amaryllis, going beyond Servius' identification of her with Rome, brings the eclogue even closer to Spenser's reworking: *Haec Roma est vel Octavianus* (*In publii Vergilii Maronis Bucolica interpretatio*, A3v).

libertatis erat ('and there was no hope of freedom', 1.32).

Galatea's scorn is of course not explicit in Eclogue 1. It is only implied by the fact that such a story makes sense of Tityrus' inability to save money, and by the intertextual relation to Theocritus' third and eleventh idylls, reinforced by the fuller and closer imitation of both in the ensuing eclogue telling of Corydon's despair and hopeless love-gifts. That is to say that Tityrus' Galatea is paralleled, across the eclogues, with Corydon's Alexis (himself modelled on Theocritus' Galatea, as well as on his scornful Amaryllis). It is therefore entirely appropriate that Spenser turns to Eclogue 2 to fill out his picture of the scornful Galatea–Rosalind. He does so by constructing his own love-triangle (55–60).

> It is not *Hobbinol*, wherefore I plaine,
> Albee my loue he seeke with dayly suit:
> His clownish gifts and curtsies I disdaine,
> His kiddes, his cracknelles, and his early fruit.
> Ah foolish *Hobbinol*, thy gyfts bene vayne:
> *Colin* them giues to *Rosalind* againe.

As E.K.'s gloss spells out for us, line 57 'imitateth Virgils verse, *Rusticus es Corydon, nec munera curat Alexis*' (quoting Eclogue 2.56, 'You're a clown, Corydon, and Alexis doesn't care for your gifts'). The allusion is extended as the 'clownish gifts' are enumerated, Hobbinol's 'kiddes' recalling Corydon's gift of the twin *capreoli* at 2.40–4, his 'early fruit' the quinces, chestnuts and plums Corydon offered to Alexis at 2.51–3. And like Corydon at line 69, Hobbinol is 'foolish'. Colin thus plays Alexis to Hobbinol's Corydon.[11]

But the final line of the stanza neatly flips the situation, and binds the love of Virgil's second eclogue to the narrative of the first, as Colin passes the gifts on to Rosalind, taking up the position of Corydon to her Alexis. Corydon's frustration and foolishness become Colin's, and in retrospect his Petrarchan lament emerges as reminiscent of Corydon's, with lines 39–40,

> The blossome, which my braunch of youth did beare,
> With breathed sighes is blowne away, and blasted

recalling Corydon's *floribus Austrum / ... inmisi* ('I have let the South Wind in to my flowers', 2.58). Meanwhile, E.K.'s long, defensive note

---

11 Theodore Bathurst's Latin translation of the *Calender*, the *Calendarium Pastorale* (dated to 1608, though not published until 1653), gives Colin the name Alexis (as does British Museum MS Harleian 532, a Latin translation of the *Aprill* lay to Elisa).

disclaiming that the homoerotic scenario implies any 'execrable and horrible sinnes of forbidden and vnlawful fleshlinesse' nevertheless observes that, as long as it remains a matter of the soul and not of the body, 'paederastice [is] much to be praeferred before gynerastice'. Thus it is clear which of the two Corydons we have here is the most *demens* or 'foolish'. The very device of the love-triangle is wittily Virgilian, for not only does it reflect the ludic interrelations both between the loves of Virgil's first and second eclogues and between the different love-objects of Eclogue 1, but the relationship in Eclogue 2 is in itself a triangle. The reason Corydon's gifts are useless is ultimately not Alexis' cruelty but the existence of a rival with whom he cannot compete. Alexis is the slave and valued catamite of his master Iollas (*delicias domini*, 2.2; Iollas named at 57) in the city. In so far as he plays the role of Alexis to Hobbinol's Corydon, then, Colin's fidelity to Rosalind, the social superior who dwells in the city, also carries muted overtones of slavery. And the idea that Colin is in a sense Rosalind's slave, while in keeping with his Petrarchan stance throughout, also fits neatly with the ambiguities surrounding the manumission of Alexis' fellow slave Tityrus, which play so significant a part in the politics of Eclogue 1.

In the following stanza the material gifts fade out of the picture, and are replaced by Colin's songs, the object of Rosalind's scorn (63–6):

> Shee deignes not my good will, but doth reproue,
> And of my rurall musick holdeth scorne.
> Shepheards deuise she hateth as the snake,
> And laughes the songs, that *Colin Clout* doth make.

The lines specifically expand the opening of Corydon's complaint, *O crudelis Alexi, nihil mea carmina curas*? ('O cruel Alexis, do you care nothing for my songs?', 2.6), and the similar accusation in Eclogue 8, where the goatherd of Damon's song (which like Corydon's alludes to the third idyll) says of Nysa *tibi est odio mea fistula* ('my pipes are hateful to you', 8.33).[12] At the same time the stanza recalls that wider equation between love-gifts and the gift of pastoral song which we saw reported in Servius' gloss to 3.71, where the ten apples Menalcas gives to Amyntas are identified as the eclogues themselves, which Virgil presents to Octavian.

---

12 The situation of Damon's song in Eclogue 8, in which the goatherd complains not merely of Nysa's resistance to his suit but of her marrying Mopsus instead, will become the more suggestive parallel for Colin's relationship with Rosalind when, in *June*, we first hear of her desertion of him in favour of Menalcas.

But where Menalcas promises to send more apples tomorrow, Colin does not (67–72).

> Wherefore my pype, albee rude *Pan* thou please,
> Yet for thou pleasest not, where most I would:
> And thou vnlucky Muse, that wontst to ease
> My musing mynd, yet canst not, when thou should:
> Both pype and Muse, shall sore the while abye.
> So broke his oaten pype, and downe dyd lye.

Of Eclogue 2's main Theocritean models, the eleventh idyll was explicitly designed to show the consoling power of song to ease the mind of the lover, while the third makes no allowance for such consolation, and the goatherd ends by declaring that he will sing no more (*Id*. 3.52). Virgil's eclogue seems to admit the possibility of consolation with Corydon's parting 'you will find another Alexis'. Colin here explicitly denies song's power to console, and like the goatherd of the third idyll abjures future song. In doing so, he reverts to the stance of Meliboeus, who as we have seen (and in the context of Eclogue 1's intimate relation to the third idyll) imitated Theocritus' goatherd in his promise to sing no more songs (1.77).[13]

Colin's farewell to song also recalls another despairing lover in the *Eclogues*. At the end of his lament in Eclogue 10, Gallus concludes that song holds no consolation and the god of love no pity for the pains of lovers (60–3):

> tamquam haec sit nostri medicina furoris,
> aut deus ille malis hominum mitescere discat!
> iam neque Hamadryades rursus neque carmina nobis
> ipsa placent; ipsae rursus concedite silvae.

['As though this could be a medicine for my madness, or that god could learn to pity the ills of men! Now once more neither the hamadryads nor our songs themselves please; even ye woods, once more farewell!']

Gallus is recognizing at last what Pan has told him of the pitilessness of the god of love earlier in the poem (28–30). As Colin abjures the pipe which, like Gallus' songs, has failed to please, he also acknowledges the fruitlessness of his earlier prayer (13–18):

> Ye Gods of loue, that pitie louers payne,
> (If any gods the paine of louers pitie:)
> Looke from aboue, where you in ioyes remaine,
> And bowe your eares vnto my dolefull dittie.

---

13 As does the goatherd in Damon's song in Eclogue 8 (l. 61).

> And Pan thou shepheards God, that once didst loue,
> Pitie the paines, that thou thy selfe didst proue.

In the course of praising his own musical skills, which he promises to pass on to Alexis, Corydon refers to Pan, and observes *Pan curat oves oviumque magistros* ('Pan cares for sheep and for the masters of sheep', 2.33). But in Colin's prayer – and in its frustration – Spenser seems to be thinking also of Gallus, with a memory coloured by Servius' commentary. At 10.28, Pan's warning to Gallus *Amor non talia curat* ('Love does not care about such sorrows'), Servius has the gloss *quasi expertus in Syringa* ('as he has experienced over Syrinx') – the pains which he himself has proved.

Virgil's tenth and final eclogue is a song for Gallus, Virgil's friend and contemporary, a celebrated poet and general. Its topic is Gallus' unhappy love for the unfaithful Lycoris, the mistress addressed in Gallus' elegies (now lost, apart from one line preserved in a late geographical writer and a fragment discovered in the twentieth century).[14] As Servius notes, the eclogue is also a close imitation of Theocritus' first idyll, the lament for the dying Daphnis.[15] The crucial difference is that Gallus is not really dying: he is in despair after hearing that Lycoris has gone off with another soldier, following the camps. When Virgil describes him as 'dying of love' (*cum Gallus amore peribat*), he is using a common elegiac hyperbole, *pereo*: 'to be madly in love' (*Oxford Latin Dictionary* 4) in such a way as to align this metaphorical dying with the literally dying Daphnis of Theocritus' first idyll. In his long soliloquy Gallus speaks of his death, but such an imagined death is a typical feature of Roman love elegy, and could probably be traced back to Gallus if his work had survived. When it occurs in later elegy an element of self-dramatizing irony is often clear.[16] Indeed Servius observes at line 46 that 'all these verses are

---

14 The surviving fragments are printed, and the testimonials on Gallus from other writers gathered, with detailed commentary, in A. S. Hollis (ed. and tr.), *Fragments of Roman Poetry c. 60 BC–AD 20* (Oxford: Oxford University Press, 2007). The term 'elegy' used in reference to classical poetry means a poem written in the 'elegiac' metre; in first-century Rome the metre was used chiefly for love-poetry. Thus, though the awareness of an historical association of the metre with death-lament in Greek poetry is sometimes also active in the subtext of Roman elegies, its strongest connotation is amatory, and we must be careful not to confuse it with the modern use of the term as synomymous with 'obsequy'.
15 The opening of Eclogue 1 also alluded to this idyll (linking the openings of the two books, and thus foregrounding his relation to his Greek predecessor), so that in a sense Virgil's collection comes full circle here. See Clausen, *Eclogues*, p. 29.
16 See for instance Tibullus 1.3 and Propertius 1.19, and T. D. Papanghelis, *Propertius: A Hellenistic Poet on Love and Death* (Cambridge: Cambridge University Press, 1987).

Gallus', brought in from his songs' (*hi autem omnes versus Galli sunt, de ipsius translati carminibus*) – though unfortunately he does not go into detail, quote Gallus or indicate how long a passage of the eclogue he is talking about – so that Virgil's poem may be seen as a kind of affectionate pastiche of his friend's work. (It has been described as 'an elegy in a pastoral mode'.)[17] This is suggestively reminiscent of Spenser's incorporation of so many tropes familiar from Petrarchan sonnets – including the trope of dying from love, which Petrarch inherited from Roman love-elegy – into his own pastoral. But at least some sixteenth-century readers of the *Eclogues* mistook the direction of the conventional love–death trope. Vives' *Interpretatio in Bucolica Virgilii, Potissimum Allegorica*, first published in 1539, recounts in the argument to Eclogue 10 the biography of Gallus which would have been familiar to him from Servius' first gloss on the poem, from his early enjoyment of Augustus' favour, his appointment as prefect of Egypt, and his poetic skill, to his spectacular fall from grace under suspicion of conspiracy against the emperor and his consequent suicide. Even despite his late dating of the *Eclogues*, Servius doesn't imagine that the eclogue was composed after Gallus' death.[18] But Vives is even more confused about chronology, and concludes his argument *Mortem hanc Vergilius deflet, sub titulo amorum* ('This his death Virgil laments under the title of his loves').[19] For readers of Vives or like him, then, Gallus' love-despair was just the final instance of many in which love allegorizes political discontent across Virgil's *Eclogues*.

Thus *Januarye* works into its imitation of Virgil's opening eclogue, which readers would have expected, a pattern of allusions to other Virgilian eclogues whose theme of love was already intertwined, either by the commentaries or by Virgil himself, with the political subject matter of the first. Conspicuously lacking Tityrus' amatory and political good fortune, he mirrors Meliboeus, Corydon and

---

17 Christine Perkell, 'The "Dying Gallus" and the Design of Eclogue 10', *CP* 91 (1996), 128–40, at 132. On the posited imitation of Gallus' elegies, see also Clausen, *Eclogues*, 290–2; Ross, *Backgrounds to Augustan Poetry*, pp. 85–106.
18 He feels moved to explain not why Virgil dared to write of his love for a supposed enemy of the state but rather why he *left it to stand* at a later date, while supposedly rewriting at Augustus' command the second half of the fourth Georgic, which he alleges had originally comprised a lengthy celebration of Gallus. However, he does suggest, in his gloss to line 74, that Virgil draws attention to the political necessity of moderating his expressions of love for Gallus in Eclogue 10: 'He says "I love Gallus, but secretly, as trees grow" ... evidently because of Caesar' (*amo, inquit, Gallum, sed latenter, sicut arbores crescunt ... scilicet propter Caesarem*).
19 *In publii Vergilii Maronis Bucolica interpretatio*, C6v.

Gallus combined, figures in whom love-despair and political discontent was already blended. But despite his apparent premature abandonment of song, which evokes the end of Virgil's collection at the beginning of Spenser's, Colin's emblem in *Januarye* holds back from final despair, as the eclogue ends with *Anchora speme*. 'Notwithstande his misfortune in loue,' E.K. glosses, 'yet leaning on hope, he is somewhat recomforted.' In the context, *Anchora speme* may remind us of the note of hope at the end of Virgil's second eclogue, 'You will find another Alexis'. After all, 'hope' (*spes*) once resided in a change of love for Tityrus, too: there was no hope of liberty while Galatea held him (1.32). Against the background of Rosalind's identification with Elizabeth, this would have very disturbing implications: Spenser would seem to be warning Elizabeth that his loyalty as a subject is hanging in the balance. Such an implication would resemble hints in Sidney's letter to Elizabeth warning against the French match.[20] And we remember that Spenser could have read Corydon's line as containing just such an insinuation. Servius reports the view that Corydon's unrequited love is an allegory for the petition to Octavian about the land confiscations, and that therefore

> volunt quidam, hoc loco allegoriam esse antiquam in Augustum, ut intelligamus, invenies alium imperatorem, si te Augustus contemnit pro agris rogantem. (*ad* 2.72)
>
> ['some want there to be an allegory on Augustus here, so that we are to understand, you will find another emperor, if Augustus scorns your petition for your estate.']

The allusion throws a closing emphasis on the political bargain of pastoral – its conditional gift of praise to a ruler, backed by the threat of a change of allegiance and the deployment of poetical powers against the regime.

June

It is in *June* that we next meet Colin, and this eclogue too is presented as a reworking of Virgil's first eclogue. But where *Januarye* transformed Virgil's dialogue into a monologue, here the dialogical

---

20 Sidney warns Elizabeth that her subjects' 'hartes will be galed, if not aliened, when they shall see you take to husband a frenchman & a papist' (Albert Feuillerat (ed.), *The Prose Works of Sir Philip Sidney* (Cambridge: Cambridge University Press, 1968), Vol. 3, p. 52); cited by Richard McCabe, '"Little booke: thy selfe present"', p. 21.

structure is restored. We have two speakers, as Colin is joined by Hobbinol, the third member of *Januarye*'s love triangle – it is the only time in the *Calender* that we see Colin and Hobbinol together. It quickly becomes clear that Colin still plays the part of the discontented Meliboeus, with Hobbinol taking up the role of Tityrus, the contented beneficiary of patronage.[21] In *Januarye* the wintry landscape reflected Colin's despair back to him (19–20):

> Thou barrein ground, whome winters wrath hath wasted,
> Art made a myrrhour, to behold my plight ...

Now, in high summer, his mood is out of kilter both with the season and with the idyllic setting, described for us by Hobbinol. It appears that Colin now has a choice, but actively chooses to remain a despairing exile.

Hobbinol's opening description of his *locus amoenus* strongly evokes the contentment of Tityrus as described by Meliboeus in Eclogue 1 (1–8).

> Lo *Colin*, here the place, whose pleasaunt syte
> From other shades hath weand my wandring mynde.
> Tell me, what wants me here, to worke delyte?
> The simple ayre, the gentle warbling wynde,
> So calme, so coole, as no where else I fynde:
> The grassye ground with daintye Daysies dight,
> The Bramble bush, where Byrds of euery kynde
> To the waters fall their tunes attemper right.

That the place can at first be summed up as a 'shade' itself recalls Tityrus' defining posture *lentus in umbra* ('reclining in the shade', 1.4), while the more detailed description which follows (1.51–8) recalls Meliboeus'

> fortunate senex, hic inter flumina nota
> et fontis sacros frigus captabis opacum;
> hinc tibi, quae semper, vicino ab limite saepes
> Hyblaeis apibus florem depasta salicti
> saepe levi somnum suadebit inire susurro;
> hinc alta sub rupe canet frondator ad auras,
> nec tamen interea raucae, tua cura, palumbes
> nec gemere aeria cessabit turtur ab ulmo,

---

21 Donald Maurice Rosenberg, *Oaten Reeds and Trumpets: Pastoral and Epic in Virgil, Spenser, and Milton* (Lewisburg: Bucknell University Press, 1981), p. 82; Alpers, *What Is Pastoral?*, p. 180.

['Lucky old man! Here among familiar streams and sacred springs you will seek out the shady cool. Henceforward, as ever, from the neighbouring boundary, the hedge whose willow-flowers are grazed by Hyblaean bees will often invite you with its soft murmur to fall asleep. Henceforth under the high-reared cliff the woodman shall sing to the breezes; nor meanwhile will your hoarse beloved wood-pigeons, or the turtle-dove, cease to moan from the lofty elm.']

with its elements of coolness, flowers, waters and harmonious birds.

Colin's reply picks up the echo: his 'O happy *Hobbinoll*, I blesse thy state' (9) is clearly a version of Meliboeus' exclamation *fortunate senex*. His own tribute to the 'Paradise' Hobbinoll has found, meanwhile, recalls earlier lines: the praise by negatives in

> Here wander may thy flock early or late,
> Withouten dreade of Wolues to bene ytost

(11–12) is reminiscent of the first half of the same speech of Meliboeus, a less idealized description which works through the implicit contrast with the ills which the dispossessed shepherds are to suffer, and which also opens with *fortunate senex* (1.46–50):

> Fortunate senex, ergo tua rura manebunt
> et tibi magna satis, quamvis lapis omnia nudus
> limosoque palus obducat pascua iunco.
> non insueta gravis temptabunt pabula fetas
> nec mala vicini pecoris contagia laedent.

['Lucky old man! So these lands will remain your own, and big enough for you, even though bare stone covers all, and the marsh cloaks them with muddy rushes. No unaccustomed fodder shall assail your ailing pregnant ewes, no foul contagions from a neighbour's flock harm them.']

'Thy louely layes here mayst thou freely boast' (13), meanwhile, links Hobbinol to the Tityrus whom we discover teaching the woods to echo 'Beautiful Amaryllis', and who boasts of his freedom to play what he wants on his rustic pipe (*ludere quae vellem calamo ... agresti*, 1.10). After Meliboeus' lengthy description of the lands Tityrus is so fortunate to enjoy, his next words describe his own fate by contrast (1.64–6):

> At nos hinc alii sitientis ibimus Afros,
> pars Scythiam et rapidum cretae veniemus Oaxen
> et penitus toto divisos orbe Britannos.

> ['But we must go hence – some to the parched Libyans, some to reach Scythia and the swift Oaxes, which snatches up chalk in its current, and the Britons, utterly cut off from the whole world.']

Colin likewise immediately goes on to contrast Hobbinol's good fortune with his own, which he now describes explicitly as exile (14–16):

> But I vnhappy man, whom cruell fate,
> And angry Gods pursue from coste to coste,
> Can nowhere fynd, to shroude my lucklesse pate.

Surprisingly, however, the lines clearly imitate not Meliboeus' lament over his exile in Eclogue 1 but rather the description of a grander exile, Aeneas, which opens the *Aeneid*.[22] We shall return to this presently.

With Hobbinol and Colin now recognizable as versions of Tityrus and Meliboeus respectively, the dialogue takes an unexpected turn, as Hobbinol invites Colin to join him in his *locus amoenus* (17–24):

> Then if by me thou list aduised be,
> Forsake the soyle, that so doth thee bewitch:
> Leaue me those hilles, where harbrough nis to see,
> Nor holybush, nor brere, nor winding witche:
> And to the dales resort, where shepheards ritch,
> And fruictfull flocks bene euery where to see.
> Here no night Rauens lodge more blacke then pitche,
> Nor eluish ghosts, nor gastly owles doe flee.

At the end of Eclogue 1, to be sure, Tityrus tentatively extends the offer of one night's hospitality to Meliboeus, but there is no suggestion that this would do more than postpone his journey into exile until morning. Here it appears that it is quite open to Colin to take up residence in these fruitful Tityrean dales 'if [he] list'. Hobbinol's further description of the enticements of the place associates it with a particular type of poetry (25–32):

> But frendly Faeries, met with many Graces,
> And lightfote Nymphes can chace the lingring night,
> With Heydeguyes, and trimly trodden traces,
> Whilst systers nyne, which dwell on Parnasse hight,
> Doe make them musick, for their more delight:
> And Pan himselfe to kisse their christall faces,
> Will pype and daunce, when Phoebe shineth bright:
> Such pierlesse pleasures haue we in these places.

22 As noted by Shore, *Spenser and the Poetics of Pastoral*, p. 75, and by Hubbard, *Pipes of Pan*, p. 287.

Virgilian negotiations

This scene is fraught with reminiscences of Colin's lay to Elisa in the *Aprill* eclogue. The lay invokes both the nymphs (37) and the Muses 'that on *Parnasse* dwell' (41); Calliope with 'the other Muses' hasten 'with their Violines' (100–3) to where Elisa sits on the green, and the graces foot it finely and 'daunce deffly' to their music. Elisa is compared to the moon by the names of 'Phoebe' (64–5) and 'Cynthia' (82–5), and Pan is mentioned twice as her father (51, 91). The woodcut to *Aprill*, meanwhile, with its bevy of richly dressed ladies surrounding a crowned and sceptre-bearing Elizabeth, makes it clear that the pastoral vision of the lay is merely a veil for an act of courtly homage. As we shall see when we come to discuss *Aprill* in more detail, the lay to Elisa is pointedly compared to Tityrus' hymning of Octavian in Eclogue 1. Evidently Hobbinol in *June* is inviting Colin not merely to enjoy the protected situation of a Tityrus with him but to return to the Tityrean poetry of political praise which, in some unspecified past remembered in the *Aprill* eclogue, he used to compose. Indeed, the one seems to imply the other, in the reciprocal exchange of praise for patronage, patronage for praise, dubbed 'prestation' and taken as paradigmatic of Renaissance pastoral by Louis Adrian Montrose.[23]

Colin's response confirms this association of the Tityrean exchange with his past. He not only rejects but reproves it as a youthful folly (36–7). We might expect from his talk of 'ryper age' and 'stayed steps' that he is taking up the stance of the censorious elder like Thenot in *Februarye*, and condemning the pleasures described by Hobbinol as smacking of worldliness and sexual desire, but Colin says he was able to enjoy such delights 'whylst youth, and course of carelesse yeeres / Did let me walke *withouten* lincks of loue' (33–4, my italics).[24] The riper age which has removed his appetite for them seems to coincide with the *onset* of love, or perhaps rather with experience of its imprisoning chains or 'lincks', rather than with his maturing beyond it. Yet when he goes on to describe how he used to partake of these pleasures, love does after all appear to be the focus (41–6):

> Tho couth I sing of loue, and tune my pype
> Vnto my plaintiue pleas in verses made:
> Tho would I seeke for Queene apples vnrype,

---

23 Louis Adrian Montrose, 'Gifts and Reasons: The Contexts of Peele's Araygnment of Paris', *ELH* 47 (1980), 433–61.
24 The surprise to our expectations is noted by Nancy Jo Hoffman, *Spenser's Pastorals: The Shepheardes Calender and 'Colin Clout'* (Baltimore: Johns Hopkins University Press, 1977), p. 65.

> To giue my *Rosalind*, and in Sommer shade
> Dight gaudy Girlonds, was my comen trade,
> To crowne her golden locks ...

The only way to resolve the obvious contradiction is to suppose that Colin was not actually *in* love when he was wont to 'sing *of* loue' and to offer the conventional lovers' gifts of verses, apples and garlands to Rosalind.[25] His apparent wooing, that is, actually represents something else: 'love is not love', as Marotti put it in his influential essay on the political function of Elizabethan love-sonnets.[26] Meanwhile, we remember that this memory of Colin's is supposed to describe a scene analogous to Hobbinol's, which itself replayed the lay to Elisa, explicitly 'made in honor of her Maiestie' (*Aprill*, Argument) – that is, poetry as courtly entertainment and political praise. The naming of the fruit as 'Queene apples' punningly reinforces the impression that Rosalind is here again none other than Elizabeth. E.K. glosses 'Queene apples vnrype' by quoting Virgil, Eclogue 2.51, *ipse ego cana legam tenera lanugine mala*, Corydon's promise to gather quinces for Alexis. Given the context, we should remember Servius' interpretation of Eclogue 2 as Virgil's wooing of Augustus under the name of Alexis, and the allegory he offers in Eclogue 3 interpreting Menalcas' similar love-gift of ten apples as Virgil's ten eclogues for Augustus.[27] Colin is remembering his former participation in the exchange of praise of Elizabeth (such as the lay of Elisa) for patronage and the protected state described by Hobbinol – a participation imaginatively placed in a time before the composition of the *Calender*, and which the 'New Poete' has never enjoyed in fact, but which the biographical allegories traditionally imposed on Virgil's eclogues have made an intrinsic and expected theme of pastoral.

What has made participation in this reciprocal relationship no longer possible for Colin is 'losse' of Rosalind, and this will be explained in more detail a little later as her betrayal of him for Menalcas. It is from *this* point, we must understand, that Colin has been forced to walk in 'lincks of loue' (34). Rosalind's scornful treatment has put Colin in chains: we feel the contrast with Hobbinol's freedom to 'boast' his 'louely lays' mentioned at line 13, and recalling as we saw Tityrus' freedom to sing, granted by Octavian. Freedom was of course a major theme in Virgil's first eclogue, where Tityrus moved

---

25 Cp. Harry Berger, *Revisionary Play: Studies in the Spenserian Dynamics* (Berkeley: University of California Press, 1988), pp. 436–7.
26 Marotti, '"Love Is Not Love"'.
27 See Servius' glosses to 2.6, 2.73 and 3.71.

from the slavery he suffered during the period when Galatea held him to *Libertas*, granted by Octavian, after he had switched his affections on to the reciprocating Amaryllis. Colin has moved in the opposite direction, from the carefree pleasures of a properly reciprocal relation between the ruler and her subjects to the chains imposed by her scorn and betrayal, a kind of slavery. The trope of the lover as slave to the mistress is certainly Petrarchan, and in Elizabethan England the Petrarchan trope had already acquired the potential to convey a political meaning. But its roots can be traced back to the poetry of Virgil and his contemporaries, and its prominent use in Virgil's first eclogue, structuring the political ideas of that eclogue on a deep level, has a significance here, in Spenser's pastoral, at least as great as the later accretions of the Petrarchan tradition.

Hobbinol responds with two stanzas in praise of Colin's poetry. He is clearly talking about the productions of Colin's 'youth', the earlier period Colin has been describing as irrevocably past. Again, the stanzas evoke an idyllic scene, but now there are hints of a very different perspective on the patronage relationship (49–56):

> Colin, to heare thy rymes and roundelayes,
> Which thou were wont on wastfull hylls to singe,
> I more delight, then larke in Sommer dayes:
> Whose Echo made the neyghbour groues to ring,
> And taught the byrds, which in the lower spring
> Did shroude in shady leaues from sonny rayes,
> Frame to thy songe their chereful cheriping,
> Or hold theyr peace, for shame of thy swete layes.

The first thing to notice about this scene is that Colin appears to create it himself by the act of singing. These 'rymes and roundelayes' were performed not in the dales, the 'pleasaunt syte' (1) praised by Hobbinol at the beginning of the poem, but on 'wastfull hylls' just like the setting of Colin's current exile, 'those hilles, where harbrough nis to see' (19), which Hobbinol has been trying to entice him to leave. But by the end of the stanza, and as if in response to his song, the bleak setting becomes filled with birds and vegetation, summer, shade and rejoicing nature. Lines 52–5 specifically evoke the scene of Tityrus enjoying his *otium* at the beginning of Virgil's first eclogue, but the emphasis here is not on the poet as fortunate recipient of favour, pleasure, shade and protection, but rather on his creative power. Spenser's image of the echoing wood and, in particular, the idea that Colin *teaches* the birds to sing in harmony with him imitate

Virgil's lines, with their bold use of the verb *doceo* ('to teach') (1.4–5),

> tu, Tityre, lentus in umbra
> formosam resonare doces Amaryllida silvas.

['You, Tityrus, at ease in the shade, teach the woods to echo "Beautiful Amaryllis".']

'Thus', Coleman comments, 'does the pastoral singer transform his surroundings.'[28] There are muted hints of Orphic power in these lines, quite different from the aura of disempowered dependency on his patron which otherwise hangs about Tityrus, and Spenser exploits them subtly but to the full. Where Tityrus emphasizes that he owes his contented leisure and his very freedom to sing to the 'god' who 'made' it for him (*deus nobis haec otia fecit*, 1.6), Colin as he appears here is in no one's debt, and rather himself acts as benefactor to the delighted audience made up of Hobbinol and the birds.

The alternative idea, in line 56, of the birds' shame at being outsung leads Hobbinol into the further scene-painting of the following stanza (57–64):

> I sawe Calliope wyth Muses moe,
> Soone as thy oaten pype began to sound,
> Theyr youry Luyts and Tamburins forgoe:
> And from the fountaine, where they sat around,
> Renne after hastely thy siluer sound.
> But when they came, where thou thy skill didst showe,
> They drewe abacke, as halfe with shame confound,
> Shepheard to see, them in theyr art outgoe.

Featuring the Muses and their instruments, this scene is reminiscent of Hobbinol's description of the dales at lines 25 to 32, which as we saw seemed to stand for the protection extended to the Queen's faithful servants. It also recalls that passage's close intertext, the lay to Elisa, as 'I sawe Calliope wyth Muses moe ... / Renne after hastely thy siluer sound' specifically echoes *Aprill* (100–2):

> I see *Calliope* speede her to the place,
>   Where my Goddesse shines:
> And after her the other Muses trace ...

---

28 Coleman (ed.), *Eclogues*, p. 73. In fact, the precise notion of the poet teaching *the birds* to sing comes from pseudo-Moschus, *Lament for Bion* (an eclogue which is among Virgil's models in Greek pastoral, and which forms a prominent intertext for Spenser's own *Nouember*, and especially his 'Astrophel'). The allusion to it here aligns Colin with Bion, whose death the Greek poem laments, and thus contributes to the strain of elegy on his own metaphorical death which is implied by Colin in this eclogue and in *December*.

The obvious difference is the object of the Muses' wonder, no longer Elizabeth but Colin's poetic skill. Even in the *Aprill* lay itself, as Thomas Cain has observed, there are suggestions that Elisa, as the daughter of Pan and Syrinx, the emblematic pastoral instrument, is in a sense to be identified with Colin's song, and thus owes her existence to him.[29] Here, just as the Muses are outdone by Colin's music, so Elizabeth is quite replaced by it.

The idea of the pastoral singer outdoing the Muses is derived from another closely related Virgilian source. At the end of the fourth eclogue, which prophesies the return of the Golden Age with the growth to maturity of a boy about to be born, Virgil hopes to live long enough to be able to sing of his deeds as a man, in which case, he anticipates (4.55–9),

> non me carminibus vincet nec Thracius Orpheus
> nec Linus, huic mater quamvis atque huic pater adsit,
> Orphei Calliopea, Lino formosus Apollo.
> Pan etiam, Arcadia mecum si iudice certet,
> Pan etiam Arcadia dicat se iudice victum.

['Neither Thracian Orpheus nor Linus shall surpass me with their songs, even should the mother of one or the father of the other come to their aid – Calliope to Orpheus, beauteous Apollo to Linus. Even Pan, if he were to contend with me with Arcadia as judge, even Pan with Arcadia as judge would own himself defeated.']

While emphasizing the superlative poetic skill which is to be displayed in the future work, the lines fundamentally constitute a promise of poetic praise. That the poem will be finer than Orpheus assisted by Calliope, Linus assisted by Apollo, or Pan himself could compose makes the gift the more valuable. But, like the song in which Menalcas promises to lift Varus' name to the stars in the fragment recited in Eclogue 9, it has not yet been written. An air of conditionality hangs over it, and, like the fragment in Eclogue 9, we might regard it as extending the offer of a bargain: 'this is what I shall do if you make my prophecy good by ruling well', for instance. Eclogue 4 is itself a gift of poetic praise, of course. Though we are not told who, exactly, the miraculous child will be, nevertheless as Servius notes it honours Pollio, under whose consulship the birth is expected, and also reflects glory on Octavian as ruler. Together with Eclogue 5 it is the most outspokenly Caesarean poem in the book, associating Octavian's

---

29 Thomas H. Cain, 'The Strategy of Praise in Spenser's "Aprill"', *SEL* 8 (1968), 45–58, at 51.

rule with supernatural blessings. But still its refusal to identify the child explicitly, leaving it to a degree open to interpretation, withholds something of the magniloquent political support which, as it demonstrates, it is in Virgil's power to bestow on Octavian if he chooses, and the as-yet-unfulfilled promise contained in the lines just quoted encapsulates this.[30] Hobbinol's memory of Colin's former poetry putting Calliope to shame alludes to this passage, and in doing so evokes the political praise-poetry of Eclogue 4. But here it is not merely an as-yet-unfulfilled promise, but rather a feat of poetic skill already attained but now explicitly renounced by Colin. Spenser amplifies the notes of ambiguity and uncertainty in the Virgilian text. His refusal in the following stanzas to resume such song amounts to an implicit refusal to perform the acts of homage to the ruler promised and partially embodied in Virgil's fourth eclogue.

Virgil's fourth eclogue opens with an address to the *Sicilides Musae* – that is, the muses specifically of the Sicilian Theocritus, and thus of pastoral poetry – which nevertheless announces that the poem is to rise a little above the lowly genre of pastoral in order to be a fitting gift for Pollio (4.1–3):

> Sicelides Musae, paulo maiora canamus.
> non omnis arbusta iuvant humilesque myricae;
> si canimus silvas, silvae sint consule dignae.

['Sicilian Muses, let us sing of things a little greater. Orchards and humble tamarisks do not please everyone. If we must sing of woods, let the woods be worthy of a consul.']

Colin's response to Hobbinol precisely reverses this promise of singing 'something a little greater' (*paulo maiora*), vowing to remain in the 'lowly grove', Virgil's *humiles myricae* (65–72):

> Of Muses *Hobbinol*, I conne no skill:
> For they bene daughters of the hyghest *Ioue*,
> And holden scorne of homely shepheards quill.

---

30 See Powell, *Virgil the Partisan*. The ambiguity which Eclogue 4 maintains over the identity of the child also insures the poem against alternative political outcomes. It was by no means obvious in 40 BCE, when this eclogue was composed, that Octavian would emerge as ruler, and Virgil works in elements which would make it readable, retrospectively, as a panegyric for Antony, should that turn out to be politically advantageous (see particularly the closing evocation of Hercules, whom Antony claimed as his ancestor). However, the poem does clearly suggest a future quasi-monarchical rule, and associate it with supernatural blessings. The techniques were to be applied explicitly to Augustus in the *Aeneid*, and for commentators working with the retrospective knowledge of Octavian's rise to power the Caesarean implications of the poem were uppermost.

> For sith I heard, that *Pan* with *Phoebus* stroue,
> Which him to much rebuke and Daunger droue:
> I neuer lyst presume to *Parnasse* hyll,
> But pyping lowe in shade of lowly groue,
> I play to please my selfe, all be it ill.

The last lines are usually read as showing that Colin's 'verse is essentially private, and ... can aspire neither to a public function nor to public fame'.[31] Often they are taken as a sign of narcissistic 'introversion' resulting from a culpable absorption in love which blinds him to public duties.[32] But this misses the narrower point of Colin's assertion, which emerges when it is read against Eclogue 4. It is not public duty which Colin renounces here, but the specific aim of pleasing the powerful. Virgil modifies his song because lowly tamarisks do not please (*non iuvant*) great consuls, but Colin will stick to the 'lowly groves' and be guided by his conscience in what he sings: it is, as Robert Lane puts it, 'a specific repudiation of the courtly strategy of ingratiation'.[33]

The Muse specifically mentioned by Hobbinol, Calliope, is the Muse associated in the Renaissance with epic poetry, and the dichotomy of Pan and Phoebus also suggests the contrast between pastoral and epic. Aspiring 'to *Parnasse* hyll' suggests, as many have pointed out, the attempt to compose epic and thus 'winne renowne' (74).[34] But Colin is not simply rejecting the higher genre in favour of the lower. He wishes to avoid any dealings with such powerful figures because of their fundamental inclemency. The Muses are like the pitiless Rosalind in their scorn for pastoral song. Phoebus, meanwhile, has shown himself to be dangerously vindictive when surpassed in song: where the Muses in the previous stanza merely

> drewe abacke, as halfe with shame confound,
> Shepheard to see, them in theyr art outgoe,

much worse could be expected of their father, Phoebus Apollo. In

---

31 Richard Helgerson, 'The New Poet Presents Himself: Spenser and the Idea of a Literary Career', *PMLA* 93 (1978), 893–911, at 900.
32 Rosenberg, *Oaten Reeds and Trumpets*, p. 82.
33 Robert Lane, *Shepheards Devises: Edmund Spenser's* Shepheardes Calender *and the Institutions of Elizabethan Society* (Athens: University of Georgia Press, 1993), p. 155. The reminiscence of lines from Theocritus' seventh idyll (37–9) which preface the ridicule of Homer's bombastic imitators (45–8), meanwhile, suggests fidelity to the Callimachean aesthetic principles which Virgil subordinates to political ends in this fourth eclogue.
34 Cheney, 'Spenser's Pastorals', p. 92; Helgerson, 'The New Poet Presents Himself'; Patrick Cullen, *Spenser, Marvell, and Renaissance Pastoral* (Cambridge, MA: Harvard University Press, 1970).

the story explicitly alluded to here, the contest of Pan and Phoebus related in Book 11 of Ovid's *Metamorphoses*, Pan in fact receives no rebuke or punishment – it is only Midas who is punished with asses' ears for preferring Pan's music. But the mention of 'rebuke and Daunger' evokes the similar contest between Phoebus and another satyr, Marsyas, earlier in Ovid's poem, and this satyr is flayed alive in punishment for his hubris.[35] Marsyas was credited, for instance in Ovid's *Fasti*, with the discovery of the *aulos*, a particular type of flute associated with pastoral poetry (mentioned for instance in Theocritus, idylls 6 and 8).[36] He was also a symbol of liberty in republican and Augustan Rome, as Servius notes in his glosses to *Aeneid* 3.20 and 4.58, and seems to have been particularly associated with class struggle and with freedom of speech.[37] Though Pan, as the god of shepherds, is more strongly connected with pastoral, it is worth noting that in Ovid's account in the *Metamorphoses* Marsyas' death elicits the mourning of shepherds, nymphs and rural deities, in a scene reminiscent of the elegy for Daphnis in the genre's founding text, Theocritus' first idyll, and of Virgil's imitations of that elegy in eclogues 5 and 10.[38] Thus the oblique allusion fits well as a warning to a pastoral singer against precisely the kind of aspiration voiced at the end of Virgil's fourth eclogue – do not try to contend in higher genres, which involve dealing with the great and powerful and praising their deeds, for they are at best scornful and at worst cruel.[39] But the music of Colin's which Hobbinol praises as outdoing the Muses, and which Colin now renounces, was, presumably, pastoral such as the lay of Elisa, and the Muses' scorn is of a piece with Rosalind's scorn for

---

35 *Metamorphoses* 6.383–400; see Pugh, *Spenser and Ovid*, pp. 14–15, 264–6. The contests of Pan and Marsyas with Apollo are like grossly unequal versions of pastoral's amoebaean song-contests. Virgil imagines himself triumphing against similar odds in the contest imagined at the end of Eclogue 4, echoed in Hobbinol's opinion of Colin reported at *December* 45–8. In the 'straight' amoebaean song-contest of the *Calender*, in *August*, Colin will win without taking part, and will do so with a song bewailing the same woes which afflict him here, teaching him not to aspire to 'Parnasse hyll'. As in Thomalin's theological argument in *Julye*, the lowly is exalted, and the pastoral *recusatio* paradoxically achieves greater heights than epic aspiration.
36 *Fasti* 6.703–8.
37 Elaine Fantham, 'Liberty and the People in Republican Rome', *TAPA* 135 (2005), 209–29, at 220–1 and n. 52.
38 A scholiast on Theocritus reports that Alexander Aetolus, one of Theocritus' contemporaries, describes Marsysas as having learnt to play the flute from Daphnis. See H. W. Prescott, 'A Study of the Daphnis-Myth', *Harvard Studies in Classical Philology* 10 (1899), 121–40, at 126.
39 On the Marsyas episode as a contest between pastoral and epic, see Andrew Feldherr and Paula James, 'Making the Most of Marsyas', *Arethusa* 37 (2004), 75–103.

'rurall musick' (*Januarye*, 64). What he abjures here is not merely future experiment in higher genres but also the *pastoral* 'pleas in verses made' he used to offer her, along with 'Queene apples' and 'girlonds' (42–5). It is the offer of poetic tribute to cruel and ungrateful potentates in *any* genre, including the attempt of Virgilian pastoral to negotiate a bargain with the powerful – a bargain which, Colin here seems convinced, they will not honour.

In place of such tribute, Colin opts to sing only 'piteous plaints' in 'rudely drest' pastoral. Here he segues into a lament on the death of 'the God of shepheards *Tityrus* ... / Who taught me homely, as I can, to make' (81–2), seeming to align his plaints with the genre of pastoral elegy. Theocritus' first idyll, we remember, was focused on an elegy for the legendary shepherd Daphnis, himself a singer 'whom the Muses loved' (Idyll 1.141).[40] Virgil imitates this eclogue twice, both in Eclogue 5's elegy for a 'Daphnis' probably (and traditionally read as) representing Julius Caesar, which makes no reference to Daphnis as a poet, and in Eclogue 10, where the poet Gallus laments his imagined or metaphorical death as a result of his beloved Lycoris' deserting him to follow another. Now, E.K. explains in a gloss 'that by Tityrus is meant Chaucer', as he also claimed in *Februarie*, and offers as proof 'that he sayth, he tolde merye tales. Such as be hys Canterburie tales.' This would be considered pretty thin evidence if E.K. were just any critic, but he is not, and no doubt Spenser approved (if he did not author) this note, for its broad gesture of affiliation to a past golden age of English poetry. But the allusion to Chaucer does not bring with it anything very significant or illuminating in the immediate context, whereas, if we continue to think of Tityrus as a character of Virgilian and Theocritean pastoral, he fits neatly into *June*'s sustained intertextual negotiations.

Firstly, the reflection that 'Tityrus' is dead harmonizes well with the renunciation that is Colin's subject, for he is after all refusing Hobbinol's invitation to take up a stance and a manner of poetry which the eclogue has clearly aligned with Tityrus' protected position and poetry of grateful praise to a ruler in Virgil's first eclogue. In fact he has been telling us that this was the occupation of his youth, a Tityrean phase of his career which is now dead and lost to him, just as this 'Tityrus' is dead. We might be reminded of the effect in Virgil of Eclogue 9's gloom after the delicate balance between Tityrus' gratitude and Meliboeus' despair in Eclogue 1. Lycidas is shocked

---

40 Diodorus Siculus, *Library of History* 4.84.3, says that Daphnis was the inventor of bucolic song.

to hear that Moeris' land has been confiscated, since he had heard that Menalcas had saved everything with his songs, suggesting a successful petition at Rome resembling Tityrus' in Eclogue 1; Moeris tells him that this was merely a false rumour, and that in fact he and Menalcas have not only been dispossessed but have narrowly escaped being killed into the bargain, prompting Lycidas to echo Eclogue 5's elegy for the dead Daphnis in his alarmed reflections on what Menalcas' death would have meant for the shepherd community. The suggestion of an overturning of Tityrus' apparent good fortune is hard to avoid (particularly since both Tityrus and Menalcas were both traditionally read as representing Virgil), and Colin's lament for the death of Tityrus here seems to imply something similar – but even more strongly, since the death has not been avoided as it has in Eclogue 9. *June*, moreover, has a relationship to *Januarye* similar to that between Virgil's eclogues 1 and 9. Despite his act of despair in breaking his pipe at the end of *Januarye*, Colin's emblem there was *Anchora speme*, glossed by E.K. with 'yet leaning on hope, he is some what recomforted'. His emblem in *June* is *Gia speme spenta*, and E.K.'s gloss makes the reversal explicit:

> You remember, that in the fyrst Æglogue, Colins Poesie was Anchora speme: for that as then there was hope of fauour to be found in tyme. But nowe being cleane forlorne and reiected of her, as whose hope, that was, is cleane extinguished and turned into despeyre, he renounceth all comfort and hope of goodnesse to come.

This extinction of Colin's hope recalls Tityrus' *spes libertatis* (1.32) which seemed partially fulfilled in Eclogue 1 but is thrown into doubt in Eclogue 9. Tityrus, one might say, embodied hope – the hope of a favourable response a poet must necessarily possess if he is to attempt to negotiate pastoral's bargain with power. To say that Tityrus is dead is on one level merely another way of saying that all such hope is spent.

An elegy on the death of Tityrus is an innovation, but nevertheless, in Theocritus, the figure of Tityrus is connected with pastoral elegy. The lament for Daphnis is sung in full by an anonymous goatherd in Theocritus' first idyll, but in Idyll 7 it is summed up in a third-hand, thumbnail sketch, as Lycidas imagines how it will form part of the musical entertainment with which he will celebrate his lover's safe arrival (7.72–7):

> ὁ δὲ Τίτυρος ἐγγύθεν ᾀσεῖ
> ὥς ποκα τᾶς Ξενέας ἠράσσατο Δάφνις ὁ βούτας,
> χὠς ὄρος ἀμφεπονεῖτο καὶ ὡς δρύες αὐτὸν ἐθρήνευν

Ἱμέρα αἴτε φύοντι παρ' ὄχθαισιν ποταμοῖο,
εὖτε χιὼν ὥς τις κατετάκετο μακρὸν ὑφ' Αἷμον
ἢ Ἄθω ἢ Ῥοδόπαν ἢ Καύκασον ἐσχατόωντα.

['And close at hand Tityrus shall sing how once Daphnis the neatherd loved Xenea, and how the hill was sorrowful about him and the oak trees which grow upon the river Himera's banks sang his dirge when he was wasting like any snow under high Haemus or Athos or Rhodope or remotest Caucasus.']

In singing an elegy for Tityrus, then, Colin is lamenting the singer of an elegy for Daphnis, in an elegant turn which recalls, for instance, the way that the *Lament for Bion* imitates Bion's *Lament for Adonis*, or, in music, the way that Gombert's lament for Josquin quotes Josquin's *Nymphes des Bois*, which itself imitates Ockeghem while lamenting his death. But the second stanza of Colin's elegy makes it clear that it is in fact merely a prelude to his personal plaint. The point of mentioning Tityrus' death is that (91–6):

> all hys passing skil with him is fledde,
> The fame whereof doth dayly greater growe.
> But if on me some little drops would flowe,
> Of that the spring was in his learned hedde,
> I soone would learne these woods, to wayle my woe,
> And teache the trees, their trickling teares to shedde.

In the context, the reminiscence in those final lines of the oak trees lamenting Daphnis in Theocritus' seventh idyll is striking, but it is his own pain Colin is talking about – it is not now Tityrus but he himself who is parallelled with the dying Daphnis, for whom nature laments. It prepares us for *December*, which is even more clearly 'an elegy for himself'.[41] It is almost as though Colin were saying 'Tityrus could have sung an elegy for me, just as he once sang an elegy for Daphnis'.

Virgil also imitates these lines of Theocritus' Idyll 7 in his tenth eclogue, adding its details of the sorrowing mountain and trees into the more sustained imitation of Idyll 1's lament it conducts (10.13–15):

> illum etiam lauri, etiam flevere myricae;
> pinifer illum etiam sola sub rupe iacentem
> Maenalus et gelidi fleverunt saxa Lycaei.

['Even the laurels, even the tamarisks wept for him; even pine-clad Maenalus and the rocks of frozen Lycaeus wept for him as he lay beneath a lonely cliff.']

---

41 McCabe, *Shorter Poems*, p. 570.

And in *June*, Colin's ensuing explanation of his woe makes it clear that he is also imitating this eclogue. In Eclogue 10, Gallus is wasting away out of love for Lycoris, who has abandoned him for another man (10.22–3). Likewise, we learn in the following stanza, Colin's grief now arises, not from the simply unrequited love that caused his Corydon-like suffering in *Januarye* but from 'the falsenesse of his louer Rosalinde, who forsaking hym, hadde chosen another' (E.K.'s gloss to line 97). It would appear that we are to imagine some period intervening between *Januarye* and *June* – or indeed since *Aprill*, for there Rosalind's love was still 'the thing he cannot purchase' (*Aprill* 159)—when Rosalind had accepted Colin's love, before 'wex[ing] light' (*June* 103) and betraying him for one 'Menalcas'. E.K.'s gloss on 'Menalcas' encourages us to seek for a real person beneath the Virgilian name, though concealing his identity: 'the name of a shepheard in Virgile; but here is meant a person vnknowne and secrete, agaynst whome he often bitterly inuayeth'. Given that the most pressing political issue at the time of the *Calender*'s publication in 1579 was Elizabeth's plan, against the advice of many of her Protestant counsellors, to marry the French Catholic Duc d'Alençon, and given the volume's strong suggestion of affiliation with the anti-Alençon camp through its dedicatee and printer, it seems entirely plausible to read this (as many since Paul McLane have done) as allegorizing Elizabeth's turn to a Catholic lover – a 'faithlesse fere' (110) – scorning her advisers and breaking faith with her Protestant subjects. Earlier in her reign, when resisting pressure from Parliament and from her counsellors to marry and produce an heir, Elizabeth had repeatedly presented herself as already married – to England.[42] Now Spenser turns her metaphor against her: the entertainment of this new, foreign suitor must constitute an abandonment of her people equivalent to adultery.

Colin's lines on the sympathetically wailing woods conflate their allusion to the laments of Idyll 7 and Eclogue 10 with an ironic echo of Tityrus' contented song in Eclogue 1, for if these woods are to weep it will be because he *teaches* them to do so. The figure, insisted upon in the rhetorical repetition of lines 95 and 96, recalls the familiar opening image of Eclogue 1 (1.4–5):

---

[42] See for example Carole Levin, *The Heart and Stomach of a King: Elizabeth I and the Politics of Sex and Power* (Philadelphia: University of Pennsylvania Press, 2013), pp. 41–2, citing Elizabeth's 1558 speech to Parliament; and Virginia Tufte, *The Poetry of Marriage: The Epithalamium in Europe and Its Development in England* (Los Angeles: Tinnon-Brown, 1970), pp. 167–8.

> tu, Tityre, lentus in umbra
> formosam resonare doces Amaryllida silvas.⁴³

['You, Tityrus, at ease in the shade, teach the woods to echo "Beautiful Amaryllis".']

Thus it ironically recalls, and rewrites in a darker key, *June*'s earlier imitation of the same lines in Hobbinol's description of Colin's verse (52–5),

> Whose Echo made the neyghbour groues to ring,
> And taught the byrds, which in the lower spring
> Did shroude in shady leaues from sonny rayes,
> Frame to thy songe their chereful cheriping ...

Here too Spenser is picking up on a hint in Eclogue 10, for its prologue ends with a recurrence of the image of the echoing woods from Eclogue 1: *non canimus surdis: respondent omnia silvae* ('we do not sing to the deaf: all the woods respond', 10.8). In Virgil, however, the tone of this echo is much less dark. Responsiveness, like that of these 'responding' woods, and sympathy constitute an important theme in the poem, creating an emphasis on friendship and community which considerably reduces the pessimistic effect of Gallus' lament. The poem is offered as a gift of friendship and condolence 'for my Gallus' (*meo Gallo*, 10.2), and is responsive to him also in echoing Gallus' own poetry (as Servius tells us in his gloss to 10.46).⁴⁴ The 'echoing' which the woods do is thus brought into the same orbit as the attentive tributes of friendship. Gallus finds some consolation in the thought that the Arcadian shepherds will sing of his loves,

---

43 In doing so, it returns Tityrus' song of happy love, *formosam Amaryllida*, to its original minor key in the despairing song of the goatherd to Amaryllis in Theocritus' third idyll, and Spenser is probably also thinking of Virgil's fuller imitations of Idyll 3. As Eclogue 2, the song of the despairing Corydon, was important in *Januarye*, so here Damon's song, which comprises the first half of Eclogue 8, seems relevant. While strongly invoking Theocritus' third idyll, as the second eclogue does, this song suggestively unites key elements which we also see brought together in Eclogue 10, Spenser's more obvious model. Like Gallus (and like Colin), the goatherd is in despair because his beloved has left him for another man (8.26–35). The lines from Idyll 7 on the hills and oaks lamenting Daphnis are recalled here too, as the goatherd reflects that the ever-speaking hills and woods of Maenalus always listen to the loves of shepherds (8.22–4), and Idyll 1 (a major model for Eclogue 10) is also evoked, as Damon's posture, leaning against an olive-tree, alludes to the posture of the singer of the Daphnis elegy there.

44 On the poem as a gift of friendship, see Paul Alpers, *Singer of the Eclogues* (Berkeley: University of California Press, 1979), pp. 127–8. On its supposed imitation of Gallus' elegies, see Clausen, *Eclogues*, 290–2; Ross, *Backgrounds to Augustan Poetry*, pp. 85–106.

as he appeals to them to do, apparently confident of their response (10.33–4):

> O mihi tum quam molliter ossa quiescant,
> vestra meos olim si fistula dicat amores!

['Oh how softly would my bones rest then, if only your pipe would sing my loves!']

Since it may well be that Gallus' collection of love elegies was titled *Amores*, what he imagines here can again be read as an echo, like that of the responsive woods – the shepherds not just singing about his love for Lycoris but actually reciting his poetry, just as Virgil in this eclogue quotes from it.[45] The idea that 'we are not singing to the deaf' is also consolatory, for the prologue has already told us that this poem is written 'for Lycoris too to read'. This would seem to imply that it is intended, like Roman love-elegy, as a persuasion to love, aimed at Lycoris and on behalf of Gallus, attempting to move her to take pity on his plight.[46] So the responsive woods suggest the hope that Lycoris too will not be deaf but rather will respond, and return, to Gallus.

Colin too imagines that, if he were as skilful a poet as Tityrus was, his words would also reach Rosalind and 'pierce her heart with poynt of worthy wight, / As shee deseures, that wrought so deadly spight' (100–1). But the express desire is only to cause her deserved pain, not to persuade her to return to him as with Lycoris in Virgil's eclogue. Likewise, Colin like Gallus appeals to the shepherds generally to repeat the gist of his song (106–12):

> Ye gentle shepheards, which your flocks do feede,
> Whether on hylls, or dales, or other where,
> Beare witnesse all of thys so wicked deede:
> And tell the lasse, whose flowre is woxe a weede,
> And faultlesse fayth, is turned to faithlesse fere,
> That she the truest shepheards hart made bleede,
> That lyues on earth, and loued her most dere.

But where Gallus imagines the beauty of the shepherds' singing consoling him after death, the point of Colin's appeal is instead that they will testify against her as if in a court of law, and blacken her name to perpetuity. If we accept that Rosalind represents Elizabeth,

---

45 F. Skutsch, *Aus Vergils Frühzeit* (Leipzig, 1901), pp. 23–4.
46 Perkell, 'The "Dying Gallus" and the Design of Eclogue 10', 132–4.

it precisely reverses Colin's appeal to the Nymphs and Muses in the *Aprill* lay, 'Helpe me to blaze / Her worthy praise' as 'The flowre of Virgins' (*Aprill* 43–4, 48): Rosalind's 'flowre is woxe a weede' (109), and Colin advertises his power to ensure that she will be remembered thus.

Hobbinol's concluding stanza (113–20) introduces the note of friendly sympathy which is so prominent in Eclogue 10:

> O carefull Colin, I lament thy case,
> Thy teares would make the hardest flint to flowe.
> Ah faithlesse Rosalind, and voide of grace,
> That art the roote of all this ruthfull woe.
> But now is time, I gesse, homeward to goe:
> Then ryse ye blessed flocks, and home apace,
> Least night with stealing steppes doe you forsloe,
> And wett your tender Lambes, that by you trace.

But it does not offer any of the consolation or compensation for suffering implied by Virgil's echoing woods and shepherds, by the affectionate gift of 'a little song for my Gallus', and by the apparent attempt to win Lycoris back for his friend. The political situation allegorized by Colin's misfortune in love is not to be alleviated so easily. Bernard, who also analyses *June*'s relation to Virgil's first and tenth eclogues, points out that 'O carefull *Colin*, I lament thy case' echoes and answers Colin's earlier line, 'O happy *Hobbinoll*, I blesse thy state' (9), and argues that a delicate balance is thus created in the eclogue between Hobbinol's Tityrean happiness and Colin's Meliboean despair.[47] But in the light of all that Colin has told us about Tityrean poetry, the echo is just as easily read as revising and replacing the earlier sanguine outlook, concluding the eclogue with condolence and shared gloom, rather than political ambivalence or 'balance'. At the same time, Hobbinol underlines the intertextual relation to Virgil's tenth eclogue by closely imitating its final line, *ite domum saturae, venit Hesperus, ite capellae* (10.77). In doing so, he confirms the analogy between Rosalind and Lycoris. Renaissance readers would have known from Servius' introductory gloss to the eclogue that Gallus' 'Lycoris' represented the courtesan Volumnia Cytheris, lover first of Gallus and then of Antony. If we accept that Rosalind represents Elizabeth, the comparison to a *meretrix* is of course far from flattering to the Queen, and itself contributes to the blackening of her

---

47 Bernard, *Ceremonies of Innocence*, p. 59. Alpers also notes that the situation of *June* recalls that of Virgil's tenth eclogue (*What Is Pastoral?*, p. 179).

name which Colin calls on the shepherds to ensure.

So although *June* is often read as a *recusatio* of higher genres,[48] its central purpose seems instead to be *accusatio*. Colin is rejecting the Tityrean pastoral of praise in favour of the alternative pastoral voice of 'plaint', as well as rejecting epic. This is not a solipsistic indulgence in private love poetry at the expense of public duty as enshrined in higher genres, but a refusal to ingratiate himself with the powerful in any genre. The refusal is motivated by, and used to highlight, the injustice of the powerful, who have shown themselves to be undeserving of such praise and unlikely to requite it. But this is still a kind of *recusatio*, and it is telling, as others have noted, that it comes in Spenser's sixth eclogue, for Virgil's sixth eclogue opens with a *recusatio*.[49] The speaker there (who turns out to be Tityrus) tells us that his muse was not ashamed, at first, to dwell in the groves (*silvas*) and play with *Syracosio versu*, pastoral poetry like that of the Syracusan Theocritus. But when he was preparing to sing the stuff of epic, *reges et proelia* (kings and battles), Apollo plucked his ear and warned him, in Callimachean terms, that shepherds should stick to fine-spun song (*deductum carmen*). So now, since there will be others who will wish to sing Varus' praises and compose sad wars, he will 'ponder the rustic muse on a slender reed' (*agrestem tenui meditabor harundine Musam*, 6.8). (A similar *recusatio* opens Eclogue 8, promising to tell of the 'pastoral muse of Damon and Alphesiboeus', while wondering whether the day will ever come when he will be allowed to sing of Octavian's great deeds.) But there are telling differences between Spenser's *recusatio* and that of Virgil's Tityrus. Virgil is obeying the order of Apollo; Colin is refusing an invitation, and one that seems to come with a promise of patronage by similarly powerful figures. Apollo's command is aesthetically motivated, appealing to the Callimachean preference for *deductum carmen* ('fine-spun song'); Colin's choice is due to his sufferings and the political discontent they allegorize. Tityrus' response *agrestem tenui meditabor harundine Musam* ('I shall meditate the rural Muse on a slender reed', 6.8) significantly echoes Meliboeus' description of his playing at the beginning of Eclogue 1 (*silvestrem tenui musam meditaris avena*), and thus implies that he is rededicating himself to the kind of pastoral praise poetry with which

---

48 E.g. Helgerson, 'The New Poet Presents Himself', 900; Harry Berger, 'Mode and Diction in the *Shepheardes Calender*', *MP* 67 (1969), 142; Alexander Leigh DeNeef, *Spenser and the Motives of Metaphor* (Durham, NC: Duke University Press, 1982), pp. 23–4; Richard Mallette, 'Spenser's Portrait of the Artist', *SEL* 19 (1979), 29.
49 Cheney, 'Spenser's Pastorals', p. 92; Hubbard, *Pipes of Pan*, p. 289.

he hymned Octavian there; Colin instead chooses a poetry of bitter complaint and accusation. Virgil says that his poem will still honour Varus, and cause him to be sung by all the tamarisks and groves, for his name appears at the top of the page (9–12); Colin disguises the names of the powerful, and talks of them only to ensure that their 'villanee' (104) is publicized by the whole shepherd community.

Finally, the *recusatio* of Virgil's sixth eclogue is, of course, explicitly a rejection (or postponement) of epic, where Colin's as we have seen is not so specific. This difference is highlighted by the startling effect, which we noted earlier, of Colin's imitation of the opening lines of the *Aeneid* at lines 14–16.

> But I vnhappy man, whom cruell fate,
> And angry Gods pursue from coste to coste,
> Can nowhere fynd, to shroude my lucklesse pate.

As well as evoking Meliboeus' exile as we expected at that point in the eclogue, the lines ennoble Colin's plight by echoing the *Aeneid*'s opening description of Aeneas, *fato profugus* ('exiled by fate', *Aen.* 1.2) from Troy, and suffering *saevae memorem Iunonis ob iram* ('because of the unforgetting anger of cruel Juno', *Aen.* 1.4). The grandeur of epic intrudes into the lowly groves of pastoral, and the sufferings of the humble shepherd are raised to the level of importance of epic's *reges et proelia* ('kings and battles', *Ecl.* 6.3). Where it might seem that the experiences of pastoral's shepherds are essentially private and individual, while those of epic's kings and leaders are of public significance, Spenser's allusion here challenges such a limiting notion of the lower genre.[50] The victimization of the humble shepherd Meliboeus, at the hand of the ruler Octavian, is conflated with the exilic suffering of the epic hero Aeneas, mythical ancestor of Octavian, in his efforts to found the Roman race – a struggle in which the destiny of Rome itself is at stake.

The apparently private and individual suffering of shepherds is suddenly dignified by the epic analogy and the perspective it brings. The complaints of Meliboeus and Colin, we realize, should provoke

---

50 Tracing echoes of the *Odyssey* and of Euripides in Virgil's first eclogue (echoes noted by Fulvio Orsini in 1567), Van Sickle observes a similar effect: 'Exile gives Virgil's project the weight of tragedy and suffered history in the system of literary relationships. It positions *Meliboeus* with greater gravity against Theocritean exits caused by love, but also against *Odysseus*, pitting the theme of revolutionary crisis against legendary but individual plight' (Van Sickle, 'Two Programmatic Plots', 45–6). Once again, Spenser is using *contaminatio* to do to Virgil what Virgil did to his sources, and if anything amplifies the effect here.

not merely our sympathy but our active concern over the public calamities for which their plights stand. Spenser suggests a reading of Virgil by which the injustice exemplified in the land-confiscations is as much a threat to the future felicity of Rome as the hostility of Juno, who strove to prevent Aeneas from reaching Italy: tyrannical behaviour on Octavian's part is capable of preventing the hoped-for Golden Age, which was depicted in the fourth eclogue as a possible outcome of his rule, but as not yet come to pass. And the scorn of Rosalind which gives rise to Colin's Meliboean despair now appears to stand for a lack of care for and responsiveness to the English people on the part of Elizabeth, who in her marriage negotiations with the 'faithlesse fere' D'Alençon has broken faith not only with Colin but with all her Protestant subjects, and threatened their collective future. It is not merely Colin's private 'comfort and hope of goodnesse to come' which is 'cleane extinguished and turned into despeyre', but that of the English nation.

Aprill

June associates the Tityrean pastoral of political praise with *Aprill*'s lay to Elisa, and it is to this we must now turn. *Aprill* is unique in *The Shepheardes Calender* in speaking openly of the Queen: its *Argument* begins 'This Æglogue is purposely intended to the honor and prayse of our most gracious soueriegne, Queene Elizabeth'. Such explicit praise of the ruler coming in the fourth eclogue of the book irresistably recalls Virgil's fourth eclogue, and many have noted the connection.[51] Within the *Calender*, as has also been often observed, the lay is linked by many echoes and reminiscences to Colin's elegy for 'Dido' in the *Nouember* eclogue,[52] and that elegy has very obvious connections with the elegies for 'Daphnis' in Virgil's fifth eclogue. Taken together, then, these two formal, public compositions by Colin recall the pair of almost openly Caesarean eclogues which form the climax of Virgil's book. But as well as being the most Caesarean politically, this pair of eclogues had also been submitted, as we noted above, to influential Christian allegorization. As we shall see, *Aprill* and *Nouember* work together to play the Christian and political

---

51 E.g. Paul Alpers, 'Pastoral and the Domain of Lyric in Spenser's *Shepheardes Calender*', *Representations* 12 (1985), 83–100, at 92; McCabe, '"Little booke: thy selfe present"', p. 27; *Shorter Poems*, p. 529; Montrose, '"The perfecte paterne of a Poete"', 40.
52 McLane, *A Study in Elizabethan Allegory*, 55, 58–9; McCabe, *Shorter Poems*, p. 565.

interpretations of the commentary tradition off against one another, and do so in order once again to tilt the supposed 'balance' of the *Eclogues*' political stance away from praise of the powerful.

Aprill introduces Elizabeth in person into the rustic setting. The shock of a royal figure thus intruding without an allegorical veil into the lowly genre of pastoral is particularly sharp in the woodcut, which depicts the Queen and her ladies-in-waiting in full court dress, Elizabeth crowned and bearing her sceptre and her ladies playing the courtly musical instruments of harp, viol, lute and side-flute. Among the other woodcuts, with their ragged shepherds, bagpipes and pan-pipes, the effect is startling, and the contrast is maintained within this illustration too, for the left margin of the picture shows a scene more appropriate to the setting, with Thenot and Hobbinol keeping their sheep, and Colin piping beside a spring. Again, the reader is reminded of Virgil's fourth eclogue, which opens by announcing its intention to stretch the boundaries of pastoral to sing something a little greater (*paulo maiora canamus*, 4.1), worthy of a consul (*consule dignae*, 4.3).

Servius evidently perceived that the fourth eclogue, with its lofty theme and style, challenges his own description of the *Eclogues* as 'humble' in style, 'in accordance with the nature of their concerns and characters', for his gloss to *paulo maiora canamus* seems calculated to defend the eclogue against any charge of a breach of pastoral decorum: 'It is well he says "a little": for though this eclogue departs from bucolic song, still, to some extent, he inserts suitable things into it.'[53] Presumably he was thinking of the mention of Pan at 58–9 (the last of the musicians Virgil boasts he will outdo, if he lives to sing of the child's mature deeds), or of the quaint idea of multi-coloured sheep, obviating the need for dye, as the kind of blessing a shepherd might imagine flowing from a returned Golden Age. There is really nothing else pastoral about the eclogue. Spenser is at more pains than Virgil to accommodate his lofty subject matter to the lowly genre, as E.K. takes care to point out:

> In all this songe is not to be respected, what the worthinesse of her Maiestie deserueth, nor what to the highnes of a Prince is agreeable, but what is moste comely for the meanesse of a shepheards witte, or to conceiue, or to vtter. And therefore he calleth her Elysa, as through

---

[53] *humilem pro qualitate negotiorum et personarum* (preface, Thilo-Hagen 2.3–4); bene 'paulo': nam licet haec ecloga discedat a bucolico carmine, tamen inserit ei aliqua apta operi (*ad Ecl.* 4.1).

rudenesse tripping in her name: & a shepheards daughter, it being very vnfit, that a shepheards boy brought vp in the shepefold, should know, or euer seme to haue heard of a Queenes roialty.

Unlike Virgil's fourth eclogue, and unlike its own woodcut, Spenser's lay is careful to maintain a pastoral tone in its praise. Though she is 'Yclad in scarlet like a maiden queen / And Ermines white', Elisa sits 'upon the grassie greene', and her 'cremosin coronet' is 'set' not with with jewels but with flowers. (Indeed the crown in the woodcut could be a garland of flowers too.) Elizabeth is herself 'the flowre of Virgins', and the same imagery returns to fill the whole of the penultimate stanza, cataloguing the flowers presented to her as gifts by the 'shepheards daughters'. The Muses similarly bring 'Bay braunches' and the nymphs 'a Coronall' of 'Oliue braunches'.

State ceremony is nevertheless distinctly evoked. Though as vegetation they are blended smoothly into the pastoral register, the symbolism of the bay or laurel as the crown both of the Muses' poets and of the imperial Caesars has unmistakable royal connotations, and the lay spells out a similarly apt significance for the olive (124–6):

> Oliues bene for peace,
> When wars doe surcease:
> Such for a Princesse bene principall.

Meanwhile, Elisa's dress as she sits 'upon the grassie greene' might recall in particular the traditional costume of crimson velvet and ermine she wore on the day of her coronation. Though here embellished with flowers, the 'Cremosin coronet' perhaps resembles the third of the crowns placed on her head that day, the personal crown represented in several portraits (including 'Queen Elizabeth I and the Three Goddesses'), whose under-cap was of crimson velvet, and which was decorated with fleurs-de-lis, the last of the flowers named in the catalogue of lines 136–44.[54] That catalogue contains other 'political puns', as Richard McCabe notes, with its 'Kingcups', its apparently invented flower, the 'chevisaunce', a word which elsewhere in Spenser means 'chivalry', and in its choice of the variant spelling 'Coronation' for 'carnation'.[55] This last is particularly telling, because other aspects of the lay are reminiscent of Elizabeth's ceremonial entry into London on the eve of her coronation, as memorialized and widely disseminated in the account written by Richard Mulcaster, the

---

54 Janet Arnold, 'The "Coronation" Portrait of Queen Elizabeth I', *The Burlington Magazine* 120 (1978), 726–41.
55 McCabe, *Shorter Poems*, p. 532.

headmaster of the Merchant Taylors' School, shortly before Spenser became one of his pupils there.

Mulcaster's text describes Elizabeth's passage past a succession of elaborate symbolic pageants. The opening and persistent emphasis is on the mutuality of the love displayed by Elizabeth and her people:

> And entryng the citie was of the people receiued marueylous entierly, as appeared by thassemblie, prayers, wishes, welcomminges, cryes, tender woordes, and all other signes, whiche argue a wonderfull earnest loue of most obedient subiectes towarde theyr soueraigne. And on thother syde her grace by holding vp her handes, and merie countenaunce to such as stode farre of, and most tender & gentle language to those that stode nigh to her grace, did declare her selfe no lesse thankefullye to receiue her peoples good wyll, than they louingly offred it vnto her. To al that wyshed her grace wel, she gaue heartie thankes, and to such as bade God saue her grace, she sayde agayne god saue them all, and thanked them with all her heart. So that on eyther syde ther was nothing but gladnes, nothing but prayer: nothing but comfort.[56]

At set stages along the route, verse tributes and symbolic gifts are proffered to Elizabeth, and she makes appropriate responses, each not only expressing gratitude but implying some pledge about how she intends to rule. The pageants are very clearly didactic, instructing her in the very virtues of good government for which they ostensibly praise her – as is occasionally made explicit by the use of the verb 'teach', for instance in the summing up of the fourth pageant:

> The fourth did open Trueth, and also taught thee whan
> The commonweale stoode well, & when it did thence slide.[57]

The meaning of each pageant as it is unfolded is repeatedly said to be 'to put her grace in remembrance of' this or that duty of the sovereign – such as to resist bribery and flattery, to tread down superstition (or Catholicism) or to consult the various estates in her government and heed their counsel.[58] There is great emphasis on how good a pupil Elizabeth is, the 'perpetuall attentiuenes' of her expression, the words and gestures which show that she takes what she is told to heart, and she is reported as promising to 'remember' the lessons embodied in the tributes and symbolic gifts, and the generosity of

---

56 [Richard Mulcaster], *The passage of our most drad Soueraigne Lady Quene Elyzabeth through the citie of London to westminster the daye before her coronacion Anno 1558* (London, 1558 [=1559]), Aii^{r-v}.
57 Ei^v.
58 Di^v; see also Ci^v; Diiii^r.

the givers.⁵⁹ Again and again we are told that these responses give her subjects great 'hope' of her good government in future, reiterating the point made explicit at the beginning: 'This her graces louing behauiour ... emplanted a wonderfull hope in them touchyng her woorthy gouernement in the reste of her reygne.'⁶⁰ The whole is an elaborately staged exchange of pledges between the new monarch and her people, in which the responses of the supposed 'audience', Elizabeth, are as much part of the theatrical display as the pageants so elaborately devised by her subjects – and this is even implicitly acknowledged by Mulcaster as he compares London to

> a stage wherin was shewed the wonderfull spectacle, of a noble hearted princesse toward her most louing people, & the peoples exceding comfort in beholding so worthy a soueraigne.⁶¹

The first verse tribute offers the 'two gyftes' of 'blessing tonges' and 'true hertes', and all that follows ostensibly flows from a spontaneous upwelling of love.⁶² But in fact the didactic pageants with their symbolic gifts are clearly understood by all parties to be a lesson in what they expect back from her, and to put her under an obligation to meet these expectations – an obligation which her responses acknowledge and accept. The fifth and final pageant reiterates and focuses on the 'hope' of the people that Elizabeth will fulfil this promise – this expectation, this pledge.

> For all men hope in thee, that all vertues shall reygne,
> For all men hope that thou, none errour wilt support,
> For all men hope that thou wilt trueth restore agayne,
> And mend that is amisse, to all good mennes comfort.⁶³

The implication that the love and loyalty of the people might be *conditional* upon this fulfilment cannot, of course, be spoken openly, but nevertheless is allowed to peep through here and there, as for instance in the 'as ... so' clauses in the final stanza of this same verse:

> and as our hope is sure,
> That into errours place, thou wilt now trueth restore,
> So trust we that thou wilt our soueraigne Queene endure,⁶⁴

---

59 Aiii^v; Diii^r.
60 Aii^v.
61 Aii^v.
62 Aiii^r.
63 Eii^r.
64 Eii^r.

or the 'if' clause in the summing up of the significance of the third pageant, on the Beatitudes:

> The third, if that thou wouldst goe on as thou began,
> Declared thee to be blessed on euery syde.[65]

Mulcaster also focuses at some length on her responses to the less formal gifts of nosegays she receives along the way from anonymous individuals among the crowds that line the streets. This is mentioned near the opening of the pamphlet, before the Queen meets with the first of the pageants:

> priuately if the baser personages had either offred her grace any flowres or such like, as a signification of their good wyll, or moued to her any sute, she most gently, to the common reioysing of all the lookers on, & priuate comfort of the partie, staid her chariot, and heard theyr requestes.[66]

And it is recurred to in more detail at the end, among the anecdotes in Mulcaster's concluding section on the marks of clemency, mercy and wisdom in Elizabeth's behaviour throughout the proceedings.

> What more famous thing doe we reade in auncient histories of olde tyme, then that mightye prync05 haue gentlye receyued presentes offered them by base and lowe personages. If that be to be wondred at (as it is passingly) let me se any writer that in any one princes lyfe is able to recounte so manye presidentes of this vertue, as her grace shewed in yt one passage through the citie. How many nosegayes did her grace receiue at poore womens handes? How ofttimes stayed she her chariot, when she sawe any simple body offer to speake to her grace? A branche of Rosemary geuen to her grace with a supplication by a poore woman about flete bridge, was seen in her chariot til her grace came to westminster, not without the merueylous wondring of such as knew the presenter, and noted the Queenes most gracious receiuing and keping thesame.[67]

These private floral gifts too, though lacking the didactic verbal accompaniments of the more elaborately devised public tributes, are offered up by Mulcaster as contributing to the hope and promise of a reign that will repay the people's love and loyalty with clemency and good government. Perhaps 'rosemary' is singled out for such specific mention precisely because of its traditional symbolic import

---

65 Ei^v. See also similar suggestions at Biii^v and Ci^v.
66 Aii^v.
67 Eiii^v.

of 'remembrance' – Elizabeth's gracious acceptance and cherishing of it symbolically underscoring her pledge to 'remember' and repay her subjects.

Mulcaster's pamphlet was commissioned by the Crown, the first edition rushed out after the coronation, and several subsequent editions following quickly after, showing its popularity and wide dissemination. It could be seen as simply a piece of state propaganda, intended, as Montrose argues of other entertainments later in the reign, to 'affirm a benign relationship of mutual interest between the Queen and the lowly', and thus to 'fortify loyalty toward the crown'.[68] But its propagandistic claim takes the form of a promise not yet fulfilled – not an insistence on the immovable Divine Right to rule, such as we see in James I's coronation procession as related by Ben Jonson and Thomas Dekker, but rather on the hopeful signs that Elizabeth will indeed rule in the way these pageants tell her she should. Whether the sanguine and rejoicing tone of the document will turn out to have been justified or misplaced is entirely dependent on the Queen's future actions, and this conditionality is quite clearly supposed to be apprehended by the reader. The gift of the people's love expects a return, and not just in the form of private patronage but in a style of government which abides by the virtues and eschews the vices described in its didactic pageants.

The floral tributes of the 'shepheards daughters' in the *Aprill* lay, humble in the exalted company of nymphs and Muses, are reminiscent of the nosegays offered by the 'baser personages' in Mulcaster's text. Alongside the more symbolic tributes of bay and olive, recalling the symbolism of the pageants Mulcaster describes, taken together with Elisa's 'cremosin Coronet' and 'Ermines white' which recall her coronation dress, and in the context of a poetic trubute calling for communal celebration of the 'maiden queen' – not to mention the apellation 'Coronation' in the flower catalogue – the reminiscence seems deliberately to evoke or allude to Mulcaster's popular text, and its occasion. E.K.'s glosses also bring out another striking point of contact. The lay returns twice to its mythological, and appropriately pastoral, genealogy for Elisa as the imagined offspring of Pan and Syrinx. On its own terms, as Thomas Cain points out, and as we have

---

68 Louis Adrian Montrose, '"Eliza, Queene of shepheardes," and the Pastoral of Power', *ELR* 10 (1980), 153–82, at 179. See William Leahy, *Elizabethan Triumphal Processions* (Aldershot: Ashgate, 2005) for further sceptical scrutiny of Mulcaster's text (pp. 60–74, 105–11) and of assumptions based on it and similar documents by modern historians and critics (pp. 25–51).

already mentioned, this identifies Elisa with pastoral song, and thus implies that she is Colin's creation. But E.K.'s long note on 'Syrinx' at line 50 draws in other considerations. Pulling back from his initial suggestion that the genealogy is devised to show 'her graces progenie to be diuine and immortall ... as the Paynims were wont to iudge of all Kinges and Princes', he concludes 'that by Pan is here meant the most famous and victorious King, her highnesse Father, late of worthy memorye K. Henry the eyght', emphasizing her relationship to her father while tactfully avoiding mention of the more ambiguous figure of her mother, Anne Boleyn.[69] When Colin compares her complexion to 'The Redde rose medled with the White' at line 68, E.K. returns to the royal genealogy:

> By the mingling of the Redde rose and the White, is meant the vniting of the two principall houses of Lancaster and of Yorke: by whose longe discord and deadly debate, this realm many yeares was sore traueiled, & almost cleane decayed. Til the famous Henry the seuenth, of the line of Lancaster, taking to wife the most vertuous Princesse Elisabeth, daughter to the fourth Edward of the house of Yorke, begat the most royal Henry the eyght aforesayde, in whom was the firste vnion of the Whyte Rose and the Redde.

Where her mother was elided, her paternal grandmother and namesake is introduced, and the unity and cessation of discord symbolized by the Tudor rose invoked. This was the explicit topic of the first of the pageants described by Mulcaster. 'Thys pageant was grounded', he tells us, 'vpon the Queenes maiesties name', linking her to Elizabeth of York, and the union that ended the Wars of the Roses and founded the Tudor dynasty: 'it was deuised that like as Elizabeth was the first occasion of concorde, so she another Elizabeth myght maintaine thesame among her subjectes'.[70] It took the form of a rose tree depicting her descent from Henry VII and Elizabeth of York through Henry VIII and Anne Boleyn. Admittedly, these historical and symbolic connotations of the Tudor Rose were common currency, but Spenser's foregrounding of them here, among other elements evoking Mulcaster's pamphlet, suggests a link between the two texts. When Colin returns to the mythological parentage of Elisa at lines 91 to 94, E.K. provides no gloss, but he does not need to – the theme of the royal genealogy and its significance have already been established.

69 Cain, 'Strategy of Praise', 50.
70 Bi^r.

Mulcaster's pamphlet, though in a different literary form, has much in common with Virgil's fourth eclogue, joyously heralding a reign which promises to bring peace and prosperity to the nation. At the same time, its political stance is very different. Virgil's wonder-child is a semi-divine creature, sent by the gods to restore a mythical Golden Age, not by adherence to traditional political virtues but as if by magic, by merely existing and being a prophesied saviour. His reign is supernaturally ordained. The only hint of conditionality in this praise is the veiled suggestion contained in the promise of future song towards the end of the eclogue, which we looked at earlier. In Mulcaster, by contrast, the emphasis is all on what Elizabeth can be, if and as long as she conforms to the precepts and traditional virtues laid down for her in the pageants. Its praise is consistently and emphatically optative, the overriding emphasis is on scrutinizing the status of the hope it holds out for a good rule, and the prevailing tone is not prophetic but didactic. Though its subject is a promise, the promise is Elizabeth's, and the text all but announces that the people have a right to hold her to it. This could scarcely be further from the supernatural trappings of Virgil's eclogue. But there is one moment in Mulcaster where tangible echoes of Virgil's fourth eclogue creep in. As Elizabeth reaches St Paul's School, she receives a speech and a verse in Latin (the only Latin texts in the pamphlet unaccompanied by an English version), strikingly different from the rest of the pageants. The speech commands the people *Huius imperiis animo libentissimo subditi estote* ('Be submissive to her authority with most willing hearts'), because *Hac imperante pietas vigebit, Anglia florebit, aurea saecula redibunt* ('With her ruling, piety will thrive, England will flourish, the Golden Age will return').[71] The verse repeats and amplifies this echo of the Golden Age theme of Virgil's prophetic eclogue:

> Anglia nunc tandem plaudas, laetare, resulta,
> Praesto iam vita est, praesidiumque tibi.
> En tua spes venit, tua gloria, lux, decus omne
> Venit iam, solidam quae tibi praestat opem.
> Succurretque tuis rebus quae pessum abiere,
> Perdita quae fuerant haec reparare volet.
> Omnia florebunt, redeunt nunc aurea saecla,
> In melius surgent quae cecidere bona.
> Debes ergo illi totam te reddere fidam,
> Cuius in accessu commoda tot capies.

71 Dii^r.

> Salue igitur dicas, imo de pectore summo,
> Elizabeth regni non dubitanda salus,
> Virgo venit, veniatque optes comitata deinceps,
> Pignoribus charis, laeta parens veniat.
> Hoc Deus omnipotens ex alto donet olympo,
> Qui coelum & terram condidit atque regit.[72]

['Now at last, England, applaud! rejoice! dance! Your life and your protection are now at hand. Lo, your hope comes, your glory, light, every splendour. Now she comes who brings you lasting help and will hasten to assist your affairs, which have sunk so low; what has been lost she wishes to repair. All things will flourish; the Golden Age now returns; those good things which have fallen will now rise up better than before. Therefore you must render her your entire faith, at whose approach you will receive so many gifts. Therefore say 'Hail!', from the very bottom of your heart. Elizabeth the virgin comes, without doubt the salvation of her kingdom. Wish that hereafter she may come attended by dear pledges, that she may come as a joyful parent. This let almighty God bestow, from high Olympus, Who created and rules heaven and earth.']

With *Elizabeth Virgo venit*, the verse exploits the opportunity of identifying the young Queen with Astraea, the goddess of justice, whose return to earth in expectation of the birth of the wonder-child heralds and symbolizes the turn in the cycle of the ages at the beginning of Virgil's fourth eclogue: *iam redit et Virgo, redeunt Saturnia regna* ('now the Virgin returns, the reign of Saturn returns', 4.6).[73] Later writers would also make hay out of this possibility, including Van der Noodt, in the dedicatory epistle to Elizabeth prefacing his *Theatre for Worldlings*, to which the youthful Spenser anonymously contributed the translations which were his first printed work. (It is an identification which Spenser himself would never quite make.) This one moment of transparent Virgilian imitation is like a foil setting off the stern didacticism of Mulcaster's text, highlighting how very different from Virgil's prophetic fervour is his own literary response to a similar political occasion. Perhaps this is why he sets it apart, as the only Latin text in the pamphlet offered up with no English version.

It is significant that *Aprill*, while bringing together Mulcaster's pamphlet and Virgil's fourth eclogue as models (apparently meant to

---

72 Dii^v.
73 On this identification in other texts of the period, see Frances Yates, 'Queen Elizabeth as Astraea', in *Astraea: The Imperial Theme in the Sixteenth Century* (London: Routledge & Kegan Paul, 1975), pp. 29–87.

be recognized as intertexts), omits any mention of this theme of the returning Golden Age in which the two texts explicitly, though briefly, converge. There is no mention of any returning Golden Age in *Aprill*, or in *The Shepheardes Calender* as a whole. Indeed, despite dealing explicitly with the sovereign, *Aprill*'s lay does not speak of reigns or of government at all, either in Virgil's laudatory and prophetic tones or in terms of Mulcaster's precepts of good government: only in E.K.'s glosses on Elizabeth's genealogy do we find any reference to real political context. For the rest, there are only touches of symbolism deftly evoking royal ceremony, such as Elisa's dress, to disturb the pastoral tone. Spenser markedly holds back from the explicitly political perspective of Virgil's fourth eclogue, the *paulo maiora* subject matter which broke the bounds of the pastoral form, and – more like Tityrus, adjured by Apollo at the beginning of Eclogue 6 – conspicuously resists the lure of epic themes to remain in an appropriately lowly register, to play on the humble reed which befits a shepherd.

But where shepherds like Tityrus do not sing of 'kings and battles', they do speak of gods. As we noted above, Spenser in *June* remembers the *recusatio* opening Eclogue 6 as a rejection of epic in favour of the kind of deifying praise of the ruler in a pastoral register indulged in by Tityrus in Eclogue 1. And in the central stanza of the lay, Colin alludes pointedly to this act of homage (95–9).

> Soone as my younglings cryen for the dam,
> To her will I offer a milkwhite Lamb:
> Shee is my goddesse plaine,
> And I her shepherds swayne,
> Albee forswonck and forswatt I am.

The passage invokes Tityrus' first speech in the first eclogue (6–10):

> O Meliboee, deus nobis haec otia fecit.
> namque erit ille mihi semper deus, illius aram
> saepe tener nostris ab ovilibus imbuet agnus.
> ille meas errare boves, ut cernis, et ipsum
> ludere quae vellem calamo permisit agresti.

['O Meliboeus, a god has made this peace for us. For to me he will always be a god; often a tender lamb from our folds shall stain his altar. He has allowed my cattle to roam, as you see, and myself to play what I will upon my rustic pipe.']

Colin's explicit deification of Elisa, though qualified like Tityrus' with the possessive article – '*my* goddesse plaine'; *erit ille* mihi *semper deus*

– seems to be interpreted quite literally by Thenot and Hobbinol in their emblems, dividing between them the first line of Aeneas' speech to Venus in Book I of the *Aeneid* (1.328):

> Thenots Embleme.
> *O quam te memorem virgo?*
>
> Hobbinols Embleme.
> *O dea certe.*

['O what shall I call you, virgin? O, a goddess, surely.']

Even in this emphatic *certe*, though, there is a little uncertainty, for at this point in the *Aeneid*'s narrative Venus is disguised as a mortal maiden out hunting; Aeneas has not yet recognized her as his truly divine mother, and his *o dea certe!* is evidently intended merely as a courteous compliment to a pretty girl. (In fact, it conspicuously imitates the Homeric lines in which the smooth-talking Odysseus greets and supplicates Nausicaa, a mortal princess about whom there is never any suspicion of actual deity, in Book 6 of the *Odyssey*.) In the lay itself, however, there are even stronger suggestions that Colin's attribution of deity to Elisa is not as 'plaine' as it might seem. In the preceding two stanzas, Colin has compared Elisa's beauty favourably with Phoebus and Cynthia, or the sun and the moon, but then drawn back from his own rhetorical excess (86–90):

> But I will not match her with Latonaes seede,
> Such follie great sorow to Niobe did breede.
>   Now she is a stone,
>   And makes dayly mone,
> Warning all others to take heede.

E.K. summarizes the story, familiar from Ovid's *Metamorphoses*:

> Latonaes seede) Was Apollo and Diana. Whom when as Niobe the wife of Amphion scorned, in respect of the noble fruit of her wombe, namely her seuen sonnes, and so many daughters, Latona being therewith displeased, commaunded her sonne Phoebus to slea al the sonnes, and Diana all the daughters: whereat the vnfortunate Niobe being sore dismayed, and lamenting out of measure, was feigned of the Poetes, to be turned into a stone vpon the sepulchre of her children. for which cause the shepheard sayth, he will not compare her to them, for feare of like mysfortune.

In Ovid's account, the hubris for which Niobe is punished consists not merely in her *scorning* the goddess Latona but in her commanding her people to worship her in Latona's place. Though framed as a warning to himself, then, Colin's comparison invokes a negative exemplum for Elizabeth – the warning example of a queen punished for hubristic aspiration to divinity, and for demanding of her subjects the kind of worship and sacrifice which Tityrus offers to Octavian in Virgil's first eclogue.[74]

A similar warning is couched in E.K.'s gloss on the reference to Rosalind at line 26, part of the eclogue's 'frame' for the lay. Returning to the riddle of Rosalind's real identity, which he had highlighted without solving in his gloss to *Januarye* line 60, he further piques our curiosity with his long note, while adding little that could help the reader identify her. The ostensible point of the note is merely one of social class, arguing

> that shee is a Gentle woman of no meane house, nor endewed with anye vulgare and common gifts both of nature and manners: but such indeede, as neede nether Colin be ashamed to haue her made knowne by his verses, nor Hobbinoll be greued, that so she should be commended to immortalitie for her rare and singular Vertues ...

But the continuation of the sentence chimes with the cautionary note which will be struck by the Niobe allusion:

> Specially deserving it no lesse, then eyther Myrto the most excellent Poete Theocritus his dearling, or Lauretta the diuine Petrarches Goddesse, or Himera the worthye Poete Stesichorus hys Idole: Vpon whom he is sayd so much to haue doted, that in regard of her excellencie, he scorned & wrote against the beauty of Helena. For which his praesumptuous and vnheedie hardinesse, he is sayde by vengeaunce of the Gods, thereat being offended, to haue lost bothe his eyes.

The sequence of examples unfolds an argument. Myrto is referred to only briefly in Theocritus' seventh idyll, before Simichidas sweeps on to other topics. She is therefore 'commended to immortalitie' only in the sense that her name is mentioned in a poem – 'made knowne by his verses', in the humblest sense, but without any accompanying praise for her 'gifts ... of nature and manners' or her 'rare and singular Vertues'. What follows develops the idea of commending a woman to immortalitie in a quite different direction, with the example of Petrarch, who does not merely grant Laura the immortality of fame 'by his verses' but attributes divinity to her with his use of the metaphor 'Goddesse' – a metaphor which of course became a conventional

---

74 Lane, *Shepheards Devises*, pp. 18–20; Pugh, *Spenser and Ovid*, p. 25.

compliment in Petrarchan poetry. The final example then interprets such attribution of divinity as idolatry, earning the vengeance of the gods.[75] Like Stesichorus, E.K. obliquely tells us, Colin would risk divine retribution if he were to attribute deity to Rosalind, as he seems to do to Elisa in the imitation of Virgil's first eclogue placed at the centre of the lay. That Tityrean moment of apparently 'plaine' deification of the monarch, then, is thoroughly hedged about with cautions about the irreligious and idolatrous nature of such a rhetoric and such a political stance.

The allusion to Eclogue 1 is also interesting from the perspective of pastoral's bargain with power. Tityrus' speech ends, as though to justify and explain his calling the youth a god, by calling Meliboeus' attention to how this youth has 'permitted' his current state of happy freedom. There is a clear exchange of praise for protection here, whatever ambiguities may suggest themselves as we read further and ponder the difference between this dependency and the Libertas Tityrus was initially seeking. In the lay, Colin likewise proceeds immediately to describe his own state, but the contrast with Tityrus' is pointed. Far from enjoying Tityrus' *otium*, Colin is 'forswonck and forswatt', which E.K. glosses as 'ouerlaboured and sunneburnt'. He refers to himself as Elisa's 'swayne', a word which in its root and its common use means not merely 'youth' but 'servant'. In the context of the analogy with Tityrus, this implication of servitude recalls Tityrus' slave-status, and contrasts with his freedom 'to play what he wants' (1.10).[76] Colin conspicuously lacks the recompense Tityrus enjoys in return for his praise and the promised lamb. The importance of requiting services thankfully, and the hope that Elisa will observe this obligation in exemplary manner, is foregrounded in the lay's iconography by the presence of the dancing 'graces' at the celebration, with the subjunctive wish or command that Elisa will become one of them (113–15), and E.K.'s long gloss spelling out their moral and didactic significance. The question of recompense, in more explicit and specific form, is the note on which the lay will end (147–53).

---

75 It is reminiscent of Elizabeth Boyle's rebuke in *Amoretti* 75 – 'Vayne man, sayd she, that doest in vaine assay, / a mortall thing so to immortalize' – responding, I would argue, to her lover's Petrarchan descriptions of her as 'goddesse', 'Saynt' and 'Idoll' in sonnets 22 and 61.

76 Bathurst, *Calendarium Pastorale*, translates 'swayne' here with *mancipium*, one Latin word for 'slave', while British Museum MS Harleian 532 uses another with the same meaning, *servus*.

> And now ye daintie Damsells may depart
>   echeone her way,
> I feare, I haue troubled your troupes to longe:
> Let dame *Eliza* thanke you for her song.
>   And if you come hether,
>   When Damsines I gether,
> I will part them all you among.

Immediately following the stanza devoted to a catalogue of the floral offerings of the 'shepheards daughters', the thanks owed by Elisa 'for her song' rolls together the duty to protect and reward her poet (the exchange embodied by Tityrus and Octavian) and the obligation to repay her subjects' symbolic gifts, in the less personal (and less material) currency of just and merciful government, which Elizabeth incurs in Mulcaster's text. With 'I feare, I haue troubled your troupes to longe', Colin recognizes the reality of his fellow commoners' labour, and he announces his intention to give them fair recompense in the form of 'Damsines'. This is no mere spontaneous effusion of love, but work that deserves payment. But the debt has also been incurred by Elisa herself, and her thanks is expressed only as Colin's hope for the future, in the subjunctive of 'Let dame *Eliza* thanke you ...' As in Mulcaster's text, the mood may be optimistic, but it remains optative – the promise is yet to be fulfilled.[77]

There is, then, already much within the lay itself to suggest *Aprill*'s distance from Virgil's fourth eclogue, and the over-simplification involved in interpretations like that of Louis Adrian Montrose, for whom the eclogue is a 'symbolic form' or 'illusion ... sanctify[ing] political power'.[78] But the lay is not the whole of the *Aprill* eclogue, and the dialogue between Thenot and Hobbinol which frames it only adds to its distance from Virgilian panegyric. The frame returns us to the doleful love-triangle sketched in *Januarye*, as Hobbinol explains to Thenot that he is grieving for Colin, still suffering because of his unrequited love for Rosalind (13–16):

---

77 Interestingly, the painters hired to embellish the conduit at Cheapside for the eve of Elizabeth's coronation seem to have withdrawn their labour in a dispute with the Crown over pay. (Thus Mulcaster's claim that the conduit was 'bewtified with pictures' (Cir) is either a deliberate falsification or evidence that he did not see the actual procession, and was only privy to the plans.) See Leahy, *Elizabethan Triumphal Processions*, pp. 72–3. This very concrete and material failure to repay the tributes of her subjects embodied in the pre-coronation procession, then, foreshadows what Spenser seems to perceive as Elizabeth's subsequent failure to discharge her duty to her Protestant subjects in her planned Catholic marriage.

78 Montrose, '"Eliza, Queene of shepheardes," and the Pastoral of Power', 168.

> Shepheards delights he dooth them all forsweare,
> Hys pleasaunt Pipe, whych made vs meriment,
> He wylfully hath broke, and doth forbeare
> His wonted songs, wherein he all outwent.

Colin himself is physically absent, just as 'his mynd was alienate and withdrawen' (in the words of the 'Argument'), and the lay to Elisa is recited by Hobbinol at Thenot's request, in the author's absence.

The first thing to note here is that, whatever thanks is hoped for at the end of the lay, the passage of time has not improved Colin's condition. If he was 'forswoncke and forswatt' in his servitude to Elisa within the lay, he is still 'plongd in payne' in his courtship of Rosalind. Of course, we can take this as a direct indication of the failure of Elisa's gratitude promised in line 150 only if we identify Rosalind, too, with Elizabeth, but her apellation here as 'the Widowes daughter' does offer some reinforcement to that already convincing interpretation: 'widow' at the time was not a gender-specific term, and Henry VIII was therefore a 'widow' several times over. The peculiar indirections of E.K's gloss here also contribute to the impression, for as we have seen it is given over largely to justifying Colin in commending Rosalind 'to immortalitie', in an argument which quickly slides from the idea of making her famous 'for her rare and singular Vertues' into that of setting her up as a goddess in idolatrous fashion. Now, although Colin often sings of his love for Rosalind, the only moments which could be construed as praise are the epithet 'fayre', in line 52 of *Januarye*, and a reference to the 'siluer sounde' of her voice at *August* 181. For the rest, we have only continual animadversions on her scornful nature, and the lengthy vilification of the 'wicked' fickleness which has turned her flower to a 'weede' in Colin's final two stanzas in *June*. Even less than Theocritus' Myrto could she be said to be made famous for her 'rare and singular Vertues'. Meanwhile, there is no suggestion anywhere in the *Calender* of calling her a goddess, even in the most rhetorical terms of Petrarchan convention, and even where, in *Januarye*, she was being paralleled in other ways with Tityrus' divine youth. The Elisa of Colin's lay, meanwhile, is immortalized in both senses, so that E.K.'s gloss on Rosalind really makes sense only if we understand it to refer to Colin's treatment of Elisa, who is explicitly acknowledged as representing Elizabeth. If '*Rosalind* hath bred hys smart,' then, there is a strong implication that Elisa has failed to pay the thanks due for her song.

To interpret the way in which she has failed more precisely, it is necessary to bear in mind the lay's striking emphasis on virginity.[79] Elisa herself is 'the flowre of Virgins' (48) and 'a mayden Queene' (57), she is compared twice to Cynthia, goddess of chastity (65, 82–5), the Muses are referred to as 'Virgins, that on *Parnasse* dwell' (41), and in fact anyone who is *not* a virgin is explicitly excluded (129–30):

> Let none come there, but that Virgins bene,
>   to adorne her grace.

The emphasis is in keeping with the lay's echoes of Mulcaster's text on the pre-coronation entry twenty years before, at which Elizabeth was a mere twenty-five years of age. If the Latin oration and verses at St Paul's School in that text looked forward to her being blessed with children (needed for stability in any hereditary monarchy), the rest of the progress makes it clear that the hope would have been for the children of a securely Protestant marriage, as Elizabeth is required again and again to commit to upholding the Protestant faith in England. What has happened to such hopes by 1579 is that Elizabeth looks set to abandon her virginity in marriage to a Catholic, endangering, as many of her Protestant subjects feared, the future of the Reformation in England. Another striking irony in the eclogue would also seem to relate to this prospect. The emblems of Hobbinol and Thenot, reproducing Aeneas' address to his mother, parallel the 'mayden Queene' Elizabeth with Venus, the Roman goddess of sexual love, a surprising and even jarring analogy in the context of the lay's insistent celebration of virginity.[80] Indeed, while we have explained Spenser's placing of the lay in *Aprill*, the fourth month, by the parallel thus created with Virgil's fourth eclogue, April is also the month dedicated by the Romans to Venus, so that the closing allusion to the goddess strikes the reader as something structural and significant. Spenser and his contemporaries would have known very well that April was Venus' month from Ovid's calendrical *Fasti*, which lays great emphasis on the dedication of its fourth book to the goddess. In fact, this book of the *Fasti* may be one of the texts which Spenser had in mind as he composed *Aprill*. In a passage towards the end of the book – and in a pastoral context, immediately following the shepherds' festival in honour of the pastoral goddess Pales – Ovid addresses Rome's prostitutes:

---

79 McCabe, '"Little booke: thy selfe present"'.
80 McCabe, '"Little booke: thy selfe present"'.

> numina, volgares, Veneris celebrate, puellae:
> multa professarum quaestibus apta Venus.
> poscite ture dato formam populique favorem,
> poscite blanditias dignaque verba ioco,
> cumque sua dominae date grata sisymbria myrto
> tectaque composita iuncea vincla rosa.
>
> (*Fasti* IV.865–70)

['Celebrate the divinity of Venus, you common girls: great Venus is concerned with the earnings of those of your profession. Having offered frankincense, ask for beauty and the favour of the people; ask to be charming and witty; give to your mistress her beloved mint, with myrtle, and chains of rushes concealed with well-arranged roses.']

The resemblance between this and Colin's call to the virginal 'shepheards daughters' to bring their floral tributes to Elisa is as shocking as it is striking. But given the context (the book devoted to April in another calendrically structured work), and the fact that Elizabeth is about to be paralleled openly with Venus in the emblems, it is possible that Spenser is deliberately echoing the Ovidian passage at 127–44. Like the implied analogy between Rosalind and the courtesan Lycoris at the end of *June*, the Ovidian *contaminatio* here associates Elizabeth's marriage plan with prostitution. The gulf, then, between the lay's celebration of Elisa's virginity (a celebration located in the past) and Elizabeth's identification with the goddess of sexual love parallels the gulf between the optimistic tribute of the lay and the current frustration of Colin's hopes, a frustration caused by Rosalind's scorn. We will learn in *June* to attribute that scorn not to icy chastity but to her fickle preference for a 'faithlesse fere' – abandoning fidelity to her subjects for a Catholic suitor.

The closing exchange between Thenot and Hobbinol casts further light on the question of thanks or payment as part of the pastoral exchange. Thenot's response to the lay (154–7),

> And was thilk same song of Colins owne making?
> Ah foolish boy, that is with loue yblent:
> Great pittie is, he be in such taking,
> For nought caren, that bene so lewdly bent

is in line with those critics who insist on moral irony at Colin's expense throughout the *Calender*, implying that Colin is an example of culpable amorous obsession leading to dereliction of duty.[81] But

---

81 For example Anthea Hume, *Edmund Spenser, Protestant Poet* (Cambridge: Cambridge University Press, 1984), p. 48; Cullen, *Spenser, Marvell, and Renaissance Pastoral*, pp. 76–111.

Hobbinol's response is more pragmatic (158–61):

> Sicker I hold him, for a greater fon,
> That loues the thing, he cannot purchase.
> But let vs homeward: for night draweth on,
> And twincling starres the daylight hence chase.

What Hobbinol sees as folly is not love but persistence in a love which is unrequited, and his metaphor 'purchase' resonates suggestively with the emphasis on payment in the final stanza of the lay. The unsuccessful wooing of Rosalind and the poetic and floral tributes to Elisa are thus drawn together into the stark light of a failed economic exchange, in which any hope of return is mere folly. The promises Elizabeth made to her subjects on the eve of her coronation – to govern well and wisely, and to uphold the Protestant faith against Catholic superstition – should be written off as a bad debt.

As a result of these disappointed hopes, Colin has broken his pipe and renounced poetry. The lay therefore becomes an example of the kind of tribute he will no longer pay, preserved only because Hobbinol 'recordes' it here as a prized fragment of the past. Such elegiac recollection of another shepherd's admired song in his absence inevitably evokes the situation of Virgil's ninth eclogue, where Moeris and Lycidas exchange fragments of Menalcas' songs as they trudge along the road, lamenting the land confiscations which have affected so many, including Moeris and Menalcas himself. The overriding theme there is the powerlessness of song against political injustice. Countering the false rumour that Menalcas had saved all the surrounding lands with his songs, Moeris bitterly reflects (11–13):

> Audieras, et fama fuit; sed carmina tantum
> nostra valent, Lycida, tela inter Martia, quantum
> Chaonias dicunt aquila veniente columbas.

['You had heard it, and so went the rumour. But our songs have as much power amid the weapons of war, Lycidas, as they say the Chaonian doves have when the eagle approaches.']

Menalcas' songs have failed not only to secure the restoration of his own and his neighbours' lands but even to avert an attempt on his own life and that of the friend who now reports the calamity. The fragment which begins the exchange of Menalcas' songs by Moeris and Lycidas is offered by Lycidas to illustrate how great a poetic talent would have been lost to the shepherd community if that attack had succeeded (just as Hobbinol's recital is prompted by his grief-stricken report to Thenot of how Colin has renounced his art). Even as it is, they recall the brief passages they recite to one another with such difficulty that Moeris reflects sadly (51–4):

> Omnia fert aetas, animum quoque; saepe ego longos
> cantando puerum memini me condere soles:
> nunc oblita mihi tot carmina: vox quoque Moerim
> iam fugit ipsa; lupi Moerim videre priores.

['Time bears everything away, even the mind. I remember that often as a boy I would close the long days in singing. Now so many of my songs are forgotten. Voice itself now flees Moeris; wolves have seen Moeris first.']

A song might be referred to by repeating only a fragment because it is so well-known, and the speaker can be confident that a brief quotation will instantly call the rest to his audience's mind, but that is not what is suggested here. These fragments are broken relics, testifying to Moeris' bleak doctrine of universal decay.

The sense of their fragmentary nature is conveyed partly by their discontinuity – they seem to have nothing to do with each other, and come from different poems. Their selection feels arbitrary, but in fact it is not. The fragments poignantly evoke both the attempt to bargain with political power by offering poetic praise and the pastoral wooing which, as Servius attests and as we have been arguing, can be read as allegorizing that attempt. The first is a direct translation of the opening of Theocritus' third idyll. As we have seen, Servius argues that Virgil uses it to refer allegorically to his own affairs, adducing his narrative of how Virgil was forced to return to Rome to appeal when the centurion who had taken over his lands refused to recognize that Octavian had revoked the confiscation order – this then is Virgil's command that his men should look after his affairs and not dare to disobey Arrius until his return. But a less strained reading still evokes the pleading of the disempowered. The everyday, practical tone of the lines masks the fact that the passage, in its original Theocritean context, introduces the despairing love-song of the goatherd of Idyll 3 to his scornful Amaryllis, a model both for Corydon's song in Eclogue 2 and for Damon's in Eclogue 8. To those who know its source, then, it evokes a tragically unsuccessful wooing.[82] Servius, of course, interpreted Corydon's wooing as allegorizing a plea to Octavian, and we have already seen that Spenser strongly implies the same interpretation by

---

82 We should remember that, while Corydon is a major analogue for Colin in *Januarye*, Damon's despairing goatherd is an analogue for Colin in *June*, since (like Gallus in Eclogue 10) he has been abandoned by his beloved for another man.

his *contaminatio* of eclogues 1 and 2 in *Januarye*. The other amatory fragment is an ecapsulation of Theocritus' eleventh idyll, also a model for Eclogue 2 and for Damon's song in Eclogue 8, so the same conclusions apply. The other, explicitly political and Roman, fragments we have already discussed, as evoking the failure of poetry's attempt to bargain with Octavian's regime by offering the kind of praise exemplified in Menalcas' elegy for 'Daphnis' in Eclogue 5 (see pp. 75–7 above).

Where the fourth eclogue optimistically celebrates the political promise embodied in a new ruler, then, the ninth records the breaking of the promise, the extinction of hope, the failure of the poetic tribute of praise to elicit any return of favour, clemency or justice from the regime. By evoking this dark picture in *Aprill*'s frame, Spenser presents his version of Virgil's panegyric in the lay to Elisa as, like the fragments of Menalcas' songs, another example of failed poetic tribute, a relic of ruined hopes.

Meanwhile, the current running through the lay and E.K.'s glosses, warning against the idolatry involved in worshipping a mortal as divine, draws attention to the fact that praise like that of Virgil's fourth eclogue can properly be offered only to God. E.K. reminds us of this from a pointedly Christian perspective in his gloss on 'Syrinx' at line 50, with the slightly disapproving tone of 'supposing (as seemeth) her graces progenie to be diuine and immortall (*so as the Paynims were wont to iudge of all Kinges and Princes ...*)' (my italics), and with the marked disjunction of the final sentence of the same gloss, on 'Pan': 'And by that name, oftymes (as hereafter appeareth) be noted kings and mighty Potentates: And in some place Christ himself, who is the verye Pan and god of Shepheardes.' In addition, the Marian overtones of 'shee is Syrinx daughter *without spotte*' (50, my italics), and the possible reminiscence of the shepherds at the Christian Nativity in Colin's offer of a lamb in the central stanza, set off the eclogue's warnings about idolatry with subtle reminders that this is the kind of poetry which should be dedicated specifically to Christ. That is, while following the political interpretation of Virgil's fourth eclogue by devoting his imitation of it to praise of his own Queen, Spenser simultaneously evokes the messianic interpretation. Only if we read Eclogue 4 as referring to the birth of Christ, he seems to say, can a conscientious Christian poet take it uncritically as a model. As a political poem it is idolatrous.

Overall, then, *Aprill* raises expectations of an imitation of Virgil's fourth eclogue which it markedly refuses to fulfil, and explains its refusal by allusion to other related texts. Such deifying tributes cannot be paid to Elizabeth, it suggests, both because such abject devotion is not a fitting model for political relationships, which are necessarily relationships between human beings, and because (in her planned marriage to D'Alençon) she has failed to fulfil the promise she seemed to her Protestant subjects to embody at her coronation.

Nouember

Death has a way of undermining claims to immortality, and death is the topic of *Aprill*'s partner-piece. The *Nouember* eclogue's lament for 'Dido' is replete with echoes of the lay for Elisa, so that the two ask to be read in connection with one another. As a pastoral elegy, it challenges the reader to compare it to Virgil's fifth eclogue, on the death of Daphnis. Thus the two examples the *Calender* gives us of Colin's public poetry (the only examples of his song which are not devoted to lamenting his personal misfortune in love) announce themselves as versions of the two eclogues in Virgil's book most obviously given over to political praise. As we shall see, *Nouember* distances itself from Virgil's veiled celebration of Caesar, just as *Aprill* distanced itself from Virgil's announcement of a new Golden Age, through ironic echoes of other eclogues in the *Calender*, through evocation of the Christian alternative to political interpretation of the Virgilian text and through memories of the ironic frame provided by Virgil's ninth eclogue.

Eclogue 5 is an exchange of songs between Mopsus and Menalcas. Mopsus first laments the death of Daphnis, in an elegy modelled on Theocritus' first idyll. Menalcas responds with a song intended to 'lift Daphnis to the stars' (52), which celebrates his apotheosis and pledges altars and regular sacrifices to the new god. As we saw in the last chapter, commentators generally agreed that Daphnis allegorized some historical figure, and the most popular candidate was Julius Caesar, who had been officially declared a god after the appearance of the *sidus Iulium* at the games in his honour in July 44 BCE, four months after his assassination. As we also noted, however, one of the alternative interpretations mooted in the sixteenth century was that the eclogue treated the death and resurrection of Christ. Both interpretations of the fifth eclogue are important to an understanding of Spenser's poem.

One thing we should notice here is that, by introducing Colin as the author of *Nouember*'s elegy, Spenser is again implicitly aligning him with Virgil's Menalcas. If Colin's lay of Elisa in *Aprill*, recited in his absence, was paralleled with the fragments of Menalcas' songs sung in his absence in Eclogue 9, *Nouember* is where Colin appears to sing his elegy in person, as Menalcas sang his hymn in person in Eclogue 5. To those who noticed the parallel between *Aprill* and the ninth eclogue, then, the continuity will be evident – contributing to the links between *Aprill* and *Nouember*, and at the same time sustaining our sense of the significance of Virgil's gloomiest eclogue in the background of Spenser's work. *Nouember* opens with a dialogue between Thenot and Colin which recalls, while adapting, the opening dialogue of Mopsus and Menalcas in Eclogue 5. Thenot begins by inviting Colin to sing, and suggesting alternative topics (7–8):

> Whether thee list thy loued lasse aduaunce,
> Or honor *Pan* with hymnes of higher vaine.

Colin rejects both (9–10):

> Thenot, now nis the time of merimake.
> Nor Pan to herye, nor with loue to playe

just as Mopsus rejects Menalcas' proposed subjects (10–13):

> *Menalcas*:
> Incipe, Mopse, prior, si quos aut Phyllidis ignis
> aut Alconis habes laudes aut iurgia Codri;
> incipe; pascentis servabit Tityrus haedos.
>
> *Mopsus*:
> Immo haec in viridi nuper quae cortice fagi
> carmina descripsi et modulans alterna notavi,
> experiar

['*Menalcas*: You start, Mopsus, if you have any songs on your flame, Phyllis, or praise of Alcon, or quarrels with Codrus. Begin: Tityrus will look after the kids as they graze. *Mopsus*: No: rather I will try these verses, which lately I carved on the bark of a green beech and noted the alternate music.']

But where Mopsus gives no reason for his rejection of Menalcas' proposed subjects (we assume that he is simply particularly proud of his 'Daphnis'), Spenser looks back to Virgil's model, Theocritus' first idyll, where the goatherd refuses to pipe because of the time of day (15–18):

Nay, shepherd, nay; at noontide pipe we may not, for fear of Pan. For then, of a surety, he is resting wearied from the chase. And he is quick of temper and bitter wrath sits ever on his nostril.

There is even, possibly, a witty gesture towards this passage in Spenser's choice of the word 'herye', which, as well as being an already very old-fashioned and rarely used word for 'praise', was a common form of the verb 'to harry' or torment.[83] Spenser adapts Theocritus' seasonal excuse to suit his own purpose, though, and we shall have more to say about the significance of Colin's 'sollein season' (17) later. The other specific echoes of Eclogue 5 are slight. Thenot's humble reference to himself as one of 'the little plants that lowly dwell' in comparison with Colin's 'higher tree' at 31–2 perhaps looks back to Menalcas' compliment to Mopsus at 16–18:

> Lenta salix quantum pallenti cedit olivae,
> puniceis humilis quantum saliunca rosetis,
> iudicio nostro tantum tibi cedit Amyntas.

['As much as the pliant willow yields to the pale olive, as much as the humble wild nard yields to the purple rose-garden, so much, in my judgement, does Amyntas yield to you.']

The mourning landscape at 124–9 is reminiscent of 5.34–9; the notion of Daphnis as *omne decus tuis* ('the glory of all your people') at 5.34 is recalled by Dido as 'the sonne of all the world' at line 67; and the flocks refusing to feed and the wailing of the forest beasts at 133–6 is modelled on 5.24–8. Structurally, the turn from mourning Dido's death in the first eleven stanzas to rejoicing at her entry to heaven in the last four recalls the way Mopsus' lament is followed by Menalcas' announcement of Daphnis' deification. But pastoral elegy is, as others have noted, a thriving genre in its own right, and Spenser's is an original reworking of motifs which have become commonplace: the direct imitation of Eclogue 5 is not as detailed and intricate as the imitation we found in *Januarye* or *June*. If it were not for its pivotal place within a work which foregrounds its relation to Virgil's eclogue book as a whole, we might be tempted to dismiss the relation between the poems as distant and insignificant.[84]

But one thing which *Nouember* has in common with Virgil's fifth eclogue is striking and unusual: it is the riddle over the identity of the dead person. Normally the whole intention of elegy is to memorialize the subject, and though he or she may be represented by a suitably pastoral name within the poem, the title will declare whose memory is really being celebrated – as for instance in Marot's elegy

---

83 See the *OED* entries for 'hery' and 'harry', with the examples they quote.
84 As Alpers does: *What Is Pastoral?* p. 109, n. 37.

for Queen Louise de Savoy, which E.K. names as Spenser's model in the 'Argument'. Virgil may have intended his Daphnis to be readily identifiable, and the stellar imagery would surely have reminded most contemporary readers strongly of the *sidus Iulium*. But as we have seen, opinion was never unanimous, and Spenser and his contemporaries would have seen the eclogue couched in the speculations of commentators – with Julius Caesar comfortably leading the betting, but only as a solution to an acknowledged riddle. Spenser's own riddling treatment of Dido's identity, headlined as an insoluble mystery in E.K.'s 'Argument' and reinforced by his gloss at line 38, would have reminded his readers of this debate, which resurfaces in all the commentaries on Virgil's fifth eclogue.

It is paradoxical but true that, precisely by evoking the Virgilian riddle, Spenser suggests a solution to his own. Readers would have been aware that Julius Caesar was by far the most popular candidate for the figure represented by Daphnis, and therefore, when provoked by E.K. to seek the answer to the parallel mystery in *this* pastoral elegy, would be predisposed to look to the very top of their own political hierarchy. E.K.'s claim that '*This Æglogue is made in imitation of Marot his song, which he made vpon the death of Loys the frenche Queene*' supports the impression that a queen is intended. But the last time a Queen of England died was twenty years earlier, and no one would suspect such an outspokenly Protestant work to mourn the passing of the Catholic Mary. Elizabeth seems the only possible candidate, but this too is riddling, for she is not dead.

As we read the elegy itself, however, the accumulating echoes of *Aprill*'s lay reinforce this impression. It has been often acknowledged that there are many resemblances, but it is worth noting them in detail here, for the specific bearing they have on our argument.[85] As in the first stanza of the lay to Elisa, we begin here with an invocation to the Muses – or rather, emphasizing the vast difference in mood, to the tragic muse Melpomene. The lay's first stanza invoked the nymphs and the Muses together, and when, in *Nouember*, the Muses return, they are once again in the company of the nymphs (143–7):

> The water Nymphs, that wont with her to sing and daunce,
> And for her girlond Oliue braunches beare,
> Now balefull boughes of Cypres doen aduaunce:
> The Muses, that were wont greene bayes to weare,
> Now bringen bitter Eldre braunches seare ...

---

85 E.g. McLane, *A Study in Elizabethan Allegory*, pp. 55, 58–9.

The passage remembers almost explicitly their tributes to Elisa in the *Aprill* lay – the 'Bay braunches' brought by the Muses 'All for *Elisa*, in her hand to weare' (104–5) and the 'Coronall' of 'Oliue braunches' offered by '*Chloris*, that is the chiefest Nymph of al' (122) – in a link so strong that it seems difficult to conceive of Elisa and Dido as separate figures. The floral imagery which was woven in with these tributes in *Aprill* is also prominent here, and also used to emphasize the distance between *Aprill's* hopeful mood and *Nouember's* despair. If the shepherds' daughters there offered flowers, now 'sike happy cheere is turnd to heauie chaunce', and (103, 108–9)

> The gaudie girlonds deck her graue,
> The faded flowres her corse embraue.

The metaphor by which Elisa was herself compared to such a flower, in *Aprill's* 'The flowre of Virgins, may shee florish long', is also brought back, with the same sad difference (75–6):

> The fayrest floure our gyrlond all emong,
> Is faded quite and into dust ygoe.

Aprill's hope of long flourishing has been dashed. And the image gives rise to the conventional reflection on mortality, common to biblical and classical traditions (83–9):[86]

> Whence is it, that the flouret of the field doth fade,
> And lyeth buryed long in Winters bale:
> Yet soone as spring his mantle hath displayd,
> It floureth fresh, as it should neuer fayle?
> But thing on earth that is of most auaile,
>   As vertues braunch and beauties budde,
>   Reliuen not for any good.

We have seen that the floral tributes of the *Aprill* lay – and the lay itself – represented the hopes which the English nation (and most especially its Protestants) placed in Elizabeth, particularly remembering the optimistic mood at her coronation twenty years earlier. It is these self-same flowers, and these hopes, which are now 'faded' and spent.

In this context, such offerings as the poetic tribute of the lay itself are no longer appropriate, and so Colin commands (77–9):

---

[86] Moschus, 'Lament for Bion', 99–104; Job 14:7–10. On the relation to Moschus, which is usually assumed to be mediated through Marot, see G. W. Pigman, *Grief and English Renaissance Elegy* (Cambridge: Cambridge University Press, 1985), p. 83; Shore, *Spenser and the Poetics of Pastoral*, p. 88; Merritt Y. Hughes, 'Spenser and the Greek Pastoral Triad'.

> Sing now ye shepheards daughters, sing no moe
> The songs that *Colin* made in her prayse,
> But into weeping turne your wanton layes,

where the direct address to the 'shepheards daughters', echoing the appeal at line 127 of *Aprill*, makes it clear that the lay 'intended to the honor and prayse of ... Elizabeth' is specifically meant. The breaking off of song is by now a familiar image in the *Calender*, but elsewhere is associated with the grief of Colin's unrequited love for Rosalind. The recurrence of the topos later in the elegy takes us directly back to two such occasions (171–2):

> Breake we our pypes, that shrild as lowde as Larke,
>   O carefull verse.

The breaking of the pipes repeats Colin's despairing gesture at *Januarye* 72, avenging himself on the pipes which cannot obtain a return of love from the scornful Rosalind, while the comparison to the 'Larke' recalls Hobbinol's description of Colin's erstwhile song in *June* (49–55):

> Colin, to heare thy rymes and roundelayes,
> Which thou were wont on wastfull hylls to singe,
> I more delight, then larke in Sommer dayes:
> Whose Echo made the neyghbour groues to ring,
> And taught the byrds, which in the lower spring
> Did shroude in shady leaues from sonny rayes,
> Frame to thy songe their cherefull cheriping ...

These are the songs which Colin can no longer sing, because Rosalind has betrayed him for Menalcas, turning his wanton lays to plaints. Before this infidelity, Colin tells us in *June*, he was wont to offer Rosalind these songs of his youth (themselves strongly recalling *Aprill*'s lay, as we have seen) together with 'gaudie Girlonds' (*June* 45), and it is clearly these same 'gaudie girlonds' which now deck Dido's grave along with the 'faded flowres' of *Aprill* at *Nouember* 108–9.

E.K.'s riddling description of the subject of Colin's elegy as 'some mayden of greate bloud, whom he calleth Dido' in the 'Argument' to *Nouember* reinforces the identification of Dido and Rosalind by the marked reminiscence of his similar remark on the identity of Rosalind in his gloss to *Aprill* 26, 'For it is well knowen, euen in spight of Colin and Hobbinoll, that shee is a Gentle woman of no meane house'. Of course, he explicitly denies such an identification in his gloss to 'Dido the greate shepehearde his daughter sheene' at line 38,

The great shepherd) is some man of high degree, and not as some
vainely suppose God Pan. The person both of the shephearde and of
Dido is vnknowen and closely buried in the Authors conceipt. But out
of doubt I am, that it is not Rosalind, as some imagin: for he speaketh
soone after of her also.

But in doing so, he draws attention to the possibility of the reading.
It is reminiscent of the way in which Servius preserves readings
he rejects merely by reporting in order to dismiss them.[87] But here
the claim is contrived, since this is the first edition of a new poem,
and the reader cannot really imagine a background of past critical
debate over its interpretation. It is quite clear elsewhere that E.K. is
misleading, and probably deliberately so (see for instance the notorious astrological inaccuracy in his gloss to *Nouember* 16, to which
we shall return). That 'he speaketh soone after of [Rosalind] also'
is unconvincing evidence – we might remember how *The Faerie
Queene* refers to Elizabeth under different names, as Spenser openly
explains in the prefatory Letter to Ralegh.[88] Indeed, the reference
to Rosalind deepens the connection, for Thenot hopes that Colin's
'rymes' for Dido will be comparable to 'those that did thy *Rosalind*
complayne' (44), and Colin's response (50–1),

> But ah to well I wote my humble vaine,
> And howe my rymes bene rugged and vnkempt

is strikingly reminiscent of the way he described his complaints of
Rosalind's betrayal in *June*, delivered 'in shade of lowly groue' (71): 'I
wote my rymes bene rough, and rudely drest' (77).

By the same token, E.K.'s gloss also disingenuously implies that
Dido is Elisa, again by suggesting (in the course of dismissing) the
identification of her father 'the great shepherd' with 'God Pan', who,
as Elisa's father in the *Aprill* lay, was explicitly identified as Henry VIII
in E.K.'s gloss to *Aprill*, line 50. Dido, Rosalind and Elisa all, it would
seem, offer different perspectives on the same figure, and we have been
explicitly informed in the Argument to *Aprill* that this figure is the
Queen. Indeed, that was the only safe place to do it, given the openly
libellous tone of *June*'s vilification of Rosalind, and given that, by an
act of 1571, it was a criminal offence to depict the Queen's death in art.

Like Rosalind's infidelity in *June*, Dido's death leaves behind a
mourning lover (113–22):

---

87 See chapter 3, 'Other Voices in Servius: Schooldust of the Ages', in Thomas, *Virgil and the Augustan Reception*, pp. 93–121.
88 McLane, *A Study in Elizabethan Allegory*, p. 28.

> O thou great shepheard Lobbin, how great is thy griefe,
> Where bene the nosegayes that she dight for thee:
> The coloured chaplets wrought with a chiefe,
> The knotted rushrings, and gilte Rosemaree?
> For shee deemed nothing too deere for thee.
>   Ah they bene all yclad in clay,
>   One bitter blast blew all away.
>   O heauie herse,
> Thereof nought remaynes but the memoree.
>   O carefull verse.

There are hints here, if we wish to hear them, that Lobbin's grief is that of the lover scorned and betrayed, rather than merely bereaved, for the image of the floral nosegays blown away by the wind echoes Colin's lament in *Januarye* (39–40),

> The blossome, which my braunch of youth did beare,
> With breathed sighes is blowne away, and blasted,

with its reminiscence of Corydon's *floribus Austrum / ... inmisi* ('I have let the South Wind in to my flowers') in Virgil's second eclogue (l. 58). Lobbin probably represents the prominent Protestant peer Leicester here, as also at 'Colin Clouts Come Home Againe', 736.[89] Leader of the faction opposed to the D'Alençon match, Leicester had once harboured hopes that he himself would marry the Queen.[90] Dido's gift to Lobbin of 'gilte Rosemaree', while possibly referring to some real jewel bestowed on Leicester by Elizabeth, carries the same symbolic connotation of 'remembrance' which we associated with the rosemary given to Elizabeth in Mulcaster's account of the pre-coronation celebrations. A material jewel would remain after the giver's death; only of the giver herself, or else of the relationship the gift symbolized, could it be said that 'nought remaynes but the memoree'. The idea that nothing but the memory remains of a pledge of remembrance fits the situation of a breach of fidelity at least as well as it fits a bereavement. Again, we might infer, Elizabeth's promises to remember and repay the loyalty of her Protestant subjects have come to nothing.

In the final stanza before the turn to rejoicing, Colin draws the general and traditional Christian moral of *contemptus mundi* (153–7):

---

89 As first argued by Mary Parmenter, 'Spenser's "Twelve Aeglogves Proportionable to the Twelve Monethes"', *ELH* 3 (1936), 190–217, at 214–16.
90 Michael Brennan, *The Sidneys of Penshurst and the Monarchy, 1500–1700* (Aldershot: Ashgate, 2006), esp. pp. 32–6.

> O trustlesse state of earthly things, and slipper hope
> Of mortal men, that swincke and sweate for nought,
> And shooting wide, doe misse the marked scope:
> Now haue I learnd (a lesson derely bought)
> That nys on earth assuraunce to be sought ...

But another echo of *Aprill* reveals that the general reflection on mortality masks a more specific, and quite different, reflection on the failure of the individual to remember and repay. It may be owing to mortality that men 'swincke and sweate for nought', but already in the lay to Elisa the discovery that Colin was 'forswonck and forswatte' (99) cast an ironic light on his promise to offer a 'milkwhite Lamb' (96) to his Queen in imitation of the contented and well-rested Tityrus – thus the phrase is a marker of the frustration of Colin's hope of thanks or repayment, which we saw reflected in *Aprill*'s frame.

The echo points up the oddity of that aspect of Dido's portrayal which seems most difficult to square with an identification between her and Rosalind, and I would argue Elisa too. For where Elisa is never seen giving anything to anybody, and Rosalind is always conspicuous for her failure to do so, Dido is remembered as generous and hospitable. In the stanza addressed to Lobbin we just looked at, although the flowers blown away by the bitter blast recall the ruined state of unrequited lovers like Colin and Corydon, they take the form of nosegays and chaplets made for him by Dido, pointedly reversing the usual direction of such gifts as the 'gaudy Girlonds' Colin offers to Rosalind in *June* (45) or the entwined herbs and flowers Corydon offers Alexis in Virgil's second eclogue (45–50). And her remembered liberality is not confined to a private love relationship, but extends to the whole community (93–102):

> She while she was, (that was, a woful word to sayne)
> For beauties prayse and pleasaunce had no pere:
> So well she couth the shepherds entertayne,
> With cakes and cracknells and such country chere.
> Ne would she scorne the simple shepheards swaine,
>   For she would call hem often heame
>   And giue hem curds and clouted Creame.
>   O heauie herse,
> Als Colin cloute she would not once disdayne.
>   O carefull verse.

Again there is a suggestion of a reversal of the familiar direction. The 'cracknells' recall those given in vain by Hobbinol to Colin, and then by Colin to Rosalind, in *Januarye* (58, 60), while the general munificence recalls the tributes of the host of 'daintie Damsells' to Elisa in the *Aprill* lay (47), followed only by the *hope* that Elisa would offer anything in return (together with Colin's more concrete pledge to pay them with 'Damsines' on his own part). Meanwhile, Dido's refusal here to 'scorne the simple shepheards swaine' or, especially, to 'disdayne' Colin himself provides a marked contrast to what we know of Rosalind.

In the context of a pastoral elegy, the remembered feast also recalls the central passage of Menalcas' hymn to Daphnis in Eclogue 5, describing the merry feasts Menalcas will hold in his honour each year, before the altars he has set up to him (65–73):

> Sis bonus o felixque tuis! En quattuor aras:
> ecce duas tibi, Daphni, duas altaria Phoebo.
> Pocula bina nouo spumantia lacte quotannis,
> craterasque duo statuam tibi pinguis oliui,
> et multo in primis hilarans convivia Baccho,
> ante focum, si frigus erit, si messis, in umbra
> vina novum fundam calathis Ariusia nectar.
> Cantabunt mihi Damoetas et Lyctius Aegon;
> saltantis Satyros imitabitur Alphesiboeus.

['Be good and auspicious to your people! See these four altars: behold, two for you, Daphnis, two altars for Phoebus. Two cups, foaming with new milk, I shall place there for you each year, and two bowls of rich olive oil, and most importantly, making the feasts merry with much wine (before the hearth if it should be cold, or in the shade at harvest-time), I shall pour out from wine-bowls the fresh nectar of Chian wine.']

The opening prayer *sis bonus o felixque tuis!* ('Be good and auspicious to your people!') tactfully indicates, even in this most deferential of eclogues, that the tribute is intended as part of an exchange, and expects a return. It is precisely this hoped-for return which Colin's feast represents, with Dido, rather than the poet and shepherds themselves, providing the hospitality. Dido's generosity recalls all that we have seen, both in Spenser and in Virgil, of tributes by the lowly to the great and powerful, rather than their enjoyment of the actual returns they hoped for. Servius' gloss on Menalcas' *sis bonus o felixque tuis!* at line 65 reminds us that the fulfilment of such hopes is far from certain in prospect, and that in retrospect it may be very much a matter of perspective:

tuis: to the shepherds, if we take it as Daphnis; if as Caesar, it is well he says 'your'. For he was very harmful to his assassins; for Augustus, his son, pursued them all.

As with the hopes of good government entertained at Elizabeth's accession, the opinions of different factions on whether or not they have been fulfilled may vary widely in the event.

What Spenser is lamenting here is not what has been and is no more, but rather that which was once hoped for but never came to pass. Like the happy Tityrean circle of poetic tribute and royal patronage which Colin projects into his youth in *June* but which the 'New Poet' has patently never experienced, this is an imagined past, a remembered projection of past hopes. Dido's 'cracknells', like the 'faded flowres' which deck her grave, are the ghosts of the tributes once offered to Elizabeth by her optimistic Protestant subjects, and of what they looked for in return. Dido's death symbolizes the death of such hopes. *Gia speme spenta* – tributes, gifts, loyalty, faith have come to nothing.

Specifically, what has dashed these hopes is the plan of marriage to the Duc d'Alençon, a marriage which Sidney warns Elizabeth, in a letter which circulated in manuscript and earned him the Queen's disfavour, could prove 'the manifest death of your estate'.[91] As Paul McLane argued and many have now accepted, the 'death' of Dido in *Nouember* is Spenser's adaptation of the same metaphor used repeatedly in Sidney's letter, most emphatically at the beginning:

> But as they say, the Irishmen are wont to tell them that dye, they are ritche, they are feare, what nede they to dye? So truely to you indued with felicities beyond all others (though shorte of your desertes) a man may well aske, what maketh you in such a calme to chaunge course, to so helthfull a body to applye such a weary medicine? what hope can recompense so hazardous an adventure? Hazardous indeed, if it were for nothing but the altering a well mainteined & well approved trade. For as in bodies naturall any soudain change is not without perill, so in this body politick wherof you are the onely head, it is so much the more as there ar more humours to receave a hurtfull impression.[92]

Sidney warns that Elizabeth's Protestant subjects, whose 'sowles live by your happy government', and who are in turn her 'chefe, if not sole, strength', will (like the 'alienate and withdrawen' Colin of *Aprill*'s

---

91 Feuillerat (ed.), *Prose Works of Sir Philip Sidney*, Vol. 3, p. 59.
92 McLane, *A Study in Elizabethan Allegory*, pp. 47–60; *Prose Works of Sir Philip Sidney*, Vol. 3, pp. 51–2.

'argument') be 'aliened' and 'diminishe much of their hopefull love they have long held in you' if the marriage goes ahead.[93] Virgil's Dido, whose other name 'Elissa' links her even more strongly with Elizabeth, dies at the end of Book IV of the *Aeneid* as a direct result of her love for a foreign prince, so that the choice of name deepens the association of this metaphorical death with the Alençon match.[94] As McLane points out, there were also fears among opponents of the match that the real, and not merely metaphorical, death of the Queen and of her Protestant subjects might ensue. The Spanish ambassador Mendoza reports in a letter dated 16 October that the majority of Elizabeth's Council believe 'the security of her person' and 'the tranquillity of her realm' to be threatened by the match: 'If she were to die, as might be feared if the French were to obtain control of her person, they would take possession of the country'; in a letter following on 11 November he predicts that the marriage 'may undoubtedly be looked upon as a divine provision to reduce this country to the Catholic religion, and to punish it by means of an intestine war'.[95] Catholics and crypto-Catholics in England may have been recovering their spirits, but the hopes of Protestants that Elizabeth would remain *bonus felixque* to their cause seemed, in late 1579, to have been tragically misplaced.

The theme of dashed hopes, the failure of the powerful to repay former tributes, and even an accompanying threat of death, suggestively recall Virgil's ninth eclogue, the darkest of all Virgil's eclogues just as *Nouember* is the darkest of Spenser's, and one which, as we have seen, overshadows *Aprill*, the partner-piece to *Nouember* in Spenser's volume. Eclogue 9 is itself related to the elegy for Daphnis intimately, though with deep irony, so that it offers Spenser a Virgilian model for the pessimistic reworking of Eclogue 5's political praise. As we have seen, the fourth fragment of Menalcas' songs which is recited in Eclogue 9 deals explicitly with the same topic of the *sidus Iulium*, making it, for those who accepted that allegory, a kind of encapsulation of the Eclogue 5 elegy with the veil removed – but in a context which aligns it ironically with misplaced tributes of purely rhetorical praise to ungrateful recipients. Of the two political song-fragments recited there, the first pledges to lift Varus' name to heaven on condition the Mantuan farmers are spared, and, since the condition has evidently not been met, it will presumably never be completed. The

---

93 *Prose Works of Sir Philip Sidney*, Vol. 3, pp. 52–3.
94 Douglas Brooks-Davies (ed.), *Edmund Spenser: Selected Shorter Poems* (New York: Longman, 1995), p. 72; McCabe (ed.), *Shorter Poems*, p. 565.
95 Quoted in McLane, *A Study in Elizabethan Allegory*, pp. 50–1.

last hails Caesar's star, promising that it will ensure the fertility of the fields and the security of the farmers, recalling Menalcas' prayer to Daphnis, *sis bonus o felixque tuis!* ('Be kind and propitious to your friends!') in Eclogue 5 (l. 65). But its confident tone is radically undermined by its closing echo of Meliboeus' bitterly ironic exclamation *insere nunc, Meliboee, piros* ('Graft your pears now, Meliboeus; plant your vines in rows', 1.73) in *insere, Daphni, piros: carpent tua poma nepotes* ('Graft your pears, Daphnis; your grandchildren will harvest your fruit', 9.50). Farmers like Meliboeus, Moeris and perhaps Menalcas himself cannot after all look forward to their grandchildren enjoying the fruits of their labour.

That *Nouember* might be intended to evoke the ninth eclogue as well as the fifth should not be surprising. Not only is it intimately connected with *Aprill*, where the recitation of an admired and absent singer's composition by a grief-stricken shepherd irresistably recalls Eclogue 9, but, just as 9 is the penultimate eclogue in Virgil's book, *Nouember* is the penultimate eclogue of the *Calender*, to be followed only by Colin's 'elegy for himself' in *December*, a poem which (as others have observed)[96] recalls the song for Gallus in Virgil's final eclogue. Moreover, as Nancy Lindheim has pointed out, though *Nouember* is the eleventh eclogue in the *Calender*, November is the *ninth* month in the official calendar of England (in which the number of the year would change on the Feast of the Annunciation, 25 March), as it was also in the earliest Roman calendar, discussed by E.K. in the *Generall Argument* prefacing the book.[97] Spenser's decision to begin his *Calender* with January rather than March is, rather oddly, the main focus of this 'generall argument', and E.K.'s account is slightly confusing. Explaining that the primitive Roman calendar had only ten months, beginning in March (and making up for the discrepancy with the solar year by the unsystematic insertion of unnamed 'intercalendrical' months), he seems at first, misleadingly, to associate the addition of January and February at the beginning of the year with Julius Caesar's calendrical reforms in 46 BCE, though a few lines later he correctly attributes it to the much earlier king, Numa.[98] The names of September, October, November and

---

[96] Rosenberg, *Oaten Reeds and Trumpets*, p. 87.
[97] Nancy Lindheim, 'The Virgilian Design of *The Shepheardes Calender*', *Spenser Studies* 13 (1999), 1–21, at 5–6.
[98] Numa's responsibility is of course a matter of the legendary past, and we cannot judge with certainty. By 'correctly' I mean that he follows classical accounts such as Ovid, *Fasti* I.27–44, and Macrobius, *Saturnalia* I.13.1–3.

December ('seventh', 'eighth', 'ninth' and 'tenth'), in the Roman and Elizabethan calendars and in our own today, are a hangover from this early ten-month calendar. The whole passage seems rather strange and under-motivated, where the reader might reasonably expect, under the heading 'The generall argument of the whole booke', some guide to the overall meaning of the work. To the reader trying to gain some purchase on how this modern pastoral collection, with its illustrations and commentary, might relate to the Virgilian eclogue-book it seems to resemble, however, one of the effects of E.K.'s discourse is arguably to associate Virgil's ten eclogues with the old Roman ten-month calendar. Virgil's eclogue-book is *not* structured calendrically at all, and the primitive ten-month calendar supposed to have been devised by Romulus was already a matter of obscure antiquarian lore by Virgil's time.[99] But from the perspective E.K. seems to encourage here, the ninth eclogue would recall the old ninth month, November. By misleadingly associating the expansion from ten to twelve months with the Julian reforms, E.K. anchors this concern in the period and the political context of the *Eclogues*' composition.

Lindheim also points out that 'Spenser may even have thought that Virgil's own use of his fifth (*Quintus*) eclogue to celebrate Julius Caesar, for whom the month of *Quintilis* was renamed *Julius* in 44 BCE, represented analogous calendrical punning'.[100] In support of such an idea, we might note that Servius prompts the reader of Virgil to connect the Caesarean eclogues to the renaming of Quintilis and Sextilis as July and August, in honour respectively of Julius Caesar and Augustus Caesar. In his gloss to 4.12, *incipient magni procedere menses* ('the great months begin to progress'), he argues that 'this touches the fact that July and August received their names in honour of Caesar and Augustus, for they were formerly called Quintilis and Sextilis. And he draws this into an argument for the golden age' (*illud tangit, quod Iulius et Augustus menses in honorem Caesaris et Augusti acceperunt nomina: nam antea quintilis et sextilis dicti sunt. et hoc etiam trahit ad argumentum aurei saeculi*). Again, commenting on the fragment of Menalcas' song on the *sidus Iulium* in Eclogue 9 (that fragment which we have called an encapsulation of Eclogue 5 with the allegorical veil removed), he argues that the promise of fertility there attributed to Caesar's star 'alludes to the month of July, which

---

99 On the history of the Roman calendar, see Jörg Rüpke, *The Roman Calendar from Numa to Constantine: Time, History, and the Fasti*, tr. David M. B. Richardson (Oxford: Wiley-Blackwell, 2011).
100 Lindheim, 'Virgilian Design', p. 6.

was named in honour of Julius Caesar: because both grapes and corn ripen' (*ad mensem alludit Iulium, qui dictus est in honorem Caesaris: quo et uvae et frumenta maturescunt*; gloss to 9.48). Spenser would also have known that, after his posthumous deification, Caesar's feast-day (that annual feast adumbrated in Menalcas' pledge at 5.65–73) was celebrated annually on 12 July. Thus Virgil's fifth eclogue, with its theme of the death and heavenly rebirth of Caesar, had distinct connotations, available to Spenser and his contemporaries, of the fifth month of the old calendar and its renaming in Caesar's honour.

For Spenser, the month of November woud also have had connotations both of death and of new beginnings. The old almanac, the *Shepherds Kalendar*, advises that November is the time when man should prepare for death.[101] More specifically, though controversially, it may be relevant that the November of 1579 was the month in which Elizabeth had a contract drawn up for her marriage to d'Alençon, making it appear a near certainty to alarmed Protestants – the true death-knell of their hopes. The *Shepheardes Calender* was entered on the Stationers' Register on 5 December, and most have assumed that its composition was completed in the first half of the year. The letter to Gabriel Harvey which prefaces it is dated 10 April 1579. But McLane hypothesizes that the dating of the letter is deliberately misleading, intended to throw the censors off the track of topical allusions to events in the last four months of the year, and that Spenser was still making additions and revisions in the period August to mid-November. Though there is no external evidence on either side of the argument, McLane's hypothesis deserves to be entertained seriously. I would suggest that the opening dialogue of *Nouember* shows evidence of a hurried late revision, in the neighbourhood of a notorious crux which throws riddling attention on to the month to which the elegy is assigned, and that this may be taken as evidence for a very precise and up-to-the-minute topical reference to the drawing up of Elizabeth's marriage contract.

The rhyme-scheme of the dialogue prefacing Colin's elegy is of interlocking quatrains, *abab / bcbc / cdcd* etcetera. It is not particularly intricate compared to others among the great variety of rhyme-schemes employed with ostentatious virtuosity in the *Calender*, but it is scrupulously sustained. Thenot at line 25 picks up the closing rhyme of Colin's last quatrain at line 24 for the beginning of his speech ('long', 'song'), and at line 49 Colin duly picks up Thenot's

---

[101] Parmenter, 'Spenser's "Twelve Aeglogves"', 194.

rhyme at line 48, neatly closing the exchange by making the even lines of his quatrain rhyme with the odd lines of Thenot's last four lines (Thenot: 'gayne', 'bynempt', 'swayne', 'contempt'; Colin: 'tempt', 'vaine', 'vnkempt', 'strayne'). But there is an anomaly at the beginning of Colin's first speech, where he ignores Thenot's closing rhyme ('vaine', l. 8) and substitutes a new one ('merimake', l. 9). We might arguably infer that some portion of this speech, starting at its first line, has been substituted for a former version which observed the rhyme-scheme, and in too much haste to make the new passage obey it fully.

Now, the second quatrain of this speech, together with E.K.'s gloss upon it, contains a much-debated crux (13–16).

> But nowe sadde Winter welked hath the day,
> And *Phoebus* weary of his yerely taske,
> Ystabled hath his steedes in lowlye laye,
> And taken vp his ynne in *Fishes* haske.

What could November have to do with Pisces, the astrological sign of the fish? It is in February to March that the sun is in Pisces. E.K.'s gloss on line 16 only worsens the reader's quandary with its blatant error, focusing her mind on the fact that there is a riddle to be pondered here: 'the sonne, reigneth that is, in the signe Pisces all Nouember. a haske is a wicker pad, wherein they vse to cary fish'. And if, as is highly unlikely, any contemporary reader was in danger of believing E.K.'s erroneous assertion, the woodcut prominently advertises the fact that November correctly belongs to Saggitarius, depicted in the sky in line with all the other illustrations. (Pisces, meanwhile, is correctly depicted in the woodcut to *Februarie*.) McLane connected the anomaly with the anti-Alençon theme by suggesting that the sun is to be understood as the conventional symbol of monarchy, and the 'Fish' represents D'Alençon because, as heir to the French throne, he bore the title 'Dauphin', the French word for 'dolphin' (which in this period was still believed to be a type of fish), or else because of the Catholic connotations of fish as Catholics' Friday fare. Thus for McLane the sun and the fish are purely allegorical, and the apparent allusion to astrology is merely a red herring.[102] Richardson sees the lines as referring to the positions of the sun when it is descending towards the winter solstice in November and when it is ascending again in March, and connects this overlaying of the ascending sun on the descending sun with Dido in the elegy, who is at once falling

---

102 McLane, *A Study in Elizabethan Allegory*, p. 54.

in death and rising to heaven.[103] So again the reference to Pisces is merely a matter of imagery, evoking the idea of spring renewal – a solution which does not tackle the riddling anomaly. Douglas Brooks-Davies follows McLane in connecting the crux to the anti-Alençon polemic, arguing that '*Fishes* haske' refers not to the *sign* of Pisces but to the twelfth astrological *house*, which is correlated with the sign of Pisces.[104] The astrological houses denote the different areas of human affairs in which planetary influences will be expressed, with the twelfth house indicating affliction or prison. The image thus suggests that the monarch (or sun) is entrapped and in dire danger. But this suggestion only worsens the astrological problem, for, where the sun passes through the zodiacal *signs* month by month over the course of the solar year, it passes through all the *houses* in each twenty-four-hour period: thus the sun would be in the twelfth house only at a certain time of day, and would be there at some point on any day of the year. But Colin calls his 'sollein season' 'sadde Winter', and defines it by contrast with 'May' and 'summer' (11–13): it clearly cannot indicate merely a fleeting hour.

As far as I am aware, it has not previously been noted in this context that D'Alençon was born on 18 March 1554, under the sign of Pisces. Thus there is an astrological reason for connecting D'Alençon to Pisces, in addition to the connotations of the 'fish' image suggested by McLane, bolstering the claim that line 16 alludes to him. Secondly, if as I have argued the break in the rhyme-scheme at lines 8–9 can be taken as evidence of a last-minute substitution of text, we might infer that Spenser has chosen to insert this passage, together with E.K.'s flagrantly erroneous gloss, specifically into *Nouember* in order both to mark the apparent triumph of the Piscean D'Alençon with the signing of the marriage contract in November 1579, and at the same time to highlight the unnatural nature of this turn of events – to present it as a mistake and an upheaval on a cosmic scale, with potential consequences for the nation's destiny comparable to those of planetary influence. The effect is similar to the wandering of 'the heauens reuolution' described in the Proem to Book 5 of *The Faerie Queene*, and its moral application:

---

103 J. M. Richardson, *Astrological Symbolism in Spenser's* The Shepheardes Calender: *The Cultural Background of a Literary Text* (Lewiston, NY: E. Mellen Press, 1989), appendix 2.
104 Brooks-Davies, *Selected Shorter Poems*, pp. 406–7.

> For who so list into the heauens looke,
>   And search the courses of the rowling spheares,
>   Shall find that from the point, where they first tooke
>   Their setting forth, in these few thousand yeares
>   They all are wandred much; that plaine appeares ...
>
> So now all range, and doe at randon roue
>   Out of their proper places farre away,
>   And all this world with them amisse doe moue,
>   And all his creatures from their course astray,
> Till they arriue at their last ruinous decay.
>
> (*The Faerie Queene* V.Proem.5–6)

Moreover, by placing the sun in the position it occupied at D'Alençon's nativity, the astrological error suggests that this November in some sense represents a repetition of his birth. We remember that Virgil's fifth eclogue, the ostensible model for *Nouember*, treated Daphnis' (or Caesar's) death and rebirth as a god. We might also remember Pliny's report that Octavian privately interpreted the *sidus Iulium* (apparently evoked by Menalcas' hymn) as signifying his own rebirth or rise to power after his adoptive father's death. While Colin's elegy, as we shall see, grants this expected apotheosis to Dido (or Elizabeth) only in the strictly Christian sense of the salvation open to all Christian souls, the suggestion of the rebirth of D'Alençon brings in its train the full political implications of the Virgilian apotheosis. If anyone's star appeared to be rising in November 1579, it was D'Alençon's, and he might reasonably look forward to wielding a power in England comparable to that of planetary influence, of the deified Caesar, or of an Octavian newly ensconced in empire.

The month of November also connoted new beginnings for Spenser and his contemporaries because, as commentators on the eclogue have noted, it was the month in which Elizabeth's Accession was celebrated.[105] This was the chief festival in the 'liturgy of state' which the regime insinuated into the calendar, partially compensating for the Catholic holidays now expunged from it, and a day paralleling Julius Caesar's feast on 12 July – also just one of a series of feast-days honouring his own family which Augustus inserted into the Roman liturgical year.[106] The irony with which Spenser writes of

---

105 See for instance Lane, *Shepheards Devises*, p. 26; A. Chapman, 'The Politics of Time in Edmund Spenser's English Calendar', *SEL* 42 (2002), 1–24, at 16.
106 Roy C. Strong, *The Cult of Elizabeth: Elizabethan Portraiture and Pageantry* (Berkeley: University of California Press, 1977), p. 115; on Augustus, Alessandro Barchiesi, *The Poet and the Prince: Ovid and Augustan Discourse* (Berkeley: University of California Press, 1997), p. 71.

the Queen's imagined death in the month traditionally consecrated to celebrating the commencement of her reign has often been remarked. The decision to do so must have been taken earlier than November 1579, and thus independently of the deepening of gloom arising for Protestants from the events of that month as they unfolded: even if the elegy had originally been composed for another month, *Nouember*'s woodcut, depicting a funeral procession under the sign of Saggitarius, could hardly have been produced at such short notice. But the mood of many at the Accession Day celebrations of 1579 must have resembled the gloom of Colin's mourning song. The irony produces an interesting contrast with Virgil's fifth eclogue. Where Virgil's poem remembers a past death merely as the premise and preface to its triumphant announcement of a new political beginning, the apotheosis of Julius Caesar heralding the glorious reign of Octavian *divi filius*, Spenser does almost precisely the opposite, commemorating the beginning of Elizabeth's reign, and the hopes attendant on it, with lamentation for a death still in the future, whose only present reality is as a metaphor and as a fear.

Colin's version of elegy sidesteps the political tribute of deification central to Menalcas'. It does so in part because *Aprill*, *June* and *October* have already taught us that there is no hope of return for such a tribute. Thus *Nouember* recalls the mood of Eclogue 9 – the *other* place where we find a song of Menalcas on the apotheosis of Caesar – the eclogue in which hope of favour and protection from rulers mortal or divine has turned out to be hollow, and which consequently and conspicuously decides not to honour a parallel promise to lift Varus, another political potentate, to the stars. In Colin's elegy the expectation of an apotheosis like that of Daphnis or Caesar is disappointed not by such a clear refusal but rather by its replacement with a Christian alternative. The last four stanzas of the lay turn from lamenting her death to celebrate the fact that 'Her soule vnbodied of the burdenous corpse' is 'into heauen hent'. Though recalling Menalcas' Daphnis on the threshold of Olympus just sufficiently to maintain the sense that *Nouember* is a reworking of Virgil's fifth eclogue, and though classicizing its heaven slightly with the appellation '*Elisian* fieldes' at line 179, this is a recognizably orthodox account of Christian salvation. Foremost among the touches which keep it so is the exclusively Christian reference to saints, bound as closely as possible to the elegy's only use of that vexed term 'goddesse' (175–6):

> She raignes a goddesse now emong the saintes,
> That whilome was the saynt of shepheards light ...

This is the closest Colin comes to reproducing the apotheosis claimed by Menalcas for Daphnis or Caesar; the accompanying Christian imagery of saints polices and qualifies it, ensuring that it remains restricted to a metaphorical sense.

In this Christian perspective, Dido's salvation is a cause for jubilation, but is quite divorced from earthly political affairs. Caesar's apotheosis is clearly an honour bestowed by the gods in recognition of his rule; no ordinary citizen could expect to follow him to Olympus. And as a god, he is expected to continue to influence events on earth: hence Menalcas' prayer *sis bonus o felixque tuis* in Eclogue 5 and his claim that Caesar's star sustains the fertility of the crops in Eclogue 9.[107] By contrast, Colin reminds us repeatedly that *this* heaven is equally open to all Christian souls, and Dido's death is even made the occasion for encouraging the lowliest on their own passage to salvation: 'Make hast ye shepheards, thether to reuert' (191). This is no special honour singling out a great ruler: Dido is merely 'gone afore (whose turne shall be the next?)' (193). And conversely, there is no suggestion that Dido will exert any influence on earthly affairs from her new abode in heaven. 'Whilome' she 'was the saynt of shepheards light' (176), 'whilome' she 'was poore shepheards pryde' (198), but this was only in the past, 'While here on earth she did abyde' (199). Now the 'poore shepheards' are abandoned and alone, like their sheep, who are chased by 'Wolues ... Now she is gon that safely did hem keepe' (136–7). The fate of Protestants is clearly what Colin has in mind here, the wolves of Protestant pastoral conventionally representing Catholics. The rejoicing in these closing stanzas is purely over the pleasures Dido is experiencing in heaven, regardless of the present and future experiences of those she has left behind. In fact, those pleasures are described in such a way as to suggest a stark contrast with the 'daunger' that besets the singer and his fellow shepherds (185–8).

> But knewe we fooles, what it vs bringes vntil,
> Dye would we dayly, once it to expert.
> No daunger there the shepheard can astert:
> Fayre fieldes and pleasaunt layes there bene ...

---

107 From a more cynical perspective a similar implication in political affairs holds true: the deification of Caesar was brought about by his adopted son Octavian for political reasons and to political ends, bolstering his own claim to absolute power – as is implied by Ovid at *Metamorphoses* 15.760–1.

It is perhaps the specific sense of this danger, and the absence of her in whom they had trusted for protection from Catholic 'wolues', rather than merely a generalized Christian *contemptus mundi*, which provokes Colin to hope for death, both on his own behalf ('Might I once come to thee (O that I might)' 181) and on behalf of his fellows ('Make hast ye shepheards, thether to reuert' 191). We could take this wish as hinting that a good death – perhaps martyrdom in that repetition of the St Bartholomew's Day massacre feared by Sidney and Stubbes, or in the civil war predicted by Mendoza – is all that is left for English Protestants to hope for.

The couplet on the saints also points up the denominational issue. In the context of the month of November, it hints at how Elizabeth's Accession Day was a kind of secular equivalent to the Catholic saints' days no longer celebrated in England, honouring the Queen in their vacated place. Now, however, she is 'emong the saintes' in a different sense – in fact in two distinct senses, both equally significant, though mutually incompatible. Firstly, if we think of Dido's death literally (perhaps as something imminent, 'as might be feared if the French were to obtain control of her person', in Mendoza's words), she is now a true 'saint' in the orthodox Protestant sense, as one of the saved souls in heaven. (This is all very well for her, but no help to the shepherds whose 'light' is thus removed, for the crucial difference between Catholic and Protestant 'saints' is that Protestant saints do not intercede with God on behalf of the living – and thus Protestants denounced as idolatry the Catholic practice of praying to saints for such intercession.)[108] When we think of the metaphorical meaning of this 'death', however, a second set of implications comes into play. Betraying her Protestant subjects with her planned marriage, Elizabeth seems to have joined the Catholics, with their idolatrous pantheon of 'saintes' – that modern Christian equivalent of the hubris with which 'the Paynims were wont' to deify 'Kinges and Princes' (*Aprill* 50 gloss), as Menalcas deifies Julius Caesar in eclogues 5 and 9. She is no longer 'the saynt of shepheards' because she has gone over to the other side – the side of the wolves. And a typically Spenserian quibble in line 176 enhances this second reading. She was once 'the

---

[108] Thomalin spells out the Protestant view of saints in *Julye*: 'nowe they bene to heauen forwent, / theyr good is with them goe: / Theyr sample onely to vs lent, / that als we moght doe soe' (117–20). On the reformed treatment of saints in the *Calender*, see Chapman, 'The Politics of Time', 15–16; and on the Protestant view of saints generally, see Robert Kolb, *For All the Saints: Changing Perceptions of Sainthood and Martyrdom in the Lutheran Reformation* (Macon, GA: Mercer University Press, 1987).

saint of shepherds' light' in the sense that she has been praised as 'the sonne of all the world' and the 'wonted light' of the earth at 67–8, recalling the comparison of Elisa to Phoebus at *Aprill* 73–81. But she has also shown herself to be 'the light (or fickle) saint of shepherds', in the sense that Rosalind is said in *June* to have 'wexe[d] so light' (103) in her infidelity to Colin, turning to the 'faithlesse fere' (110) Menalcas.

These consolatory Christian stanzas evoke the alternative Christian allegorization of Virgil's fifth eclogue, with Dido's resurrection *in* Christ taking the place of the resurrection *of* Christ which Vives found in the apotheosis of Daphnis.[109] The substitution is not as blasphemous as it might sound, since (especially from a Protestant perspective) the passage of Dido's, and of any, soul to heaven is predicated upon the death of Christ, which Vives sees as the true subject of Mopsus' lament. As in *Aprill*, Spenser seems to be suggesting that Virgil's eclogue is fit to be imitated by a Christian poet only if interpreted in this religious sense, and not as political praise. But as religious poetry, these four stanzas offer consolation only on a metaphysical level. They provide no solution to the political discontent adumbrated in the rest of the elegy, and, as we have seen, they too hide sour reflections on the political situation just beneath their surface. In any case, they are greatly outnumbered by the eleven stanzas of lament which precede them – in contrast with Virgil's fifth eclogue, where Mopsus' lament and Menalcas' hymn are exactly equal in length.

Despite the invocation of Christian salvation at the end of the elegy, then, the prevailing mood of the eclogue is gloomy, and the emphasis is on the seemingly desperate political situation of English Protestants in this world, whatever consolation might await them in the next. This emphasis on despair at the expense of the hopeful message of Christian salvation is reflected even more obviously across the *Calender* as a whole. When, in the General Argument, E.K. invokes the birth of Christ in late December, 'renewing the state of the decayed world', as a justification for beginning the year in January, he passes swiftly on to the discussion of the Roman calendar, to which he devotes significantly more space and attention. His mention of Christmas, moreover, acts as a foil to the body of the work itself, which conspicuously fails to mention it anywhere. *December* ends the work by circling round to the same despair which began it, with the monologue of a

---

109 *In publii Vergilii Maronis Bucolica interpretatio*, B7r.

solitary Colin delivered in the same stanza-form as *Januarye*, and in this month to which Christmas belongs we are left neither with any sense of the cyclical 'renewing' of the natural seasons nor with the spiritual renewal of Christian redemption (143–4):

> Winter is come, that blowes the bitter blaste,
> And after Winter dreerie death doth hast.

As in *Nouember*, the 'sollein season' offers only the prospect of death.[110]

The failure to register the Christian hope symbolized by Christmas has often been adduced as evidence of Colin Clout's mental and emotional shortcomings by critics who take a psychologistic approach to the text.[111] He is accused of solipsism, immaturity and unchristian despondency. But the death imagined in the 'sollein season' of *Nouember* marks (as I join many others in arguing) the betrayal of Protestants in England to their Catholic enemies, threatening an overturning of the Reformation. If, as Mendoza predicts, the French were to take the marriage 'as a divine provision to reduce this country to the Catholic religion, and to punish it by means of an intestine war', Elizabeth's subjects would be threatened not only with physical death but with spiritual death too. Only Protestants, Protestants believed, could hope to be resurrected in Christ (and if this in itself sounds rather solipsistic, it is the solipsism not of a character, nor even of an author, but of an age). It is not that Colin is a sulky adolescent fixated on his personal problems, while Spenser is capable of a more sanguine and balanced or Christian view. Neither is it merely – though this is closer to the mark – that the *Calender*'s political concerns stand apart from an essentially otherworldly Christian consolation, so that the promise of heaven may be acknowledged in *Nouember* but cannot alleviate the gloom neccessarily arising from the nation's prospects in the here and now. Rather, the political danger is precisely a spiritual danger: from the perspective of Elizabethan Protestants, salvation can no longer be looked forward to with confidence by future generations of English men and women, who may in future be 'nousell[ed]' in such 'ignorounce' that they will fail to 'smell out the vntruth' of Catholicism's 'packed

---

110 Contrast the claims made for the promise of salvation as the *Calender*'s fundamental message by R. A. Durr, 'Spenser's Calendar of Christian Time', *ELH* 24 (1957), 269–95, among others.
111 Notably Johnson, *The Shepheardes Calender: An Introduction*; Durr, 'Calendar of Christian Time'; Isabel MacCaffrey, 'Allegory and Pastoral in *The Shepheardes Calender*', *ELH* 36 (1969), 88–109; Cullen, *Spenser, Marvell, and Renaissance Pastoral*, pp. 76–111; Mallette, 'Portrait of the Artist'.

pelfe and Massepenie religion' (*June* 25 gloss) and thus forfeit their souls. Colin's subjunctive 'Might I once come to thee (O that I might)' (181) registers an uncertainty newly vivid to English Protestants, and there is reason for 'ye shepheards' to 'Make hast' with special urgency 'thether to reuert' (191), before their consciences are subjected to trials they might prove unable to bear.

And here we could hazard another – perhaps even darker – significance of *Nouember*'s imagining of Elizabeth's death. Perhaps it would be better, we might read the *Calender* as implying, if she were to die now, a Protestant and a virgin, before she has had the chance finally to undermine the Reformation in England and imperil her subjects' souls, or has been 'vnderfong' (*June* 103) by her spouse to convert to Catholicism and lose her own. Perhaps such a hope also underlies the choice of the name Dido. For, as has often been noted, it was well known to Spenser's contemporaries that Virgil had fabricated his story of the widow Dido's affair with Aeneas, who was historically separated from her by several centuries.[112] The competing account of her legend, regarded as more reliable by sixteenth-century humanists, has her commit suicide in order to avoid a second marriage, out of fidelity to her dead husband Sychaeus. Even in Virgil's account, the final word is given to this wifely fidelity: our last glimpse of Dido is in the Underworld, where her shade turns angrily away from Aeneas to return to Sychaeus' company in the groves of the Mourning Fields (*Aeneid* 6.472–4). In her plan to marry D'Alençon, Elizabeth too has been presented by Spenser as unfaithfully abandoning her first and true spouse – her kingdom – for another, 'faithlesse fere'. The only glimmer of hope in *Nouember* is that Elizabeth may yet return to her true husband, or prove faithful to him after all, and a possible implication of the elegy is that this might be achieved by her hasty passage to the other world.

---

[112] As Servius notes in his *Aeneid* commentary. Spenser would also have been familiar with Petrarch's, Boccaccio's and Chaucer's treatments of the subject. On the tradition of the chaste Dido, see A. S. Pease (ed.), *Aeneidos liber quartus* (Cambridge, MA: Harvard University Press, 1935), pp. 65–7; Mary Louise Lord, 'Dido as an Example of Chastity: The Influence of Example Literature', *Harvard Library Bulletin* 17 (1969), 2–44, 216–32; Craig Kallendorf, *In Praise of Aeneas: Virgil and Epideictic Rhetoric in the Early Italian Renaissance* (Hanover, NH: University Press of New England, 1989), pp. 58–76.

3

Virgilian structure in *The Shepheardes Calender*

In what goes before, I have focused on the eclogues which exhibit a very strong and direct relation to Virgil's, and these happen to be ones where Colin Clout features prominently. I have opposed ironic readings of Colin, which put the gloom of his eclogues largely down to his psychological shortcomings as a solipsistic or worldly adolescent, and argued that it represents instead an intensification of the Virgilian attempt to negotiate a bargain with power, amplifying the exilic gloom of Meliboeus and Moeris, and dampening the optimistic, Caesarean or Tityrean strain by projecting it into the past, identifying it with youthful hopes which have already proved vain, and that Spenser does this for a specific religious and political purpose – a rearguard action against the forces which threaten the Protestant Reformation in England, focused particularly on Elizabeth's planned marriage to the Duc d'Alençon. It may be objected that this is a selective reading, and that there are other concerns, other eclogues and other shepherds in the *Calender*. To cite only one instance, my discussion so far has only glanced at *October*, which may strike some as strange, given that it is here that Virgil is spoken of directly by Cuddie. This is because, unlike the eclogues treated in the last chapter, this eclogue is not a close *imitation* of Virgil: however, I shall discuss it in more detail later in this chapter. Most would accept that Colin is given priority by being explicitly identified with the author, and by having the first and last words. But it is worth pointing out a striking structural symmetry which underlines how fundamental Colin is to the conception of the entire work. To make this as clear as possible, I shall often refer to the eclogues of the *Calender* by number rather than by name in this chapter. (Note that this is also E.K.'s usual method in his glosses, making it easier for readers to draw the kinds of parallels and discriminations between the *Calender*'s structure and that of Virgil's eclogue-book I shall be arguing here.)

Colin appears in person in eclogues 1 (*Januarye*), 6 (*June*), 11 (*Nouember*) and 12 (*December*). In addition, other shepherds recite his songs in 4 (*Aprill*) and 8 (*August*). If we put in parentheses the eclogues where Colin is absent but one of his songs recited, this gives us the following:

1   (4)   6   (8)   11   12

12 here looks like a coda, added after the end of a completed pattern – and that fits the nature of the *December* eclogue, which reviews the seasons of the year and of Colin's life. The perfect symmetry of this pattern surely cannot be accidental.

Now this symmetry in the *Calender*, which as far I can find has not been pointed out before, is strikingly reminiscent of the concentric structure which modern classicists observe in Virgil's *Eclogues*. Paul Maury was the first to describe this, in 1944, and it has since been widely accepted and refined. According to this theory, eclogues in the second half of Virgil's eclogue-book mirror the eclogues in the first half, in a kind of 'ring composition' (a structural technique pervasive in classical literature all the way back to Homer).[1] Eclogues 1 to 9 follow this pattern:

  i Roman: land-confiscations
    ii Theocritean: frustrated erotic passion
      iii Theocritean: amoebean song-contest
        iv: mythological: supernatural prophecy
          v: deification of Daphnis/Caesar
        vi: mythological: song of the god Silenus
      vii: Theocritean: amoebean song-contest
    viii: Theocritean: frustrated erotic passion
  ix: Roman: land-confiscations

---

1 See Paul Maury, 'Le secret de Virgile et l'architecture des Bucoliques', *Lettres d'Humanité* 3 (1944), 71–147; O. Skutsch, 'Symmetry and Sense in the Eclogues', *Harvard Studies in Classical Philology* 73 (1969), 153–69; Otis, *Virgil: A Study in Civilized Poetry*, 128–43; John Van Sickle, *The Design of Virgil's Bucolics* (Rome: Edizioni dell'Ateneo & Bizzarri, 1978), pp. 20–4, 27–9. On ring composition in Homer, see Cedric Whitman, *Homer and the Heroic Tradition* (Cambridge, MA: Harvard University Press, 1958), and Julia Haig Gaisser, 'A Structural Analysis of the Digressions in the *Iliad* and the *Odyssey*', *Harvard Studies in Classical Philology* 73 (1969), 1–44.

The final eclogue, 10, stands apart as a kind of coda, like Spenser's *December*; as Otis points out, it also forms a pair with the central eclogue, both being conspicuously marked as imitations of Theocritus' first idyll. Eclogue 5, treating the apotheosis of Daphnis/Caesar, stands at the centre of the book, in the same way that we find the godlike *iuvenem* who so clearly represents Octavian in precisely the central line of Eclogue 1, line 42. It is suggestively comparable that Spenser's naming of Elisa as a 'goddesse', in direct imitation of Eclogue 1, occurs in the central stanza of the *Aprill* lay (stanza 7 out of 13).[2] All these phenomena answer to the 'triumphal' symmetry analysed at length by Alistair Fowler, and identified by him as distinctively Virgilian in origin, and as common in Renaissance practice particularly where the theme is celebration of a sovereign.[3]

Let us pause to note that, though it took so long to appear in print, most of this symmetry should be eminently obvious to anyone inclined to look for structure and pattern in Virgil's *Eclogues*. 1 and 9 are explicitly on the same topic; 2 and the first half of 8 are versions of the same Theocritean idyll, no. 3; that 3 and 7 are both Amoebean song contests places them quite distinctly in their own subgenre; and 4 and 6 are the two eclogues which in their mythological subject matter strain the boundaries of pastoral altogether, and are associated not with shepherds' songs but with divine singing or inspiration.[4] What held it back, surely, was a combination of two factors. Firstly, modern criticism has been very slow to analyse the *Eclogues* as a book rather than as a series of discrete poems; this habit of thought is reflected even in the usual but non-classical title *Eclogues*, which means 'selections' – suggesting an arbitrary gathering of bits and pieces, without a unified design – instead of the classical title *Bucolica*.[5] Spenser was unusual among Renaissance poets in choosing to write an eclogue-*book*, rather than merely individual pastoral poems, and he gives a marked emphasis to its 'proportioned' nature in the title, so it seems highly probable that he

---

2   The corresponding use of the term 'goddesse' in the *Nouember* elegy occurs *not* at its centre but in its thirteenth stanza. This, too, is interesting in the light of what I shall have to say about the number thirteen below.
3   Alastair Fowler, *Triumphal Forms: Structural Patterns in Elizabethan Poetry* (Cambridge: Cambridge University Press, 1970), esp. pp. 62–4.
4   One might even speculate that the superficial obviousness of all this may be one factor which prevented scholars – always keen to display their ingenuity in revealing what is hidden from open view – from describing it until such a late date.
5   On approaching the *Eclogues* as a book, and the implications of the alternative titles, see Van Sickle, *Design*, pp. 25–7.

would have approached Virgil's *Eclogues*, his principal model, as a structured book. Indeed, I have been unfaithful to Spenser's volume in using the familiar term 'eclogue' to refer to its poems, for in 'The generall argument of the whole booke' E.K. is at pains to point out that 'they be not termed Eclogues, but Aeglogues', deriving the term from the Greek for 'Goteheards tales', and explicitly dismissing the implication of the more common term that such poems are 'extraordinary discourses of vnnecessarie matter'.[6] Secondly, structure as pattern, harmony and number was arguably not as important to nineteenth- and twentieth-century modes of thinking about literature as it has been to other ages. Chief among those 'other ages' is the Renaissance, and Spenser himself loomed large in the criticism of the 1960s and 1970s which reminded us of this fact.[7] One of the most assiduous exponents of the elaborate numerological structure of Virgil's eclogue-book speculates that Spenser may have 'mastered some of its essentials'.[8]

If we look for precisely the same symmetrical structure in *The Shepheardes Calender* that we have described in Virgil, we find it as we have seen in Colin's songs, but it doesn't elucidate all the remaining eclogues.[9] I suggest, however, that Spenser has adapted the symmetry of Virgil's ten-eclogue book to fit his own twelve-eclogue calendar in another way, creating a pattern which is overlaid on to the symmetry of Colin's more precisely Virgilian contributions. This second pattern is most easily shown in a diagram:

---

6   McCabe, *Shorter Poems*, p. 32.
7   See A. Dunlop, 'The Unity of Spenser's Amoretti', in A. D. S. Fowler (ed.), *Silent Poetry: Essays in Numerological Analysis* (London: Routledge & Kegan Paul, 1970), pp. 153–69; Maren-Sofie Røstvig, 'The Shepheardes Calender – A Structural Analysis', *Renaissance and Modern Studies* 13 (1969), 49–79; Alastair Fowler, *Spenser and the Numbers of Time* (London: Routledge & Kegan Paul, 1964); A. Kent Hieatt, *Short Time's Endless Monument: The Symbolism of Numbers in Edmund Spenser's 'Epithalamion'* (New York: Columbia University Press, 1960). Numerology has fallen out of fashion in Spenser studies as in classics, although in both fields some of the discoveries made during its brief vogue are still accepted and widely cited. In both disciplines it is time for an objective reappraisal of the value of the approach.
8   Van Sickle, *Design*, p. 24.
9   2 and 10 go together well: in each we have a discontented Cuddie in debate with another shepherd who argues against his disgruntlement. The pairing of 4 and 8 is suggestive in other ways than only their containing recitations of Colin's songs, since Perigot and Willye's roundelay contains many echoes of the *Aprill* lay. 5 and 7, too, go together obviously as Protestant Church satire. But the pairing of 3 and 9 is a sticking point: these eclogues seem to have nothing in common.

Virgilian structure

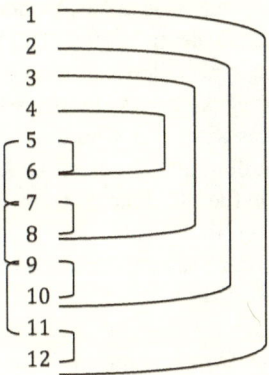

Let me explain my rationale. I shall deal first with the four major pairs, linked by the long lines on the right, taking them in turn.

- 1 and 12 go together very obviously: both are monologues from Colin, using the same stanza form, and critics almost universally observe that Eclogue 12 marks a closing of the circle, a return to the point of 1, just as the cyclical nature of the calendar would in fact require.
- In 2 and 10, we have a discontented Cuddie debating with another, apparently older, shepherd (Thenot, Piers), who tries to make him give up complaining about external circumstances.
- In 3 and 8, we have Willye condoling with another shepherd (Thomalin in *March*, Perigot in *August*), who has been smitten by the arrow of love, causing a wound that 'rancketh more and more' (*March* 100, *August* 101). Though 3 is not a song-contest as 8 is (for Spenser has only one song-contest for the pair which Virgil gives us in his third and seventh eclogues), nevertheless 3 quotes prominently from Virgil's third eclogue (lines 40–2 translate Virgil, Eclogue 3.33–4, as E.K. explains in his gloss), while 8 imitates the same Virgilian eclogue in its stakes (a sheep on one side, a richly carved cup on the other), and by ending in a draw, with the prizes exchanged.
- In 4 and 6, we have Hobbinol expressing sympathy for Colin, and the description of courtly/pastoral 'Heydegyues, and trimly trodden traces' of nymphs and Muses, together with all the references in *June* back to the the *Aprill* lay and its Tityrean poetics which we explored in the last chapter.

The fulcrum is at Eclogue 5, as in Virgil's book, but where in Virgil that point marks the great central vision of the apotheosis of Daphnis/Caesar, here any such expectation is displaced by what turns out to be merely the first in a regular series of bitter satires, from a Protestant perspective, on abuses within the Church, spilling over in 9 to wider social ills and concluding in *Nouember*'s lament for the death of the Protestant nation. On the left of the diagram, I have shown this series of satires (5, 7, 9, 11), interpolated regularly before the answering term in each of the four primary pairs of eclogues which mimic the concentric structure of Virgil's book.

The placing of the individual satirical eclogues within this series is also determined by their relation to those answering eclogues, as shown in the short brackets on the right, linking 5 to 6, 7 to 8, 9 to 10, and 11 to 12:

- In 5 and 6, Piers and Colin both make a principled rejection of a scene of merrymaking and festivity. That scene is also notably reminiscent, in each case, of the lay in 4. The catalogue of flowers gathered by the young people in Palinode's description overlaps with *Aprill*'s flowers in its roses (*Maye* 14, *Aprill* 60) and its 'Sopps in wine' (*Maye* 14, *Aprill* 138), and his May Queen attended by 'A fayre flocke of Faeries, and a fresh bend / Of louely Nymphs', who in the woodcut are shown dancing in a ring around her and her consort, is distinctly reminiscent of '*Elisa*, Queene of shepheardes' (*Aprill* 34).
- 7 is linked to 8, in its pairing with 3, for the following reason. 8 brings back Willye, *one* of the figures in Eclogue 3, and reproduces its situation. But Willye's interlocutor in 3, Thomalin, is replaced by the similarly afflicted Perigot in 8, and Thomalin himself is displaced into 7, now complaining about the state of the Church rather than his own amatory plight.
- 9 is linked to 10, because both are complaints about poverty and economic injustice – Diggon's in 9 about poverty in the nation generally, Cuddie's in 10 about the poverty of aspiring poets. Just as 10 answers 2 because both feature the complaining Cuddie, so 9 also recalls 2 in its emphasis on the cold weather: 'the Westerne wind [which] bloweth sore' (*September* 49), exacerbating the destitute Diggon's 'poore … plight' (*September* 8), echoes the 'bitter blasts' of 'Winters rage' which provoke Cuddie's complaint at the opening of *Februarie*.
- 11 is linked to 12 not only because Colin is the main speaker but

also because it is on the subject of death. As we have seen, 12 is Colin's 'elegy for himself', modelled on Virgil's song for the dying poet Gallus in his own final eclogue (an eclogue which Spenser also invokes in the first term of the 1/12 pair, *Januarye*, as we saw in the last chapter). Virgil's tenth eclogue shares its chief model – Theocritus' lament for Daphnis in Idyll 1 – with the fifth eclogue, on the death and apotheosis of Daphnis/Caesar, which is the basis for 11 with its elegy for Dido. And again, details of 11 also recall the first term in the 1/12 pair, as both appeal to the correspondence between 'sollein season' and 'sadder plight' (*Nouember* 17), 'carefull case' and 'sadde season' (*Januarye* argument), and *Nouember*'s imagery of 'faded flowres' (*Nouember* 109) recalls the wasted buds and blasted blossome of Colin's youth in *Januarye* (38–40). As we have seen, *Nouember*'s imitation of Virgil's fifth eclogue amplifies the mournful mood of its first half, Mopsus' lament, and radically diminishes the joyful celebration of Menalcas' hymn. Hence it is placed, not at the triumphal fulcrum as the Daphnis/Caesar elegy was in Virgil's book, but in connection with the gloomy ending of the work – the final eclogue on the death of the poet which recalls the ending of Virgil's *Eclogues*.

The upshot of all this is that, while close imitation of Virgil's individual eclogues is concentrated in Colin's eclogues, and other models are important in some of the other eclogues (Mantuan particularly in 5, 7 and 9, but also Aesop in 2 and 5, and the native satirical tradition represented by *Piers Plowman*, the pseudo-Chaucerian *Plowman's Tale* and Thomas Churchyard in 9), nevertheless the structure of Spenser's *Calender* as a whole is designed to evoke the structure of Virgil's eclogue-book. Whether or not the ordinary reader was intended to be fully conscious of the structure of the *Calender* and of its correspondence with the structure of Virgil's book is another question, but it is demonstrable that they are there, to be discovered in whole or in part according to how closely the individual reader examines the book, perhaps even to take their effect at a subconscious level. In *October*, E.K. glosses line 27, Piers' description of how Cuddie's music bereaves his audience of sense:

> what the secret working of Musick is in the myndes of men ... appeareth, hereby, that some of the aunciant Philosophers, and those the most wise, as Plato and Pythagoras held for opinion, that the mynd was made of a certaine harmonie and musicall nombers, for the great compassion and likenes of affection in thone and in the other ...

The gloss suggests that the effect of numerical structure and patterning is irresistible precisely because it operates at a level beneath consciousness and readerly control. E.K. proceeds to offer the example of Alexander roused to warlike fury and then immediately calmed once more by the varied strains of the musician Timotheus: such control over his own ruler's moods and actions is of course the ultimate aim of Spenser's structural choices, as of the rest of his complex poetic strategy in the *Calender*. A reader who had absorbed the structural rhythm of Virgil's eclogue book would feel a small shock of disappointment when, after *Aprill*'s evocations of the fourth eclogue, she was met *not* by a version of the triumphal *Daphnis* but instead with *Maye*'s ecclesiastical satire. The disappointment would become positively nagging with the regular return of the topical and satirical voice in the remaining odd-numbered eclogues, only to reach a climax in 11, when the long-delayed version of Virgil's Daphnis finally appears, but transforms Virgil's political praise into the *Calender*'s bleakest and most doom-laden vision of the current crisis of the nation. The rude and harsh voice of sharply topical satire which intrudes so insistently in 5, 7 and 9 is at first kept separate from the voice of the skilled poet Colin, his own similar discontents marked off by the veil of allegory from their more direct confrontation of social ills. But in 11, finally responding for the first and only time in the volume to a direct request for song (like that which opens the founding poem of bucolic, Theocritus' first idyll), he assumes the mantle of a public poet precisely by identifying his voice with this satirical strain, sounding the final note in the sequence, and transforming it into high art.

Returning to our first, narrower topic of Colin's contributions, we need now to notice an even odder structural feature. The first eclogue has 13 stanzas, and this sets up a pattern which is borne out in a surprising way throughout the book. For the eclogues in which Colin appears in person – with the notable exception of 6, at the very centre of that symmetrical pattern which marked Colin's part in the *Calender* – each have a total number of lines which is divisible by this number, 13:

1 (*Januarye*): 78 lines (= 6 × 13)
11 (*Nouember*): 208 lines (= 16 × 13)
12 (*December*): 156 lines (= 12 × 13)

Moreover, Colin's songs recited by others in 4 and 8 also turn out to have lines numbering multiples of 13:

4 (*Aprill*) lay: 117 lines (= 9 × 13)
8 (*August*) sestina: 39 lines (= 3 × 13)

(All sestinas, of course, must have this number of lines, and some might argue that this fact weakens its significance here, but we could equally argue that the number furnishes another reason for Spenser's decision to include a sestina at all.)

The prominence of this structural motif goes further, too. The dialogue preceding Colin's elegy in 11 (*Nouember*), and, in 8 (*August*), *both* the dialogue preceding Colin's sestina *and* the dialogue preceding Willye and Perigot's roundelay, each have line totals divisible by 13:

11 opening dialogue: 52 (= 4 × 13)
8 dialogue before roundelay: 52 (= 4 × 13)
8 dialogue before sestina: 26 (= 2 × 13)

And two further eclogues have *total* line numbers also divisible by 13, like the ones where Colin appears in person:

3 (*March*): 117 (= 9 × 13)
8 (*August*): 195 (= 15 × 13)

These two eclogues are related in being one of the pairs we noted above: they are also set apart by being the only two eclogues in the book apart from Colin's which are about love-suffering (Thomalin's in *March*, Perigot's in *August*).

Meanwhile, what appears as the sole exception to the basic pattern of thirteens as regards *Colin's* appearances – the total number of lines in our central eclogue 6 (*June*) – is remarkable in another way. Its length is 120 lines, which is eye-catching not only for its roundness as the product of 10 and the calendrically significant 12[10] but

---

[10] In Renaissance number theory, multiplication by 10 is often held not to affect the significance of the initial number. 10 in itself, however, also has symbolic importance as a form of the Pythagorean *tectractys* (since 1 + 2 + 3 + 4 = 10) and the number of perfection. 10 and 12 are also, of course, the number of eclogues in Virgil's and Spenser's books respectively, so the line total 120 could also connote the product of Spenser's refashioning of Virgil's *Eclogues* in his own book. This must remain merely suggestive and hypothetical, but an analogy suggests itself with an interesting numerical moment in Virgil. Corydon specifies in Eclogue 2 that the instrument bequeathed him by Pan is made up of seven pipes held together with wax (2.36), which contrasts with the 'nine-voiced' pipe in his Theocritean source, Idyll 8.18, and Van Sickle suggests that 'seven' thus becomes 'a sign of Virgil's difference from Theocritus' (p. 235). We could expand on this by observing that 63, the length of the pivotal Eclogue 4, is the product of this Theocritean 9 and

also because it is the only line-total in the *Calender* shared by two eclogues: Eclogue 10 (*October*) also has 120 lines. Thus there are strong reasons to see the apparent exception as a product of design, rather than as invalidating our suggested pattern.

Two questions arise immediately. Is this deliberate or a coincidence? And if deliberate, what might it be intended to signify? Well, the chances of its being coincidental must be infinitesimally small. At the risk of stating the obvious, only one in thirteen numbers is divisible by thirteen, and since it is a prime number (and not one of the smallest), its points of overlap with numbers whose multiples we might expect to encounter commonly in a poetic context, such as multiples of 4 or 6, are rare. For it to occur by chance in a pattern-forming, predictable way as it does in the context of Colin's appearances and songs would be freakish in the extreme; the further occurrences beyond this strict pattern (in the dialogues of 8 and 11, and in the line totals of the two eclogues on the *Calender*'s other suffering lovers, 3 and 8) are merely the icing on an already rich cake of improbability.

Now, the structure identified by modern scholars in Virgil's *Eclogues* also extends to a pattern of line numbers.[11] In the first four eclogues – the opening terms of all the pairs identified in the concentric structure – we find the number 63. Eclogue 1 has 83 lines, or 5 + 5 + 63 + 5 + 5. Eclogue 2 has 73, or 5 + 63 + 5. Eclogue 3 has 63 lines of dialogue, surrounding the 48 lines of the actual singing match. Eclogue 4 is 63 lines long. At this point another pattern commences, as we find that three regularly spaced eclogues, beginning with Eclogue 4, have line totals in increments of 7. Eclogue 4 has 63 lines, Eclogue 7 has 70, and Eclogue 10 has 77. These also happen to be the only three poems in the book which mention Arcadia. In addition, the sums of the four pairs in the concentric structure obey a pattern (though here the sums are not *quite* exact). In all this, multiples of 7 are obviously important, and especially 9 x 7, or 63. As to the significance of this fact, the existence of the pattern clearly reinforces the sense of structure in the book; Van Sickle has also argued that the incremental series 4–7–10 highlights the growth of the theme of Arcadian song, which he sees as replacing the Tityrean pastoral of political praise first adumbrated at the beginning of the collection

---

this Virgilian 7, so that what we have is not merely 'a sign of ... difference' but the fruit of the meeting of the two poets – we might almost say the offspring of cross-breeding, 'by Virgil out of Theocritus' (and we could say the same of 120 in the *Calender*, as symbolizing this poetic fruit bred 'by Spenser out of Virgil').

11 See Maury, Skutsch, and Van Sickle (offering a useful summary) in note 1 above.

and reaching a climax in Eclogue 4.[12] The number 7 often occurs in Virgil in solemn and ceremonial contexts.[13] In a recent discussion of Horace's *Carmen Saeculare*, Alessandro Barchiesi points out more specific connotations which are also obviously relevant to interpretation of Virgil, calling it 'the powerful number that unites the ... gods Apollo and Diana with Rome and, implicitly, with Augustus'.[14] Servius Danielis' gloss on *numero deus impare gaudet* ('the god rejoices in odd numbers') at Eclogue 8.75 lists examples of the divine associations of the numbers 3 and 7, connecting the latter with the seven strings of Apollo's lyre and the seven planetary spheres. If we hypothesize that Spenser noticed some part or all of Virgil's pattern of sevens, we could safely assume that it would also have carried connotations for him unavailable to Virgil and his contemporaries, since 7 is the number of the Sabbath, God's day of rest after the creation of the universe, and thus symbolic of completion and divine perfection.[15] To reject out of hand the hypothesis that he may have noticed it would seem rash, when we are dealing with a poet capable of producing, from a similar system of counting line numbers, the elaborate structure of the *Epithalamium*.[16]

So what could Spenser's pattern of multiples of 13 be intended to signify? Thirteen seems to have had very little significance in Renaissance numerology or in the Pythagorean, Platonic, Augustinian, cabbalistic or astrological ideas it drew on. The only strong connotation that the number 13 ever seems to have borne is the one it still carries popularly today, the belief that it is an 'unlucky' number, and there is evidence in Montaigne that this superstition was current in the sixteenth century, though a matter of folklore rather than an integral part of the 'science' of number symbolism.[17] We should not be

---

12 Arcadian song for Van Sickle represents 'an idea of pure and unique poetic skill' (*Design*, p. 193), 'an image of self-sufficiency and ordered work and play and love within bucolic confines' (19,4) in which Roman ideology, with its attributes of 'struggle and ambition', is renounced, 'giving rise to a sweet dream of peace' (p. 164). For Spenser's response to this strain in the *Eclogues*, see Chapter 5 below on 'Colin Clouts Come Home Againe'.
13 Skutsch, 'Symmetry and Sense in the *Eclogues*', p. 158.
14 Alessandro Barchiesi, 'Lane-switching and Jughandles in Contemporary Interpretations of Roman Poetry', *TAPA* 135 (2005), 135–62, at 158.
15 On the divine symbolism of seven as the number of the Sabbath, see Philo Judaeus, *On the Allegories of the Sacred Law* 2 and *Creation* 7, 23; Augustine, *De civitate Dei* XI.31.
16 Hieatt, *Short Time's Endless Monument*.
17 Vincent Foster Hopper, *Medieval Number Symbolism: Its Sources, Meaning and Influence on Thought and Expression* (New York: Columbia University Press, 1938), pp. 130–3, quoting Montaigne, *Essais* 3.8, 'On the Art of Conversation', at 131.

surprised to find Spenser drawing on popular lore in a work which mingles its classical humanist learning with rural dialect, vernacular traditions and their concern for the peasantry, and whose very title combines the 'olde name' of *The Kalender of Shepherdes*, a popular almanac, with an emphasis on classical number and proportion in 'Conteyning tvvelue Aeglogues proportionable to the twelue monethes'. What is going on here, I would argue, is simply that Spenser is replacing the suggestions of Apollonian harmony and Roman patriotism in Virgil's sevens with a numerical ground bass of gloom and foreboding in his own work, sounded whenever Elizabeth or the politically charged topic of love comes to the fore, and reinforcing his sombre warning of the disaster that will follow the French marriage.

So far, we have not fully explored the relation of Spenser's pairs of eclogues to those of Virgil, and there are still further things to say. Virgil pairs 1, the loss and recovery of the homestead, with 9, on the homestead's recovery and loss, the latter reversing the hopeful movement of the former. Spenser's corresponding pair begins in despair, with Colin as a combination of the despairing Meliboeus and a Tityrus whose hope has *not* been fulfilled. Answering this, 12 can only confirm the resignation and despair, and generalize it through the analogy of Colin's life to the seasons (but without the hope of spring renewal). Virgil's ninth eclogue also exerts its influence in other places in the *Calender* – in fact, in all of the eclogues which formed part of that first pattern we identified in relation to Colin. Its motif of remembered song as a melancholy reminder of broken promises overshadows the remembered hopes enshrined in the lay in 4, recital of the work of the absent master-singer is also a feature of 8, and its ironic reworking of the apotheosis of Daphnis/Caesar inflects Spenser's own reworking of the same elegy in 11. Meanwhile, the *emblem* in 1 still holds out a (Tityrean?) hope missing from Colin's monologue itself, and it is in the emblem to 6 (that *other* reworking of Virgil's first eclogue) that we are told (as in Virgil's ninth) that this hope is lost. We could say that this Virgilian pair, 1 and 9, whose position at the beginning and end of Virgil's concentric structure (before the parting coda of Eclogue 10) already gives it such prominence, acquires an even greater significance in *The Shepheardes Calender*, overshadowing and governing Colin's part in the whole work.

Virgil pairs 2 and 8, while Spenser pairs 2 and 10. The opening terms of these pairs are not close. Spenser has already bound much of the substance, form and significance of Corydon's lament into

Januarye, where Colin is a Corydon as well as a Meliboeus, the love-anguish of Eclogue 2 is closely interwoven with the political misfortunes of Eclogue 1 (amplifying the hints we observed in Virgil in our opening chapter), and the monologue form of Eclogue 2 displaces the dialogue of Virgil's first eclogue. Rather than merely repeat the soliloquy of the despairing lover, Spenser opts here to lighten the tone, generalize the complaint to the common cares of physical discomfort in winter and tensions between youth and eld, and reinstate the dialogue form from Virgil's Eclogue 1 to depict less tendentious subject matter – differences arising not from political injustice but merely from the limited perspectives of ordinary individuals suffering the common lot of humankind. Cuddie's complaints about the cold, which spark his argument with Thenot, could nevertheless be seen as taking their cue from an aspect of Eclogue 2 which is crucial to its mood and the scene it paints, for Corydon's soliloquy is delivered in the seasonal discomfort of the burning noonday sun, when all but he are relaxing in the shade. In Virgil's eclogue, this heat works most strongly on a figurative level, as it comes to stand for the burning passion which consumes Corydon from within. Spenser strips away this more serious figurative level, the aspect of the eclogue he has already deployed in relation to Colin, and reserves for Cuddie only the superficial, literal, physical discomfort (here of cold instead of heat).

The relation between the answering terms in Spenser's and Virgil's second pairs, however, is much stronger. The body of Virgil's eighth eclogue is made up of Damon's despairing love-song which so closely resembles Corydon's, and Alphesiboeus' own imitation of another Theocritean idyll glanced at in Eclogue 2. But it opens with a lengthy *recusatio*, which emphasizes the theme of patronage (8.6–13):

> Tu mihi seu magni superas iam saxa Timaui,
> sive oram Illyrici legis aequoris, en erit umquam
> ille dies, mihi cum liceat tua dicere facta?
> en erit, ut liceat totum mihi ferre per orbem
> sola Sophocleo tua carmina digna coturno?
> a te principium, tibi desinam. accipe iussis
> carmina coepta tuis, atque hanc sine tempora circum
> inter victricis hederam tibi serpere laurus.

['But you, my friend, whether you are now passing the cliffs of the great Timavo, or skirting the coast of the Adriatic Sea: oh, will that day ever come when I shall be allowed to tell of your deeds? Will it ever be that I am allowed to bear through the whole world the fame of your songs, uniquely worthy of the buskin of Sophocles? In you was my beginning; in you I shall end. Accept the songs undertaken at your command, and permit this ivy to creep among the victor's laurels around your head.']

Spenser's tenth eclogue is also a *recusatio*, recalling Colin's version of *recusatio* in 6, but putting it now in explicitly and precisely generic terms, as Virgil does. Cuddie ends with a vision of what he might aspire to if the necessary patronage were forthcoming (109–18):

> Thou kenst not Percie howe the ryme should rage.
> O if my temples were distaind with wine,
> And girt in girlonds of wild Yuie twine,
> How I could reare the Muse on stately stage,
> And teache her tread aloft in buskin fine,
> With queint Bellona in her equipage.
>
> But ah my corage cooles ere it be warme,
> For thy, content vs in thys humble shade:
> Where no such troublous tydes han vs assayde,
> Here we our slender pipes may safely charme.

The focus on the writing of tragedy, through the metonymy of the tragic buskin or *coturnus*, the image of the ivy entwining (*serpere*) his temples (*tempora*), and the wistful subjunctive mood of the whole vision, are obviously intended to evoke the Virgilian passage.[18] Indeed, lest we should fail to notice, E.K. quotes *Eclogues* 8.10 in his gloss on 'buskin' at *October* 113. At the same time, there is a poignant contrast. Virgil advertises the fact that this pastoral song has itself been commissioned by his addressee, whom Servius identifies as Octavian, whereas the whole burden of Cuddie's song is that he has no patron, and at the exact centre of the eclogue we find his lament, precisely, that both the benign system of patronage which supported Virgil and the great deeds which he took as his subject (as promised and deferred in Eclogue 8's *recusatio*) are now consigned to the past (55–66):

> Indeede the Romish *Tityrus*, I heare,
> Through his *Mecænas* left his Oaten reede,
> Whereon he earst had taught his flocks to feede,
> And laboured lands to yield the timely eare,
> And eft did sing of warres and deadly drede,
> So as the heauens did quake his verse to here.

---

18 Noted Hubbard, *Pipes of Pan*, p. 296.

> But ah *Mecœnas* is yclad in claye,
> And great *Augustus* long ygoe is dead:
> And all the worthies liggen wrapt in leade,
> That matter made for Poets on to play:
> For euer, who in derring doe were dreade,
> The loftie verse of hem was loued aye.

As in *Februarye*, Cuddie focuses on material needs. He is not lovelorn like Corydon in Eclogue 2 or the protagonists of Damon's and Alphesiboeus' songs in Eclogue 8: this role is reserved for Colin. But nevertheless, a correspondence between the material and amatory plights is worked into the eclogue as, in response to Piers' recommendation that he turn to religious poetry, Cuddie gives only a nod to the conventional modesty topos to explain his own refusal, and chooses to dwell instead on the reason why *Colin* cannot follow such advice. He is, Cuddie argues, understandably incapacitated from rising to such poetry by his amatory despair. Cuddie himself is not a lover, and his focus is on the obstacle in his own path, the lack of patronage – that is, on the failure of the high and mighty to heed their obligations to the lowly. But this is precisely, as we have argued, the failure allegorized in Colin's unrequited love, and in Corydon's as interpreted by Servius. In so far as Cuddie in 10 departs from the amatory theme of Virgil's eighth eclogue, then, we can see it as a laying bare of the political concerns underlying the allegorical veil of love.

We have already spoken of the correspondences between the next pairs, Virgil's third and seventh eclogues on the one hand, and Spenser's third and eighth on the other. While *March* is not a song-contest, it quotes from Virgil's third eclogue, and shares its light tone and treatment. *August* draws conspicuously on the same eclogue in the draw and the exchange of gifts between Willye and Perigot (as E.K. emphasizes by quoting *Eclogues* 3.109 in his gloss to line 131), while nevertheless contriving to end with acclaim for the absent singer Colin, recalling the victory of Corydon at the end of Virgil's seventh. Or rather, acclaim for both the poet Colin and the singer Cuddie, who recites the song in Colin's absence: 'thou shalt ycrouned be / In *Colins* stede, if thou this song areede', Willy tells him. (145–6). In *October*, referring back to this recitation, E.K. will tell us

> I doubte whether by Cuddie be specified the authour selfe, or some other. For in the eyght Aeglogue the same person was brought in, singing a Cantion of Colins making, as he sayth. So that some doubt, that the persons be different.

Perigot's comment on the sestina pointedly accords the compliment paid to Virgil's Corydon by his Meliboeus equally to both. Virgil's Eclogue 7 ends *ex illo Corydon Corydon est tempore nobis* ('from that time forth, it is "Corydon! Corydon!" with us', 7.70). Perigot's verse mimics the striking repetition of 'Corydon' twice, once for Colin and once for Cuddie (190–3):

> O *Colin, Colin*, the shepheards ioye,
> How I admire ech turning of thy verse:
> And *Cuddie*, fresh *Cuddie* the liefest boye,
> How dolefully his doole thou didst rehearse.

We might even speculate that there is a witty play here on the other possible reading of Virgil's line, which can also be interpreted 'from that time, Corydon is a Corydon to us', with the second 'Corydon' used as a predicate, with the metaphorical meaning 'the ideal poet' – or, as we might put it with the argument to *October*, 'the perfecte paterne of a Poete'. Colin and Cuddie, figures presented in *October* as so riddlingly interchangeable or identical, seem in Perigot's quatrain to be almost generated out of the repeated 'Corydon', with its two senses, in this second reading of Virgil's verse, even as they are accorded equal praise with the doubled exclamatory vocatives imitated from the first reading of the same verse ('it is "Corydon! Corydon!" with us'). Meanwhile, Virgil's *Corydon, Corydon* at 7.70 echoes his *a, Corydon, Corydon, quae te dementia cepit* ('Oh, Corydon, Corydon, what madness has seized you?') at 2.69. Whether this is significant and intended to be noticed in Virgil's text or not, in Spenser's context it is striking and suggestive: *Januarye* has already carefully paralleled Corydon's despairing love in Eclogue 2 with Colin's, which is also the subject of Colin's doleful monody just recited by Cuddie; and the apostrophe of 2.69 is recalled and applied to Colin, once by himself in *December*'s 'Ah vnwise and witlesse Colin Clout', and twice by Hobbinol, in *June*'s 'Oh carefull Colin, I lament thy case', and in *September*'s 'Ah for Colin, he whilome my ioye', which resonates particularly closely with line 190 above.

With regard to the central pair, 4 and 6, in each book, we have discussed the relations of both Spenserian eclogues to Virgil's fourth at length in the previous chapter. It remains for us here to consider the relation between the answering terms in the two pairs – the sixth eclogue of each – and again, as in our consideration of Virgil's eighth and Spenser's tenth, contrast rather than similarity seems to predominate. We have seen that there is a *kind* of *recusatio* in *June*, reminiscent of the *recusatio* which opens Virgil's sixth eclogue, though we have also seen that it is not a *recusatio* in specifically generic terms, of epic in favour of pastoral. But what Tityrus goes on to sing in Eclogue 6 after his *recusatio* is very different from the choice which Colin makes. Like the *paulo maiora* of 4, it rises above the humble subject matter of pastoral; like 4, it is mythological. It relays the song of the god Silenus, a Callimachean medley of Greek amatory and metamorphic myths: both the god himself and a nymph appear in person, and Servius argues that the two boys Chromis and Mnasyllos are themselves fauns or satyrs. However, it replaces the political, Roman mythology of 4's prophecy with an apolitical, backward-looking review of myth, which has been described as 'a deliberate reversion to something intellectually prior or aside from the ideological (historical-heroic) vision of the first half-book (an ironic reconstruction of a world "as before" and without Rome)'.[19] As we have seen, Spenser's own rejection in *June* of the panegyrical poetics of his fourth eclogue is carried out in a very different – and indeed a more political – way. As in the relation between Virgil's eighth and *October*, Spenser chooses to follow and expand upon the terms of the opening *recusatio* rather than the body of the eclogue, returning to the topic of Tityrean praise as exemplified in Eclogue 1, and the question of whether it is truly the proper path for a pastoral poet to follow.

It is in Spenser's sixth and tenth eclogues, then, that we find a marked *contrast* in theme with the corresponding terms in Virgil's concentric structure, alongside the similarities. While evoking the *recusatio* from the opening of Virgil's sixth eclogue, Spenser's sixth eclogue does not follow Virgil's retreat into apolitical mythology, but chooses instead the politically oppositional stance of plaint; and in Spenser's tenth eclogue, Cuddie, while echoing the *recusatio* of Virgil's eighth, pointedly focuses on his lack of the patronage which Virgil, even in this *recusatio*, claims to enjoy. It is striking that these are also the two eclogues which, as I have mentioned, are structurally linked by their identical length of 120 lines. This odd connection between 6 and 10 cuts across the structure of Virgilian pairings.[20]

---

19 Van Sickle, *Design*, p. 157. Cp. Otis, *A Study in Civilized Poetry*, p. 131: 'it is clear ... that *Eclogues* 1–5 are relatively forward-looking, peaceful, conciliatory, and patriotic in a Julio-Augustan sense. *Eclogues* 6–10, on the contrary, are neoteric, ambiguous or polemic, concerned with the past and emotively dominated by *amor indignus*, love which is essentially destructive and irrational and is implicitly inconsistent with (if not hostile to) a strong Roman-patriotic orientation.'
20 Virgil also suggests a structural link between his sixth and tenth eclogues, for both end with the command to drive the flock back to the fold, because the evening star

What is its significance?

June marks a radical departure from the Virgilian model, as Spenser makes clear his decision to continue on the political path of censure and critique, rather than to retreat into an other-worldly aesthetic Arcadia, as Virgil does in Eclogue 6. In doing so, he also announces that he is returning Virgil to the drawing board, by modelling this eclogue primarily, again, on Virgil's first, the Tityrus–Meliboeus dialogue, which was less unexpectedly the main model for *Januarye* (combined with allusion in both to Virgil's last). He is simultaneously abjuring both the types of song identified with Tityrus, the figure commonly identified in the commentaries as Virgil's persona: both the deifying praise of the ruler from Eclogue 1 and the escapist fairy-tales of Eclogue 6.

October, meanwhile, stands out as being the place where Spenser discusses the question of imitating Virgil directly. It is explicitly metapoetic in a way no other eclogue in the *Calender* is, as is highlighted in E.K.'s *Argument*, with its sketch of the Platonic theory of poetry's divine inspiration and its promise of future publication of the author's 'booke called the English Poete', and by his glosses, with their discourses on the titles of *Vates* and 'Poetes or makers' (gloss to line 210), on the 'honor … Poetes always found in the sight of

---

is approaching. As we have seen, Spenser's sixth eclogue also ends on this note, and, in the context of Rosalind's infidelity which Colin has just been lamenting, that ending is clearly an allusion to the end of the 'Gallus', Virgil's Eclogue 10; *December*, in which Colin is obviously intended to recall the Gallus of Eclogue 10, ends on the same note (ll. 147–8). The version that we encounter at the end of Virgil's Eclogue 6, meanwhile, contains an ambiguity which should by now catch our eye, for Vesper commands the shepherds to pen their flocks *numerumque referre*, which we could translate as 'and count their number' (as Menalcas tells us in Eclogue 3 his father and jealous stepmother do each evening – an indignity also suffered by Willye in *March*), or else as 'recite their song', with *numerum* referring to the feet of metrical verse. (A closely similar scene at *Georgics* 4.433–6 contains a similar ambiguity in the phrase *numerumque recenset*, occurring in the same position in the line.) But this word *referre*, from *re-* + *ferre* 'to bear back', has a connotation of backward movement, and we might read it as a hint that, at this point, the first eclogue of the second half-book and the first of the mirror-eclogues in Virgil's concentric structure, we must begin to count the poems backwards, as we encounter reflections of Eclogue 4, then of 3, then of 2, then of 1 – until finally, in Eclogue 10, the full-fed goats are returned to their fold and the genre of pastoral is put away in the same final line. So we have a Virgilian precedent for a special marker distinguishing eclogues 6 and 10 from the other eclogues and linking them together, and one which coincides with a ludic reminder of the numerical structure of Virgil's book – the very concentric structure that this linking cuts across. Virgil's sixth and tenth eclogues also contain his two treatments of Gallus, whose poetic career is a foil to his own. This will be central to Spenser's articulation of his own role in his later pastorals: see Chapters 4 and 5 below.

princes and noble men' (gloss to line 65), and on Pythagoras' theory of the power of 'harmonie and musicall nombers': 'Such might is in musick' (gloss to line 27). And at its exact centre, stanzas 10 and 11 out of 20, we find Cuddie's lament for the death of Virgil, of his patron Maecenas and of 'great *Augustus*', and with them of all 'worthies' who provided both fit matter for song with their 'derring doe' and necessary support and protection for the poets they revered. Here then is the place where Spenser explains directly the fundamental reason for the revision of and departures from his Virgilian model in the *Calender* as a whole – his society is lacking in the 'vertue' (67) which merits and sustains optimistic or triumphal poetry, and his must be a gloomy pastoral for a debased age.

Since 'Princes pallace' provides neither the pattern of virtue nor the patronage which could support a Virgilian ascent to epic, Piers suggests that Cuddie pursue a different path (83–4):

> Then make thee wings of thine aspyring wit,
> And, whence thou camst, flye backe to heauen apace.

In the context of *October*'s imitation of the opening *recusatio* of Eclogue 8, this strikingly recalls line 11 of that poem: *a te principium, tibi desinam* ('from you is my beginning, in you I shall end'), a line which, in its Virgilian context, is thoroughly embedded in the politics of patronage, and partakes of the Caesarean extreme of the *Eclogues*' two-sided political negotiation. Under a surface which appears merely to acknowledge Octavian's patronage and promise future epic praise in return, Virgil insinuates a hyperbolical compliment. For his readers would have recognized the line as alluding to the opening of Theocritus' seventeenth idyll, a fulsome panegyric to his patron Ptolemy which opens

> Ἐκ Διὸς ἀρχώμεσθα καὶ ἐς Δία λήγετε Μοῖσαι,
> ἀθανάτων τὸν ἄριστον ἐπὴν αὐδῶμεν ἀοιδαῖς·
> ἀνδρῶν δ' αὖ Πτολεμαῖος ἐνὶ πρώτοισι λεγέσθω
> καὶ πύματος καὶ μέσσος· ὁ γὰρ προφερέστατος ἄλλων.
> (*Idylls* 17.1–4)

[From Zeus let us begin, and with Zeus in our poems, Muses, let us make end, for of immortals he is the best; but of men let Ptolemy be named, first, last, and in the midst, for of men he is most excellent.]

Virgil has already imitated the opening line at 3.60, without its political baggage (*Ab Iove principium, Musae*).[21] By applying it to his

---

21 As noted by Eobanus Hessus, *In P. Vergilii Maronis Bucolica*, ad 3.60.

addressee here, he implies the same analogy and near-identification of ruler and god made more explicitly in Theocritus' poem. (Horace would also imitate the Theocritean passage at *Carmina* 3.5.1–4, with explicit panegyrical application to Augustus.) When Piers uses the image to represent precisely an *alternative* to political praise poetry, the contrast is pointed: he is suggesting a poetry in which religious worship and divine inspiration would not be perverted for political ends.

After a conventional resort to the modesty topos on his own behalf, Cuddie explains Colin's inability to take this course because of his frustrated love (89–90):

> He, were he not with loue so ill bedight,
> Would mount as high, and sing as soote as Swanne.

The continuous allegory by which Colin's amatory cares figure his political discontent means that these lines evoke the song fragment addressed to Varus in Eclogue 9 (27–9):

> 'Vare, tuum nomen, superet modo Mantua nobis,
> Mantua vae miserae nimium vicina Cremonae,
> cantantes sublime ferent ad sidera cycni.'

['Varus, if only Mantua remains to us (Mantua, alas, too near wretched Cremona), singing swans shall bear your name on high to the stars.']

But it is not quite the same. Cuddie and Piers are explicitly *not* discussing epic or political praise poetry any more, and there is no mention of Colin's swan lifting anyone else's name in its flight. Menalcas will exercise his will in refusing fame to Varus if his political suit is not granted, but Colin here is simply thwarted. It is as if he cannot exercise his poetic gift freely and to the full because he is trammelled and clogged, not merely by his own principled decision to withhold tribute strategically under adverse circumstances but by the very model of poetry as negotiation which his Virgilian pastoral wooing symbolizes. The idea of future poetic flight projected in the *Eclogues* is predicated on the expectation that it will lift up the names of patrons and potentates, anticipating the Virgilian *cursus* with its drive towards deifying praise of the ruler in heroic epic. The *Eclogues*' strategy is to keep open the possibility that the poet will refuse this path, but only by positing an alternative path of cursing and satire – poetry like the *Dirae*, which would 'Beare witnesse' to the 'wicked deede[s]' of rulers, but which is still fundamentally shaped by their actions. The constraints of this model afford no opportunity for a flight of truly inspired poetry, even on religious themes, which is not bound up in that close relation of dependence between ruler and poet.

Piers responds with an appeal to neoplatonic love as a means of transcendence, reminiscent of the movement of Petrarch's *Canzoniere*. Rosalind is herself an 'immortall mirrhor' who could 'rayse' Colin's 'mynd aboue the starry skie' (93–4), and constitute the Platonic divine inspiration alluded to in the *Argument*, if only Colin and poets like him were receptive to her influence. (It implies the same charge voiced by those critics who see the *Calender*'s prevailing gloom, and Colin's apparent unwillingness to ascend to higher genres, as evidence of his psychological shortcomings.) The imagery of Cuddie's reply again insists on the political constraints underlying any neoplatonic poetics which bases itself on a mystification of Elizabeth's power: such love is not 'lofty' (96) but 'lordly', a 'Tyranne fell' (98) opposing and limiting the poet's own Orphic 'power' (97). Whatever inspiration she ought to provide, Elizabeth is currently an obstacle who prevents generic ascent, whether to epic or to hymn: the political crisis of the nation is too urgent a concern for Colin simply to turn his back on the real affairs of 'Princes pallace'. Clogged by pastoral's implication in the demands of political praise, of lifting the ruler or patron 'to the stars', the poet cannot make this flight himself.

The two perspectives on love are incompatible, and it has been argued that Cuddie fails to perceive the value of Piers' 'immortal mirrhor' because he is mired in his own gross material needs. But a telling ambiguity, veiled beneath a typical misdirection, in E.K.'s gloss on this 'immortall mirrhor' suggests that the problem is not a moral failing on Cuddie's part, but rather the limitations enforced on poetry by dependence on political power – a dependence which Virgil's pastoral negotiations fail to escape:

Immortall myrrhour) Beauty, which is an excellent obiect of Poeticall spirites, as appeareth by the worthy Petrarchs saying.

> Fiorir faceua il mio debile ingegno
> A las sua ombra, et crescer ne gli affanni.

The quotation is Petrarch, *Rime Sparse* 60.3–4, which McCabe translates '[the noble tree] made my weak wit blossom in its shade and grow in my troubles'. The noble tree is the laurel, representing Petrarch's beloved, Laura. E.K. spells out only the positive side of this deeply conflicted statement, so that Piers' idea of Elizabeth as a source of inspiration is paralleled with the protecting and nurturing aspect of the tree. But Petrarch yokes this image paradoxically with a suggestion of the tree's simultaneous, baleful influence in the speaker's growing troubles. E.K.'s quotation, offered ostensibly to support Piers' argument that Elizabeth can provide Petrarchan or Platonic inspiration, thus reveals the flipside of Petrarchan poetics, the criticism of Laura's cruelty and pride which could be deployed in the service of political complaint.

Moreover, when the Petrarchan lines are quoted in the context of a Virgilian eclogue book, we are encouraged to read them as themselves alluding to Virgil (not a far-fetched notion when dealing with a humanist scholar and laureate poet, who composed both pastoral and epic as well as this love-poetry). And indeed, closer scrutiny reveals that, even in this direct quotation from Petrarch, the *Calender* is looking back through him to Virgil. The resemblance between the positive side of the Petrarchan image and the scene of Tityrus singing at ease in the shade at the opening of Virgil's book is very strong – the more so when E.K. effectively reapplies it to identify the tree with not Laura but Elizabeth, the ruler to whom Spenser might look for protection and patronage such as Octavian has granted Tityrus. When we come to the negative side of Petrarch's image, the baleful influence of the tree which make the speaker's troubles grow, we might surmise that Petrarch is combining the allusion to the beginning of Virgil's first eclogue with an allusion to the close of his last. For the ending of Eclogue 10, followed only by the final line's command to the goats to go home because Hesperus approaches, we have a surprisingly negative reprise of that opening *umbra* (75–6):

> surgamus: solet esse gravis cantantibus umbra,
> iuniperi gravis umbra; nocent et frugibus umbrae.

['Let us arise: shade is wont to be harmful to singers. The shade of the juniper is harmful; shades damage the crops.']

Petrarch is identifying Virgil's opening, beneficent shade with his closing, baleful shade in order to turn it to his own, amatory purpose, in the service of his distinctively conflicted and oxymoronic depiction of the painful pleasure and pleasant pain of love. But by applying Petrarch's lines to Elizabeth, E.K. brings out the political possibilities of the identification of the two shades which frame Virgil's book. The Queen who should provide the shelter to poets afforded by Octavian to Virgil, E.K.'s quotation implies, is herself their bane.

In this light, we can see that Cuddie's and Colin's *recusatios*, their refusal to follow the Virgilian *cursus* by ascending to higher genres (or indeed to indulge in Virgilian praise in any genre), is not the result of their psychological failings, but rather a response to unsupportable external conditions. Cuddie in *October* focuses on the most material aspect of these conditions, the lack of patronage, but Colin's protest is broader and more political, and targeted in particular at the Queen's own threatened recusancy in her plan to marry a Catholic, which casts a blight over the nation. Under such circumstances, not only is Tityrean gratitude to the ruler misplaced but Tityrus' very dependency on such a ruler for personal protection in return for deifying praise (the shade of Eclogue 1) is pernicious and damaging to the poet (like the shade of Eclogue 10). The implications go beyond the personal and material concerns of Cuddie in *October*, for the problem evoked here is not merely the failure of the Queen to extend patronage to poets. Colin himself was offered such Tityrean patronage in *June*, and actively rejected it. It is the condition of reliance on the monarch, with the obligations it brings and the constraints it places on the poet's freedom to 'sing what he wants', which is harmful – whether Cuddie's meat and wine is forthcoming or not.

Even as the *Calender* negotiates its Virgilian bargain with political power, then, it is wary of the constraints which that negotiation could place upon the poet. In the wake of the breaking off of the D'Alençon match, Spenser was to fulfil the expectations raised by E.K. in the 'Letter to Harvey' and dealt with so ambivalently in the rest of the *Calender*, by pursuing the Virgilian *cursus* and 'ascending' to epic with his *Faerie Queene*. When, in 1595, he interrupts that epic and throws the Virgilian *cursus* into reverse with a return to pastoral, it is a new kind of pastoral, which shrugs off the traces of dependency inherent in the model of negotiation, and lays claim to the independence which comes of a supreme, vatic authority. In his final pastorals, Spenser climbs to the stars without the obligation to carry his ruler with him, and enjoys access to divine inspiration by a direct route which altogether bypasses the political power-system. But he will not turn his back on politics in a Petrarchan transcendence of worldly concerns: rather he will assert his own political authority to critique Elizabeth's government and to influence her subjects, arising from his Orphic poetic power. These poems will take the form not of bargain, but of prophecy.

4
Reshaping the Virgilian *cursus*: pastoral vocation in 'Astrophel'

last eclogue of *The Shepheardes Calender*, as we have seen, imitates Virgil's tenth and final eclogue, comparing Colin's despair to the love-death of Gallus. Virgil's book ends on a note which, at least to later readers familiar with the subsequent trajectory of his career, clearly suggests a farewell to pastoral and the promise of an ascent to higher genres (70–7).

> Haec sat erit, divae, vestrum cecinisse poetam,
> dum sedet et gracili fiscellam texit hibisco,
> Pierides ...
> Surgamus; solet esse gravis cantantibus umbra;
> iuniperi gravis umbra; nocent et frugibus umbrae.
> ite domum saturae, venit Hesperus, ite capellae.

['This will be enough, divine Muses, for your poet to have sung, while he sits and weaves a basket of slender hibiscus ... Let us arise: the shade is wont to be oppressive to singers; the shade of the juniper is wont to be oppressive, and shades harm the crops. Go home, well-fed goats, go home – the evening star is coming.']

Spenser too would 'rise' to epic, and opens his *Faerie Queene* with an imitation of those lines appended to the opening of Virgil's *Aeneid* in sixteenth-century editions, in which Virgil reviews his generic ascent.[1] But where Virgil never wrote another eclogue, *December* was not Spenser's final exercise in pastoral. Sixteen years later, in 1595, he published another pastoral volume, containing the long eclogue

---

1 *Ille ego qui quondam gracili modulatus avena / carmen et egressus silvis vicina coegi / ut quamvis avido parerent arva colono, / gratum opus agricolis, at nunc horrentia Martis / arma virumque cano ...* ('I am he who once played my song on a slender oaten reed, and leaving the woods made the neighbouring fields fruitful for the eager settler, a work welcome to farmers, but now of bristling arms and the man I sing ...'). The lines are imitated in *The Faerie Queene*'s opening stanza, I.Proem.1.

'Colin Clouts Come Home Againe', a pastoral elegy for Sidney entitled 'Astrophel', and several elegies for Sidney by fellow poets, three of which had previously appeared in *The Phoenix Nest* in 1593. The conception of the volume as a whole, and the substance of the two Spenserian poems which dominate it, engage deeply with Virgilian pastoral, and particularly with Virgil's tenth eclogue. In doing so, they revisit and revise the major themes of Virgil's pastoral work, including the very values enshrined in the notion of the generic ascent from pastoral to epic, and vaunt a radically new vision of the relation between the poet and political power. Eschewing the path taken by the *Aeneid* towards greater dependence on and compromise with the monarchical patron, they carve out a space in which the poet may wield an independent moral, social and religious authority, and act directly on a print-consuming public to right those ills complained of in the *Calender* and in the *Eclogues*' more critical strains.

Spenser's pastoral elegy for Sidney has received very little critical attention. When it is discussed, it is as a free-standing piece (including the 'Lay of Clorinda', the attribution of the latter to Mary Sidney now being widely recognized as a Spenserian fiction), and on those terms it is generally found slight and mediocre – suffering possibly in part from critical discomfort with its mixture of the serious mode of elegy with light Ovidian epyllion, and in part from comparison with *Nouember*'s more orthodox and more obviously artful exercise in pastoral elegy. Its function as part of a composite volume was not considered until Patrick Cheney's brief but suggestive piece in the 2010 *Oxford Handbook*.[2] Outside this essay, 'Colin Clouts Come Home Againe', too, is always discussed independently of the rest of the volume, and it is only relatively recently that this poem itself started to emerge from centuries of neglect, as critics began to perceive an overarching design and significance in what had often been dismissed as a rambling and disunified poem. When we consider the volume as a whole, however, a greater sense of unity

---

2 Patrick Cheney, '*Colin Clouts Come Home Againe, Astrophel,* and *The Doleful Lay of Clorinda*', in Richard McCabe (ed.), *Oxford Handbook of Edmund Spenser* (Oxford: Oxford University Press, 2010), pp. 237–55. See also, on the unity of the volume approached from a book-history perspective, Elizabeth Chaghafi, 'Spenser and Book History', in Paul Hecht and J. B. Lethbridge (eds), *Spenser in the Moment* (Teaneck, NJ: Fairleigh Dickinson University Press, 2015), pp. 67–99, at 75–95. Though Raphael Falco, *Conceived Presences: Literary Genealogy in Renaissance England* (Amherst: University of Massachusetts Press, 1994), refers to the volume as a whole (p. 106), it pays no attention to *Colin Clouts Come Home Againe* beyond noticing its mentions of Astrophel: in fact, Falco goes on to call the volume 'the *Astrophel* collection' (p. 191).

emerges – a unity in which even the elegies by other hands play a token role – and the relation between the poems adds both sharpness and depth to their key themes. (In my own effort to encourage a contextual sense of these poems as parts of a single volume, I have decided to break with critical tradition in the presentation of their titles. The title-page to the whole volume bears the title *Colin Clouts Come Home Againe*, and names the author as 'Ed. Spencer', with no mention of the other poems, or of the names of the authors of the other elegies for Sidney which follow 'Astrophel'. A dedicatory epistle to Ralegh, which seems to refer only to the eclogue 'Colin Clouts Come Home Againe' follows, immediately before the eclogue, with the title at its head, begins. After this, we have a separate title-page for 'Astrophel', with a separate dedication to Sidney's widow, by now Countess of Essex, but with no imprimatur or date, and therefore clearly never intended to be published separately. Other elegies for Sidney by other hands are then introduced, but with no separate title-page. I posit that 'Colin Clouts Come Home Againe' is intended *both* as the title of the first eclogue *and* as the title of the volume. Therefore I have chosen to use italics only when referring to the whole volume, and to refer to the individual poems within it by using quotation marks and not italics: thus, when I am talking about the opening eclogue, it will be 'Colin Clouts Come Home Againe'.) It is no accident that this holistic perspective also brings out Spenser's engagement in both his contributions with Virgil's tenth eclogue, the work which before all others underlies the conception of the volume. It is in 'Astrophel' that the relation to Virgil's poem is closest to the surface. For this reason, and also since of the two poems it is the more neglected and so the most likely to be overlooked, this is where we shall begin.

'Astrophel' is an elegy for a friend and fellow poet: that the subject was the poet's own friend is emphasized ('dearest vnto mee', 150), as is also the fact that he was a skilled poet himself (31–4). Among the prominent models for pastoral elegy available to Spenser, Theocritus' first idyll laments the death of the legendary poet Daphnis, but with no suggestion that Thyrsis knew him personally. Virgil's elegy for Daphnis in Eclogue 5, like many Renaissance elegies, is clearly for a political potentate, with no suggestion either of personal friendship or of shared poetic vocation. The *Lament for Bion* often ascribed to Moschus meets both criteria, as pseudo-Moschus laments a poet he describes as his teacher and precursor in pastoral song, frequently echoing Bion's own *Lament for Adonis* (a poem which itself has been identified as the source of several passages in 'Astrophel').³ But the author of the *Lament for Bion* is so hyperbolic in his praise of his subject – who, he suggests, excels all other poets of Greek antiquity, and even Pan himself – as to make his own claimed inheritance of Bion's skill sound insecure.⁴ This, as we shall see, is quite different from Spenser's tone regarding Sidney in 'Astrophel'. Much closer to Spenser's elegy is Virgil's lament for Gallus.

As we have already seen, Virgil's tenth eclogue is not a true elegy, because Gallus is not literally dead or dying in the poem: rather, he is imagined figuratively as dying from the pains of love, in what was to become the conventional stance of the poet–lover in amatory elegy, and which was almost certainly already a feature of his own elegies to his mistress 'Lycoris'. Virgil's poem clearly aligns this metaphorical death with the real deaths lamented in Theocritean pastoral elegy, however, by imitating and alluding to the elegy for Daphnis in Idyll 1 (as Servius points out), and (as we have also seen) to the sketch of a similar elegy in Idyll 7. As the very play on this elegiac trope suggests, Gallus' status as a skilled poet himself is fundamental to Virgil's poem. Servius tells us that the speech given to Gallus, which takes up half of the eclogue, contains quotations from Gallus' poems. When at lines 31–4 Gallus begs the Arcadian shepherds to sing his *amores*, he probably means not only to sing about his love but also to recite his elegies, which may well (like Ovid's later collection) have been titled *Amores*.⁵ The 'shepherd' Virgil, by echoing Gallus' poetry, is thus providing precisely the sort of consolation which Gallus

---

3 Merritt Y. Hughes, 'Greek Pastoral Triad'; T. P. Harrison, Jr, 'Spenser, Ronsard, and Bion'; Michael O'Connell, '*Astrophel*: Spenser's Double Elegy'. Hughes and Harrison are both sceptical about Spenser's direct knowledge of the Greek pastoralists, and prefer to see the influence as mediated through Virgil and the Pléiade poets. (This is unsurprising: the same Hughes, after all, was unable in his *Virgil and Spenser* to find any evidence that Spenser had more than the dimmest recollection of anything in Virgil beyond the pseudo-Virgilian *Ciris*.) But O'Connell points out that 'The Greek pastoral poets were available in a handy edition by Henri Estienne with Latin translations on facing pages, *Theocriti Aliorumque Poetarum Idyllia* (1579), which contained both Bion's Lament for Adonis and Moschus's Lament for Bion' (p. 28), and intriguingly suggests that 'Pentheia', Spenser's name for the flower into which Astrophel is transformed, may allude to the refrain of Moschus' *Lament for Bion* (p. 33).

4 I find Harold Bloom's theorization of literary influence as Oedipal 'anxiety' reductive and unhelpful when applied to many (or even most) imitative poets, but this is one case which it seems to fit well: the author of the *Lament for Bion* is notably not a 'strong poet' in Bloom's sense. See Harold Bloom, *The Anxiety of Influence: A Theory of Poetry* (Oxford: Oxford University Press, 1973).

5 A point first made by F. Skutsch, *Aus Vergils Frühzeit* (Leipzig: Teubner, 1901), pp. 23–4.

imagines the Arcadians' singing will bring him, enabling his bones to rest softly (33). In the course of reflecting wistfully that his life and loves would have been happier had he been a shepherd, reclining in the shade with some Phyllis or Amyntas, or inviting Lycoris herself to join him in his pastoral idyll, Gallus even fantasizes briefly about becoming a pastoral poet himself (50–4):

> Ibo, et, Chalcidico quae sunt mihi condita versu
> carmina, pastoris Siculi modulabor avena.
> certum est in silvis, inter spelaea ferarum
> malle pati, tenerisque meos incidere amores
> arboribus; crescent illae, crescetis, amores.

['I shall go, and the songs I composed in Chalcidian verse I shall play on the oaten reed of the Sicilian shepherd. Certainly it is better to suffer in the woods, among the dens of wild beasts, and to carve my loves on the young trees. You, my loves, will grow, as they will grow.']

The sylvan setting standing in here for the genre of Virgilian pastoral (*silvae* are a distinctive recurring feature of Virgil's landscape throughout the *Eclogues*), the suggestion is clearly that his sufferings are due in large part to his choice of genre, and that pastoral – partly because of the easy-going promiscuity of pastoral love, in which Phyllis and Amyntas and Lycoris are interchangeable – both expresses and fosters greater contentment and less acute pain than the self-destructive intensities of elegiac passion for a single mistress. The fantasy is renounced as Gallus realizes that it could not cure the insane extremity of his love (*nostri ... furoris*, l. 60), and he yields to the pitiless god Amor, bidding farewell to the pastoral *silvae* and to song itself. Virgil describes his eclogue as 'a few verses for my Gallus' (*pauca meo Gallo ... carmina*, 10.2–3), framing the whole as a gift of friendship, and ends with an emphasis on his love for his friend, which grows (73–4):

> tantum ... crescit in horas,
> quantum vere novo viridis se subicit alnus.

['by the hour, just as the green alder shoots up in the early spring.']

The reminiscence, in this arboreal image, of Gallus' earlier idea of carving his love on trees (53–4) suggests a comparison and contrast between Gallus' frenzied elegiac love and this sympathetic pastoral friendship. Meanwhile, the sympathy embodied in Virgil's gift, condoling with Gallus' sorrows and echoing his songs, is reflected in the pastoral landscape, which not only weeps as it did for Daphnis, but hears and 'responds' with echoes to the eclogue itself: *non canimus surdis, respondent omnia silvae* ('We do not sing to the deaf: all the woods respond', 8). Thus the eclogue combines three emphases. Firstly it is an elegy for a friend and fellow poet, and secondly it is a record of sympathetic friendship and exchange of song by imitation and as gift (an exchange itself recalling the pastoral tradition of amoebaean song).[6] Thirdly it represents a meeting of and negotiation between the different genres of pastoral and love elegy, in which the latter is characterized by self-destructive passion leading ultimately to the abandonment of song and to death, while the former is associated with consolation and with the inspiration of the Muses, and espoused by the author, but only as a prelude to his own renunciation of it in favour of higher genres.[7] All these aspects will be significant to our reading of Spenser's volume.

'Astrophel', as Raphael Falco has shown, marks a significant turning point in the posthumous image of Sidney in the emphasis it throws on his poetry rather than his military and diplomatic career.[8] But though Spenser's elegy presents Sidney as a shepherd 'borne in *Arcady*' (1), it insistently invokes not Sidney's pastoral *Arcadia* but his sonnet sequence *Astrophil and Stella*, simply relocating his amatory persona and relationship with his mistress in Spenser's own pastoral setting. It is as a sonneteer that Sidney is here remembered. Sidney's distinctive style in the sonnets is subtly evoked, as Michael O'Connell has shown.[9] Astrophel's relation to the pastoral setting is shifting and uneasy. We see him first in the conventional posture of a shepherd-poet of pastoral poetry, wandering 'About the grassie banckes of *Haemony*' (3) keeping his sheep. 'Haemony', actually an ancient name for Thessaly, is here imagined as a river, and we remember such scenes as Corydon and Thyrsis singing beside the Mincius in Virgil's seventh eclogue, Gallus wandering on the banks

---

6 Alpers, *Singer of the Eclogues*, pp. 127–8.
7 S. J. Harrison, *Generic Enrichment in Vergil and Horace* (Oxford: Oxford University Press, 2007), ch. 2; Colin G. Hardie, 'The Tenth Eclogue', *PVS* 6 (1967), 1–11.
8 Raphael Falco, 'Spenser's "Astrophel" and the Formation of Elizabethan Literary Genealogy', *Modern Philology* 91 (1993), 1–25. My reading of 'Astrophel' is indebted to Falco at many points.
9 O'Connell, 'Spenser's Double Elegy', 34, drawing attention to Sidney's frequent use of feminine rhyme, and his insistent use of repetition of words and phrases and of repetitive rhetorical *schema*. (On the latter, see Colin Williamson, 'Structure and Syntax in *Astrophil and Stella*', *RES* 31 (1980), 271–84.) Such echoes are, however, more subdued than we might expect in an elegy for a poet (contrast Ovid's *Amores* 3.9 on the death of Tibullus, or Virgil's tenth eclogue itself), for reasons which will become clear in our discussion of literary influence and the trope of fertility below.

of the Permessus in his sixth or Colin himself piping 'by the *Mullaes* shore' in 'Colin Clouts Come Home Againe' (59). Yet as we go on to hear of Astrophel's virtues as he grows up over the next three stanzas, pastoral references quickly fade from the picture. There is a reference to his learning to feed his mother's lambs at the beginning of the third stanza, but in the fourth it is not specifically 'all shepherds' but 'all men' who are won by his graces, and he is remarkable for being unassailable even by 'Spight it selfe that all good things doth spill', a foe not traditionally found among the shepherds of pastoral, but one which 'Colin Clouts Come Home Againe' has already taught us to associate with court, 'Where each one seeks with malice and with strife, / To thrust downe other into foule disgrace' ('Colin Clouts Come Home Againe', 690-1). By the fifth stanza it appears that the circle in which Astrophel shines is indeed the court, and not a pastoral community at all, for we are told (27-8) that

> he himselfe seemd made for merriment,
> Merily masking both in bowre and hall.

There are no bowers in pastoral poetry, and there are most certainly no halls – these are the traditional settings of courtly romance, and of course of the real entertainments put on for Elizabeth and her courtiers, in which Sidney often participated. Spenser allows the historical Sidney of the court to peep through the pastoral mask, and at the same time allows the momentary breach of generic decorum subtly but pointedly to bring the discrepancy between the two to our attention. For the original readers, coming to this poem immediately after reading 'Colin Clouts Come Home Againe', where such a contrast between the court and the 'shepheards nation' is so central a focus, the discrepancy would surely have carried distinctly sinister overtones. However 'innocent' Astrophel's 'ioyance' might appear, such a reader may well be reminded of the preceding eclogue's satire against courtiers who 'their dayes to ydlenesse diuide, / Or drownded lie in pleasures wastefull well' (762-3), who compose love poetry 'But as a complement for courting vaine' (790), and rely on the gaudy display of wealth and gay garments to (726-8):

> purchase highest rowmes in bowre and hall:
> Whiles single Truth and simple honestie
> Do wander vp and downe despys'd of all.

A sense emerges that the pastoral fiction of Spenser's elegy may mask a morally tainted reality.

The following three stanzas focus on Astrophel's poetic gifts, and here we return firmly to a pastoral setting – indeed the passage specifically and strongly evokes Spenser's own earlier pastoral, *The Shepheardes Calender*. Astrophel's skill is now not to 'mask ... in bowre and hall' but to (31–3)

> pipe and daunce, and caroll sweet,
> Emongst the shepheards in their shearing feast:
> As Somers larke ...

The simile recalls Colin's reference to his 'pypes, that shrild as lowde as Larke' before they were broken from grief in the *Nouember* elegy (71), and through it Hobbinol's comparison of his own delight at Colin's former songs (which 'taught the byrds ... Frame to thy song their chereful cheriping') to that of the 'larke in Sommer dayes' (*June* 51–5). In the next stanza (41–2), the maidens' promise

> to dight for him,
> Gay chapelets of flowers and gyrlonds trim

if he will agree to make rhymes for them, or to name them in his rhymes, recalls the pastoral exchange of gifts for song so highlighted throughout the *Calender*, particularly the 'coloured chaplets' given by Dido to Lobbin in *Nouember* (115), the 'gaudy Girlonds' 'dight' for Rosalind in *June* (45) and all the floral gifts of *Aprill*. So do the presents of spring flowers and 'mellow fruit' brought by the nymphs in the next stanza, in a scene which is also strongly reminiscent of the *Calender* (43–8):

> And many a Nymph both of the wood and brooke,
> Soone as his oaten pipe began to shrill:
> Both christall wells and shadie groues forsooke,
> To heare the charmes of his enchanting skill.
> And brought him presents, flowers if it were prime,
> Or mellow fruit if it were haruest time.

The whole stanza recalls the same speech by Hobbinoll in *June*, where he relates (57–64) how

> I sawe *Calliope* wyth Muses moe,
> Soone as thy oaten pype began to sound,
> Theyr yuory Luyts and Tamburins forgoe:
> And from the fountaine, where they sat around,
> Renne after hastely thy siluer sound.
> But when they came, where thou thy skill didst showe,
> They drewe abacke, as halfe with shame confound,
> Shepheard to see, them in theyr art outgoe.

In all of this, there are crucial differences at work. The lark simile in the *Calender* only ever occurs in the context of remembering the songs of happier days which are now no longer possible to an embittered and grief-stricken Colin. The gifts of chaplets and garlands in the *Calender* are, as we saw in Chapter 2, always tributes *to* the mistress or the potentate, and used to mark conspicuously the recipient's failure to reciprocate the gift. The single exception, the 'chaplets' once given by Dido to Lobbin, is grimly qualified by being consigned to the past (for 'nought remaynes' of them 'but the memoree' (*Nouember* 121), and as I have argued to a past that was never actual, but only optative. And where the nymphs offer concrete rewards of flowers and fruit to Astrophel, the similar scene in *June* showed them recoiling in apparent scorn and envy on finding that the musician was a simple shepherd – a moment leading Colin to refer to the more damaging jealousy of Apollo in his competitions with Pan and Marsyas. Astrophel, it would seem, is blessed with the same poetic gift as Colin, but has none of his cause for complaint.

Yet this pastoral gift-exchange fails as surely as do those of *The Shepheardes Calender*. Where in the *Calender* this was owing to the ingratitude of Rosalind, however, here the scorn and ingratitude are Astrophel's (49–54):

> But he for none of them did care a whit,
> Yet wood Gods for them often sighed sore:
> Ne for their gifts vnworthie of his wit,
> Yet not vnworthie of the countries store.
> For one alone he cared, for one he sight,
> His lifes desire, and his deare loues delight.

The stanza is marked by the kind of ironic reservations and corrections which will emerge as characteristic of the poem, quietly but insistently marking the distance between the attitude of the protagonist and the judgement of the narrator. The first 'Yet' clause, recalling Priapus' reminder to Daphnis in Theocritus' first idyll that he is foolish to die (whether from an unrequited love or a resistance to love – the situation is not explained, and the mythological tradition varies) when a love-stricken woman is pursuing him, is ambivalent in tone. It could imply that Astrophel does an injustice to beauty which is worthy of love, but on the other hand it could equally imply approbation for Astrophel's discriminating taste and unspotted fidelity to his chosen Stella. The second 'Yet', similarly, could approvingly mark Astrophel's high standards and suitably high estimation of his own worth as truly excelling even the richest produce of the countryside. The alternative interpretation, by which Spenser is correcting Astrophel's underestimation of the worth of the gifts, is however a little more strongly present here: where the desirability of the nymphs and maidens was merely the subjective opinion of the (notoriously susceptible) wood-gods, it is stated as a matter of objective fact that their gifts are 'not vnworthie of the countries store'.[10]

The reason for Astrophel's scorn is his exclusive devotion to Stella (65-6):

> Her, and but her of loue he worthie deemed,
> For all the rest but little he esteemed

– and here too the indications are ambivalent. On one hand, the passage recalls Colin's great central paean to his love in 'Colin Clouts Come Home Againe':

> To her my thoughts I daily dedicate,
> To her my heart I nightly martyrize:
> To her my loue I lowly do prostrate,
> To her my life I wholly sacrifice:
> My thoughts, my heart, my loue, my life is shee,
> And I hers euer onely, euer one:
> One euer I all vowed hers to bee,
> One euer I, and others neuer none
> ('Colin Clouts Come Home Againe', 472-9)

with its repetitions and rhetorical schemes echoed closely in

> For one alone he cared, for one he sight,
> His lifes desire, and his deare loues delight ...
> To her he vowd the seruice of his daies,
> On her he spent the riches of his wit:
> For her he made hymnes of immortall praise,
> Of onely her he sung, he thought, he writ.
> ('Astrophel', 53-4, 61-4)

Who the object of Colin's love in the preceding eclogue may be is of course open to interpretation, though I shall argue with Burchmore and others that it is Spenser's new wife Elizabeth Boyle, celebrated in the *Amoretti* and *Epithalamium* in the same year.[11] But nevertheless, the reminiscence of this passage would seem to suggest sympathy and approval for such a love on the part of the narrator (since we

---

10 On the question of the worthiness of the gifts, see Falco, 'Spenser's "Astrophel"', 21.
11 David W. Burchmore, 'The Image of the Centre in "Colin Clouts Come Home Againe"', *RES* 28 (1977), 393-406.

are surely intended to regard Colin as the narrator of this poem). On the other hand, however, Astrophel's scorning of the rural gifts also recalls Colin's scorn for the gifts proffered by Hobbinol in *Januarye* because of his own desperate and unrequited love for Rosalind, and this love is consistently presented as foolish and self-destructive throughout the *Calender*.[12]

If we judge Astrophel's love by its fruits, the more negative implications are those which will ultimately emerge more strongly. It is already worth noting that, until Stella's display of grief after his death, there is no indication that she returns Astrophel's love. The fact that he 'sight' for her (53), indeed, suggests that the relationship is as painfully unfulfilled as it is in Sidney's *Astrophil and Stella*. In the sonnet sequence, Stella is a married woman, who virtuously resists Astrophil's adulterous advances. Sidney's sequence differs very markedly from Petrarch's, the original of the genre, in the unscrupulous tactics of its protagonist (who steals a kiss when his mistress is sleeping, berates himself for failing to seize the opportunity to rape her, and uses threatening and manipulative rhetoric throughout) and in his continuance in bondage to his own sexual desire, never achieving the transcendence of physical love afforded Petrarch's speaker after Laura's death. Indeed, Astrophil rhetorically exploits more Platonic or spiritual conceptions of love in the service of his attempted seduction, before cynically and humorously rejecting them: compare, for instance, sonnets 25 and 52. He thus remains in deep despair and suffering when Stella continues to refuse him.[13] In our context, the contrast with Spenser's own sonnet sequence, appearing in print in the same year as this pastoral volume, is also striking and surely relevant. Spenser's *Amoretti and Epithalamium*, while similarly eschewing the transcendence of physical love and the turn towards *contemptus mundi* of Petrarch in the *Rime sparse*, relate his successful wooing of his second wife. Her initial resistance and his suffering continue only until he has relinquished the selfish urge to mastery and the

---

12 It also (and particularly) recalls what Roche describes as the 'self-seeking demented hyperbole' of the recurring, refrain-like 'Only for you', 'Onely by you', 'Onely to you' etc. in Song 1 of *Astrophil and Stella*, 'the very extravagance of which turns the reader to the only One [God] to whom they rightly belong', revealing the 'idolatrous blasphemy' of Astrophil's love (Thomas P. Roche Jr, 'Astrophil and Stella: A Radical Reading', in Dennis Kay (ed.), *Sir Philip Sidney: An Anthology of Modern Criticism* (Oxford: Clarendon Press, 1987), pp. 185–226, at 204; the article was first published in *Spenser Studies* 3 (1982), 139–91).
13 See Roche, 'A Radical Reading'; A. Sinfield, 'Astrophil's Self-Deception', *EIC* 28 (1978), 3–17.

violent and manipulative rhetoric evident in the earlier sonnets (and reminiscent of Sidney's Astrophil), and thereafter the sequence ends with the consummation in marriage of a mutual love presented as a reflection of the reciprocal love between God and man.[14] The unhappiness of Spenser's persona at the beginning of his sequence is thus revealed in retrospect to have been a symptom and consequence of moral and spiritual blindness.

Astrophel's sighing at line 53 of the elegy is the first explanation we have in the poem of a curious note struck in its initial description of him, where he is said to excel other shepherds in every way but one (9–12):

> Far passing all the pastors of his daies,
> In all that seemly shepheard might behoue.
> In one thing onely fayling of the best,
> That he was not so happie as the rest.

This 'happy' is ambiguous, and so piques the reader's curiosity. On one hand, it may mean 'fortunate', and refer forwards to his early death. On the other, it may mean 'contented', and refer to his present mental and emotional state. The true identification of either kind of felicity will become a focal concern later in the poem, at lines 79–80 ('in hunting such felicitie, / Or rather infelicitie he found'), and again at 101 ('Full happie man (misweening much) was hee'), where Astrophel explicitly misjudges what constitutes good fortune and happiness. In 'Colin Clouts Come Home Againe', too, a quibble over the word 'happy' marks the turning point of the poem from praise to satire, as Colin answers Thestylis' question, 'Why didst thou euer leaue *that happie place* ...?' (654) by revealing the 'enormities ...'

> The which in Court continually hooued,
> And followd those *which happie seemd to bee*.
> ('Colin Clout', 665–6; my italics)

The question of what we perceive as our own happiness is evidently an important one to Spenser in this volume and at this point in time, and one with moral ramifications connected to his critique of contemporary court culture. Here it is tempting to read Astrophel's unhappiness as a reference to the moral condition and resultant mental state of Sidney's persona in *Astrophil and Stella*, and to see

---

14 Dasenbrock, 'The Petrarchan Context of Spenser's Amoretti'; W. C. Johnson, 'Gender Fashioning and the Dynamics of Mutuality in Spenser's *Amoretti*', *English Studies* 74 (1993), 503–19; Klein, 'Protestant Marriage and the Revision of Petrarchan Loving in Spenser's *Amoretti*'.

Spenser as implying a comparison between those sonnets and the effusions of Cynthia's corrupt courtiers (776-92):

> For all the walls and windows there are writ,
> All full of loue, and loue, and loue my deare,
> And all their talke and studie is of it.
> Ne any there doth braue or valiant seeme,
> Vnlesse that some gay Mistresse badge he beares:
> Ne any one himselfe doth ought esteeme,
> Vnlesse he swim in loue vp to the eares.
> But they of loue and of his sacred lere,
> (As it should be) all otherwise deuise,
> Then we poore shepheards are accustomd here,
> And him do sue and serue all otherwise.
> For with lewd speeches and licentious deeds,
> His mightie mysteries they do prophane,
> And vse his ydle name to other needs,
> But as a complement for courting vaine.
> So him they do not serue as they professe,
> But make him serue to them for sordid vses.

This may seem excessively jaundiced in relation to the way Astrophel's love is depicted in the elegy, which is never openly condemnatory, but the hints we have seen connecting Astrophel with the court are real enough, and the point should seem more plausible when considered in relation to Sidney's own deeply ironic treatment of his persona in the sonnet sequence – an intertext which Spenser would surely have expected his readers to bear in mind. Another notable feature of that persona is his evident and continuous concern – despite his claims to be oblivious to anything but his desire for Stella – for his competitive relationships with other male courtiers (see for instance his bragging about the stolen kiss in sonnet 74, and Stella's plea in sonnet 81 that he will not thus destroy her reputation). Sidney's sonnets were themselves, of course, circulated in manuscript at court (their only form of publication until the unauthorized print edition in 1591), and seem therefore to have been conceived largely as 'homosocial' exercise, a means of displaying Sidney's wit for the purpose of self-promotion in that competitive environment.[15] With their identification of Stella

---

15 This is not to suggest that Astrophil's display of wit is identical to Sidney's, however: through his ironic persona, Sidney shows at once that he is capable of Astrophil's rhetorical ingenuity *and* that he has the wit and judgement to reveal and satirize its moral failings through humour at the expense of his persona. Where Astrophil's wit is slave to his 'infected will', Sidney's 'erected wit' shows us something better (to use the terms of the *Apologie*). For the concept of 'homosocial desire' underlying

as Penelope Devereux, Lady Rich, in the puns of sonnets 24 and 35, which would have been scandalous if the narrative had been taken as true, it indeed seems unlikely that their readers were intended to take them as anything more than such an exercise. It seems likely that Sidney himself might not have demurred from the suggestion that his sonnet sequence used the 'ydle name' of love 'for other needs, / But as a complement for courting vaine' ('Colin Clouts Come Home Againe' 789–90).

The hunting expedition which proves Astrophel's doom is conceived as a means of wooing Stella, as described in a stanza which once again, and more explicitly, highlights the gap between Astrophel's judgement and values and those of the narrator (67–72):

> Ne her with ydle words alone he wowed,
> And verses vaine (yet verses are not vaine)
> But with braue deeds to her sole seruice vowed,
> And bold atchieuements her did entertaine.
> For both in deeds and words he nourtred was,
> Both wise and hardie (too hardie alas).

The parenthetical 'yet' clause here carries no possible ambiguity: it is a direct contradiction by the narrator of the view (evidently that of Astrophel) that words are idle and verses vain. Despite the serious tone with which Astrophel's poems for Stella were described in the previous stanza as 'hymnes of immortall praise' (63), we discover here that he actually regards poety as a trivial and valueless pursuit, or at the least yields easily to social pressure (whether emanating from Stella or from his wider community) to concede that it is so.[16] It would seem that Astrophel and the court society to which he belongs conceive of poetry as merely a part of that merry 'masking both in bowre and hall' in which he shines. Thus Astrophel progresses to 'braue deeds' as more worthy and significant, reflecting what Richard Helgerson has influentially identified as the 'prodigal' career trajectory typical of the generation of English poets immediately preceding Spenser, for whom poetry merely furnished a medium in which they could advertise their wit and rhetorical skill as a means of obtaining, and before progressing to, some form of public office.[17] This *vita activa* commonly deemed worthier than poetic production takes

---

love-poetry, see Eve Kosofsky Sedgwick, *Between Men: English Literature and Male Homosocial Desire* (New York: Columbia University Press, 1985).
16 Falco, 'Spenser's "Astrophel"', 13, 19.
17 Richard Helgerson, *The Elizabethan Prodigals* (Berkeley: University of California Press, 1976) and *Self-Crowned Laureates*.

the form here, and in Sidney's life, of a military venture, and the way the elegy presents it shows little admiration for such exploits.[18] Presented as a hunting expedition, it appears as merely a particularly dangerous example of the competitive 'sports' in which Astrophel is accustomed to 'vanquish' his peers, like 'wrestling', 'renning' and 'swimming' (73–4). It is a 'perilous game' (91), undertaken to 'entertaine' Stella (70) – and thus itself emerges as nothing more noble than another form of that 'meriment' by which the court recreates itself. No mention is made of any principle or objective motivating the venture, to correspond to the Protestant aims of the military intervention in the Netherlands in which Sidney fell, beyond Astrophel's 'proud desire of praise', seeking 'His mistresse name, and his own fame to raise' (86, 88). If the pride here is already morally dubious, Astrophel soon emerges as not only reckless but also culpably cruel (111–12):

> Ill mynd so much to mynd anothers ill,
> As to become vnmyndfull of his owne.

'Ill mynd' is the most open condemnation of Astrophel in the poem, and it is open indeed. What is evinced here is not so much Spenser's low opinion (despite his strong Protestant sympathies) of Leicester's campaign in the Netherlands (even though by this time it was widely regarded as having been a failure), but rather his rejection of the set of values, characteristic of the 'prodigal' generation, by which military exploits were considered as inherently more worthy than the writing of poetry. Even in Sidney's *Apologie for Poetry*, poetry is praised as 'the companion of the camps', and the virtuous action which it inspires is repeatedly associated with military action.[19] Here, such military endeavour is shown to be no more than prideful homosocial competitiveness and cruel violence when not inspired or necessitated by a valid political goal. The question of the rights and wrongs of the particular campaign are bracketed off, so that the relative value of poetry and the military *vita activa* can be considered directly. Coming to this poem immediately after 'Colin Clouts Come Home Againe', the reader's understanding of the parenthetical 'yet verses are not vaine' will meanwhile be freighted with that poem's demonstration of the poet's valuable and influential public role as 'Priest' and teacher of society – a demonstration which triumphantly bears out

---

18 Falco, 'Spenser's "Astrophel"', 11–13.
19 See Robert W. Maslen's introduction to *An Apology for Poetry*.

Spenser's understated claim in the dedicatory letter to Ralegh that a poem can constitute proof that its author is 'not alwaies ydle as yee thinke'. It is the potential to fulfil just such a role – and not merely to facilitate courtly 'meriment' – which Astrophel has thrown away by losing his life in this rash and foolish venture.

It is at this point, when Astrophel is lying wounded on the field of battle, that a clear allusion marks the relation of Spenser's elegy to Virgil's tenth eclogue (127–32).

> Ah where were ye this while his shepheard peares,
> To whom aliue was nought so deare as hee:
> And ye faire Mayds the matches of his yeares,
> Which in his grace did boast you most to bee?
> Ah where were ye, when he of you had need,
> To stop his wound that wondrously did bleed?

The lines are obviously intended to be recognizable as an imitation of lines 9–12 of Virgil's poem:

> Quae nemora, aut qui vos saltus habuere, puellae
> Naides, indigno cum Gallus amore peribat?
> nam neque Parnasi vobis iuga, nam neque Pindi
> ulla moram fecere, neque Aoniae Aganippe.

['What forests, or what mountain passes, did you keep, you virgin nymphs, while Gallus was perishing from an intolerable love? For neither any peak of Parnassus nor of Pindus caused you to delay, nor Aonian Aganippe.']

Virgil's lines themselves are based on the similar question in Theocritus' first idyll (66–9):

> πᾷ ποκ' ἄρ' ἦσθ', ὅκα Δάφνις ἐτάκετο, πᾷ ποκα Νύμφαι;
> ἦ κατὰ Πηνειῶ καλὰ τέμπεα; ἦ κατὰ Πίνδω;
> οὐ γὰρ δὴ ποταμοῖο μέγαν ῥόον εἴχετ' Ἀνάπω,
> οὐδ' Αἴτνας σκοπιάν, οὐδ' Ἄκιδος ἱερὸν ὕδωρ.

['Where were ye, nymphs, where were ye, when Daphnis was wasting? In the fair vales of Peneius or of Pindus? for surely ye kept not the mighty stream of Anapus, nor the peak of Etna, nor the sacred rill of Acis.']

But the motivation for the rebuke seems very different in the two poems. Ogilvie has suggested that Theocritus' local nymphs would have been able to save his Daphnis, had they been present in these Sicilian settings, because his death is a death from drowning in their waters: he interprets the river which enfolds Daphnis in line 140, and which has posed something of a riddle to commentators, as the

Sicilian river the Anapos referred to earlier in the idyll, rather than as a reference to the Styx, the more widely accepted reading.[20] (Thus the situation is analogous to that of Damon's song in Virgil's eighth eclogue, where the speaker ends by announcing that he will fling himself into the sea.) But Gallus is not in danger of drowning, so that there is no obvious reason why water nymphs should have been able to save him. But the eclogue has opened with Virgil invoking one particular nymph, Arethusa, to inspire his song, as if she were a muse, and now the expected haunts of these nymphs, Parnassus and the Aganippe, suggest that they are to be identified with the Muses. The Muses are often identified with nymphs in classical poetry.[21] This is indeed Servius' interpretation:

> quia diximus easdem esse nymphas quas etiam musas, videtur hoc dicere, quia, si cum ipso fuissent musae, id est si dedisset operam scribendis carminibus, non incidisset in tantas amoris angustias.

> ['because we say that these nymphs are the same as the muses. He seems to say this because, if the muses had been with him – that is, if he had paid attention to writing songs – he would not have perished in such agonies of love.']

In Servius' reading, the Muses are addressed because they would have been in a position to intervene to save Gallus, in the sense that dedication to them and to poetry would have prevented his amatory sufferings. The implication is that Gallus has actively chosen his self-destructive passion in preference to a poetic vocation.[22]

Vives picks up Servius' suggestion that Gallus' abandonment of his poetic vocation is to blame for his misfortunes, but elaborates it to produce a biographical allegory (implausible because guilty of anachronism). He reads Gallus' love for Lycoris as an allegory for his relationship with Augustus, her desertion of him representing Gallus' fall from favour after the accusation that he had been involved in a plot against the emperor, and the metaphorical love-death as Gallus' enforced suicide. For Vives, the meaning of the eclogue is that Gallus would have survived and been happy if he had clung to the *vita contemplativa* of a poet, and never abandoned it for the *vita activa* which exposed him to the envy and malicious slander of the

---

20 Robert M. Ogilvie, 'The Song of Thyrsis', *JHS* 82 (1962), 106–10. For the commoner reading, see Gow *ad loc.*
21 Pauly-Wissowa, *Real-Encyclopädie der klassischen Altertumswissenschaft*, s.v. 'Musai'.
22 Hardie, 'The Tenth Eclogue'.

political class.[23] Vives' reading requires an impossibly late date for the eclogues, which were actually composed long before Gallus' death, and it seems probable that Spenser would have realized this. But it also seems likely that this widely available commentary, which makes the tenth eclogue into a real elegy for a fellow poet actually and not merely metaphorically dead, may have caught Spenser's attention as he planned his elegy for Sidney. The notion that Virgil is gently chastising Gallus for abandoning his poetic calling he would certainly have known from Servius. Vives' further notion that it is abandoned not merely in favour of passionate love but in the pursuit of public life and courtly advancement also resonates suggestively with Spenser's portrayal of Astrophel. In Spenser's elegy Astrophel's love remains a literal love (like that of Servius' Gallus), but although it is not an allegory for the courtly public life (as in Vives' reading), it is nevertheless presented as a symptom of it.

Now, both Servius' and Vives' interpretations are surely inspired by reading the tenth eclogue in connection with Gallus' earlier appearance in Virgil's book. For at the climax of Silenus' song in the sixth eclogue we find him again, a lone Roman figure in a catalogue of Greek myths, undergoing a ceremony of poetic initiation (64–73).[24]

> Tum canit, errantem Permessi ad flumina Gallum
> Aonas in montis ut duxerit una sororum,
> utque viro Phoebi chorus adsurrexerit omnis;
> ut Linus haec illi, divino carmine pastor,
> floribus atque apio crinis ornatus amaro,
> dixerit: 'Hos tibi dant calamos, en accipe, Musae,
> Ascraeo quos ante seni, quibus ille solebat
> cantando rigidas deducere montibus ornos:
> his tibi Grynei nemoris dicatur origo,
> ne quis sit lucus, quo se plus iactet Apollo.'

['Then he sings of how, as Gallus wandered by the rivers of Permessus, one of the sisters led him into the Aonian mountains, and of how the whole choir of Phoebus rose in the man's honour; of how Linus, the shepherd of divine song, his hair adorned with flowers and bitter

---

23 *In publii Vergilii Maronis Bucolica interpretatio, potissimum allegorica*, C6v.
24 The initiation scene forms part of a 'poetic genealogy', as Ross describes it, which Virgil constructs through allusion and imitation in Eclogue 6 (*Backgrounds to Augustan Poetry*, pp. 27–33, at p. 27). The line descends from Apollo, through Orpheus and Linus, to Gallus, taking in Callimachus and the Alexandrian poets beloved of the neoterics on the way, and 'delicately ... include[s]' Virgil himself (J. P. Elder, '*Non iniussa cano*: Virgil's Sixth Eclogue', *Harvard Studies in Classical Philology* 65 (1961), 109–25, cited by Ross above).

parsley, said to him "The Muses give you these pipes – see, take them – which once they gave to the old Ascraean, with which as he played he used to draw the hard ash-trees down the mountains. With these let the origin of the Grynean wood be told by you, so that there shall be no sacred grove in which Apollo takes more glory."']

The passage begins firmly in the pastoral register, with Gallus in the traditional position of the shepherd-poet who wanders along the banks of a river, tending his sheep. This was one of the examples we invoked as an analogy for Astrophel keeping his sheep 'About the grassie bancks of *Haemony*' at the beginning of Spenser's elegy. But Gallus is no mere shepherd, and the scene quickly threatens to burst the bounds of the pastoral mode as the Muses themselves lead him to the Aonian mount, and the divine singer Linus bestows on him the pipes of Hesiod, here described as wielding the Orphic power to draw trees down the mountain-side. This is the same son of Apollo whom Virgil boasts that he will equal, if he should live to sing one day of the mature deeds of the miraculous child heralded in Eclogue 4 (55–7). Virgil is alluding to the opening of Hesiod's *Theogony*, where he tells how he received his poetic vocation. While still a real, humble shepherd, he encounters the Muses as he tends his flock, and is given a staff (not, as in Virgil, a set of pipes) and inspiration to divine song. Thereafter, Hesiod becomes the author of the *Theogony* and the *Works and Days*, an epic and a large-scale didactic poem on farming, respected as highly as Homer by Virgil's contemporaries. (Hesiod was indeed taken as the preferred model by Callimachus, whose poetics were especially revered and followed by the Roman 'neoteric' poets of Virgil's generation.) It is just such an Hesiodic or Callimachean didactic and etiological poem which Gallus is instructed by Linus to sing. What we have here is a vision of an ascent to a higher genre, and in fact precisely the ascent that Virgil would make when he progressed from the *Eclogues* to the *Georgics*, a work whose obvious Greek forebear is the *Works and Days* of Hesiod. Though Servius assumes that Gallus must in reality have composed such a poem on this topic of the origins of Apollo's sacred grove at Grynea, and identifies it with the 'Chalcidian verse' Gallus refers to in the tenth eclogue (promising to rewrite it as pastoral), there is no evidence that he ever did write such a work, and from what Virgil went on to do it would seem that what he offers here is a recommendation and a statement of his own ambitions.

It is for this reason that the Muses of Aonian Aganippe could, in Eclogue 10, have been expected to take a special interest in their

Gallus' fate, yet as Servius notes they are conspicuously absent, and thus Gallus, unable to escape his obsession with love, bids farewell not only to pastoral but to poetry (62-3) and dies. Meanwhile, however, they are present in the frame of the tenth eclogue. The nymph Arethusa, as noted above, is invoked in place of a Muse at the beginning of the poem, where she is chosen because of her association, as a Sicilian nymph, with Theocritus, and specifically as the stream apostrophized by the dying Daphnis in Idyll 1. In the *Lament for Bion*, pseudo-Moschus had already transformed her stream into the source of inspiration for pastoral poetry, corresponding to the Helicon as the source of Homer's epic inspiration.[25] At the close of the eclogue Virgil addresses the Muses directly as the *divae Pierides* (70-2), giving them charge of his song, and dubbing himself *vestrum poetam* (70). If Gallus has deserted the Muses and betrayed the vocation described in Eclogue 6, Virgil himself has taken up the mantle and been embraced by them.

The movement of Spenser's elegy clearly indicates a similar abandonment of true poetic vocation and waste of inspiration on Astrophel's part. At lines 31 to 48, as we have seen, Astrophel's poetic skill closely recalled that of Colin in *The Shepheardes Calender* – 'Colin, the shepheards ioye' (*August* 190), who has been 'watered at the Muses well' (*Nouember* 30); Colin whose skill, 'If that *Hobbinol* right iudgement bare', is, like Virgil's in the boast at the end of the fourth eclogue, superior even 'To *Pan* his owne selfe pype' (*December*, 45-6). The level of inspiration implicit in Astrophel's resemblance to Colin puts him on a par with the Gallus hailed by the Muses in Eclogue 6. We might remember too the more explicit tribute paid Sidney by Verlame in *The Ruines of Time* (332-6), where she imagines that

> thou now in *Elisian* fields so free,
> With *Orpheus*, and with *Linus* and the choice
> Of all that euer did in rimes reioyce,
> Conuersest, and doost heare their heauenlie layes,
> And they heare thine, and thine doo better praise.

evoking both Virgil's fourth eclogue (55-9) and Gallus' initiation in the sixth. But like the Gallus of Eclogue 10, Astrophel in the elegy renounces the Muses' gift, as a result both of a love of which the author does not seem entirely to approve (recalling Servius' interpretation of the eclogue) and of the misplaced ambitions and mistaken values which he absorbs from a corrupt courtly milieu (recalling

---

25 *Lament for Bion*, 71-84.

Vives' interpretation). By alluding to Virgil's lines on the absence of the Muses from the scene of Gallus' languishing, Spenser brings out the analogy between the two figures. To the reader who recognizes the allusion, it clinches and adds depth and coherence to the subtle hints of criticism with which he has coloured his portrayal of Astrophel – and Spenser could rely on many such readers in a period when Virgil's *Eclogues* were not only a supremely prestigious text but also one studied by all schoolboys from an early age.

The implicit contrast with Colin is also striking. It is true that Colin in the *Calender* broke his pipes and abjured poetry himself, but this was as a result of hardships to which Astrophel is not subject, receiving scorn and envy in place of the gifts and admiration which Astrophel receives from the nymphs and maidens, and which constitute the marked difference between the 'Astrophel' stanzas and the corresponding passages in the *Calender* to which they allude. Moreover, in 'Colin Clouts Come Home Againe' the reader has seen Colin triumphantly rededicated to his vocation, a confident conduit of divine song. In the narrative of that poem, Colin emerges unscathed from the temptations and corruption of Cynthia's court, maintaining his moral and poetic integrity, and fulfilling his potential to use his inspiration for the public good of his community. Astrophel, by contrast, has succumbed to the distorted value system of the court, with its focus on trivial pleasure and prideful rivalry, and as a result has failed to take his poetic vocation seriously, squandering his talent and throwing away his life. As Falco has argued, one of the central motivations underlying Spenser's elegy is to construct Sidney as a failed predecessor: 'By creating a flawed poetic original, Spenser illumines his own superior poetic achievement.'[26] In doing so, he is self-consciously and allusively imitating the use to which Virgil puts Gallus in his pastoral elegy for his friend.

When the Lay of Clorinda succeeds Colin's own lament, the tone shifts. There is a general consensus among most critics that the Lay is an act of ventriloquism, authored not by Mary Sidney (or 'Clorinda'), as Colin claims, but by Spenser himself. As we shall see, it is conspicuously and deeply indebted to Spenser's own earlier pastoral elegy in the *Nouember* eclogue (and responds, like that poem, to the elegy for Daphnis in Virgil's fifth eclogue); indeed we can say that, as in 'Astrophel' itself, Spenser's true subject here *is* his own poetry. Yet the notional change of speaker is striking and significant, and Clorinda's

---

26 Falco, 'Spenser's "Astrophel"', p. 25.

subject is different. An ironic gap is opened between the inconsolable grief of Astrophel's sister and the full meaning offered to readers.

The opening stanzas of the 'Dolefull Lay' bring out a stark difference between the speakers and the rhetorical situations of their songs. The speaker of 'Astrophel' (whom I have been calling Colin) opens his poem with an address to the shepherd community, begging them to 'place my dolefull plaint your plaints emong' (6), and anticipating that it will 'empierse' their hearts 'with dolours dart for death of *Astrophel*' (10). The version of the modesty topos which ensues imagines the possibility of a wider audience – evidently the audience of Spenser's print readers. Since his 'rymes bene rudely dight' (12), he knows they are fit only for an audience of shepherds, but he anticipates a greater one (13–18):

> Yet as they been, if any nycer wit
> Shall hap to heare, or couet them to read:
> Thinke he, that such are for such ones most fit,
> Made not to please the liuing but the dead.
> And if in him found pity euer place,
> Let him be moou'd to pity such a case.

His excuse for the alleged roughness of his style is that his poem does not seek approval or admiration from contemporaries as a literary work, indeed is not concerned at all with its contemporary reception, but is intended rather as a simple tribute to his 'dead' friend; yet he hopes none the less to achieve the same rhetorical effect on this wider audience which he anticipated among his fellow shepherds, moving them to pity. The reader of these lines, following on immediately as they do from 'Colin Clouts Come Home Againe', is evidently intended to identify this shepherd audience with the community which peopled that eclogue and was so large a part of its focus. This last stanza adds an idea which was encouraged but never stated in the previous poem, implying that this community – and Colin's rhetorical power and moral authority over it – extends to Spenser's wider readership wherever his books are seen. Colin is confident of a wide and attentive audience, sure in his rhetorical purpose, and sure too of his power to accomplish it.

By contrast, 'Clorinda' seeks only personal comfort for herself, and opens with a lengthy refusal to address any audience outside herself because none is capable of providing that comfort.

> Ay me, to whom shall I my case complaine,
> That may compassion my impatient griefe?

> Or where shall I vnfold my inward paine,
> That my enriuen heart may find reliefe?
> Shall I vnto the heauenly powres it show?
> Or vnto earthly men that dwell below?
>
> ('Lay of Clorinda' 1–6)

She can expect no sympathy from the heavens, which are the 'workers of my vnremedied wo' (8), and no comfort from men, who are 'like wretched' and themselves in need of comfort, because alike subject to mortality. She is therefore reduced to a solipsistic plaint:

> Then to my selfe will I my sorrow mourne,
> Sith none aliue like sorrowful remaines:
> And to my selfe my plaints shall back retourne,
> To pay their vsury with doubled paines.
> The woods, the hills, the riuers shall resound
> The mournfull accent of my sorrowes ground.
>
> ('Lay of Clorinda' 19–25)

The stanza is reminiscent of Colin's sestina in *August*, but the situation is very different. There, Colin was imprisoned in the sterile echo-chamber of his lonely song because of his reliance on a sympathy which was really denied – sympathy from a single source, the scornful Rosalind. But Clorinda's claim that none can compassion her grief because none fully share it is highly dubious: the lay has been introduced as merely the first of many laments made by the entire shepherd community, who 'euery one did make exceeding mone, / With inward anguish and great griefe opprest' ('Astrophel' 205–6), and will conclude with two stanzas introducing the elegies by other hands as similar 'dolefull layes', made 't'expresse their inward woe' ('Lay of Clorinda' 105–6). The image of the echoing woods returning her plaints, though most closely akin to the *Calender*'s sestina, also recalls the echoing landscape of Virgil's tenth eclogue: *non canimus surdis, respondent omnia silvae* ('We do not sing to the deaf: all the woods respond', 8). But there, as we have seen, the echo is part of a pervasive pattern of responsiveness running through the poem, which tempers the extremity of Gallus' woe with the consolatory assurance of sympathy – from the comforting singing of the Arcadians at 31–4, to the speaker's own echoes of Gallus' poems, and the very notion of his song as a gift for his friend. This reminiscence too, then, ironically highlights Clorinda's near-sightedness in her denial of the shared and communal nature of her grief. Indeed, if the memory of Virgil's echoing woods also reminds the reader that the whole of Virgil's eclogue is a gift of sympathetic friendship (because it is part of this same pattern of response and reciprocation), then the allusion also highlights the contrasting selfishness and self-absorption of Clorinda's song, made for herself alone.

Like Virgil in the tenth eclogue – though omitting the address to the absent Muses, with its critical implications – Clorinda passes on to the motif of the grieving landscape. This is a commonplace of pastoral elegy, familiar from the (central) eighth stanza of the elegy for Dido in *Nouember*, but also bearing a long classical pedigree. We have seen that Virgil's use of it at 10.13-15 is indebted to Theocritus' first and seventh idylls. It receives its fullest Virgilian treatment in Eclogue 5, where Mopsus at ll. 34-9 describes the barrenness of the countryside after Daphnis' death, and in Menalcas' reply the same landscape rejoices at his apotheosis, the very woods and mountains proclaiming *deus, deus ille, Menalca!* The trope is thus closely bound up in that eclogue with the hyperbole of political deification which we have seen subjected to such sceptical scrutiny in the *Calender*. Since the *Calender* is such a prominent intertext of the 1595 volume, and in the context of the other hints of Clorinda's lack of objectivity described above, it is possible to see this evocation of a piece of panegyric which Colin has already found suspect as implying that Clorinda's admiration for her dead brother is similarly exaggerated. In the context of Eclogue 10, meanwhile, the mourning woods and mountains occur in close proximity to the reference to the absent Muses, which as we have seen looks back to the scene of Gallus' investiture as a divine poet in Eclogue 6, where the same Muses gave him the pipes with which Hesiod drew trees down mountain-sides. The memory of this Orphic potential makes the animation of nature to mourn him in Eclogue 10 the more plausible. As we have seen, Astrophel too was once an inspired singer, his resemblance to Colin implying that he too had perhaps been 'watered at the Muses well' (*Nouember* 30). But Clorinda has not yet made any allusion to his being a poet, and when she does it will not be in such a way as to place great importance on it. Rather, her invocation of the commonplace of the mourning landscape takes a different turn, as we are told that the fields are mourning Astrophel as their 'fairest flowre', now lost. Though the trope progresses naturally enough (we might expect personified 'fields' to be grieved by the loss of their 'fairest flowre'), when read, as educated contemporaries would have read it, against its classical models it marks a surprising diminution. Where those models lead us to expect a reference to Astrophel's quasi-divine power over the landscape, like a Daphnis or an Orpheus, he is instead reduced to the status of its smallest and most vulnerable part. From an outcry against the loss of nature's informing and sustaining principle, the wailing of the fields is also reduced to the level of self-pity over a lost possession, recalling the implied selfishness of Clorinda's own grief. And indeed, beneath the artifice which is a given of such conventional tropes, we might see Spenser as implying another layer of artificiality, for by introducing the image of the mourning landscape *immediately and directly* through the image of the landscape as merely *echoing* the plaints of the isolated and self-absorbed Clorinda back to her, in the preceding stanza, the poem encourages us to speculate that the landscape is not animate, and not mourning, at all – that its apparent wailing is no more than a 'resound[ing]' of 'The mournfull accent' of Clorinda's sorrow. (23–4) The flower to which Astrophel is reduced, meanwhile, is the traditional, pathetic image of man's helpless mortality. Here it particularly echoes Colin's use of the same image in the elegy for Dido, 'the fayrest floure our gyrlond all emong' (*Nouember* 75), also evoking its development in the following stanza of that elegy as a highly generalized and conventional lament for mankind's mortal condition:[27]

> Whence is it, that the flouret of the field doth fade,
> And lyeth buryed long in Winters bale:
> Yet soone as spring his mantle hath displayd,
> It floureth fresh, as it should neuer fayle?
> But thing on earth that is of most auaile,
>   As vertues braunch and beauties budde,
>   Reliuen not for any good.
>
> (*Nouember* 83–9)

What is really being mourned here, the allusion may be taken to imply, is merely the condition of mortality common to all, not the death of an especially remarkable or important individual.

The echoes of *Nouember* now begin to flow thick and fast. The next stanza brings in that other dimension of the flower image as it was employed in the *Calender*, the garlands of the 'shepherd lasses' and their replacement in *Nouember* with funeral wreaths. *Nouember* makes great play on the fate of the floral tributes and garlands offered to Elisa by the 'shepheards daughters', nymphs and Muses in the *Aprill* lay:

---

27 Spenser was there drawing this image from pseudo-Moschus, *Lament for Bion*, 99–104.

> The gaudie girlonds deck her graue,
> The faded flowres her corse embraue ...
>
> The water Nymphs, that wont with her to sing and daunce,
> And for her girlond Oliue braunches beare,
> Now balefull boughes of Cypres doen advaunce:
> The Muses, that were wont greene bayes to weare,
> Now bringen bitter Eldre braunches seare ...
>
> *(Nouember* 107–9; 143–7)

The echoes in Clorinda's 'Dolefull Lay' are very conspicuous:

> Breake now your gyrlonds, O ye shepheards lasses,
> Sith the faire flowre, which them adornd, is gon:
> The flowre, which them adornd, is gone to ashes,
> Neuer againe let lasse put gyrlond on.
> In stead of gyrlond, weare sad Cypres nowe,
> And bitter Elder, broken from the bowe.
>
> ('Lay of Clorinda' 37–42)

In the *Calender*, as we saw, the floral tributes were carefully developed throughout the volume as a symbol of the hopes of Elizabeth's Protestant subjects and the trust they placed in her at her coronation, now dashed by her apparent abandonment of their cause with the plan to marry the Duc d'Alençon. The invocation of the same pattern of imagery here invites a comparison to that situation. Not only is the emphasis thrown again on to the sense of waste and squandered hopes in Astrophel's needless death, but we may infer that the mourning of Sidney in the present volume similarly functions as a conduit for the communal mourning of wider social ills. Even Clorinda will finally realize – after the consolatory vision of Astrophel's soul happily ensconced in heaven – that she and the other elegists are 'Mourning in others, our owne miseries' (96). As befits her self-absorbed grief, she defines that misery only as 'his priuate lack' (89), and the sense which emerges strongly in 'The Mourning Muse of Thestylis' (first of the elegies by other hands to follow 'Astrophel' – the author is Lodowick Bryskett) that Sidney's death is a synecdoche for the lamentable loss of heroic Protestant spirit from Elizabethan politics is absent from her lay. Prompted, however, by memory of the mood of *Nouember* and the social criticism in which it played so important a part, the first readers of the volume are very likely to have connected this grief with the bleak view of affairs at Cynthia's court offered in 'Colin Clouts Come Home Againe', and its more veiled satire of the dominant influence of Lord Burghley in the 1590s.[28]

But the ensuing echoes of Spenser's earlier poetry develop and qualify this suggested resemblance to the earlier satirical intent of the *Calender* in interesting ways. The next stanza echoes *Nouember*'s

> Sing now ye shepheards daughters, sing no moe
> The songs that Colin made in her prayse,
> But into weeping turne your wanton layes,
>
> (*Nouember* 77–9)

but again with a striking diminution of effect. There, the inappropriateness of such songs as *Aprill*'s lay for Elisa arose not merely from a difference in mood resulting from personal grief but from a disastrous change in the political situation and a threat to society as a whole. Moreover, even as the praise of the *April* lay is consigned to the past, its author is singing a new song to reflect that change and its effect on the community, as part of a volume in which Spenser seeks through warning satire to avert the threat. (We might even argue that he did so successfully, as canto viii of the first book of *The Faerie Queene* seems to suggest.)[29] Astrophel's songs, by contrast, are consigned to the past for quite different reasons (43–8):

> Ne euer sing the loue-layes which he made:
> Who euer made such layes of loue as hee?
> Ne euer read the riddles, which he sayd
> Vnto your selues, to make you mery glee.
> Your mery glee is now laid all abed,
> Your mery maker now alasse is dead.

The songs remembered here are such poems as *Astrophil and Stella*, presented as composed for trivial recreational purposes—the courtly 'meriment' of 'masking both in bowre and hall', which was Astrophel's occupation at the beginning of *Astrophel* (27–8). Their current inappropriateness is merely a result of their inadequacy to any situation but that of trivial merrymaking, their failure to aspire to any status or social purpose higher than mere entertainment. They do not fit the mood. Moreover, the dismissal of Astrophel's songs comes as a shock in the context of an elegy for a poet. In Virgil's tenth eclogue, we recall, Gallus is comforted by the thought that Arcadians will continue to sing his verses, and indeed it is usual in elegy for a dead writer to allude to the immortality of his work. In the *Lament for*

---

28 On the satire against Burghley, see Linn Kelsey, 'Spenser, Ralegh, and the Language of Allegory', *Spenser Studies* 17 (2003), 183–213.
29 Pugh, *Spenser and Ovid*, pp. 67–8; 'Reinventing the Wheel'.

Bion, for instance, Bion's potential successors, and even Pan himself, do not dare to touch his pipes 'For thy lips and thy breath live yet, and in those straws the sound of thy song is quick' (53ff.). Compare again Callimachus' Epigram 2, on the death of Heraclitus:

> αἱ δὲ τεαὶ ζώουσιν ἀηδόνες, ἧσιν ὁ πάντων
> ἁρπακτὴς Ἀίδης οὐκ ἐπὶ χεῖρα βαλεῖ.
>
> ['Still are thy pleasant voices, thy nightingales, awake;
> For Death, he taketh all away, but them he cannot take.']³⁰

In Ovid's lament for Tibullus (*Amores* 3.9) we are told that songs escape the funeral pyre, and the closing vision of Tibullus adding to the 'numbers' of the blessed shades in a poet's Elysium significantly echoes Ovid's earlier promise (*Amores* 1.15) that Tibullus' poetic 'numbers' will be learnt by all succeeding generations.[31] For a familiar English example, we might look to Jonson writing of Shakespeare for the 1623 folio edition of his works: 'Thou art alive still while thy book doth live, / And we have wits to read and praise to give.' That Clorinda, in such a context, echoes the 'Sing no moe' figure of *Nouember* instead of an assurance that Astrophel's songs will survive and continue to be sung is a conspicuous disappointment of readerly expectations, and one explained by the (supposed) shortcomings of those songs, to which she unwittingly calls our attention.

But if Astrophel's poetic production while alive was too trivial in its ambitions to earn a promise of immortality, Clorinda's ensuing vision imagines him as the recipient, in heaven, of a nobler inspiration. Once more the progress of the 'Dolefull Lay' follows that of the *Nouember* elegy, in its passage from mourning to the consolatory Christian vision of the soul's ascent to heaven. In fact the turn happens at precisely the same point: if we consider Clorinda's elegy proper as extending up until line 90 (with the final, deflationary stanza in her voice, addressing Sidney directly, as a kind of coda), it is like the elegy for Dido fifteen stanzas long, and the heavenly vision begins at stanza 12, the point in the *Nouember* elegy where Colin's refrain switched from 'heauie' to 'happye', 'carefull' to 'ioyfull'. But where Colin told merely of Dido's spirit walking among the saints in Elysian fields, Clorinda gives us a much fuller and more detailed

---

30 Trans. William Johnson Cory, in T. F. Higham and C. M. Bowra (eds), *The Oxford Book of Greek Verse in Translation* (Oxford: Clarendon Press, 1942), p. 584.
31 Pugh, 'Supping With Ghosts: Imitation and Immortality in Herrick', in Ruth Connolly and Tom Cain (eds), *'Lords of Wine and Oile': Community and Conviviality in the Poetry of Robert Herrick* (Oxford: Oxford University Press, 2011), pp. 220–49, at 222–6.

account of what Astrophel's spirit enjoys. The passage is rich and worth quoting at length (67–88):

> Ah no: it is not dead, ne can it die,
> But liues for aie, in blisfull Paradise:
> Where like a new-borne babe it soft doth lie.
> In beds of lillies wrapt in tender wise.
> And compast all about with roses sweet,
> And daintie violets from head to feet.
>
> There thousand birds all of celestiall brood,
> To him do sweetly caroll day and night:
> And with straunge notes, of him well vnderstood,
> Lull him a sleep in Angelick delight;
> Whilest in sweet dreame to him presented bee
> Immortall beauties, which no eye may see.
>
> But he them sees and takes exceeding pleasure
> Of their diuine aspects, appearing plaine,
> And kindling loue in him aboue all measure,
> Sweet loue still ioyous, neuer feeling paine.
> For what so goodly forme he there doth see,
> He may enioy from iealous rancor free.
>
> There liueth he in euerlasting blis,
> Sweet spirit neuer fearing more to die:
> Ne dreading harme from any foes of his,
> Ne fearing saluage beasts more crueltie.
> Whilest we here wretches waile his priuate lack,
> And with vaine vowes do often call him back.

Astrophel is here the recipient of visions with strong neoplatonic overtones, visions of divine beauty kindling pure but fervent love in his soul. It is reminiscent of the allusions to neoplatonic love in *Astrophil and Stella*, which were, however, there repeatedly undercut and actively rejected by Astrophil in his recalcitrant lustfulness. This newly neoplatonic love experienced by Astrophel's soul is fully consummated, although (and because) it is independent of the flesh: it is the pure love of the soul offered by Stella in sonnets 62 and 69, but there scorned by her lover. It is therefore free of the 'paine' and 'iealous rancor' which so tormented Astrophil in the sonnet sequence. It is the stuff of potential 'loue-layes' (43) different to those Sidney actually wrote, a sonnet sequence with a more serious – or at least a more direct – moral and didactic purpose.[32] But even were

---

32 Here as throughout the poem I see Spenser as wilfully misrepresenting *Astrophil*

Astrophel's soul in heaven to translate these visions and this love into such purer lays, they could not be transmitted to an audience on earth, except through Clorinda's second-hand imaginings (which themselves are not intended for any audience beyond herself). We are reminded of *Nouember*'s insistence on the radical disjunction between the joys experienced by Dido in heaven and the sufferings of those left on earth, and its striking omission of any suggestion that she might intercede in or influence worldly affairs after her death, as Daphnis/Caesar is said to do in Virgil's fifth and ninth eclogues.

Yet, at the same time (and unintentionally on Clorinda's part, though intentionally on Spenser's), the passage reminds us forcefully of another poet who has already successfully transmitted such visions, without having to die first in order to enjoy them. That poet is Spenser himself. The peculiar image of Astrophel's soul lying 'like a new-borne babe' wrapped and compassed in flowers strikingly evokes the Garden of Adonis as described in Book III of *The Faerie Queene*, published in 1590, with its 'thousand thousand naked babes' (III.vi.32.3), 'planted' (33.2) among its 'goodly flowres' (30.1). The carolling birds of the following stanza are a familiar component of the conventional *locus amoenus*, but also recall the Garden of Adonis, where 'the ioyous birdes ... their true loues without suspition tell abrode' (42.7–9). The suggestively sexual image of Astrophel 'tak[ing] exceeding pleasure' of the 'Immortall beauties' in the next stanza evokes the perpetual lovemaking of Venus and Adonis in the bower at the centre of the Garden. His freedom from 'iealous rancor' (84) is that of the denizens of the Garden, who enjoy their loves 'Without fell rancor, or fond gealosie' (III.vi.41.6), and also of those of the Temple of Venus in Book IV of *The Faerie Queene*, which was to be published the following year (see IV.x.28.5), while his immunity to death and any future 'harme' from 'saluage beasts' in the next recalls the same immunity on the part of Adonis (48.1–6).

> There now he liueth in eternall blis,
> Ioying his goddesse, and of her enioyd:

---

and Stella, in which Sidney's exposure of Astrophil's moral shortcomings amounts to a satire with moral purpose. That Spenser in reality appreciated Sidney's irony at the expense of his persona, and its didactic function, is amply suggested by his treatment of his own speaker in the *Amoretti*, progressing, under the tutelage of his beloved, from the ironically portrayed aggression of the earlier sonnets to the Christian love with which the volume ends. See note 14 above. Spenser's identification of Sidney with his sonnet-persona in *Astrophel* is, among other things, a means to further his goal of presenting Sidney as a 'failed predecessor' in order to advance his own claims (Falco, 'Spenser's "Astrophel"', 14).

> Ne feareth he henceforth that foe of his,
> Which with his cruell tuske him deadly cloyd:
> For that wilde Bore, the which him once annoyd,
> She firmely hath emprisoned for ay,
> That her sweet loue his malice mote auoyd,
> In a strong rocky Caue, which is they say,
> Hewen vnderneath that Mount, that none him losen may.

The vision of the Garden of Adonis is a climactic one in the first instalment of Spenser's epic – though remarkable for its transcendence of the political goals we associate with the motivating visions of the *Aeneid* and epics in the Virgilian mould.[33] But the Garden of Adonis is not restricted to Spenser's epic poetry. It figures also in the visionary *pastoral* poetics of 'Colin Clouts Come Home Againe', where it introduces the great hymn to love which forms the climax of the eclogue, as we hear of the birth of Cupid:

> For him the greatest of the Gods we deeme,
> Borne without Syre or couples of one kynd,
> For *Venus* selfe doth soly couples seeme,
> Both male and female though commixture ioynd.
> So pure and spotlesse *Cupid* forth she brought,
> And in the gardens of *Adonis* nurst ...
>
> ('Colin Clout' 799–804)

Cuddy recognizes Colin's discourse as a divinely inspired vision:

> Shepheard it seemes that some celestiall rage
> Of loue (quoth *Cuddy*) is breath'd into thy brest,
> That powreth forth these oracles so sage,
> Of that high powre, wherewith thou art possest....
> Well may it seeme by this thy deep insight,
> That of that God the Priest thou shouldest bee:
> So well thou wot'st the mysterie of his might,
> As if his godhead thou didst present see
>
> ('Colin Clout' 823–6, 831–4)

and Colin's response confirms this sense that his poetry has access to higher truths, inaccessible to the 'reason' of ordinary mortals:

> Of loues perfection perfectly to speake,
> Or of his nature rightly to define,
> Indeed (said *Colin*) passeth reasons reach,
> And needs his priest t'expresse his powre diuine.
>
> ('Colin Clout' 835–8)

---

33 See Pugh, *Spenser and Ovid*, pp. 135–6.

We are reminded of the peculiarly ambiguous status of the vision of the Garden of Adonis in *The Faerie Queene*, where its location and ontological status in relation to Faerie lond is indeterminate, and our experience of it is due ambiguously to the narrator's experience of it ('by tryall') or else to mythological tradition ('they say'). This is both a place to which no mortal has ever had direct access in life, and a place with which Spenser himself is privileged, through his exceptional inspiration, to be familiar.

The connection between Clorinda's depiction of the afterlife and Spenser's Garden of Adonis is startling because the Garden, in its context in *The Faerie Queene*, is not explicitly an image of heaven, but rather an (admittedly mysterious) allegorical image of procreative love sustaining creation (which is also the main emphasis in the hymn to love in 'Colin Clouts Come Home Againe'). The 'babes' planted in its flowerbeds are there not souls, but 'forme[s]' (37.3) – if they were taken as souls Spenser would have to be read as preaching a doctrine of reincarnation, for the babes are repeatedly 'sent into the chaungefull world' (33.7) and return to be planted again in the garden for another thousand years, in a continuous cycle imitating that described by Anchises in Book VI of the *Aeneid*.[34] Nevertheless *The Faerie Queene*'s Garden of Adonis is here clearly evoked while being reworked as a vision of heaven, omitting the babes' cyclical return to earth. On another level the allusion is not surprising at all, because the narrative of Astrophel's life and death has been conspicuously modelled on that of Adonis throughout, a modelling particularly highlighted by its heavy indebtedness to Bion's *Lament for Adonis*.[35]

Bion's *Lament for Adonis* has exerted an enormous influence on subsequent lament poetry, largely because of its close relationship with the slightly later *Lament for Bion*. It is in itself not strictly part of the genre of funerary elegy, but a devotional song representing the type of songs performed on the second day of the annual festival of Adonis, when Adonis' death was recounted, after the first day's celebration of his wedding with Aphrodite in observances and songs such as those relayed in Theocritus' fifteenth idyll.[36] However, the *Lament for Bion*, which is modelled on it and alludes

---

34 On Renaissance responses to the cycle of reincarnation in Anchises' speech, see Wilson-Okamura, *Virgil in the Renaissance*, 173–90.
35 First pointed out by Robert Shafer, 'Spenser's Astrophel', *Modern Language Notes* 28 (1913), 224–6.
36 Margaret Alexiou, *Ritual Lament in Greek Tradition* (Cambridge: Cambridge University Press, 1974), p. 56.

to it throughout, effectively founded the genre of pastoral elegy for a dead fellow poet (as distinct from the elegy for a legendary singer we find in Theocritus' first idyll). Often ascribed to Moschus, the *Lament for Bion* depicts its subject in such a way as to identify him with various of the characters who presumably peopled his poems (now mostly lost), and most strikingly with his own Adonis. Subsequent funerary elegies composed for fellow poets, in classical and in English literature, frequently compare their subjects to Adonis – a list would culminate in the particularly obvious example of Shelley's *Adonais*, a lament for Keats by a poet who had translated parts of both Greek texts into English – and such gestures can often reliably be read as a combined allusion to Bion's *Lament for Adonis* and to its partner-piece, the *Lament for Bion*.[37] Indeed, we can already see this at work in the tenth eclogue, where Virgil obliquely compares Gallus to Adonis with (17–18):

> nec te poeniteat pecoris, divine poeta; –
> et formosus ovis ad flumina pavit Adonis

['do not be displeased by the flocks, divine poet – even the beautiful Adonis grazed his sheep beside the river'.]

and the list of deities who come to him, headed by Apollo, alludes to pseudo-Moschus as well as Theocritus 1.[38] Another classical example would be Ovid's elegy for Tibullus in *Amores* 3.9, where, as Reed observes, by frequent allusion to Bion's lament, and 'by a comparison to Adonis reminiscent of Pseudo-Moschus, Ovid transforms his subject into Bion.'[39] The very way in which both Virgil and Ovid identify their subjects with the emotions and experiences of their *personae* as recounted in their poems – Virgil's Gallus hoping that the ice of the Alps will not cut Lycoris' feet, in a line which Servius tells us is taken from one of Gallus' elegies, and Ovid imagining Tibullus' second love, Nemesis, as boasting that it was *she* who clasped his hand as he died, precisely as he had promised his first love, Delia, that she would do – is ultimately derived from pseudo-Moschus' identification of Bion with his own characters, and of course it is the same technique which Spenser uses when he chooses to call Sidney by the name of his sonnet-persona.

37 Geoffrey Miles, *Classical Mythology in English Literature: A Critical Anthology* (London: Routledge, 1999), p. 205.
38 See Clausen, *ad loc*.
39 Joseph D. Reed, 'Ovid's Elegy on Tibullus and Its Models', *Classical Philology* 92 (1997), 260–9, at 267.

As almost a convention of the genre, the comparison to Adonis implies a subtext of literary filiation, a kind of shorthand by which the author of such an elegy compares his relationship with the dead poet to the relationship between pseudo-Moschus and Bion, implicitly invoking pseudo-Moschus' claim to be the sole and privileged heir of the dead poet's talent:

> αὐτὰρ ἐγώ τοι
> Αὐσονικᾶς ὀδύνας μέλπω μέλος, οὐ ξένος ᾠδᾶς
> βουκολικᾶς, ἀλλ ἄντε διδάξαο σεῖο μαθητὰς
> κλαρονόμος Μοίσας τᾶς Δωρίδος, ᾇ με γεραίρων
> ἄλλοις μὲν τεὸν ὄλβον, ἐμοὶ δ' ἀπέλειπες ἀοιδάν.
> (*Lament for Bion* 93–7)

['as for Ausonia's mourning, 'tis the song I sing thee now; and 'tis no stranger to the pastoral poesy that sings it, neither, but an inheritor of that Dorian minstrelsy which came of thy teaching and was my portion when thou leftest others thy wealth but me thy song.']

In the examples just mentioned, for instance, Ovid's poem ends with a gathering of poets in Elysium which constructs a literary genealogy of his own genre, Roman love-elegy, with the implication that it culminates in himself, heir and imitator of Tibullus' verses.[40] In Eclogue 10, meanwhile, we have seen how the poem, and indeed the book, lead up to Virgil's dubbing himself the Muses' own poet, as he assumes the divinely inspired status accorded Gallus in Eclogue 6 but since abandoned by him – a status which was already presented there as fulfilling the ambitions of Virgil's own speaker at the end of Eclogue 4. Spenser's very decision to model the narrative of Astrophel's life on that of Adonis, then, is a crucial part of the strategy Raphael Falco has discerned in the poem, whereby Spenser 'casts Sidney, by a kind of genealogical back-formation, as a vernacular predecessor'.[41] By evoking the pair of Greek texts which stand at the beginning of the genre in which he is so self-consciously working, the very use of the Adonis myth seems to position Spenser as Sidney's literary son and heir.

Yet the suggestion is as elusive as it is allusive. As Falco rightly emphasizes, although a sense of his own belatedness shadows Spenser's treatment of Sidney both here and in the earlier *Ruines of Time*, Spenser does not seem to have to struggle hard to overcome the Bloomian anxiety which arguably gets the better of pseudo-Moschus

---

40 Pugh, 'Supping With Ghosts'.
41 Falco, 'Spenser's "Astrophel"', 1.

(for whom even Pan does not dare to touch Bion's pipe). Sidney as Astrophel is a deeply flawed predecessor, already confidently surpassed by his elegist and putative 'son'.[42] The allusions to Spenser's treatments of the Garden of Adonis in Clorinda's lay bring this out in more ways than one. For in addition to showing that Spenser has already attained the fullness of divine inspiration which can be Sidney's only in death (and only in Clorinda's speculative imagination), they also evoke what Astrophel *lacks* of a true Adonis-figure. I have compared the narrative of 'Astrophel' to an Ovidian epyllion above, and its emphasis (up to the beginning of Clorinda's lay) on the tragic love-story, with its climax in the poignant metamorphosis, is akin to Ovid's treatment of the myth in the *Metamorphoses*. Supervening on this we have the associations with literary inheritance flowing from Bion and pseudo-Moschus. But there is another aspect of Adonis to which 'Astrophel' conspicuously omits any allusion, and this is his cult as a god of fertility and the cycle of the seasons, figured in his annual death and resurrection celebrated in the Adonia, the underlying subject of Bion's *Lament* as of Theocritus 15 – a cult well known and thoroughly glossed by Renaissance commentators.[43] It was of course perfectly possible for Renaissance poets to ignore this religious significance, as Ovid had done in the *Metamorphoses*, without its registering as a significant silence – Shakespeare's *Venus and Adonis* epyllion furnishes a ready example. But when Clorinda's lay reminds us of the Garden of Adonis as it has figured in Spenser's previous work, the omission becomes marked as something the reader needs to notice and interpret, for the significance of Adonis in Book III, canto vi of *The Faerie Queene* is precisely as such a figure, guarantor of the perpetual fertility and cyclical rebirth of nature. He is 'eterne in mutabilitie' (III.vi.47) because he represents the principle of procreation through which nature is perpetually replenished and life succeeds death in a continuous cycle (and though Adonis himself does not appear in 'Colin Clouts Come Home Againe', Cupid there plays a similar role). Spenser's Adonis is 'the Father of all formes', who 'liuing giues to all' (III.vi.47). This aspect of Adonis is missing from Astrophel, and has been carefully (and necessarily) excised in Clorinda's reworking of *The Faerie Queene* III.vi.

---

42 'In Spenser's version, it is necessary for Sidney to be a failed predecessor, so that Spenser can simultaneously claim the existence of a lineage and overgo the immediate past' (Falco, 'Spenser's "Astrophel"', 14).

43 See for example George Sandys, *Ovid's Metamorphosis: Englished, Mythologiz'd, and Represented in Figures* (Oxford, 1632), pp. 366–7.

The memory of Spenser's earlier depiction of Adonis contrasts strikingly with Astrophel, the fertility of the one highlighting the sterility of the other. As befits the conversion of the Garden of Adonis into a vision of heaven (and not a Catholic heaven), the lay must exclude *any* notion of Astrophel's soul exerting an influence on the lives of those remaining on earth – in the same way that any suggestion of Dido's intervention in earthly affairs after her death is pointedly excluded in *Nouember* – let alone the sexual replenishing of creation figured in the allegory of *The Faerie Queene* III.vi. But Astrophel's *poetry* might be expected to exert such an influence, and in the time-honoured metaphor a *seminal* influence, begetting future generations of literary 'sons'. As a poet, he could have hoped to attain the status of 'Father' of future poetic 'forms' – the very status which Spenser's evocation of Bion and pseudo-Moschus has hinted that this poem may accord him.[44] Yet instead, Clorinda has expressly forbidden and cut off any hope of this kind of fatherhood, with her command 'Ne euer sing the loue-layes which he made ... Ne euer read the riddles, which he sayd' (43–5), underlining as she did so the triviality which unsuited his poetry to such an afterlife. Her evocation of Spenser's own verse, meanwhile, in her vision of the nobler raptures enjoyed by Astrophel's unbodied soul, demonstrates (through the fiction that Spenser is not the author of the 'Dolefull Lay') how seminal *his* work is by contrast, in that it has already spawned such imitations. Where such elegy might be expected to display the living influence of the dead poet by conspicuously imitating his songs (as Virgil's tenth eclogue imitates Gallus, and as Ovid's *Amores* 3.9 imitates Tibullus), such evocations of Sidney's style in 'Astrophel' are distinctly muted and subtle. The direction of influence is effectively reversed by the way in which Astrophel's post mortem visions are so conspicuously modelled on Spenser's own poetry. In effect, Spenser is casting aspersions on Sidney's literary manhood in what may seem a mean-spirited way when it is spelt out like this, but nevertheless the poise, and serious wit, with which he does so precisely through a play on his own allegorical vision of male fertility in *The Faerie Queene* must be admired.[45]

---

44 The suggestion of immortality through literary influence is already bound up with Adonis as a figure of renewal in nature in the *Lament for Bion*, where the herb gardens of lines 99–104 (the passage imitated at *Nouember* 83–9) are recognizable as the 'gardens of Adonis' used in the Adonia celebrations. See Pugh, 'Adonis and Literary Immortality in Pastoral Elegy', in Syrithe Pugh (ed.), *Conversations: Classical and Renaissance Intertextuality* (Aberdeen: Aberdeen University Press, forthcoming).
45 We might note, however, that here too Spenser is responding to and developing a

The tenor and vehicle of this trope are, moreover, inextricably intertwined. The influential power of Spenser's verse, which outdoes Sidney's in its metaphorical, literary 'fertility', is due in large part to its visionary subject matter, an inspired apprehension of the true nature and purpose of love implicitly contrasted with that of the Petrarchan tradition, including Sidney's *Astrophil and Stella*. The love celebrated in *The Faerie Queene*'s Garden of Adonis (III.vi.34) is the procreative force underpinning God's creation, obeying

> the mightie word,
> Which first was spoken by th'Almightie lord,
> That bad them to increase and multiply ...

The hymn to Love in 'Colin Clouts Come Home Againe' tells us, similarly, that it was by Cupid, 'in the gardens of *Adonis* nurst' ('Colin Clouts Come Home Againe', 804), that 'the world was made of yore, / And all that therein wondrous doth appeare' (841–2), and that it is sustained by his influence, 'which with delight / Doth man allure, for to enlarge his kynd' (870–1). This love, which the shepheards nation honour 'with chaste heart' (888), is contrasted with the Petrarchan abuse of love at Cynthia's court, in a way which is strongly linked to Spenser's revision of Petrarchan love in the *Amoretti and Epithalamium* volume, published in the same year. The alternatives offered by Petrarchan poetry amount only to a transcendence and rejection of the worldly and the physical, such as that achieved by Petrarch in the sonnets after Laura's death, or else Astrophil's self-consciously depraved wallowing in selfish and obsessive lust. Both attitudes are founded in the same denigration of sexual love as counter to all that is morally good. The *Amoretti* and *Epithalamium* go beyond these sterile polarities, to embrace sexual love in the context of faithful marriage as 'the lesson which the Lord vs taught'. This love surpasses Petrarchan love both in its emphasis on mutuality and care for the other rather than the self (where 'mutuall good will, / seekes with sweet peace to salue each others wound', Amoretti 65.11–12), and in its focus on procreation. Where we leave Sidney's Astrophil, at the end of his sequence, in sterile despair, Spenser's volume closes

---

quite self-conscious and deliberate aspect of Sidney's self-presentation, and of his persona in *Astrophil and Stella*. As Tom McFaul has compellingly argued, Sidney consistently presents himself as trapped in an infantile and therefore non-procreative love to expose the 'maternal tyranny' of the Queen who prevents the maturation of her subjects' masculinity (*Poetry and Paternity in Renaissance England: Sidney, Spenser, Shakespeare, Donne and Jonson* (Cambridge: Cambridge University Press, 2010), pp. 63–94; quotation at 66).

with the *Epithalamium*'s triumphant vision of the couple's future progeny peopling heaven.[46] That vision might even seem a mirror image of Adonis' replenishing of earth from his garden in *The Faerie Queene*, accomplishing in reverse that influence of the translated soul on the mortal world which we deemed necessarily impossible once the Garden of Adonis had been reworked as heaven in Clorinda's lay. Biologically as well as figuratively, Spenser proves himself more fertile than his predecessor.[47] His literary influence meanwhile, by his example as a lover in the *Amoretti* volume, as well as by precept in his other poems, promotes the will of his community to procreate itself physically.

Finally, an ironic light is cast on the extremity of Clorinda's 'impatient griefe' (2). For all that she is wrong to present herself as a solitary mourner, nevertheless the shepherd community has already been granted some of the comfort and restitution which she believes impossible. This is another implication of the allusions to Spenser's Gardens of Adonis which we have been examining, for they remind us that not only are Astrophel's imagined heavenly visions available to the inspired Spenser but through him they have been made available to his readers – the very audience represented in the shepherd community. The radical disjunction between the joys of souls in heaven and the woes of those left on earth is thus eroded. When Clorinda concludes (92–4)

> giue vs leaue thee here thus to lament:
> Not thee that doest thy heauens ioy inherit,
> But our owne selues that here in dole are drent,

the disparity appears less obvious in the light of the references to Spenser's earlier works. Readers of *The Faerie Queene* and 'Colin Clouts Come Home Againe' have themselves already 'inherit[ed]' such 'heauens ioy' as comes from partaking of these visions, and

---

46 McFaul reflects interestingly on the interconnection of biological procreation and literary posterity in Spenser, particularly in relation to this passage (*Poetry and Paternity in Renaissance England*, pp. 95–129, esp. 123–5), though ultimately he overemphasizes the personal aspect at the expense of the public, didactic and prophetic (calling the *Amoretti* 'private poetry', 123). Similarly, he follows the traditional reading of the return to the pastoral mode in the *Colin Clouts Come Home Againe* volume as a retreat into the private sphere (125). McFaul does not discuss 'Astrophel' (and makes only a passing reference to 'Colin Clouts Come Home Againe').
47 The implied calumny is of course false on both counts: Sidney exerted a profound influence on his poetic successors (on which see Gavin Alexander, *Writing After Sidney: The Literary Response to Sir Philip Sidney 1586–1640* (Oxford: Oxford University Press, 2006)), and also left a daughter behind him.

thus cannot seem quite as 'drent' in 'dole' as Clorinda thinks. Indeed, Clorinda herself is evidently imagined as one of these readers, or she would not have been able to imitate the relevant passages. Since she is Astrophel's sister, it would perhaps be too harsh to suggest that she is obstinate in failing to appreciate and accept this as a mitigation of her own sense of bereavement, but we can no longer see her inconsolable grief as a model for others to follow. In a way, her blood-relationship thus really does place her in that exceptional and isolated position which we have said she was wrong to assume, but it is not for the reasons she gave, and it remains true that her perspective is shown, largely through her imitations of Virgil's *Eclogues* and Spenser's *Nouember*, to be limited and distorting. And indeed, if we return to the most dubious and exaggerated moment of her lay, the image of the landscape mourning Astrophel's absence, we have a very particular reason for seeing that it cannot be taken seriously by the shepherd community. For one of Spenser's fullest handlings of the motif has opened the present volume, in Hobbinol's speech to Colin at the beginning of 'Colin Clouts Come Home Againe' (22–31):

> Whilest thou wast hence, all dead in dole did lye:
> The woods were heard to waile full many a sythe,
> And all their birds with silence to complaine:
> The fields with faded flowers did seem to mourne,
> And all their flocks from feeding to refraine:
> The running waters wept for thy returne,
> And all their fish with langour did lament:
> But now both woods and fields, and floods reuiue,
> Sith thou art come, their cause of meriment,
> That vs late dead, hast made againe aliue.

The desolation of the landscape during Colin's absence is there immediately recognizable as an imitation of that topos of funeral elegy exemplified in Mopsus' lament for Daphnis in Virgil's fifth eclogue. The fields mourn Colin's absence just as Clorinda will claim that they mourn the dead Astrophel. Yet as it is spoken it has already been undone and reversed, with Colin's return reviving the landscape, restoring life to it and to its inhabitants. There are more humble analogues too – the gloom shared by Amaryllis and the landscape during Tityrus' absence in Eclogue 1 (36–9), the response of the countryside to the departure and the arrival of the contestants' beloveds in Eclogue 7 (53–60). But the dominant allusion is to the mourning topos, with the Orphic, quasi-divine power over the landscape it ascribes to the dead. Thus the revival on Colin's return recalls the rejoicing of nature at Daphnis' deification in Menalcas' hymn in Eclogue 5, the beneficent influence of Caesar's star in Eclogue 9, and the overcoming of death and replenishment of nature symbolized by Adonis in *The Faerie Queene* III.vi. Thanks to the presence of the divinely inspired poet and the teachings conveyed in his songs, the shepherd community and their pastoral setting have already been redeemed from the doleful desolation brought by awareness of mortality. Where Clorinda sees herself and the other shepherds as stranded in the desert of the mortal world and cut off from the joys of heaven, the rest of the community – and Spenser's readers – can see that the desert has already sprung into flower under the influence of divinely inspired songs which transmit those visionary joys.

Spenser's songs – in the hymn to love in 'Colin Clouts Come Home Againe' as in *The Faerie Queene*'s Garden of Adonis – convey a consolatory message about the limited power of death in created nature, which is providentially sustained, 'eterne in mutabilitie', through procreative love. This procreative love in the service of Cupid and embodied in Adonis, which Spenser in 'Colin Clouts Come Home Againe' elides with Christian faith, is defined in contradistinction not only to the courtly love satirized and condemned in 'Colin Clouts Come Home Againe' but also to the love which drives Astrophel to his death in the elegy – the fruitless 'love which reaches but to dust' depicted in Sidney's sonnet sequence, and which is reformed as procreative married love in Spenser's *Amoretti* and *Epithalamium*. Underlying the elegy and the volume is Virgil's tenth eclogue, with its implicit criticism of Gallus frenzied elegiac love, and its promotion of sympathetic friendship in its place. But Spenser's claims go beyond the ambitions and the boasts of Virgil's eclogue, and take a different attitude to love. Where Virgil's assumption of the mantle of poetic inspiration at the end of his eclogue book is there associated with the renunciation of sexual love and the future ascent to higher genres, Spenser reworks his model to identify his triumphal assumption of the role of the Muses' own poet with a reaffirmation both of sexual love in the context of procreative marriage, and of pastoral as a goal at least as worthy as epic.

5
Reimagining the pastoral muse in 'Colin Clouts Come Home Againe'

When 'Colin Clouts Come Home Againe' is read in conjunction with 'Astrophel', it becomes clear that they have in common not only their central themes but also their major intertexts, both in Virgil and in Spenser's other works. They are in fact complementary parts of the same project, constructing their meaning and their poetic programme through allusive dialogue both with Virgil and with each other. Despite the fact the 'Colin Clouts Come Home Againe' is not in any sense an elegy, Virgil's tenth eclogue is again the most important Virgilian intertext here, as a kind of *locus classicus* of ethical negotiation between different kinds of amatory poetry, as a meditation on the sympathetic friendship of the pastoral community in Virgil's imaginary Arcadia, and as the place where Virgil both lays claim to the status of the Muses' poet and abandons pastoral for higher genres.

As we saw at the end of the last chapter, Clorinda's lay was a conventional elegy, which followed the structure of Virgil's fifth eclogue and Spenser's *Nouember* in its movement from lament for Sidney's death to celebratory vision of his immortal soul in bliss. But, as we also saw, her attempted apotheosis of Sidney was severely qualified by the closely intertwined facts that, firstly, as in *Nouember*, the Protestant conception of heaven does not allow the beatified Sidney to intervene on earth to ameliorate the condition of those left on earth (as Virgil's Daphnis is said to do), and secondly that Sidney's merely recreational poetry (as it is presented in Spenser's poem) is ephemeral and cannot comfort or sustain his abandoned community. Thus the vision of heaven in stanzas 12 to 15 draws on Spenser's poetry, and in doing so implicitly attributes to Spenser himself the power to console a community otherwise 'wretched' in the face of its own mortality. Through its intertextual relations to the myth of Adonis as it figures in the *Lament for Bion* and in Spenser's *Faerie Queene* and 'Colin Clouts Come Home Againe', 'Astrophel' aligns this poetic power with the divine power to revivify nature itself, commonly figured in Orpheus' animation of the landscape, and attributed to Adonis in the *Adonia* and to Daphnis in Menalcas' hymn in Virgil's fifth eclogue. We ended by looking back to the opening of the dialogue of 'Colin Clouts Come Home Againe', where Hobbinol describes at length the mourning of a landscape and a community left 'dead in dole' in Colin's absence (22), but restored to life by his return (29–31):

> But now both woods and fields, and floods reuiue,
> Sith thou art come, their cause of meriment,
> That vs late dead, hast made againe aliue ...

These are the very 'Woods, hills and riuers' which 'now are desolate' in their 'widow state', according to Clorinda's lay. Astrophel/Sidney could only leave the landscape in the mourning condition described in Mopsus' lament in the first half of Eclogue 5 (20–8, 34–9), but Colin has the power to animate it and make it rejoice, like the deified Daphnis of Menalcas' hymn. (5.58–64) With this reworking, Spenser not only anticipates the companion poem's argument for his superiority to Sidney but also implicitly claims for himself some measure of the divinity accorded the political potentate at the Caesarean centre of Virgil's eclogue-book: his poetic authority displaces political power.

It is perhaps only in retrospect that this intertextual reverberation becomes fully audible, however. On a first reading, the humbler evocation of Tityrus from Virgil's first eclogue is more obvious. It is to Tityrus (traditionally Virgil's *alter ego*) that the poem explicitly compares Colin in its opening lines (1–2):

> The shepheards boy (best knowen by that name)
> That after *Tityrus* first sung his lay ...

Tityrus too, we recall, was mourned in his absence not only by his lover Amaryllis but also by the very pines, fountains and orchards (1.36–9). Hobbinol's request that Colin 'repeat / The passed fortunes, which to thee befell / In thy late voyage' (33–5) recalls Meliboeus' questioning in Eclogue 1, and the story of Colin's travels as it unfolds mirrors Tityrus' round trip to Rome and back.

This trip of Tityrus' was earlier reworked by Spenser in *Januarye*, with Colin's visit to 'the neighbour towne' (50). That visit brought Colin only 'bane' (53), the opposite of the good fortune received by Tityrus from the godlike youth Octavian, and as a result *Janu-*

arye's imitation of Eclogue 1 excised Tityrus' glad gratitude and collapsed Virgil's dialogue into a gloomy Meliboean soliloquy. Here, by contrast, Colin and his interlocutors seem to enjoy Tityrean contentment (despite what we are later told of the ills which beset the 'shepheards nation' in their Irish home (312–19)). The poem gestures towards political implications like those of Tityrus' happiness, as Colin 'feed[s]' in memory 'on sweet contentment of [the] sight' of 'that Angel' Cynthia (43, 40), recalling Tityrus' assertion that the memory of Octavian's countenance will never fade from his heart (*Eclogues* 1.63). But as the poem unfolds we come to realize that this resemblance is chimerical. If Tityrus' gratitude in Eclogue 1 reflects his reprieve by Octavian, so that the pleasant Theocritean life of ease evoked nostalgically by Meliboeus maintains a tenuous foothold in the reality which has shattered it for the other herdsmen, here, by contrast, any suggestion that the happiness of Colin and his community is owed to Cynthia, as Tityrus' is owed to to the beneficence of the godlike youth, has no more substance in external reality than a mental image. As the true nature of Colin's experience at court is revealed, it becomes clear that the shepherds' contentment is the result of a radical *inversion* of the dependence on political power symbolized in Tityrus' *otium*. In his decision to return 'home againe', Colin, like Melibee in Book VI of *The Faerie Queene*, actively rejects the court and a life of dependency upon its patronage, while to the rest of the 'shepheards nation' (17), fictionalized as a wholly independent realm, Cynthia and her land are merely an exotic traveller's tale, capable of provoking wonder and moral reflection, but exerting no real-world influence upon them outside of Colin's narrative. So far from being a subject colony, this imagined Ireland (in so far as the setting of the poem can be mapped on to Ireland) does not even have trading relations with Elizabeth's England. As Colin shrugs off the court and a life of Tityrean dependency, so Spenser's poem rejects the Virgilian model of pastoral as a means of negotiating with political power – that model in which, as we saw at the end of Chapter 3, the Virgilian poet remains trammelled by his dependency on that power, even as he asserts the mutual interdependence of the relationship in order to drive his bargain.

Pastoral here is no longer a bargain with power. Thus there are no gifts in this Irish setting – those garlands and lambs which symbolized the pastoral negotiation in the *Calender*. In the dedicatory epistle to Ralegh, the poem itself *is* still figured as a 'present', but it is neither a wooing gift nor a tribute to a ruler, but a gift of friendship:

> SIR, that you may see that I am not alwaies ydle as ye thinke, though not greatly well occupied, nor altogither vndutifull, though not precisely officious, I make you present of this simple pastorall, vnworthie of your higher conceit for the meanesse of the stile, but agreeing with the truth in circumstance and matter. The which I humbly beseech you to accept in part of paiment of the infinite debt in which I acknowledge my selfe bounden vnto you, for your singular fauours and sundrie good turnes shewed to me at my late being in England, and with your good countenance protect against the malice of euill mouthes, which are alwaies wide open to carpe at and misconstrue my simple meaning. I pray continually for your happinesse. From my house of Kilcoman, the 27. of December. 1591.

This 'present' is less like Tityrus' or Menalcas' propitiatory sacrifices to a potentate and more like the 'few verses for my Gallus' (*pauca meo Gallo carmina*, *Ecl.* 10.2–3) which are the token of Virgil's affection for his friend and fellow poet – the humble pastoral symbolized in the poem's closing lines (as Servius notes) by the basket woven from slender hibiscus (*gracili fiscellam hibisco*, 71), which the Muses will make a worthy gift for him. Though Spenser goes on to describe his poem as part payment of a debt incurred by Ralegh's favours, yet there is less humility here than we might expect, and more than a suggestion of near-equality, from the air of friendly banter in the opening riposte to a remembered teasing accusation from Ralegh, to the signature 'from my house of Kilcolman', which (as Montrose observes) proudly underlines Spenser's admittance to the ranks of the landed gentry with the acquisition of his Irish estate.[1] It is almost as though the humble posture required by debts incurred 'at my late being in England' becomes merely a friendly (and purely voluntary) rhetorical gesture, now that he has 'come home againe' to his own domain.

The opening riposte in the epistle, though jocular in tone, nevertheless broaches the serious question of the public value of poetry and the *vita contemplativa* which will be so prominent in 'Astrophel'. It implicitly balances Spenser's official duties as Sheriff of Cork against the poetic industry which has produced this poem and volume. We understand that Ralegh has rebuked Spenser for neglecting the former; Spenser's reply contends that what he has been doing instead

---

[1] Louis Adrian Montrose, 'Spenser's Domestic Domain: Poetry, Property, and the Early Modern Subject', in Margreta de Grazia, Maureen Quilligan and Peter Stallybrass (eds), *Subject and Object in Renaissance Culture* (Cambridge: Cambridge University Press, 1996).

also fulfils a duty, and urges a reconsideration of their respective value.[2] It is not surprising, in the light of the poem's depiction of the Shepherd of the Ocean, that Ralegh should be cast by Spenser as sharing some of that courtly prejudice against poetry as a serious pursuit which will form such a prominent part of the theme of 'Astrophel', nor that, dependent on Elizabeth's patronage and his office for his own social position, he should be inclined to insist on officiousness in government service. His own poetics and his movements within the poem, as we shall see, make it clear that he remains tied to Elizabeth's apron strings.[3] In reality, of course, Spenser does too: he owes his living to his official post as part of the Queen's colonial government. In fact, since Spenser's and Ralegh's Irish estates were confiscated from the Earl of Desmond in punishment for his part in the recent uprising, both, in the terms of Virgilian pastoral, could be said to resemble neither Tityrus nor Meliboeus so much as the *barbarus miles* who takes over Meliboeus' farm.[4] But the landscape of the poem both is and is not the real world. In the manner typical of Spenserian allegory, it 'agrees with the truth' only partially and shiftingly. Within this semi-fictional world Colin both elides his own implication in the violence of the *barbarus miles* by figuring himself as a native denizen of the land (even making gestures of affiliation to native Irish culture), and escapes the dependency to which Spenser remains materially, if not mentally, subject. The doubleness of the

2 Hadfield reads the epistle as expressing hostility and rebuke within a deteriorating relationship (*Edmund Spenser: A Life* (Oxford: Oxford University Press, 2014), pp. 231–5, 239–40). Though I disagree with him strongly about the tone of the epistle, I do find a marked but friendly difference of opinion over the relative values of the *vitae activa* and *contemplativa* registered here. On Spenser's relationship with Ralegh, see Katherine Koller, 'Spenser and Ralegh', *ELH* 1 (1934), 37–60, for a meticulous presentation of the documentary evidence. William Oram, 'What Did Spenser Really Think of Sir Walter Ralegh When He Published the First Installment of *The Faerie Queene*?', *Spenser Studies* 15 (2001), 165–74, and 'Spenser's Raleghs', *Studies in Philology* 87 (1990), 341–62, treats the relationship with measured scepticism, as a friendship allowing room for criticism; Wayne Erickson, 'Spenser Reads Ralegh's Poetry in (to) the 1590 *Faerie Queene*', *Spenser Studies* 15 (2001), 175–84, is less sceptical about the degree of affection, seeing their intertextual engagement as mutual 'serious fun' (p. 176).
3 On Ralegh's Petrarchan poetics as a mark of this dependency, see Leonard Tennenhouse, 'Sir Walter Ralegh and the Literature of Clientage', in Guy Fitch Lytle and Stephen Orgel (eds), *Patronage in the Renaissance* (Princeton: Princeton University Press, 1981), pp. 235–58.
4 Cp. James P. Bednarz, 'The Collaborator as Thief: Ralegh's (Re)Vision of *The Faerie Queene*', *ELH* 63 (1996), 279–307, who argues that Ralegh is capable of joking cheerfully about their mutual status as Hermes-like cattle thieves. Spenser, I would argue, is less sanguine and more hypocritical when it comes to acknowledging the violent origins of his wealth.

setting of Spenser's poem is interestingly related to an important current in Virgil's *Eclogues* which reaches its climax in Eclogue 10, and we shall discuss Spenser's engagement with and correction of this aspect of Virgil later in this chapter.

Ralegh as Gallus

Certainly, in Colin's domain as it is imagined in the fiction of the poem, the obligations of hierarchy give way to the spontaneity and equality of friendship in the meeting of the two poets. Colin relates their meeting as two simple shepherds in a quintessentially pastoral scene, as Colin keeps his 'sheepe amongst the cooly shade, / Of the greene alders by the *Mullaes* shore' (58–9). 'Thither led' by pure chance or by sheer, meritocratic admiration for the 'pleasing sound' of Colin's music (62–3), the Shepherd of the Ocean joins him in an exchange of song. If any hierarchy is suggested here, it is the reverse of what the patronage relationship sugested in the epistle would lead us to expect, with the Ralegh figure 'aemuling' (striving to emulate or rival, 72) Colin's pipe. But the exchange is most distinctive for its *lack* of the rivalry implicit in pastoral's amoebaean song contests. Colin acknowledges his fellow shepherd to be 'as skilfull in that art as any' (75), and as the two take turns at singing and accompanying, the aim and result is mutual delight (76–9):

> He pip'd, I sung; and when he sung, I piped,
> By chaunge of turnes, each making other mery,
> Neither enuying other, nor enuied,
> So piped we, vntill we both were weary.

As Colin reports the content of the other shepherd's song, the reader, primed of course by the dedicatory epistle, recognizes it as Ralegh's *Ocean to Cynthia*,[5] a poem about his troubled relationship with Eliza-

---

5 See Spenser, *The Shorter Poems*, ed. William Oram *et al.* (New Haven: Yale University Press, 1989), p. 532. On the relation between 'Colin Clouts Come Home Againe' and Ralegh's poem, see also Patrick Cheney, 'The Laureate Choir: The Dove as a Vocational Sign in Spenser's Allegory of Ralegh and Elizabeth', *Huntington Library Quarterly* 53 (1990), 257–80, and three essays in Christopher M. Armitage (ed.), *Literary and Visual Ralegh* (Manchester: Manchester University Press, 2013): Wayne Erickson, 'Spenser and Ralegh: Friendship and Literary Patronage'; James Nohrnberg, 'Ralegh in Ruins, Ralegh on the Rocks: Sir Wa'ter's Two Books of Mutabilitie and Their Subject's Allegorical Presence in Select Spenserean Narratives and Complaints'; and Thomas Herron, 'Love's "emperye": Ralegh's "Ocean to Scinthia", Spenser's "Colin Clouts Come Home Againe" and *The Faerie Queene* IV.vii in Colonial Context'.

beth which itself frequently echoes *The Shepheardes Calender*, and to which Spenser has already given honourable mention in the Proem to Book III of *The Faerie Queene*.[6] Spenser's song-exchange scene evokes Virgil's tenth eclogue, with its ventriloquized lament transposing the amatory despair and the very language of Gallus' elegies into the setting and metre of pastoral. Virgil's eclogue echoes and pities Gallus, just as the Arcadian landscape and shepherd community within the poem echo and pity him, and Gallus in turn longs to become a shepherd and to 'modulate' his former songs 'on a Sicilian shepherd's pipe' (*pastoris Siculi modulabor avena*, 51). That is, Gallus, granted an honorary space within Virgil's pastoral book and landscape, longs to adopt the Theocritean and therefore Sicilian mode of pastoral, taking up the *avena* ('oaten reed') which is Tityrus' distinctive instrument in Eclogue 1, just as Ralegh, transformed into a shepherd and welcomed into Spenser's pastoral domain, 'tooke in hond' Colin's 'pipe' (72–3), which has already been described as an 'oaten reed' (13). The mutual sympathy of Spenser's shepherds within the narrative resonates with this sympathetic reciprocity pervading Virgil's eclogue. The very alders beneath which they sit together recall the green alder (*viridis alnus*, 10.74) to which Virgil compares his love for Gallus.

Ralegh's relationship with the Queen is also allegorized in the Timias/Belphoebe story of *The Faerie Queene*. Ralegh's patronage by and devotion to Elizabeth is figured in Book III, where Belphoebe heals Timias' physical wound while unwittingly inflicting a new wound of love. In Book IV's continuation, Belphoebe happens upon Timias tending to the wounded Amoret, and flounces off in an apparently jealous rage, leaving the diconsolate Timias to retreat into the woods, losing his identity, all trappings of civility and even the power of speech. The episode figures Ralegh's disastrous fall from grace in 1592, when the Queen discovered his secret marriage to Elizabeth Throckmorton, one of her ladies in waiting, and had the couple thrown into prison, where they remained until Arthur Throck-

---

6 At least, a reader with privileged access to networks of manuscript exchange would recognize it as such; readers restricted to the consumption of print would see only a general evocation of Petrarchan complaints about Ralegh's relations with the Queen, which would suffice. The reference to a poem available only in manuscript also contributes both to our sense of the personal friendship foregrounded in the volume and to Spenser's claim to elevated social status. On the social dynamics of print references to manuscript poems in Jonson, see Pugh, 'Jonson and the Cavalier Poets', in Cathy Bates (ed.), *Blackwell Companion to Renaissance Poetry* (Oxford: Blackwell, forthcoming).

morton, Ralegh's brother-in-law, won their release by presenting the Queen with a heart-shaped ruby as a token of the family's loyalty. In Spenser's episode the ruby appears as the lure with which Belphoebe is led back to Timias by a dove, traditional symbol of the love poet, here representing Spenser himself.[7] The dove has been Timias' companion in his banishment, offering sympathy and jointly singing with him a 'lamentable lay'. The phrase is one of several echoes of 'Colin Clouts Come Home Againe' in the Book IV episode, which mark the dove's intervention as reciprocating in kind the favours shown to Colin by the Shepherd of the Ocean, as he pities Colin's 'banishment' and leads him to Cynthia to gain her grace with song. Like 'Colin Clouts Come Home Againe', the Book IV episode aligns Ralegh with the Gallus of Eclogue 10, as Timias carves Belphoebe's name into the bark of trees (IV.vii.46). Though this had become something of a commonplace of amatory pastoral by 1596, it is best known from Gallus' fantasy of escape into a pastoral life (10.53–4):

> ... tenerisque meos incidere amores
> arboribus: crescent illae, crescetis, amores.

['and to carve my loves on the young trees: they will grow; you, my loves, will grow'.]

The importance of the image in Virgil's poem is underlined by the way it is echoed in Virgil's closing comparison of his ever-increasing love for Gallus to the growth of the green alder. In Virgil's eclogue-book as a whole, meanwhile, it harks back to Mopsus' lament for Daphnis/Caesar in Eclogue 5, which he introduces as a song *in viridi nuper quae cortice fagi ... descripsi* ('which I marked recently in the green bark of a beech-tree', 5.13–14), so that the image contains the potential for a linking of amatory and political devotion which we see in Spenser's use of it in the Timias episode (and indeed later in 'Colin Clouts Come Home Againe' too).

Difficulties over dating the composition of 'Colin Clouts Come Home Againe' have led to uncertainty and debate over what specific instance of 'vsage hard' the Shepherd of the Ocean is lamenting. The dedicatory epistle is signed 'the 27. of December. 1591', inviting any reader acquainted with Spenser's and Ralegh's movements to recognize the 'truth' it agrees with 'in circumstance and matter' as the events of 1589–91, when Ralegh, in temporary disgrace arising from his rivalry with the Earl of Essex, was apparently driven to Ireland, where

7 Cheney, 'The Laureate Choir'.

he renewed his friendship with Spenser, and persuaded him to return with him to court. Ralegh's introduction of Spenser and his poetry to the Queen on this visit resulted in Elizabeth's grant to Spenser of an annual stipend of £50. The sample of his epic which Spenser read to the Queen on this occasion, represented in the eclogue at lines 360–7, where Colin recites his 'simple song' to Cynthia, may well have been the Timias/Belphoebe episode of Book III. Ralegh's secret marriage did not take place until 1591, its discovery and punishment not until the following year. But despite the dating of the dedicatory epistle, Spenser's poem was not published until 1595, and contains lines which could not have been written before April 1594,[8] so that we know it must have been at least revised much closer to the date of publication. It is possible, therefore, but unprovable, that the 'vsage hard' of which the Shepherd of the Ocean complains is the punishment of Ralegh's marriage also fictionalized in Book IV of *The Faerie Queene*. The episode may also underlie Colin's song of Bregog and Mulla, as Oram has persuasively argued.[9] At any rate, the reader of the published volume is free, and in a position, to apply the poem to subsequent events, even if the 1591 dating cautiously disclaims reference to such a contentious topic. A reciprocal supportive friendship is evident in Spenser's defence of the disgraced Ralegh in the 1596 *Faerie Queene*, in the dedication of this volume, in the Letter to Ralegh appended to the 1590 *Faerie Queene* and in the commendatory poems by Ralegh printed in both editions of the epic, and this friendship is articulated through continual mutual allusion to one another's poems, in an intertextual relationship which Patrick Cheney describes as 'one of the most remarkable literary exchanges during the sixteenth century'.[10] It is natural that Spenser should represent this intertextual friendship in his pastoral through an imitation of Virgil's treatment of his friendship with Gallus.

Like Astrophel/Sidney in the companion poem, then, the Shepherd of the Ocean / Ralegh is here aligned with Virgil's Gallus. If we look beyond the eclogue and into the wider dialogue between the two poets across their works, we can see a very close mirroring of Virgil's affectionate critique of Gallus as it unfolds between eclogues 6 and 10 in Spenser's dedicatory sonnet to Ralegh in the 1590 *Faerie Queene*, where Spenser admires his friend's poems 'of thy loues

---

8 See McCabe, *Shorter Poems*, p. 650.
9 Oram, 'Spenser's Raleghs', 360–2.
10 Cheney, 'The Laureate Choir', p. 269. On their mutual allusions, see also Bednarz, 'Collaborator as Thief'.

praise', but suggests that it would be 'Fitter perhaps' for Ralegh 'to thonder Martiall stowre, / When so thee list thy lofty Muse to raise' (10–12), lines which have been read as a 'muted criticism' of Ralegh's failure to ascend to epic.[11] This of course recalls Gallus' squandering in Eclogue 10 of the Muses' gift he received in Eclogue 6. But within 'Colin Clouts Come Home Againe', the critique of Ralegh's Gallus-like *indignus amor* has a different emphasis. As in 'Astrophel', Spenser's depiction of his friend and fellow poet contributes to his poem's critique of Petrarchan love, and of Elizabeth's Petrarchizing court, modelled on Eclogue 10's critique of amatory elegy.[12] But the depiction of Ralegh is both less laudatory than Virgil's eclogues or even 'Astrophel', and less harshly critical than 'Astrophel' was of its subject. There is no suggestion here that Ralegh is divinely inspired, such as we find in the scene of Gallus' initiation in Virgil's sixth eclogue, or in the praises of Astrophel's poetry which flatteringly compare him to the Colin of the *Calender*, 'watered at the Muses well'. The Shepherd of the Ocean *is* reminiscent of the Colin of the *Calender*, but is a quite different way – because of his undeserved suffering at the hands of a fickle and cruel mistress (in fact, the same mistress under a different allegorical veil). To bring out this resemblance, Colin begins his account of his own part in the song-exchange by reminding us of the unhappy love for Rosalind which dominated his persona in the earlier work, as he explains his choice of different subject matter now (88–95):

> Nor of my loue, nor of my losse (quoth he)
> I then did sing, as then occasion fell:
> For loue had me forlorne, forlorne of me,
> That made me in that desart chose to dwell.
> But of my riuer *Bregogs* loue I soong,
> Which to the shiny *Mulla* he did beare,
> And yet doth beare, and euer will, so long
> As water doth within his bancks appeare.

The choice of dwelling in a 'desart' is the choice Colin made in *June*, but his current perspective is less bitter. This love has lost him as much as he has lost it (or her), and the fiction of 'Colin Clouts Come Home Againe' will transfigure England into a space of exile

---

11 Oram, 'Spenser's Raleghs', 345.
12 On Ralegh's distortion of Spenser's epic to fit his own Petrarchizing poetics in the commendatory sonnet 'Methought I saw the grave, where *Laura* lay', see Bednarz, 'Collaborator as Thief', 284–5.

(its corrupt denizens thrust out of Cupid's court as 'exuls', 894), and the Irish 'waste' (183) into a home, with Colin's round trip beginning and ending in the pastoral space, away from Cynthia and her court. Thus Colin chooses a different theme for his part in the song-exchange, ignoring Rosalind altogether. The Shepherd of the Ocean's own circular journey beginning and ending in England, conversely, marks his continuing dependence on Cynthia.[13] Like the Colin of the *Calender*, Ralegh, in his choice of a Petrarchan version of pastoral in *The Ocean to Cynthia*, figures his happiness as dependent on the Queen's response, for all that he mixes satirical bitterness with his expressions of dutiful love. Thus he remains vulnerable to 'scorne and foule despite' (905) such as Colin suffered at Rosalind's hands. From the limited perspective imposed by his dependency, the Shepherd of the Ocean can only pity Colin's distance from Cynthia as banishment (181–3):[14] it is as though he is seeing only the bitter Colin of the *Calender*, and cannot appreciate that the situation in this poem is different, that this Colin has gained his independence. Like Colin in the *Calender*, he is the blameless victim of an *indignus amor*, an unworthy love, and suffers through no positive fault of his own. He has not abandoned a calling like Astrophel or Gallus, but what he experiences is nevertheless the wrong kind of love, and makes him vulnerable to the same accusations of folly levelled at Colin in the *Calender* (*Aprill* 25, 155, 158).

When, later in the poem, Colin's description of Cynthia's court turns to satire, we will learn to identify this Petrarchism, practised innocently by the Shepherd of the Ocean, with the corrupt, competitive and perniciously hierarchical court environment. The way in which Elizabeth's courtiers routinely negotiated their relations with the Queen through Petrarchan discourse has been much discussed.[15] Ralegh's *Ocean to Cynthia* is often cited as an example. Spenser depicts

---

13 The figure resonates suggestively with the Theocritean homage to Zeus at the opening of Idyll 17, which Virgil imitates as a direct political compliment to Octavian in the proem to Eclogue 8, *a te principium, tibi desinam* ('from you is my beginning, in you I shall end', 8.11). This prefaces Damon's song of the suicidal goatherd lamenting his own *indignus amor* (8.18) for a fickle mistress, which closely anticipates Gallus in the final eclogue. Spenser pointedly corrects the idolatrous gesture of 8.11 in *October* 84: see Chapter 3 above.
14 A point made by Oram, 'Spenser's Raleghs', 347.
15 Leonard Forster, *The Icy Fire: Five Studies in European Petrarchism* (Cambridge: Cambridge University Press, 1969); E. C. Wilson, *England's Eliza* (Cambridge, MA: Harvard University Press, 1939); Catherine Bates, *The Rhetoric of Courtship in Elizabethan Language and Literature* (Cambridge: Cambridge University Press, 1992); Marotti, 'Elizabethan Sonnet Sequences and the Social Order'.

the practice here as at once a kind of allegory and as morally corrupt.[16] Cynthia's courtiers bandy words of love about freely (776–8):

> For all the walls and windows there are writ,
> All full of loue, and loue, and loue my deare,
> And all their talke and studie is of it.

But the very frequency with which they use the word betokens lightness and insincerity. They are not speaking of the 'mightie mysteries' (788) of the God of Love, held in such awe by the 'shepheard nation'; rather (789–90) they

> vse his ydle name to other needs,
> But as a complement for courting vaine.

They abuse the name, and mean something else by it. On one level, this 'something else' is 'disloyall lust' (892), the 'sordid vses' (792) and 'licentious deedes' (787) which are the goal pursued by Paridell with Hellenore (*Faerie Queene* III.ix.27–31, x.5–11), or by Sidney's ironic persona in *Astrophil and Stella*. On another, it is the desire for promotion in the social hierarchy, 'courting vaine' as the attempt to get ahead at court, as they adopt the stance or persona of a lover as a 'badge' to make a 'braue' show and win 'esteem' (779–81), in the system of homosocial rivalry we have already seen held up to sceptical scrutiny in 'Astrophel'.

The courtier's use of Petrarchan discourse to negotiate their social climbing amounts to the same allegory which governed the *Calender*, but where Spenser used it there to avoid the 'ieopardee' of the invidious court (*Calender* 'To His Booke') in the service of the public interest, here it is used for self-serving ends, and denounced as hypocrisy. This is allegory as imagined in Puttenham's suggestively double definition, first as 'the Figure of False Semblant or Dissimulation', and then as 'the Courtier or Figure of Fair Semblant'.[17] It is part and parcel of the more general hypocrisy of the competitive courtiers described a little earlier (699–702):

> To which him needs, a guilefull hollow hart,
> Masked with faire dissembling curtesie,
> A filed toung furnisht with tearmes of art,
> No art of schoole, but Courtiers schoolery.

---

16 William Oram's reading of 'Colin Clouts Come Home Againe' in the excellent 'Spenser's Raleghs' chimes closely with my own, though he sees 'Ralegh-as-Shepherd' in the poem as rather more 'morally ambiguous' (350) and 'compromise[d]' by his association with the corrupt Petrarchism of the court than I do.
17 Puttenham, *Art of English Poesy*, 3.18 (p. 271) and 3.25 (p. 379).

Such 'speaking otherwise' (*allegoria*) as sheer dishonesty and hypocrisy is embodied in the figure of Archimago, who 'of pleasing wordes had store, / And well could file his tongue as smooth as glas' (*Faerie Queene* I.i.35.6-7), and whose fashioning of deceptive images (chiefly the beauteous image of Una, whose real-life counterpart is another idealized avatar of Elizabeth) is a perversion of poetic 'making'. (The word *poesis*, as Sidney reminds us in the *Apologie*, comes from the Greek *poiein*, 'to make'.)[18]

Their busy self-promotion is likewise part and parcel of the general culture of invidious ambition at Cynthia's court also described in the earlier passage (690-8):

> Where each one seeks with malice and with strife,
> To thrust downe other into foule disgrace,
> Himselfe to raise: and he doth soonest rise
> That best can handle his deceitfull wit,
> In subtil shifts, and finest sleights deuise,
> Either by slaundring his well deemed name,
> Through leasings lewd, and fained forgerie:
> Or else by breeding him some blot of blame,
> By creeping close into his secrecie ...

The lines are strongly reminiscent of Philotime's golden chain in the House of Mammon, on which

> Some thought to raise themselues to high degree,
> By riches and vnrighteous reward,
> Some by close shouldering, some by flatteree;
> Others through friends, others for base regard;
> And all by wrong wayes for themselues prepard.
> Those that were vp themselues, kept others low,
> Those that were low themselues, held others hard,
> Ne sufferd them to rise or greater grow,
> But euery one did striue his fellow downe to throw.
>
> (*The Faerie Queene* II.vii.47)

Though by necessity Cynthia is not explicitly linked to the corruption of her court in 'Colin Clouts Come Home Againe', Spenser's evocation of his earlier allegory (an echo of *The Faerie Queene* which he surely expected readers of this volume to recognize) implies that she

---

18 The observation was first made by A. Bartlett Giamatti, *The Play of Double Senses: Spenser's* Faerie Queene (Englewood Cliffs, NJ: Prentice-Hall, 1975), p. 119, and has been widely echoed; see also David Quint, 'Archimago and Amoret: The Poem and Its Doubles', in Patrick Cheney and Lauren Silberman (eds), *Worldmaking Spenser* (Lexington: Universiy Press of Kentucky, 2000), pp. 32-42.

stands in the same relation to it as Philotime to the courtiers viewed by Guyon. The daughter of Mammon sits enthroned in 'soueraigne maiestye', casting brightness over the scene with the 'broad beauties beam' of her face, which 'wondrous faire did seeme to bee' (44.5, 45.1–2).[19] Indeed, we are told (45.7–8)

> most heauenly faire in deed and vew
> She by creation was, till she did fall;
> Thenceforth she sought for helps, to cloke her crime withall.

This evolutionary retrospect, unusual for an allegorical personification, might already in the *Faerie Queene* have reminded readers of their ageing queen, who by 1590 relied heavily on cosmetics to maintain her beauteous public image, just as Philotime's beauty is now 'wrought by art and counterfetted shew', in an attempt 'more louers vnto her to call' (45.5–6). The change wrought by age in Elizabeth is interpreted in Philotime as the result of a 'fall' akin to Lucifer's fall by pride. In the eclogue, only the idealized beauty of her youth is remembered and described, a vision of 'her lookes … like beames of the morning Sun' (604) introduced specifically as mere 'remembrance' (46) in Colin's opening words – those words recalling Tityrus' devotion to the memory of Octavian's face in Eclogue 1. But Cynthia is implicated as surely as Philotime in the satire on her ambitious courtiers, both as symbolic love-object and as head and arbiter of the social hierarchy they aspire to climb. 'Honour and dignitie from her alone / Deriued are' (*Faerie Queene* II.vii.48.7–8), Guyon is told, but, like Colin rejecting life at court in favour of a virtuous life and pious devotion to the god of true love in his pastoral home in this poem, Guyon there rejects the offer of her love and preferment out of fidelity to another 'loue auowd' (50.7).

The memory of Philotime's association with Lucifer's aspiration to godhead, her alignment with the Zeus of Homer's *Iliad* (8.18–27) in her control of the golden chain, and Mammon's claim that she is 'Worthy of heauen and hye felicitie, / From whence the gods haue her for enuy thrust' (II.vii.29.5–6), also cast a shadow over the Tityrean rhetoric of deification which attends Colin's idealizing descriptions of Cynthia as 'that Angel' (40), 'Much like an Angell in all forme and fashion' (615). We are reminded of *Aprill*'s sceptical alignment of Tityrus' *erit ille mihi semper deus* ('he will always be my god', *Ecl.* 1.7) with idolatry, including Petrarch's worship of Laura, and with

---

[19] Michael O'Connell, *Mirror and Veil: The Historical Dimension of Spenser's Faerie Queene* (Chapel Hill: University of North Carolina Press, 1977), pp. 105–7.

punishable hubris like that of the self-deifying queen Niobe. But here the reader is left to draw her own conclusions, from the disparity between the glorious vision of the Queen and the satire on her corrupt court, and the disparity between the two heavenly figures praised in the poem – on one hand Cynthia, with her undesirable connections to a corrupt court and to a sinister intertext, and on the other Cupid, the god of love worshipped piously by the devout shepherds.

This Petrarchism is Spenser's equivalent, here as in 'Astrophel', for Gallus' *indignus amor* in Virgil's tenth eclogue.[20] Again we can see his reading as coloured by the interpretations of Servius and Vives, for Cynthia's courtiers pursue this 'Courtiers schoolery' *instead of* the 'art of schoole' (702), and despise learning and the learned. Also relevant to Spenser's poem is Servius' interpretation of *indigno* at line 10 as *meretricio* ('[love] of a prostitute'). His biographical note on Gallus at the head of the eclogue explains that Gallus' mistress Lycoris is to be identified as *Cytheridem meretricem, libertam Volumnii* ('the prostitute Cytheris, freedwoman [i.e. former slave] of Volumnius'), and goes on to claim that beneath the consolation of Gallus on the surface lurks vituperation of Gallus' 'shameful love' (*turpis amoris*), and also of Antony, Cytheris' subsequent client and Gallus' rival in the eclogue, whom she accompanied in his military camp against Roman custom (*quem contra Romanum morem Cytheris est in castra comitata*). The social shame of too serious or public an attachment to a mere prostitute can be felt in Cicero's second Philippic, where Cicero pours scorn on Antony's indecorous disregard for the social hierarchy in allowing the same Cytheris to attend him in his public procession, and making his mother walk with her as if she were his wife (*Philippics* 2.58). Though Cynthia is as far above Ralegh and the other courtiers as Lycoris is beneath Gallus, nevertheless the tribulations arising from inequalities of rank in the hierarchical social system are as relevant to Spenser's poem as to Virgil's, and this hierarchical arrangement, so different to the bonds of equal friendship and meritocratic respect organizing the 'shepheards nation', is central

---

20 Perhaps we might even see an interlingual pun on the name of Gallus, as representative of this *indignus amor* and the pains it brings, in the picture of the courtiers 'fraught with enuie that their *galls* do swell' (760). This would recall the pun on 'gall' and 'Gaul' or Frenchman in Thomalin's emblem to *March*, part of the *Calender's* strategy warning Elizabeth against marriage to the French D'Alençon (McCabe, *Shorter Poems*, p. 527). 'Gaul' or 'Frenchman' is the literal meaning of Gallus' name. Rosalind's Lycoris-like desertion of Colin in favour of her Frenchman D'Alençon caused him to assume the posture of Virgil's Gallus, dying from a bitter love, in *Januarye*, *June* and *December*.

to the satirical vision of Cynthia's court. Indeed, with the reversal in social status, the shame of prostitution adheres to Ralegh and the other courtiers, who abuse the language of love to gain preferment and wealth themselves.

Spenser's alternative to this *indignus amor* and Petrarchan idolatry is true love, figured as right worship of Cupid. This Cupid clearly reflects the Christian God (in the light of the biblical 'God is Love'). Born 'long before the world' (839), he is reminiscent of Christ in his 'pure and spotlesse' conception (800–2)

> without Syre or couples of one kynd,
> For *Venus* selfe doth soly couples seeme,
> Both male and female though commixture ioynd.

Colin's hymn praises him as creator of the world (841) and as sustaining it by inspiring all creatures with sexual desire, causing them to procreate (863–72). As in *The Faerie Queene*'s Garden of Adonis, and in the *Amoretti and Epithalamium*, published in the same year as this volume, mutual procreative love is identified with God's will and Christian piety, and Colin's teaching here is the same as that of the sonnet sequence: 'let vs loue, deare loue, lyke as we ought, / loue is the lesson which the Lord vs taught' (*Amoretti* 68.13–14).[21] This Cupid, or Christian God, is the source of Colin's vatic inspiration (823–38):

> Shepheard it seemes that some celestiall rage
> Of loue (quoth *Cuddy*) is breath'd into thy brest,
> That powreth forth these oracles so sage,
> Of that high powre, wherewith thou art possest …
> Well may it seeme by this thy deep insight,
> That of that God the Priest thou shouldest bee:
> So well thou wot'st the mysterie of his might,
> As if his godhead thou didst present see.
> Of loues perfection perfectly to speake,
> Or of his nature rightly to define,
> Indeed (said *Colin*) passeth reasons reach,
> And needs his priest t'expresse his powre diuine.

---

21 The notion of Colin as a teacher of love recalls Bion, both in Bion's poem 10, on his role as 'tutor' to Eros (in which the tables are humorously turned, and Bion learns love from his student while trying to teach him bucolic song), and in the *Lament for Bion*, where Bion is described as having 'taught the lore of kisses'. Bion's version of bucolic, with its high valuation of love which so influenced the Roman elegiac poets (Fantuzzi and Hunter, *Tradition and Innovation*, pp. 170–90), provides a suggestive exemplar for Spenser's revision of Virgil's antierotic *Eclogues*.

If the Shepherd of the Ocean is aligned with the Gallus who suffers the torments of love in Virgil's tenth eclogue, it is Colin (here as in 'Astrophel') who receives the divine inspiration accorded Gallus in Eclogue 6 and finally claimed by Virgil himself at the end of his book. In his choice of subject for his part in the song-exchange with the Shepherd of the Ocean, Colin eschews Petrarchism and the political wooing of the *Calender* in favour of a song which adumbrates the faithful mutual love he will praise in the climactic hymn, in its celebration of the triumph of Bregog and Mulla over the oppressive potentate Mole. On the surface, the song may seem 'ydle' enough (to use the terms of the disagreement registered in the opening epistle), merely a recreative toy or 'mery lay' as Thestylis calls it (157). But these 'verses are not vaine' ('Astrophel' 68); they contribute as much as any in the poem to Spenser's critical engagement with Virgil and to the unfolding of his volume's poetic programme.

Diverting the pastoral source

The story of the 'deceitfull traine' (118) by which Spenser's river Bregog gains the love of the nymph Mulla, evading the 'watchfull ward' (136) of her jealous father by conveying his streams underground 'Till they into the *Mullaes* water slide' (144), has often been compared to the myth of Alpheus and Arethusa. It is normally discussed in relation to Ovid's version in the *Metamorphoses*. But Arethusa plays an earlier, and important, role in pastoral poetry, and this is a crucial context for interpreting Spenser's river marriage.

Virgil's Arethusa is a symbol of the divine inspiration to which he lays claim at the end of the tenth eclogue: there, he calls himself the Muses' poet, but at the beginning of the poem it is Arethusa whom he invokes, as if she were a muse, to inspire his song (10.1–6):

> Extremum hunc, Arethusa, mihi concede laborem ...
> sic tibi, cum fluctus subterlabere Sicanos,
> Doris amara suam non intermisceat undam,
> incipe; sollicitos Galli dicamus amores ...

['Permit me this last work, Arethusa ... If, when you shall slide beneath the Sicanian billows, you would not have the bitter Doris (i.e. the sea) mingle her water with yours, begin: let us tell the troubled loves of Gallus.']

The Arethusa is a spring on Ortygia, an island in the bay of Syracuse which formed the ancient centre of the city, in Theocritus' native Sicily. Servius' gloss to line 1 observes that *per Arethusam autem musam Siculam, id est Theocritium invocat carmen* ('by Arethusa, moreover, he invokes the Sicilian muse, that is the song of Theocritus'). In Theocritus' first idyll, which will be an important model for Eclogue 10, the dying Daphnis bids farewell to Arethusa, as one of the local nymphs (117), and before Virgil the stream had become a symbol of Theocritean pastoral inspiration. In the lament ascribed to Moschus (discussed in Chapter 4), Bion, as a writer of Theocritean pastoral, is said to have drunk from the Arethusa just as Homer drank from the Hippocrene (77), in that passage which claims for pastoral a status comparable to epic, as an alternative but equally worthy form of hexameter poetry.

Virgil appropriates this symbol in a radical way, by connecting it to the myth of Arethusa and Alpheus, familiar to him from other Greek sources,[22] and at the same time boldly rewriting the myth. Servius' gloss on line 4 highlights Virgil's departure from his sources here:

> Opinion varies, for some say that Alpheus comes through the seas from Elis to Arethusa, a nymph of Sicily, following whom one says 'the tradition is that this Alpheus is a river of Elis'. Others say that this Arethusa, now transformed into a spring, fled Alpheus and came from Elis into Sicily, which now he follows.

In fact, there is no known account prior to Virgil's *Eclogues* in which Arethusa herself crosses the sea from Elis, the region neighbouring Arcadia in Greece – in earlier mentions, she is always already located in Sicily. Ovid takes up Virgil's innovation in his well-known account in the *Metamorphoses*, so that by Servius' time it was equally familiar, but Virgil seems to have been the originator here, not a follower.[23] In Book 3 of the *Aeneid* (694–6) Virgil alludes to the myth again, as Aeneas passes Ortygia during his escape from a sinister and threatening Sicily dominated by the Cyclopes and the thundering of Aetna, and here, though he emphasizes the union of Alpheus and Arethusa (elided in the eclogue), there is no suggestion that Arethusa too came from Greece.[24] It is Alpheus here who drives his course across the sea to mingle his waves with an indigenous nymph in hostile territory, just as Aeneas will achieve the mingling of the Trojan and Latin races

---

22 Pausanias 5.7.2–3, Moschus fragment 3.
23 See John Van Sickle, 'Staging Vergil's Future and Past', *Classical Journal* 93 (1998), 213–14.
24 Arethusa is again apostrophized at *Aeneid* 3.696, however, reminding the reader of the Eclogue 10 invocation. This section of the *Aeneid* is also an important intertext for Spenser's poem, and we shall discuss it below ('Epic Nymphs and Sources').

by wedding Lavinia after a bitter war (and with the help of another Arcadian exile, the king Evander).

In the *Aeneid* the earlier version of the myth suits Virgil's purposes. In the eclogue, Virgil's innovative idea that Arethusa also originated in Arcadia serves several purposes germane to his current project. Firstly, the notion of Arethusa herself being transported connotes the idea of the pastoral genre (of which she is the fount in the *Lament for Bion*) being brought to a new land, as Virgil imports Greek (and Sicilian) bucolic into his own native culture and language. It is like Horace's boast in *Carmina* 3.30.13–14 that he is *princeps Aeolium carmen ad Italos / deduxisse modos* ('first to have brought Aeolian song to Italian measures'), and Virgil's own at *Georgics* 3.10–11, *primus ego in patriam mecum ... / Aonio rediens deducam vertice Musas* ('I first, returning to my country, will lead the Muses with me from the Aonian peak').[25] At the same time, and even more boldly, he asserts the priority of his reworking of pastoral over its source.[26] The tenth eclogue is set in Arcadia, and in this invocation Arethusa is imagined as not having yet made her journey to the land where she will become the inspiration of Theocritus and his Greek followers. This is similar to the way in which Milton in *Paradise Lost* trumps his

---

25 Compare also *Prima Thalia*, Eclogue 6.1–2, and Propertius 3.1.3–4 (remembering the Virgilian and Horatian passages). The verb shared by the *Georgics* passage and the Horatian ode, *deduco*, has several significant connotations. Firstly, it gestures pointedly to the refinement of Callimachean poetics as practised by both poets – the *deductum carmen* of Eclogue 6.5. Secondly, it connotes the celebration of a Roman military triumph (*Oxford Latin Dictionary*, *deduco* 10 a, 'To bring (a person, army) back with one to Rome'). Both Horace and Virgil have this sense in mind, also: Horace's ode ends with the demand that Melpomene crown him with the the laurels traditionally granted the *triumphator* (*Carmina* 3.30.15–16), while the proem to *Georgics* 3 immediately goes on to imagine Virgil as *victor* (*Georgics* 3.17) driving a hundred chariots and leading a triumphal procession celebrating Octavian's military victories. As Ryan Krieger Balot puts it, 'Virgil emphasizes that he is returning to Rome with the spoils of poetic warfare ... in his train' ('Pindar, Virgil, and the Proem to Georgic 3', *Phoenix* 52 (1998), 83–94, at 90; see also A. Hardie, 'The *Georgics*, the Mysteries and the Muses at Rome', *PCPS* 48 (2002), 165–208, at 194–206). Thirdly, *deduco* can mean 'to draw or lead (water) off, divert' (*Oxford Latin Dictionary*, *deduco* 2 b). As nymphs, the Muses can appropriately be figured as water-courses, and the contexts of the Horace and *Georgics* passages both feature rivers prominently: Horace speaks of the *violens Aufidus*, an Italian river whose raging current shows how sorely Italy needs the Callimachean refinement Horace is now importing (3.30.10), and Virgil announces his intention to set up a marble temple to Octavian beside the Mantuan river Mincius (3.13–15) – the setting for the song-contest of Eclogue 7.
26 See John Van Sickle, *Virgil's* Book of Bucolics, *the Ten Eclogues Translated into English Verse, Framed by Cues for Reading Aloud and Clues for Threading Texts and Themes* (Baltimore: Johns Hopkins University Press, 2011), pp. 72, 226.

classical models by locating the source of his inspiration at the beginning of time, and presenting Greek mythology as a later falsification of the original myth he reports truly: 'Thus they relate, / Erring: for he with this rebellious rout / Fell long before' (*Paradise Lost* 1.745-8).²⁷

Virgil's Arethusa also contributes to the tenth eclogue's reflections on love and on love poetry. Arethusa's journey beneath the sea is the journey taken only by Alpheus in the earlier version of the myth, so it evokes her resistance to his rapacious advances in the myth. In fact, Virgil is imitating lines from Moschus' miniature epyllion describing Alpheus' journey:

> Ἀλφειὸς μετὰ Πῖσαν ἐπὴν κατὰ πόντον ὀδεύῃ,
> ἔρχεται εἰς Ἀρέθοισαν ἄγων κοτινηφόρον ὕδωρ,
> ἕδνα φέρων καλὰ φύλλα καὶ ἄνθεα καὶ κόνιν ἱράν,
> καὶ βαθὺς ἐμβαίνει τοῖς κύμασι, τὰν δὲ θάλασσαν
> νέρθεν ὑποτροχάει, κοὐ μίγνυται ὕδασιν ὕδωρ,
> ἁ δ' οὐκ οἶδε θάλασσα διερχομένῳ ποταμοῖο.
> κῶρος λινοθέτας κακομάχανος αἰνὰ διδάσκων
> καὶ ποταμὸν διὰ φίλτρον Ἔρως ἐδίδαξε κολυμβῆν.

['When Alpheus leaves Pisa behind him and travels by the sea, he brings Arethusa the water that makes the wild olives grow; and with a bride-gift coming, of pretty leaves and pretty flowers and sacred dust, he goeth deep into the waves and runneth his course beneath the sea, and so runneth that the two waters mingle not and the sea never knows of the river's passing through. So is it that the spell of that impish setter of nets, that sly and crafty teacher of troubles, Love, hath e'en taught a river how to dive.']²⁸

Moschus' mildly antierotic warning is amplified in Virgil's poem, and figuratively reflected in her reluctance, in Virgil's version, to let her waters be contaminated with brine. The sea-water is described as *amara* ('bitter'), a word apparently never applied to the sea before this,²⁹ but commonly used of the pains of love, as for instance by Palaemon in Eclogue 3 (line 110).³⁰ In the context of a pastoral elegy for a fellow poet, it also evokes, by pointed contrast, the opening line of the *Lament for Bion*, where pseudo-Moschus calls on the

---

27 Of course, it also resembles the triumphal connotations of the third *Georgic* and the Horatian ode noted above.
28 It is worth noting that Henri Estienne's Latin translation of this fragment in his *Theocriti Aliorumque Poetarum Idyllia* (1579) uses some of the vocabulary of Virgil's passage to render Moschus' Greek, in *subterlabitur ... fluctus*. Estienne's reading of the Moschus fragment is coloured by his memory of Virgil's allusion.
29 As Clausen notes, *ad loc.*
30 A point made by Harrison, *Generic Enrichment*, citing different examples.

'sweet Dorian waters' to lament Bion; Virgil's metonymy 'Doris' for 'sea' (also original to Virgil here) also evokes this 'Dorian', by which pseudo-Moschus refers to the seas around Sicily, colonized by Doric-speaking Greeks.[31] The *Lament* characterizes Bion's Doric pastoral as chiefly concerned with love, as we saw in Chapter 4: Virgil is revaluing this subject matter as not sweet but bitter. And the word *fluctus*, which I translated as 'billows' above, has more turbulent connotations than the Latin *undae* ('waves'), to the extent that it is commonly used, as a dead metaphor, to mean commotion or disorder, so that it strikes a chord with the description of Gallus' *amores* as *sollicitos* ('agitated', 'troubled') two lines later.[32] In Virgil's eclogue, as Virgil (according to Servius) adapts lines from Gallus' elegies, the genres of pastoral and love elegy intermingle for a while, only to separate finally as Gallus finds himself unable to break free from the tyranny of Love, and Virgil ends in a securely pastoral register with the image of his poem as a basket woven by a shepherd from hibiscus. (Basket weaving was one of the normal labours of a shepherd which Corydon rebukes himself for neglecting in his love-frenzy at the end of Eclogue 2.) As Harrison observes, Virgil in this poem resembles his own Arethusa, ultimately keeping his pastoral pure as it passes through the turbulent emotional sea of elegy.[33]

Colin's song of Bregog and Mulla engages with all these aspects of the muse of Virgil's final eclogue. Far from being a mere entertainment, detachable from the rest of the poem, it is our key to the way in which Spenser positions himself in relation to Virgilian pastoral. Most obviously, his story reverses the antierotic implications of the myth as Virgil uses it. The love of Spenser's rivers is equal and mutual: indeed, Mulla's love for Bregog is mentioned first ('Full faine she lou'd, and was belou'd full faine'), the syntactical balance of the line emphasizing the mutuality of the love. Even in the lines which seem most critical of Bregog, explaining his name as a badge of shame for his misconduct, agency is ambivalent and could be seen as shared by the lovers (118–19):

[31] Duncan Kennedy makes the connection with this line from the *Lament for Bion*: 'Arcades ambo: Virgil, Gallus and Arcadia', *Hermathena* 143 (1987), 47–59, at 48. Kennedy's article reads the Arethusa invocation as figuring the generic interaction of pastoral and love elegy in Virgil's poem, but makes the opposite identification to that which I, agreeing rather with S. J. Harrison, see in the lines: for Kennedy, Arethusa represents elegy, the sea water pastoral.
[32] Compare Dido, who *fluctuat aestu* ('swells, or seethes with passion') at *Aeneid* 4.532.
[33] Harrison, *Generic Enrichment*, p. 62.

> So hight because of this deceitfull traine,
> Which he with *Mulla* wrought to win delight.

This 'traine' ('snare' or 'trap') could be wrought by Bregog to win (his own) delight 'with Mulla', or enjoyment of her; just conceivably it could be read as practised *on* her. But it is more natural to read the lines as attributing agency to both, to Bregog 'with Mulla', to win delight for both of them. The trick is played, of course, on her father Mole, and it is his stern authority which Mulla must resist in Colin's tale – in contrast to the amatory advances of Alpheus which are the object of Arethusa's resistance. Mole is ostensibly 'more carefull of her good' (120), but what this means is that he wishes to force her against her will into an arranged marriage for the sake of social preferment (121). The 'neighbour flood' (122) Broadwater is imagined as a noble match, bargained for long and hard, with Mole's 'continuall paine' (124), and the planned marriage as a fundamentally financial transaction ('The dowre agreed', 126). Which side Spenser is on is strongly indicated by the narratorial comment 'For loue will not be drawne, but must be ledde' (129), with its reminiscence of *The Faerie Queene* (III.i.25.7–9):

> Ne may loue be compeld by maisterie;
> For soone as maisterie comes, sweet loue anone
> Taketh his nimble wings, and soone away is gone.

In the context of a pastoral song, and in the context of a piece of mythologizing landscape etiology, these references to social hierarchy and money are jarring, even comical. They belong to the world of the court as it appears in the satirical passages later in the poem, and Mole shares with the corrupt courtiers their selfish ambition to 'purchase highest rowmes in bowre and hall' (726). In an interesting article on Colin's river story in relation to the myth of Arethusa, Lynn Kelsey has argued persuasively that Mole represents Lord Burghley, who was notorious for his abuse of wardships, effectively selling off his many wards in arranged marriages in order to amass wealth for himself. Thus Colin's song continues the anti-Burghley satire which had resulted in the banning of *Mother Hubberds Tale*, but by more cautiously allegorical means, which Kelsey compares to Bregog's persistence in his forbidden love through literal, and Alpheus-like, subterfuge.[34] Like Diggon's satire in *September*, the fable is an exercise

---

34 Lynn Kelsey, 'Spenser, Ralegh, and the Language of Allegory'. See also below (and Oram, 'Spenser's Raleghs') on the tale as an allegory of Ralegh's marriage to Elizabeth Throckmorton.

in what the poet might 'dare vndersaye' (*September* 91).

If Mole's self-serving perversion of matrimony is closely related to the abuse of love by Cynthia's ambitious Petrarchizing courtiers (and thus an aspect of that *indignus amor* from which Ralegh, though innocently, also suffers), the mutual desire of Mulla and Bregog, bent on and consummated in marriage, is in keeping with the virtuous love celebrated in Colin's hymn to Cupid, as also in Book III of *The Faerie Queene*, and in the *Amoretti and Epithalamium*, also published in 1595. And indeed, Bregog's love for Mulla, in Colin's initial statement of his theme, resonates strongly with Colin's description of his love for his new wife, Elizabeth Boyle, which forms the triumphal centre of the poem (92-5, 476-9):[35]

> But of my riuer *Bregogs* loue I soong,
> Which to the shiny *Mulla* he did beare,
> And yet doth beare, and euer will, so long
> As water doth within his bancks appeare.
>
> My thoughts, my heart, my loue, my life is shee,
> And I hers euer onely, euer one:
> One euer I all vowed hers to bee,
> One euer I, and others neuer none.

The marriage of Bregog and Mulla chimes with Spenser's own recently consummated marriage. In the context of the song exchange, and Ralegh's 'lamentable lay', it also recalls Ralegh's own marriage to Elizabeth Throckmorton, which had resulted in the disfavour of the Queen the Shepherd of the Ocean laments in his own lay.[36] Mole, as a figure of Burghley, is an agent of Elizabeth's oppressive power, and his interference with the young lovers also reflects the Queen's opposition to the private loves of her favourite courtiers.[37] Robert Ellrodt has argued on the basis of a stylistic analysis that the Bregog and Mulla tale was a late addition to the poem, and Oram, accepting this, argues that it allegorizes Ralegh's secret marriage, so that 'The inset story … revises the picture advanced in the rest of the poem' – for Oram sees the Shepherd of the Ocean as inculpated in the court's corrupt Petrarchism to a greater extent than I do – 'regarding him

---

35 See David W. Burchmore, 'The Image of the Centre in "Colin Clouts come home againe"', *RES* 28 (1977), 393–406, on the concentric structure of the poem, and for a defence of the identification of Elizabeth Boyle as the subject of these central lines.
36 See Spenser, *The Shorter Poems*, ed. William Oram *et al.* (New Haven: Yale University Press, 1989), pp. 523–4, 532.
37 In *March*, Spenser had already glanced at an earlier example of this jealous control by Elizabeth, her disapproval of Leicester's marriage to Lettice Knollys.

with urbane and tempered praise'.[38] If the Shepherd of the Ocean is represented in the poem as wholly subject to the allegorical love he bears towards Cynthia, nevertheless Spenser's reminder to Ralegh of the genuine value of true marital love, and the wisest attitude to overbearing monarchical authority, relies in part on the decision Ralegh has already made and should not regret, a choice of love over worldly advantage which Spenser figures in the choice made by his watery lovers. In keeping with the way in which Spenser and Ralegh continually respond to each other's poems, his method can also be seen to play off Ralegh's lyric 'Our passions are most like to Floods and streames; / The shallow Murmur but the Deep are dumb'. The lyric is an example of Ralegh's Petrarchan courtship of his Queen, and Michael O'Connell connects it to Timias' lament in *The Faerie Queene* III.v.[39] In Spenser's story of his passionate streams in 'Colin Clouts Come Home Againe', he wittily redirects the current of Ralegh's simile, making it into an allegory approving Ralegh's decision in 1591 to put his private, literal and sincere love above his Petrarchan courtiership and courtly ambition. In *The Faerie Queene*'s treatment of the affair at IV.vii–viii, it is Amoret who represents Elizabeth Throckmorton and inspires Belphoebe's jealousy: Amoret, whose wider significance in the poem far exceeds this temporary personal identification, has been brought up in the Garden of Adonis, that visionary climax of Spenser's celebration of married love within his epic which forms such a key intertext of the present volume. By marrying his own Elizabeth, as Spenser would also do, Ralegh has embraced not just a woman but a principle, and one of supreme and symbolic importance to Spenser's religious vision and poetics. Ralegh is not merely contrasted with Colin as an exemplar of *indignus amor* in this poem but rather presented as torn between the two contrasted kinds of love. Spenser is gently advising him to end his suffering by adjusting his priorities, and choosing the virtuous private love to which both poets already share an allegiance.

Spenser's reworking of the Arethusa myth also reflects the temporary mingling of, and discrimination between, different genres in his poem, in a way which plays off Virgil's use of his invocation of Arethusa to figure the meeting of pastoral and amatory elegy in Eclogue 10. In 'Colin Clouts Come Home Againe', pastoral mingles its stream temporarily with Ralegh's Petrarchism, which, as we have

---

38 Robert Ellrodt, *Neoplatonism in the Poetry of Edmund Spenser* (Geneva: E. Droz, 1960), pp. 219–23; Oram, 'Spenser's Raleghs', 360–2 (quotation at 362).
39 O'Connell, *Mirror and Veil*, pp. 111–12.

seen, is aligned in Spenser's poem with the frenzied and *indignus amor* of Gallus' love elegies, through which Virgil's eclogue passes before emerging in pastoral purity, like his virginal Arethusa passing uncontaminated through the turbulent sea. Colin and his pastoral, too, emerge unscathed from their encounter with Petrarchism. In the wider poem, Spenser thus also resembles Virgil's Arethusa. In fact, Spenser spells this out more clearly than Virgil does himself, in the fiction of Colin's voyage. Colin crosses a literal sea in the company of the Shepherd of the Ocean, whose very name recalls Virgil's implicit analogy between Gallus' *sollicitos amores* and the *fluctus* ('billows') of *Doris amara* ('the bitter sea'). Not only does he survive the voyage, but he rejects the *indignus amor* of Petrarchism in the sinister form it takes in Cynthia's court, and returns, uncontaminated by his encounter with courtly vice, to his innocent pastoral home. But where Virgil like Arethusa rejects love *tout court*, Spenser and Colin reject debased Petrarchan love in favour of the true love celebrated in his hymn to Cupid. Thus Spenser is more like his own Mulla, who embraces mutual love and rejects the abuse of matrimony for the sake of social preferment, part of that court culture which perverts love for political ends.

He is also like Bregog, who after all is the one who, like Alpheus, actually goes underground in Spenser's reworking of the myth. Where Alpheus' descent was motivated by rapacious desire, however, Bregog is driven to these means in order to avoid oppression by hostile powers, like Colin removing himself from a life of servitude in Cynthia's corrupt court, and like Spenser (as Kelsey observes) cautiously insinuating his critique of power under cover of allegory. Spenser is not so cautious as Kelsey suggests, however: the allegory of Burghley as Mole may be buried rather deeply, but those of Ralegh as Shepherd of the Ocean and Cynthia as Elizabeth lie very close to the transparent surface. No reader could miss the force of his satire on Elizabeth's court. And 'who knowes not *Colin Clout*?' (*Faerie Queene* VI.x.16.4) There is no need for the glosses of an 'E.K.' here to alert us to secret meanings, because they are an open secret at best. The key thing about Bregog is not his secrecy but his independence, his successful disobedience in the face of oppression. After all, he does not ultimately go unespied or unpunished, but nevertheless *is* successful. The angered Mole (149–55)

> In great auenge did roll downe from his hill
> Huge mightie stones, the which encomber might

> His passage, and his water-courses spill.
> So of a Riuer, which he was of old,
> He none was made, but scattred all to nought,
> And lost emong those rocks into him rold,
> Did lose his name: so deare his loue he bought.

The punishment suggests that Bregog has lost his name and his status as a river, but it is precisely *as* Colin's 'riuer *Bregog*' that he is first introduced (92), and Colin there asserts that Bregog will bear his love to Mulla 'so long / As water doth within his bancks appeare' (94–5), so that he clearly still has banks and thus the form of a river.[40] Meanwhile, the scattering of his streams was already accomplished by himself as part of his 'deceitfull traine' (118), sharing his water into 'little streames so broken' (141), the better to convey them secretly underground and into the Mulla. He does not, in fact, seem to suffer anything at the hands of Mole. Spenser's preservation of his name despite its supposed erasure by punitive justice is reminiscent of the case of Bonfont in Book V of *The Faerie Queene*, another figure of the poet as a watery 'fount' or spring, who also stands at the threshold of a representation of Elizabeth's court (V.ix.26):

> Thus there he stood, whylest high ouer his head,
> There written was the purport of his sin,
> In cyphers strange, that few could rightly read,
> BON FONT: but *bon* that once had written bin,
> Was raced out, and *Mal* was now put in.
> So now *Malfont* was plainely to be red ...

Bonfont's original name is preserved, and highlighted by capital letters, in the very stanza which tells how that name has been 'raced out'; Spenser's typography renders it more 'plainely to be red' than the condemnatory '*Malfont*', 'title of a Poet bad' (25.8) assigned to him by the powers he has offended with his 'rayling rymes' (25.9). It is significant, too, that it is this name Bon Font, 'good fountain' or 'good poet', which is technically identified as 'the purport of his sin', if we are attending carefully: the grammar of Spenser's sentence tells us that what this court counts as punishable sin is *precisely* the moral integrity and veracity of good poetry, which dares to criticize the powerful. It takes Spenser, describing and interpreting this scene for us, to help us to 'rightly read' this truth, despite the attempt of judicial power to deface and distort it. So with Bregog, who is granted the

---

40 Lines 94–5 have almost the same force as Tityrus' adynata at *Ecl.* 1.59–63, so redirecting Virgil's gesture of loyalty to Octavian once more on to private love.

eternal enjoyment of his love by Spenser's mythopoeic imagination, as a part of the landscape in which Spenser figures his own poetic and mental freedom.[41]

Epic nymphs and sources

The story of Bregog and Mulla is also deeply informed by epic intertexts which bring out another generic contention of Spenser's poem and volume – the contention between pastoral and epic, and with it the hierarchy of genres on which the idea of the Virgilian career as ascent rests. These intertexts are episodes in Ovid and Virgil which take place in Sicily, the archetypal setting of Theocritean pastoral. When the angry Mole whelms Bregog with 'Huge mightie stones' (150), which nevertheless fail to prevent him from continuing to enjoy Mulla (92–5), he recalls Ovid's jealous Polyphemus in Book 13 of the *Metamorphoses*, who crushes his rival Acis with a massive rock torn from the hill – described as *partem e monte revulsam* ('part of the mountain, torn away', 13.882) and as a *moles* ('huge mass or boulder', 887, 890). (Spenser's 'Mole' is a play on this Latin word, as Kelsey points out.) He does this after threatening to tear Acis limb from limb and cast him into the sea, so that he may 'mingle' with Galatea, identifying the sea-nymph with her waters (13.866): his grim pun on

41 This Alpheus-like Spenser also suggests a connection with Spenser's other Irish river marriage, the story of Mulla's sister Molanna in the *Mutabilitie Cantos*. For helping the Spenser-like Faunus (Pugh, *Spenser and Ovid*, ch. 7) to spy on Diana bathing, Molanna suffers Bregog's punishment, being 'whelm'd with stones' (*Faerie Queene* VII.vi.53.4), but like Bregog is not prevented from union with her beloved Fanchin (accomplished by Faunus as her reward), nor deprived of her status: '(both combined) themselues in one faire riuer spred' (53.9). Among many classical currents infusing this episode, one not previously been noted has a peculiar relevance to our topic. In his tour of Arcadia, Pausanias reports another story about Alpheius, to explain a local cult of Artemis Alpheia at Letrini: 'Legend has it that the goddess received the surname for the following reason. Alpheius fell in love with Artemis, and then, realizing that persuasive entreaties would not win the goddess as his bride, he dared to plot violence against her. Artemis was holding at Letrini an all-night revel with the nymphs who were her playmates, and to it came Alpheius. But Artemis had a suspicion of the plot of Alpheius, and smeared with mud her own face and the faces of the nymphs with her. So Alpheius, when he joined the throng, could not distinguish Artemis from the others, and, not being able to pick her out, went away without bringing off the attempt' (6.22.9). When considered in conjunction with this lesser-known Alpheus myth, Faunus' irreverent intrusion on the same goddess, suggestively mirroring Spenser's risque exposure of his Diana-like Queen throughout his poems (not least in the *Mutabilitie Cantos* and in 'Colin Clouts Come Home Againe'), resonates with Spenser's self-presentation as an Alpheus-like figure in the eclogue – not only in the Bregog who defies a potentate to achieve his love but also in the Colin who attends Cynthia's revels and comes away again.

the figurative sexual sense of *miscere* echoes the rape of Arethusa in Book 5, where Alpheus resumes his watery form *ut se mihi misceat* ('so as to mingle himself with me' (5.638). Galatea, who loves Acis and hates Polyphemus, transforms her lover into the god of a new river, which still bears his name. But, although this denouement would seem to promise eternal union with the sea-nymph as a perfectly viable possibility, it is treated as tragic, and Galatea speaks of it as her *luctus* ('cause of grief', 13.744). All this, of course, happens in Sicily, home to the Cyclopes as well as to Theocritus, and Ovid's episode playfully combines the horrifying monster of the *Odyssey* with the comically love-stricken Polyphemus who woos Galatea in Theocritus' eleventh idyll, while adding the pathos of Acis and Galatea's mutual love as his own, original ingredient.[42] Where Idyll 11 already represents a triumphant and comic accommodation of the matter of heroic epic (Homer's monster) to the form of Theocritus' new bucolic *epos*, Ovid's episode is a virtuosic polyphony of the pastoral, elegiac and epic genres, with the emphasis not so much on accommodation as on the variously comic and poignant clash between them.[43] Ovid amplifies the horrific epic aspects of Polyphemus, which Theocritus softens, bringing out the incompatibility with his pastoral role. Even the *fistula* ('pastoral pipe'), which he takes up to sing his exaggerated version of Theocritean song, is *harundinibus compacta centum* ('made up of a hundred reeds', 13.785), combining the *septem compacta cicutis / fistula* of Virgil's Corydon (*Ecl.* 2.36-7) with the epic poet's conventional wish for a hundred mouths.[44] Likewise, he resembles the conventional lover of amatory elegy, in his bitter jealousy, and in his careful toilette: when he combs his hair (with a rake) and cuts his beard (with a scythe) (*Met.* 13.764-5), he is following Ovid's advice to lovers in the *Ars amatoria* (1.518).[45] But his elegiac features too are grotesquely exaggerated in the direction of epic. He burns with love, a

---

42 Note that Spenser uses the name of the Sicilian nymph Galatea for the Irish Lady Kildare whom he finds, on her own temporary visit, among the ladies at Cynthia's court (520), in keeping with the way in which his Ireland is imagined as a recreation of the traditional Sicilian setting of pastoral.
43 Joseph Farrell, 'Dialogue of Genres in Ovid's "Lovesong of Polyphemus" (*Metamorphoses* 13.719-897)', *AJP* 113 (1992), 235-68.
44 See for example, Homer, *Iliad* 2. Persius brings out how hackneyed a convention of epic it became: *vatibus hic mos est, centum sibi poscere voces, / centum ora et linguas optar in carmina centum* ('This is the way of poets, to wish they had a hundred voices, mouths and tongues for their poems', Persius, *Satires* 5.1-2). Farrell notes the reminiscence of Corydon's pipe, but does not mention the 'hundred mouths' connotation.
45 Noted by Farrell, 'Dialogue of Genres'.

metaphor already in Theocritus (Idyll 11.50–3) and a hugely familiar topos of love-elegy; but he describes this burning with an epic trope:

> uror enim, laesusque exaestuat acrius ignis,
> cumque suis videor translatam viribus Aetnen
> pectore ferre meo, nec te, Galatea, moveris.
>
> (*Met.* 13.867–9)

['For I burn, and the flame rages the more fiercely, injured by your scorn, and I seem to bear Aetna, with his violence, transplanted (*translatam*) in my breast, and you, Galatea, are not moved.']

Since *translatio* is the Latin rhetorical term for the Greek 'metaphor',[46] Polyphemus is effectively calling himself a personification allegory of Aetna. The activity of Sicily's volcano is explained in Virgil's *Aeneid* (3.578–82) and elsewhere in the *Metamorphoses* (5.346–53) by the rebel giant imprisoned by Jove beneath it (Enceladus in Virgil, Typhon in Ovid): thus Polyphemus' *translatam* may also indicate 'brought across from the other epic texts'.[47] The fire of Polyphemus' elegiac love is here aligned with the Gigantomachy, one of the archetypal subjects for heroic epic, in a way reminiscent of the *Aeneid*'s continual alignment of passionate love with the chthonic forces which threaten the ordered cosmos.[48] Acis and Galatea, meanwhile, exhibit the mutual love of the ideal elegiac couple, and occupy the quintessential position of pastoral lovers, as they lie in one another's arms at the foot of a cliff, listening to Polyphemus' *pastoria sibila* ('pastoral flutings', 785). They, and their very world, are the victims of Polyphemus' epic violence (which imitates Homer's Polyphemus, hurling rocks at Odysseus' ships as they depart): the *silvae* themselves, symbol of Virgilian pastoral, are terrified by the monster (760). As Farrell observes at the end of his essay, the tragic narrative participates in the *Metamorphoses*' recurrent contrast 'between a pluralistic, anti-authoritarian stance and an aggressive, domineering, and, as it were, monologic force', reflecting 'the increasingly authoritarian climate of the late Augustan principate', in the clash between epic and lower genres and between vulnerable victims and powerful gods and monsters.[49]

Spenser's animate mountain Mole literalizes the figurative self-comparison of Ovid's Polyphemus to Aetna, while he imitates him in hurling rocks to crush the young lover. His concern for wealth and

---

46 See for instance Quintilian, *Institutes* 8.6.4.
47 Farrell points out the specifically epic associations of the Aetna reference (though he does not note the suggestions of metaphor and intertextuality in *translatam*).
48 Philip Hardie, *Virgil's Aeneid: Cosmos and Imperium* (Oxford: Clarendon Press, 1986).
49 Farrell, 'Dialogue of Genres', 268.

social status recalls Polyphemus' pride in his possessions and divine descent, a central emphasis of his wooing in Ovid, greatly amplified from the Theocritean original (13.810-30 (especially 823-4) and 854-5).[50] His victimization of the young lovers, with its evocation of the epic register (the rock-hurling monsters of the *Odyssey* and the *Metamorphoses*) and attempt to destroy the innocent pastoral jouissance of their mutual love, is linked to the idea of contemporary political oppression (as Farrell suggests of Ovid's episode) in the way he anticipates the corrupt ambition of Cynthia's court, and in the allegorical undercurrents traced by Kelsey and Oram, associating him with Burghley and Elizabeth. But Spenser transforms Ovid's tragic ending, exploiting the paradox I noted above: as a river, Bregog is invulnerable to Mole's rocks, and, in their watery forms, Bregog and Mulla can mingle easily, just as the metamorphosed Acis should logically have been able to do with his beloved nymph.

Spenser is remembering Ovid's episode in combination (no arbitrary combination, as we shall see) with Virgil's treatment of Aetna and Polyphemus in Book 3 of the *Aeneid*, as Aeneas makes his first, brief landfall on Sicily. Only eight lines separate the end of this episode from Virgil's reference to the myth of Alpheus and Arethusa, as Aeneas' departing ships pass Ortygia in the bay of Syracuse. It opens with a terrifying description of Aetna and the Giant Enceladus, monster of injustice and violence, who lies buried beneath it. It continues with the rescue of Achaemenides, one of Odysseus' companions accidentally left behind on the Cyclopes' island, and his account of his sojourn with Odysseus in Polyphemus' cave. Finally we have the horrifying vision of Polyphemus himself, followed by the other Cyclopes, as they come down to the shore and Aeneas' company flees. The Cyclopes are insistently compared to the fiery mountain itself, as the same words are used to describe both. Collectively, the Cyclopes are called the 'Aetnean brothers' (*Aetnaeos fratres*, 3.678). Polyphemus is described as 'vomiting' (*eructans*, 632) meat and wine, like Aetna 'vomiting' rocks (*eructans*, 576); in his great height he strikes the stars (*pulsat sidera*, 619-20) as Aetna's fires lick the stars (*sidera lambit*, 574);[51] both groan (*gemitu*, 577, 664). Enceladus' heaving makes all Trinacria quake (*intremere*, 581), as Polyphemus' roar makes the sea quake (*contremuere*, 673) and terrifies Italy. Both Aetna and Polyphemus

---

50 It is as though Ovid's Galatea had had a stern father who commanded her to forsake Acis and to marry Polyphemus!

51 Homer's Odysseus compares Polyphemus to a mounatin in his great stature: *Odyssey* 9.187f.

are *ingens* ('huge', 579, 658), and both are called *moles*, a huge mass or rock (579, 656). Virgil's episode is a self-conscious reworking of Book 9 of the *Odyssey*, a fact wittily underlined by the reference to Achaemenides' retracing or 'rereading' of his former wanderings with Odysseus (*relegens*, 3.690). Virgil's Aetna flings molten rocks to the sky (*liquefactaque saxa sub auras*, 576). Though the Cyclopes of the *Aeneid* do not throw stones at Aeneas' ships, his readers would have vividly remembered that Odysseus' escape was almost prevented by the mighty boulders hurled by Homer's Polyphemos (imitated by Ovid in the boulder with which Polyphemus crushes Acis in *Metamorphoses* 13). During the storm of *Aeneid* 1, moreover (which chronologically follows immediately after the departure from Sicily at the end of Book 3), Aeneas reminds his men that they *have* experienced the rocks of the Cylopes (*vos et Cyclopia saxa / experti*, 1.201-2), as though he has merely omitted to mention this incident in Book 3. Spenser's rock-flinging Mole is a reworking of the twin *moles*, Aetna and Polyphemus, as they appear in both Ovid's and Virgil's treatments.

Now, Ovid's Polyphemus episode is much more closely linked to Virgil's than might appear from what we have said so far. It forms half of the long, amatory, mythological and etiological digression[52] which interrupts his own 'little *Aeneid*', his account of Aeneas' wanderings in books 13 to 14 of the *Metamorphoses*. The digression begins as Aeneas and his fleet, after leaving Buthrotum, make landfall on Sicily at *Met.* 13.723-7. This is the same moment treated at the beginning of Virgil's episode, at *Aen.* 3.569-70. The mention of Scylla, plague of the Sicilian seas, at *Met.* 13.730-4 (lines closely modelled on Helenus' warning about Scylla at *Aen.* 3.420-8,[53] and

---

52 Effectively this digression is an epyllion, resembling Colin's similarly amatory and etiological lay of Bregog and Mulla. If Bregog and Mulla is in part an imitation of the Galatea section of Ovid's digression, the poem which launched the Elizabethan vogue for erotic epyllion – Lodge's *Scillaes Metamorphosis* (1589) – is an imitation of its other half. Lodge and the other authors of Ovidian epyllia in the 1590s were similarly using Ovid to engage critically with the ideological imperatives enshrined in Virgilian epic: see Enterline, 'Drama, Pedagogy, and the Female Complaint'. On the song-exchange of Colin and the Shepherd of the Ocean as an exchange of epyllia, see Cheney, 'Spenser's Pastorals', p. 99.
53 Noted by R. D. Williams, *P. Vergilius Maronis: Aeneidos Liber Tertius* (Oxford: Clarendon Press, 1962), *ad* 3.420f. Servius gloss on Helenus' warning *ad* 3.424 tells the story of Scylla's transformation as we find it in the *Metamorphoses*. Interestingly in our context, the same gloss also gives another version in which Scylla was *a Neptuno amatam, cum illa Glaucum amaret, rivalitatis dolore in hoc monstrum mutatam* ('loved by Neptune, who turned her into this monster in jealous anguish, since she would love Glaucus'). This version is not found in exactly this form elsewhere, though there is a version in which Scylla has an affair with Neptune, and is trans-

corresponding to Anchises' mention of her immediately before their arrival at the Cyclopes' island at *Aen.* 3.559), leads to Ovid's narration of the sympathetic conversation between Scylla and Galatea, before Scylla had been transformed into a monster, in which Galatea tells the tale (entirely in the first person) of her love for Acis and his death at the hands of Polyphemus. (The episode could in fact be called Galatea's 'lamentable lay', recounted to the sympathetic audience of her friend Scylla.) After this, we have Ovid's narrative (returning to the third person of the poet's voice) of how Scylla was subsequently transformed by the jealous Circe, and then, at 14.75, we return to Aeneas, and are told of how he bypassed Scylla and Charybdis and was blown ashore on the Libyan coast. This corresponds to the end of Virgil's Cyclops episode, where at *Aen.* 3.683–5 they give their sails to the following winds and pass Scylla and Charybdis; at 3.692–6 they pass Ortygia, and we have Virgil's account of Alpheus and Arethusa, and after a mere eighteen lines charting his progress around the Sicilian coast he reaches Dido's shore at line 715. What happens in the *Aeneid* in the space taken up by Ovid's long digression, in other words, is precisely Aeneas' first visit to Sicily: Ovid's Polyphemus episode conspicuously replaces, or stands in for, Virgil's.[54] It is therefore not surprising that he echoes and imitates Virgil's description of Polyphemus in *Aeneid* 3, but looking closely at this imitation brings out a more surprising aspect of Virgil's episode.

Ovid's Polyphemus sits down on a cliff, as he does in Idyll 11 (line 17), but what follows is Virgilian (*Met.* 13.781–6):

> lanigerae pecudes nullo ducente secutae.
> cui postquam pinus, baculi quae praebuit usum,
> ante pedes posita est antemnis apta ferendis
> sumptaque harundinibus conpacta est fistula centum,
> senserunt toti pastoria sibila montes,
> senserunt undae ...

---

formed by his jealous wife Amphitrite, resembling Ovid's story of the jealous Circe: see pseudo-Virgil, *Ciris* 70–6, and the comments of R. O. A. M. Lyne, *Ciris: A Poem Atrributed to Vergil*, Cambridge Classical Texts and Commentaries 20 (Cambridge: Cambridge University Press, 2004), *ad loc.* Servius' love-triangle of Scylla, Glaucus and Neptune makes the story of Scylla's transformation closely resemble Ovid's tale of Acis, Galatea and Polyphemus (all the more when we remember that Polyphemus is the son of Poseidon/Neptune in Homer). If Servius was getting it from a lost older treatment of Scylla, this may have been a model for Ovid's innovative narrative elaboration of the situation of Theocritus' idyll.

54 Ovid's Scylla episode, meanwhile, forms an extended discursus on the Virgilian references to Scylla which frame Virgil's Polyphemus episode at 3.558–9 and 684–5, in combination with Helenus' description of Scylla at 3.420–32. See further below.

['his woolly sheep following him without being led. Then, after laying at his feet the pine tree which serves him as a staff – fit for a ship's yardarm – he took up his pipe, made up of a hundred reeds. All the mountains, all the waves, felt his pastoral flutings …']

Compare Aeneas' first sight of Polyphemus in Virgil (*Aen.* 3.655–61):

>   summo cum monte videmus
> ipsum inter pecudes vasta se mole moventem
> pastorem Polyphemum et litora nota petentem,
> monstrum horrendum, informe, ingens, cui lumen ademptum
> trunca manum pinus regit et vestigia firmat;
> lanigerae comitantur oves; ea sola voluptas
> solamenque mali.

['when we saw on the mountaintop the shepherd Polyphemus himself, moving himself with his vast bulk among his sheep and seeking the familiar shore, a monster horrendous, deformed, enormous, robbed of his eye. A stripped pine tree guides his hand and supports his steps. His woolly sheep accompany him; they are his only delight and solace of his ill.']

The details of Ovid's passage which are not in Theocritus are all supplied from the Virgil text. Introduced specifically as a shepherd (*pastorem*, *Aen.* 3.657), Virgil's cyclops, like Ovid's and unlike Theocritus', is accompanied by his flock, which like Ovid's are 'woolly' (Ovid: *lanigerae pecudes secutae* (13.781); Virgil: *inter pecudes* (656), *lanigerae comitantur oves* (660)). In both passages he carries a pine trunk as a staff (as he does not in Homer or Theocritus). The mountains and waves 'feeling' his *pastoria sibila* (which are evidently, and comically, much louder than your typical pastoral flutings), meanwhile, look forward a few lines in the Virgil to the *clamorem immensum* he raises at Aeneas' departure, making the sea and all its waves tremble, and terrifying Italy (3.672–4).[55] Moreover, in sixteenth-century editions, the half-line at *Aeneid* 3.661 was supplemented, so that 660–1 read *lanigerae comitantur oves; ea sola voluptas / solamenque mali de collo fistula pendet* ('his sheep accompany him; they are his only delight, and a shepherd's pipe, solace of sorrow, hangs from his neck'). Editions preserved the supplement, though also including the comments of Servius and later commentators questioning its authenticity.[56] As Spenser would have known Virgil's Polyphemus, then, he shared the *fistula* which makes Ovid's

55 All these echoes are noted by Farrell, 'Dialogue of Genres', 248–9.
56 See Adkins, 'Spenser's Humanist Virgil', ch. 1, on the half-line and its implications for sixteenth-century approaches to Virgil.

and Theocritus' cyclopes pastoral musicians finding in song a remedy for the griefs of love. Modern editors reject the supplement, chiefly on grounds of epic decorum.[57] Though ultimately agreeing with its rejection, Richard Thomas comments that 'it must, however, have been made by a reader of some empathy, since it would Alexandrianize the couplet in a way quite familiar from elsewhere in Virgil'.[58] I would go further and suggest that Ovid's inclusion of the *fistula* within these few lines of dense allusion to the *Aeneid* 3.655–61 argues for its authenticity. Thomas glances at the *fistula* half-line in the course of his argument that Theocritean intertextuality in the *Aeneid* demonstrates the permeability of genres in Augustan as in Hellenistic poetry, and thus the limited usefulness of genre as a critical concept (which resembles the larger point being made by Farrell's article in relation to the *Metamorphoses*). We might say, in other words, that Ovid's polyphonic interplay of genres in his Polyphemus episode is picking up on, and amplifying, a dialogue between pastoral and epic already in the Virgilian episode it replaces, making more visible to us the Theocritean aspect of Virgil's *pastorem Polyphemum*, which is so in tension with his more obviously (indeed, exaggeratedly)[59] epic monstrosity in *Aeneid* 3.

Once this has been recognized – that is, when we return to the *Aeneid* after our lesson from the literary critic Ovid – we are in a position to notice a further peculiarity in Virgil's episode. As Aeneas' ships make their escape, Polyphemus tries to pursue them (3.670–3),

> verum ubi nulla datur dextra adfectare potestas
> nec potis Ionios fluctus aequare sequendo,
> clamorem immensum tollit, quo pontus et omnes
> contremuere undae ...

['But when no power is given him to lay hold with his hand, and he cannot keep up with the Ionian floods in his pursuit, he raises an enormous shout, at which the sea and all its waves tremble ...']

---

57 R. D. Williams, for instance, rejects the supplement with the comment 'the pastoral and bucolic touch is completely out of place in Virgil's picture' (note *ad* 661). Earlier (*ad* 617) he has said 'Virgil's version [of the Cyclops] here is that of Homer ... There is no trace of the ... half-pathetic amorous Polyphemus who loved Galatea.' Note the circularity of the argument: we must reject this trace of the bucolic, because there is no trace of the bucolic here.
58 Richard Thomas, *Reading Virgil and His Texts: Studies in Intertextuality* (Ann Arbor: University of Michigan Press, 1999), p. 262, n. 38.
59 Williams describes Virgil's episode as 'a passage of rhetorical and grandiose writing' of a kind 'the Silver Age loved' but which 'Virgil uses ... far less often' (*ad* 588f.). The exaggeration of epic grandiosity would also suggest that Virgil is deliberately foregrounding the issue of genre in this episode. (Cp. Williams's notes *ad* 623, 627.)

This sea across which Aeneas is fleeing is home to the sea-nymph Galatea, and can be identified with her in her watery form. If we remember Theocritus' Polyphemus, suitor of the unwilling Galatea, it may not surprise us that it is specifically the sea and all its waves which tremble at his roar.[60] Even his pursuit is described as though its object were the water (or nymph) itself rather than Aeneas and his men. The object of *adfectare*, ('to lay hold (on)') if it is to be taken as the ships, is elided; but we can equally read it as sharing the object *Ionios fluctus* ('the Ionian floods') with the verb *aequare* ('to keep up with') in the following line. *Adfectare* is related to *adficio*, 'to affect' or 'move': Polyphemus' pastoral attempt to woo the unwilling nymph underlies his Odyssean pursuit of Aeneas' ships. The pastoral intertexts of Virgil's Polyphemus (for Virgil is arguably recalling his own Corydon, modelled in part on Theocritus' Polyphemus, as well as Idyll 11 here) have been used by Richard Thomas to argue against the rigid compartmentalization of genres in Virgil.[61] But if the generic interplay of Ovid's episode reflects Farrell's anti-authoritarian dialogism (as I think it does), I would suggest that Virgil's episode retains the sense of generic demarcation – and hierarchy – which Thomas questions. Even if Virgil himself is giving a sign of his continuing engagement with Hellenistic pastoral in this episode, nevertheless his hero Aeneas is fleeing from it, leaving Theocritus' monstrous shepherd and his Sicilian home firmly behind to pursue his epic Roman destiny.[62] In

---

60 Williams notes *ad* 672 that as an instance of 'pathetic fallacy' this is reminiscent of Hellenistic pastoral and of the *Eclogues*; see below on the echoing landscape ('*Sit Tityrus Orpheus, Orpheus in Silvis*').

61 Thomas, *Reading Virgil and His Texts: Studies in Intertextuality*, ch. 9, 'Genre Through Intertextuality: Theocritus to Virgil and Propertius', pp. 246–66, at 261–3, with observations on the *fistula* half-line at n. 38. Renaissance commentators noted the relation of Eclogue 2 to Idyll 11 as well as to Idyll 3: see for instance Eobanus Hessus, *In P. Vergilii Maronis Bucolica*.

62 The demonization of Sicily also has political significance, since it had been the stronghold of Octavian's republican enemy Sextus Pompeius (see Anton Powell, *Virgil the Partisan*). Virgil's description of Aetna at the beginning of this episode includes several phrases borrowed from *Georgics* 1.471–3, where Virgil is describing the eruptions after Caesar's assassination, presented as a sign of nature's woe (466), and leading to a fulsome prayer for Octavian. (See Williams, *Aeneidos Liber Tertius, ad* 574 and 580.) These intratextual allusions in the *Aeneid* adduce the recent civil war, and suggest an alignment of Octavian's last republican enemy with Aetna's trapped rebel Giant, Enceladus, and by extension with the monstrous Polyphemus. Powell points out that victims of the land confiscations, like Virgil's Meliboeus and Moeris, and other disaffected Romans fleeing the Rome of the second Triumvirate, went mostly to Sicily to join Sextus Pompeius' army. So, until his defeat at the Battle of Naulochus in 36 BCE, discontented shepherds in Sicily had exerted very real violence against Octavian's regime.

Aeneid 3, Virgil's Sicily aligns pastoral with the insane love which flows from Theocritus' Polyphemus (*Id.* 11.11, 72) to his own Corydon, to Damon's goatherd, and ultimately to Gallus: from here Aeneas' escape is towards what will become Rome, and to epic, though first he must encounter, and make a similar escape from, a more explicit tangle with amatory *furor* in the shape of Dido and the setting of Carthage.[63] In the broader context of Spenser's poem, Colin will make a comparable but opposite escape, when he flees the moral corruption of England, the neighbouring seat of imperial power, to return to this mythologized Ireland.[64] Only here can he fulfil his better, pastoral vocation, the pursuit of a *vita contemplativa* in the service of his community, guiding them according to amatory pastoral values conceived as true religion. These values are represented in the very landscape of Spenser's imaginary Ireland, in the triumph of Bregog and Mulla over Mole. Ovid's episode can be seen as critiquing Virgil's wholesale denunciation of love as monstrous *furor*, by distinguishing between the violent desire of Polyphemus and the pathetic mutual love of Acis and Galatea; at the same time, it challenges the generic

---

63 In Eclogue 10, Gallus attempts to escape into Virgil's imaginary Arcadia, conceived as an alternative to Theocritus' Sicily as a setting for pastoral, and associated with the icy virginity of Arethusa. (Note too that Aeneas' onward epic journey will be via an Arcadian community in exile.) We will discuss the Arcadian setting of Eclogue 10 below. But the continuity of Gallus' *insanus amor* with these pastoral precedents (Theocritus' Polyphemus, Virgil's Corydon and the suicidal goatherd of Eclogue 8) suggests an underlying commonality beneath Eclogue 10's surface opposition between the genres of elegy and pastoral. This is also reflected in Servius' gloss to 10.28, Pan's warning to Gallus *Amor non talia curat* ('Love does not care about such sorrows'): *quasi expertus in Syringa* ('as he has experienced over Syrinx') – the pains which he himself has proved, as Spenser puts it in *December*. Even the god of pastoral has suffered from such love; and the shepherds Gallus implores to sing his *Amores* after his death are quite used to singing such stuff on their own account. An escape into Arcadia would perhaps not be much of an escape after all – and this helps to explain why Virgil himself abandons Arcadia, and pastoral, at the end of the eclogue.

64 Colin's escape from the England of Cynthia (or Elisa, as he calls Elizabeth in *Aprill*) also resembles Aeneas' escape from Elissa's (Dido's) Carthage, which will follow so soon after his escape from Polyphemus, and is prefigured by it. Meanwhile, and conversely, from the Shepherd of the Ocean's perspective, he is rescuing Colin from a wild place of banishment to take him to the centre of imperial civility. This recalls not only Aeneas' onward voyage to Italy, but also his rescue of Achaemenides, who (according to Virgil – he is apparently Virgil's invention) had been accidentally left behind by Odysseus, to live in poverty and fear on the Cyclopes' island. Notice that Achaemenides' speech begins by explaining that he went to Troy to seek his fortune because his family was poor (3.614–15), chiming with the relatively lowly origins of both Spenser and Ralegh, from which they rose through governmental and military service and royal patronage. Colin's perspective is not the same as the Shepherd of the Ocean's, however.

hierarchy implicit in Virgil's episode, identifying epic with the violent power which oppresses the innocent denizens of elegy and of pastoral.[65] Spenser is doing something very similar with his Bregog and Mulla, but where Ovid ultimately laments the vulnerability and helplessness of the pastoral/elegiac couple, Spenser's optimistic reworking reflects a pastoral (and a devotion to love) which is triumphantly invulnerable to political oppression, and free to flow on in its course. Galatea's 'lamentable lay' becomes Colin's 'mery lay' – not in the sense of a trivial entertainment but because of this fundamental optimism.

At a further remove, but nevertheless significant to the poem's reconsideration of the values encoded in the generic hierarchy of pastoral and epic, another animate Ovidian mountain connected to Spenser's Mole is Tmolus, who presides as judge over the music contest between Pan and Apollo in Book 11 of the *Metamorphoses*. This is a contest between the genres of pastoral and epic, symbolized by Pan's pipes and Apollo's lyre. Tmolus decides in favour of Apollo, while Midas demurs and favours Pan, for which Apollo punishes him by giving him ass's ears. Ovid's episode strongly encourages an interpretation opposite to the traditional moral of Midas' folly. Apollo has already been revealed in the *Metamorphoses* as a violent and dangerous god, a character established early on in his attempted rape of Daphne, to which this episode alludes (165). Great emphasis is laid here on his rich and bejewelled appearance (165–9). Tmolus may be swayed by fear of Apollo's power and awe at his wealth; in his judgement he effectively acts as Apollo's henchman (just as Mole/Burghley is Elizabeth's). Midas, meanwhile, has learned from his earlier experience, his truly foolish wish that everything he touched should turn to gold, which nearly resulted in his death from thirst and starvation,

---

65 There is a similar dynamic in the neighbouring Scylla episode, Ovid's strongly sympathetic portrayal of Homer's and Virgil's terrifying monster as an innocent victim. Helenus' description of Scylla at *Aen.* 3.426–8 is strongly sexualized (in a radical departure from his Homeric source), and Ovid's description of how she has been turned into a monster by Circe's *carmina* (at once 'spells' and 'songs', 14.44) implicitly comments on Virgil's demonization of women, of sexuality, and specifically of Dido, the next woman Aeneas will encounter. (See Philip Hardie, 'The Self-Divisions of Scylla', *Trends in Classics* 1 (2009), 118–47.) The Dido episode was seen in classical times (and in the Renaissance) as a gross slander on the chaste historical Dido, misrepresnting her as a woman given up to sexual passion. Macrobius decries *fabula lascivientis Didonis, quam falsam novit universitas* ('the tale of Dido's wantonness, which the whole world knows to be false', *Saturnalia* 5.17.5). Again, Ovid is picking up on hints of such self-critique in the *Aeneid* itself: see Pugh, 'Reinventing the Wheel: Spenser's Virgilian Career'.

and is described as his 'sin' at lines 132 and 134. Released from that curse by Bacchus, he learned to scorn gold, and took up a simple life in the countryside, worshipping Pan, which is how he has acquired his taste for pastoral music (146-7). His pastoral life evokes memories of the Golden Age described at the beginning of Ovid's poem (1.89-112). Against this background, his preference for Pan's music is aligned with the ideal virtue of the Golden Age, and Apollo's music, backed up by its trappings of wealth and its threat of force, aligned by implication with the violence and lust for gold associated with the Age of Iron (1.127-50). This challenge to the Virgilian hierarchy of the genres, in the context of a music-contest which reworks the amoebaean contests of pastoral on a grand (and grossly unequal) scale (*certamen inpar*, *Met.* 11.156), is also part of the background to Spenser's reworking of the generic hierarchy in this volume.[66] Colin's voyage to England will make a similar alignment of pastoral and epic with the Golden and Iron Ages. Innocent of seafaring, the horrified Colin wonders (209-11) that

> Bold men presuming life for gaine to sell,
> Dare tempt that gulf, and in those wandring stremes
> Seek waies vnknowne, waies leading down to hell.

It is a commonplace of classical accounts of the declining ages that the invention of ships came about after the end of the Golden Age, as a sign of man's moral depravity and a result of his newfound lust for wealth. In Ovid's Golden Age (*Met.* 1.94-6),

> nondum caesa suis, peregrinum ut viseret orbem,
> montibus in liquidas pinus descenderat undas,
> nullaque mortales praeter sua litora norant ...

['Not yet had the pine, felled on its mountains, descended into the liquid waves to visit the world as a foreign tourist, and no humans knew any shores except their own ...']

Only with the Iron Age and its *amor sceleratus habendi* ('wicked love of possession') (*Met.* 1.131-4),

> vela dabant ventis nec adhuc bene noverat illos
> navita, quaeque prius steterant in montibus altis,
> fluctibus ignotis insultavere carinae ...

['Men gave sails to the winds, though the sailor was not yet well acquainted with them, and keels which had previously stood on high mountains mocked the unknown floods ...']

66 See also *June*'s reference to the contest of Pan and Apollo, and Chapter 2, n. 35.

In Virgil's fourth eclogue, as the Golden Age gradually returns, *pauca ... suberunt priscae vestigia fraudis, / quae temptare Thetim ratibus ... iubeant* ('a few traces of former crime will remain, which urge men to test the sea in ships', *Ecl.* 4.31–3), until finally, when it has truly arrived, *cedet et ipse mari vector, nec nautica pinus / mutabit merces* ('even the trader will leave the sea, nor shall the ship of pine exchange merchandise', 4.38–9). The description of Colin's voyage thus figures Colin's pastoral domain in Ireland as a place of Golden Age innocence, and Cynthia's England, with its fleet of ships and captains like Ralegh, as a place of moral decline. The simplicity of pastoral life, especially as represented (in exquisitely artificial form, for the delectation of the highly civilized elite of Alexandria) in Theocritus' *Idylls*, was always associated with the Golden Age, and Donatus' *Life of Virgil* (appended to Renaissance editions of Virgil's works) speculates influentially that the genre arose during the primitive first age of man.[67] Thus Colin's voyage (with its epic overtones, recalling the stormy seas of the *Aeneid*)[68] to Cynthia's land (with its courtly poetics) is also a narrative of generic progression as moral decline, rather than as Virgilian ascent. Colin's return to the pastoral setting, reflecting Spenser's return to the traditionally 'low' genre, is therefore a recovery of moral innocence tantamount to a return of the Golden Age, or a personal rebirth or salvation.

---

[67] *illud erit probabilissimum bucolicum carmen originem ducere a priscis temporibus, quibus vita pastoralis exercita est et ideo velut aurei saeculi speciem in huiusmodi personarum simplicitate cognosci* ('It will be most probable that bucolic song takes its origin from ancient times, in which the pastoral life was practised, and for this reason an image of the Golden Age can be recognized in the simplicity of this sort of people').

[68] Particularly the Sicilian sea immediately before the Polyphemus episode of Book 3 – compare 'Colin Clouts Come Home Againe' line 211 with *Aeneid* 3.564–5, where Aeneas' ships are lifted to heaven and sink down *ad Manis* ('to the Underworld') by the waves – but also the same sea immediately after it, that is, during the storm with which the whole poem opens. I have elsewhere compared Colin's voyage with Ovid's voyage into exile in *Tristia* 1.2: Ovid was himself imitating both Virgilian passages, and Spenser is undoubtedly remembering the Ovidian and Virgilian voyages together, recognizing their interrelation. Similarly, Ovid's physical exile and mental freedom in the exile elegies underlie Spenser's newly imagined pastoral setting in 'Colin Clouts Come Home Againe', as well as the pastoral settings of Theocritus' Sicily and Virgil's Arcadia which concern me more nearly here. See Pugh, *Spenser and Ovid*, ch. 5.

Landscapes of the mind

Where Virgil's tenth eclogue shrugs off pastoral for an ascent towards Roman epic, Spenser returns from epic to pastoral, as Colin returns from imperial England to his pastoral home. And where Virgil's Arethusa shrugs off love, Colin, in his own uncontaminated passage across the sea, shrugs off the Petrarchan brand of love he encounters at court, which is the cultural form taken there by the social hierarchy and political authority resisted in the river story by his Arethusa-like Bregog. But unlike Virgil's Arethusa, and like Bregog and Mulla, he embraces true love in its place, making it the foundation for a new form of pastoral. Spenser's mythologization of his Irish setting also proclaims the novelty of this reimagined pastoral, and asserts its independence from Virgil, by imitating the very means by which Virgil asserts his own priority over Theocritus. By invoking Arethusa as a virgin nymph in Arcadia, Virgil claimed poetic precedence over his Sicilian model, and constructed Arcadia as the imaginary locale of his pastoral poetics. In his reworking of the myth, Spenser stakes an even bolder claim, with both literary and political significance. His Irish home, animated by his originary mythopoeic imagination, replaces Arcadia and Sicily as his source of inspiration, and thus symbolizes independence from his major precursor, as well as from the political authority of Cynthia's court. Where Virgil draws on the same body of Greek myth which Theocritus relied on for his Roman poetry, Spenser's animation of a specifically Irish landscape, with Irish rivers and place names, constitutes a defiant (though perhaps superficial) replacement of the classical heritage with an imagined indigenous culture.[69] Another intratextual echo subtly points this up, when Spenser describes (112–15) how Mulla takes her course past and gives her name to

> that aunciernt Cittie,
> Which *Kilnemullah* cleped is of old:
> Whose ragged ruines breed great ruth and pittie,
> To travailers, which it from far behold.

We are reminded of Verlame's mourning, in *The Ruines of Time*, for her Roman city,

---

[69] On the extent of Spenser's knowledge of Gaelic culture and his conflicted attitude towards it, see Richard McCabe, *Spenser's Monstrous Regiment: Elizabethan Ireland and the Poetics of Difference* (Oxford: Oxford University Press, 2005). Christopher Highley sees Spenser as adopting the stance of an Irish bard in Colin Clout (*Shakespeare, Spenser, and the Crisis in Ireland* (Cambridge: Cambridge University Press, 1997), pp. 29–36).

> Of which there now remaines no memorie,
> Nor anie little moniment to see,
> By which the trauailer, that fares that way,
> This once was she, may warned be to say.
> (*Ruines of Time*, 4–7)

The poet's sympathy for Verlame in that poem is limited by our sense of her inflated and too worldly pride in the Roman imperial past; as if reflecting this, wayfarers are oblivious to her when not accosted by her apparition, as the speaker of the poem is accosted, and even the rivers have abandoned her. The genuine 'pittie' of 'travailers' beholding the sight of Kilnemullah's ruins suggests, by the contrast, a place and an alternative tradition more worthy of cherishing.

The landscape of Spenser's poem both is and is not Ireland. To understand its role in Spenser's new pastoral, we must consider it in relation to Virgil's elusive Arcadia, the setting of his tenth (and only his tenth) eclogue. The Arcadian setting of Eclogue 10 is a curiosity which has puzzled commentators. It is the third reference to Arcadia in Virgil's book, following the speaker's boast in the *recusatio* at the end of Eclogue 4 that his possible future song will be such as would even vanquish Pan, in a contest with Pan's native Arcadia itself as judge, and, in Eclogue 7, the introduction of the singers Corydon and Thyrsis as *Arcades ambo* ('Arcadians both'), despite the setting explicitly beside the Italian river Mincius. The Arcadian setting of the final eclogue forms a marked contrast particularly with the darkest of the eclogues, 1 and 9, where the impact of contemporary politics on real Italian provinces is felt with such shocking force, disrupting (in a precise, allusive manner, as we saw in Chapter 1) any expectation of escapist Theocritean idyll. This contrast seems to have been Virgil's point. If he was looking for an imaginary space away from the disruptive pressures of history, Theocritus' Sicily – by now a familiar Roman province, and deeply implicated in the current political troubles as the stronghold of Sextus Pompeius – could not provide it. The geographical region of Arcadia was supposed the birthplace of Pan, the shepherds' god, and had its own minor tradition of music-making and pastoral poetry, but the main motivation for Virgil's innovative relocation of pastoral in this obscure region in his final eclogue seems to have been a need for a landscape 'remote from experience', which Arcadia, 'obscure and wild, with its old poetic mountains' afforded him.[70] Virgil is not so much denoting specifically the Arcadia which

---

70 Clausen, *Eclogues*, p. 289. For a good survey of the possible reasons for Virgil's

exists physically in Greece as evoking in his readers a nostalgia for a deliberately vague and poetic fantasy. Indeed, an influential current in twentieth-century criticism of the *Eclogues* used this Arcadian 'dreamland' as paradigmatic for the whole of Virgil's book, seeing his real topic as imaginative escape into a 'spiritual landscape'.[71] The main problem with this view is that only the final eclogue is set there, and it is mentioned only in two other places: the troubled landscape of contemporary Italy, with its pressing political questions, looms larger in the collection as a whole. But in the tenth eclogue itself, physical setting does exhibit a tendency to dissolve into the metaphorical representation of mental states. For instance, to take a notable crux of the poem, Gallus laments that, where he might have enjoyed the life of a shepherd here among the Arcadians (10.44–8),

> Nunc insanus amor duri me Martis in armis
> tela inter media atque adversos detinet hostes:
> tu procul a patria (nec sit mihi credere tantum!)
> Alpinas, ah dura, nives et frigora Rheni
> me sine sola vides ....

['Now mad love of harsh Mars keeps me in arms amongst weapons and surrounded by opposing foes. You, far from your homeland (and I should hardly believe it!), oh unfeeling one, alone without me, look on Alpine snows and the frosts of the Rhine.']

Clearly Gallus is not literally surrounded by armies – we have been told that he is in Arcadia, accompanied only by sympathetic shepherds and gods. Servius' explanation in his gloss to line 45 is that *ex affectu amantis ibi se putat, ubi amica est* ('because of the passion of the lover, he thinks himself to be where his beloved is') – Gallus is thus, mentally, in a real though distant military setting (because Lycoris has followed another general on campaign), while his body is in Arcadia.

---

choice of Arcadia as a setting, see Rosenmeyer, *Green Cabinet*, pp. 232–8 (with the *caveat* that Rosenmeyer – in keeping with his idea that a simple and Epicurean contentment in a *locus amoenus* is the essential and 'original pastoral impulse' (p. 273) – writes here as though Arcadia were the setting of entire eclogue book, and not solely of the tenth eclogue).

71 Bruno Snell, 'Arcadia: The Discovery of a Spiritual Landscape', in *The Discovery of the Mind* (Oxford: Blackwell, 1953), pp. 281–309. Snell's fundamentally Romantic reading of the *Eclogues* exerted an influence which can be felt both in theories of pastoral as a sentimental or escapist mode, such as Renato Poggioli, *The Oaten Flute: Essays on Pastoral Poetry and the Pastoral Ideal* (Cambridge, MA: Harvard University Press, 1975), and in the emphasis on 'pastoral suspension' or 'transcendence' of conflicting political views in the critics of both Virgil and Spenser cited in Chapter 1, n. 53.

But Servius' gloss on 'nunc insanus amor' suggests a further implication: *hinc usque ad finem amatoris inconstantia exprimitur* ('from here right to the end the changeable state of the lover is expressed'). This gloss implies a metaphorical equivalence between the volatile mental state of the lover and the *insanus amor Martis* of which Gallus speaks. It probably reflects Servius' awareness that Virgil is also referring here to the trope of love as warfare, common in Roman elegy and thus plausibly a feature of Gallus' poems. As modern commentators suggest, Gallus is beset by the mental turmoil of frenzied elegiac love allegorized as battle, which keeps him from enjoying the mental peace figured in Arcadia.[72] Virgil's Arcadia in Eclogue 10 does represent an ideal and escapist 'spiritual landscape', then; but even here it is merely a glimpsed alternative to a harsher reality, seen directly only in the context of Gallus' painful inability to become a part of its contentment, and only in the *extremum laborem* at the end of which Virgil himself will abandon pastoral for ever.

In the works of Sannazaro and Sidney, Arcadia as an imaginary, symbolic region would become a conventional setting for pastoral. Apart from his one reference to 'Arcady' as the birthplace of Astrophel, Spenser never explicitly participates in this tradition, but the semi-fictional Irish setting of 'Colin Clouts Come Home Againe' responds to and revises Virgil's Arcadia, exploiting its role as a space of freedom from the pressures exerted by political power in the real world, but transforming it from a place of recreative retreat into a space of empowerment for the politically engaged poet. The poem's depiction of Ireland is double, just as its depiction of England is double. On the one hand, Ireland is a place of banishment, a 'waste' (182–3), torn by nightly bodrags and infested with wolves and thieves, from which Spenser as Colin comes 'home' to Spenser's native England as a place of peace, learning and civility (308–26), epitomized in the idealized portrait of Cynthia and of her court as it is first presented (at lines 332–455 and 485–615). On the other, Cynthia's court is a space of exile from virtue and true religion (894), a place where learning and Truth are despised, (703–30) from which Colin comes 'home' to Ireland as the ideal setting of a virtuous

---

72 See for instance Harrison, *Generic Enrichment*. This metaphorization of Gallus' mental state is not so far from the allegories of Gallus' abandonment of the Muses and the *vita contemplativa* in Servius and Vives, which I have suggested influence Spenser's handling of Eclogue 10 in this volume. As I argued in Chapter 1, Servian and Renaissance allgoresis is not so quaint or far-fetched as it is often considered to be, and its superficially odd but often quite rational readings can illuminate Spenser's rational dialogue with Virgil.

community who honour their poet and worship Love aright.[73] The two perspectives play the biographical reality of Spenser's position in Ireland off against an allegorical vision of his mental freedom and social role as a poet. In the terms we have seen raised in the dedicatory epistle to Ralegh, Spenser's Ireland as imagined pastoral space represents the duties and achievements of his poetic *vita contemplativa*, as opposed to the duties of the *vita activa*, imposed on him by his official post as a colonial adminstrator of England's imperial power. This is the contemplative life envisioned not as a retreat from public concerns but as the source of supremely authoritative, divinely inspired guidance to his community – not just his neighbours in the real, geographical space of Ireland but the transnational community of his readers, wherever his print volumes find an audience of 'nycer wit[s]' who 'couet them to read' ('Astrophel' prologue 13–14), and who are willing to follow his teaching.

Like Virgil's Arcadia, this is a mental landscape constructed in opposition to a harsh political reality. But Virgil envisages his Arcadia only as a retreat from political concerns, a wistfully desired, and poignantly elusive, imaginary space of pure recreation, which ultimately seems merely a more idealized and fugitive version of Theocritean idyll. Outside the pseudo-Virgilian *Dirae*, with its politically oppositional (and purely negative) pastoral poetics, the only paths leading away from this escapist fantasy in Virgil's career are the unequal negotiations of the eclogue-book itself, which leave the poet either victimized like Meliboeus or enslaved like Tityrus, and the path Virgil subsequently took – the path, announced in Eclogue 10's closing *surgamus*, leading to 'higher' genres, to the renunciation of *amor* in favour of *Roma*, and to increasing reliance on courtly patronage in return for deifying praise of the emperor. All these paths lead, in one way or another, to Rome. By creating and entering his own pastoral space, a semi-mythical Ireland conceived as an alternative to Theocritus' Sicily *and* Virgil's Arcadia, Spenser takes the road not taken by Virgil, giving a local habitation and a name to a Republic of Letters, in which he can exercise his poetic powers freely, beyond the obligations imposed by a relationship with the great. He might well say now of Elizabeth, too, as he will soon say of Burghley, 'To such therefore I do not sing at all' (*Faerie Queene* IV.Proem.4.1).

---

73 I have elsewhere explained this double vision with reference to a similar dynamic in Ovid's exile poetry. Ovid was himself a perspicacious reader of Virgil, and his exile elegies also engage allusively with Virgil's *Eclogues*. See *Spenser and Ovid*, ch. 5.

Whatever Spenser's official obligations as Sheriff of Cork, in his newly imagined pastoral domain Colin and his songs are not subject to negotiation, or to Elizabeth. Within this domain he enjoys the moral and social authority to engage seriously with political concerns from a perspective critical of the centre of power. It is not a retreat, but a space empowering engagement. Even the harsh reality of conditions in Ireland, its famine and bodrags, is admitted into the poem in the service of this engagement, for what Spenser would identify in the *Viewe of the Present State of Ireland* as Elizabeth's dangerous mismanagement of her Irish colony is part of his critique of her government, and Ireland conceived as the geographical space of exile continues to symbolize Cynthia's or Elizabeth's injustice, the veiled subject of Colin's and the Shepherd of the Ocean's mutual condolence.

Spenser's imaginary Ireland is home to a pastoral community who embody a set of political values conceived in opposition to Cynthia's corrupt court. In place of the social hierarchy which so governs the vicious behaviour of Cynthia's courtiers, Colin's fellow shepherds are bound by ties of equal friendship, based on affection, sympathy and respect for poetic skill. Colin's frequent exchanges with many interlocutors throughout the poem generalize the portrait of his evolving personal friendship with the Shepherd of the Ocean, drawing on the theme of friendship and mutual sympathy so emphasized in Virgil's tenth eclogue, but giving it political force through the contrast with the selfish ambitions of the court.[74] The egalitarian nature of this pointedly un-hierarchical community is underlined by the inclusion of shepherdesses among the interlocutors – another departure from Virgilian pastoral, in which there are no female voices.[75] On one level, this community with their shared values, respect for poetry and religion may reflect the society of the New English in the reality of Ireland, which has been described as a fortuitous assemblage of forward-thinking humanists animated by shared ideals distinct from

---

74 As Patrick Cheney puts it, the friendship of Colin and the the Shepherd of the Ocean 'models the "mery" temperament that should order ... a civilized society' ('*Colin Clouts Come Home Againe, Astrophel*, and *The Doleful Lay of Clorinda*', in McCabe (ed.), *The Oxford Handbook of Edmund Spenser*, pp. 237–55, at 244). The same can be said for the 'shepheards nation' as a whole.

75 (Except those ventriloquized by Virgil's herdsmen.) Cheney, '*Colin Clouts Come Home Againe, Astrophel*, and *The Doleful Lay of Clorinda*', p. 241, notes the originality and significance of the inclusion of shepherdesses as speakers in a Virgilian pastoral. In the sense that Colin is revered for his exceptional skill and divine inspiration, the community could be called meritocratic rather than egalitarian, but it is important to note that he exercises no power over his fellows, only moral authority.

those which dominated the English court.⁷⁶ But it is more than this. Hobbinol, for instance, is a prominent member of the community, and the first to speak: we know from the *Calender* that he represents Gabriel Harvey, but Harvey never even visited Ireland. The 'shepheards nation' of the poem transcends national and geographical boundaries to embrace a literary community of like-minded readers and authors. Colin's revered position among them reflects Spenser's confident authority as a respected poet; his singing to his fellows, Spenser's access via print to a wide public; his religious guidance, Spenser's influence over that public, offering them a path to mental (if not physical) freedom from the corrupt values of monarchical courts. It includes any of Spenser's contemporary readers who wish to join – and it includes us. But this audience is not construed as passive: again reflecting the egalitarianism and liberty of Spenser's imagined community, hearing and speaking, reading and writing, are equally part of its distinctive occupation 'by chaunge of turnes' (77). The volume as a whole embodies this community, as a co-authored collection including elegies for Sidney by Lodowick Bryskett, Matthew Roydon, Ralegh and either Edward Dyer or Fulke Greville, and one in dialogue form which may itself have been co-authored by Bryskett and Spenser, reflecting in miniature the collaborative authorship structuring the volume and thematized within it.⁷⁷ As in the song-exchange of Colin and the Shepherd of the Ocean, as in the amoebaean song-contests of pastoral (but without their invidiously competitive motivation), as in the wider intertextual relations between Ralegh and Spenser across their poems, and as in the mutual poetic imitation figured between Virgil and Gallus in Eclogue 10, 'Colin Clouts Come Home Againe' and the volume as a whole represent the reader's or audience's response as a collaborative and creative act, and the act of poetic creation as a response to literary precursors. Poetic imitation and both the reading and the writing of poetry itself are conceived as participation in an ongoing dialogue. Within this

76 Highley, *Shakespeare, Spenser, and the Crisis in Ireland*, ch. 1, 'Spenser's Irish Courts'.
77 In her article '*Astrophel*' in A. C. Hamilton *et al.* (eds), *The Spenser Encyclopedia* (Toronto: University of Toronto Press, 1990), Katherine Duncan-Jones suggests Spenser's coauthorship (with Lodowick Bryskett) of 'A pastorall Aeglogue upon the death of Sir Phillip Sidney Knight, &c.', a dialogue poem between Lycon and Colin. Frederic Tromly, though not actually suggesting coauthorship, reads the 'Pastorall Aeglogue' as responding sympathetically to Spenser's 'Astrophel', and as constituting 'an act of homage to Spenser as well as to Sidney' (F. B. Tromly, 'Lodowick Bryskett's Elegies on Sidney in Spenser's *Astrophel* Volume', *RES* 37 (1986), 384–8, at 387).

dialogue there is room *both* for recognition of Colin's or Spenser's authority, as a supremely skilled and divinely inspired poet, *and* for the democratic openness of this community of readers and writers, in which everyone who cares to speak – even if she is female! – has a voice.

Colin as one Gallus or another

There is occasional disagreement among the shepherds in 'Colin Clouts Come Home Againe'. And, despite what I have said about the transparency of the poem's allegory, there is also disagreement among modern critics about the identity of two of its most important female characters (if they are indeed two) – the beloved to whom Colin expresses his devotion at the centre of the poem, and Rosalind, to whom he expresses his devotion when her name is, rather unexpectedly, raised at the end. This disagreement plays a part in the wider critical debate about Spenser's attitude to political power both in this poem and in the *Calender*, sparked of course by the unstable mixture of satire and panegyric which characterizes both works. If we attend carefully to the disagreements between the shepherds in this eclogue, however, we can see that they cast light on the modern critical debate, and remind us why the ambiguity which has given rise to it was necessary in the first place. We shall focus particularly on two passages expressing contention: Cuddie's comment on Colin's praise of Cynthia, and Lucid's disagreement with Hobbinol over Rosalind. Both are revealing on the topic of Spenser's repositioning of pastoral with regard to political power, which is the most fundamental concern of the eclogue.

Cuddie criticizes Colin for breaching the lowly register appropriate to pastoral in his praise of Cynthia (616–19):

> *Colin* (said *Cuddy* then) thou hast forgot
> Thy selfe, me seemes, too much, to mount so hie:
> Such loftie flight, base shepheard seemeth not,
> From flocks and fields, to Angels and to skie.

The criticism recalls the proem to Virgil's sixth eclogue, where Apollo reigns in a Tityrus who was – after the Caesarean flights of the preceding two eclogues – preparing to sing heroic epic (*reges et proelia*, 'kings and battles', 6.3), admonishing him in Callimachean terms to stick to *deductum carmen* ('fine-spun song', 6.5). Cuddie's interventions are always double (compare 80ff. and 96ff., where he asks Colin to recite his part in the song-exchange; and 289ff. and 303ff., where he marvels that another land should exist), and this is no exception, for it asks to be considered in combination with his final intervention at 823ff., commenting on Colin's description of the God of Love (823-34):

> Shepheard it seemes that some celestiall rage
> Of loue (quoth *Cuddy*) is breath'd into thy brest,
> That powreth forth these oracles so sage,
> Of that high powre, wherewith thou art possest.
> But neuer wist I till this present day
> Albe of loue I alwayes humbly deemed,
> That he was such an one, as thou doest say,
> And so religiously to be esteemed.
> Well may it seeme by this thy deep insight,
> That of that God the Priest thou shouldest bee:
> So well thou wot'st the mysterie of his might,
> As if his godhead thou didst present see.

Cuddie is describing here the same kind of elevated style, in which Colin exceeds the bounds of pastoral to talk of heavenly things (like the *paulo maiora* of Virgil's genre-stretching fourth eclogue). But where he criticized the first, he praises the second in hyperbolical terms, identifying Colin as divinely inspired and submitting to his prophetic teachings. The disparity invites our scrutiny of the two heavenly bodies praised by Colin, Cynthia and Cupid, and of their relation.

Colin accepts both Cuddie's criticism of his praise of Cynthia, and his admiration at his praise of Cupid. The criticism, when we consider it closely, seems to take issue with the rhetoric of the political panegyric, which ended with the (rather measured) simile describing Cynthia as 'Much like an Angell in all forme and fashion' (822). This is the kind of deifying rhetoric indulged in in Virgil's fourth eclogue, which begins by foregrounding its departure from the humble register usual for pastoral, and explaining it as necessary to please his patron, the consul Pollio, for 'humble tamarisks and orchards are not pleasing to all' (2). Spenser's reader is free to surmise that Colin's elevated style is driven by a similar desire to 'please', for we have already been told that, in Cynthia's corrupt court (707-10),

> Ne is there place for any gentle wit,
> Vnlesse to please, it selfe it can applie:
> But shouldred is, or out of doore quite shit,
> As base, or blunt, vnmeet for melodie.

Cynthia may have deigned graciously to listen to Colin's humble pipe (360-2), but we may gather from the other side of his depiction of her court that it may be acceptable only if larded with the flattery of such stylistic excess. Colin's immediate response to Cuddie's criticism is to accept it (620-7):

> True (answered he) but her great excellence,
> Lifts me aboue the measure of my might:
> That being fild with furious insolence,
> I feele my selfe like one yrapt in spright.
> For when I thinke of her, as oft I ought,
> Then want I words to speake it fitly forth:
> And when I speake of her what I haue thought,
> I cannot thinke according to her worth.

The excuse of an involuntary *enthusiasmos* brought on by the idea of Cynthia, recalling the treatment of 'celestiall inspiration' in the argument to *October* and Piers' claim in the same eclogue that 'Rosalind' is an 'immortal mirrhor' (93) who should give Colin Platonic access to the divine, merely repeats the deifying rhetoric to which Cuddie has just objected. (And it is not by mere coincidence that Cuddie was Piers' sceptical interlocutor in *October*.) Such flattery is still necessary, of course, for whatever the fiction of the poem claims for Spenser's and his readership's freedom from subjection to Cynthia's court, they remain Elizabeth's punishable subjects in the real world. The lines which follow (624-7) can be read as insinuating such a necessity. At first they convey a vague impression of the distance between Elizabeth's transcendent 'worth' and the limited capacity of fallen 'words' to express it. But the more closely one looks at them, the more confused and riddling they appear. His emphasis on how he 'ought' to think of her, and on how to speak his thoughts 'fitly', in particular, seems to admit the possibility that what he is struggling with is not the tension between transcendent good and inadequate language, but rather the tension between his private thoughts about her true 'worth' on the one hand, and what it would be decorous and permissable for him to utter. Construed in this way, the lines warn his audience not to take his deifying praise too literally.

This rhetoric, and the compulsion behind it, plunge Colin back into the world of the *Calender*, with its poles of deifying praise (as in the Tityrean centre of the *Aprill* lay) and the threat of punishment for illicit speech ('Harme may come of melling', *Julye* 208; 'thou speakest to plaine', *September* 136). So it is significant that this passage immediately leads to Colin's self-presentation as a version of the Gallus of Virgil's tenth eclogue, that persona which, in the *Calender*, figured the strain and bitterness of his subjection to those pressures (628–47):

> Yet will I thinke of her, yet will I speake,
> So long as life my limbs doth hold together,
> And when as death these vitall bands shall breake,
> Her name recorded I will leaue for euer.
> Her name in euery tree I will endosse,
> That as the trees do grow, her name may grow ...
> And long while after I am dead and rotten:
> Amongst the shepheards daughters dancing rownd,
> My layes made of her shall not be forgotten,
> But sung by them with flowry gyrlonds crownd.
> And ye, who so ye be, that shall suruiue:
> When as ye heare her memory renewed,
> Be witnesse of her bounty here aliue,
> Which she to *Colin* her poore shepheard shewed.

The bitterness and despair are absent here, but the allusions to Virgil's tenth eclogue are nevertheless unmistakable. Colin is immediately prompted to think of his death, and of leaving her name carved in trees, imitating Gallus' fantasy in Eclogue 10 (52–4):

> certum est in silvis, inter spelaea ferarum
> malle pati, tenerisque meos incidere amores
> arboribus; crescent illae, crescetis, amores.

['Certainly it is better to suffer in the woods, among the dens of wild beasts, and to carve my loves on the young trees. You, my loves, will grow, as they will grow.']

The vision of the shepherds singing his lays of Cynthia while his body rots in the earth, meanwhile, clearly evokes Gallus' wish that the Arcadian shepherds will sing his *Amores* (his elegies for Lycoris) (10.31–4):

> 'Tamen cantabitis, Arcades,' inquit
> 'montibus haec vestris: soli cantare periti
> Arcades. O mihi tum quam molliter ossa quiescant,
> vestra meos olim si fistula dicat amores!'

['Yet you, Arcadians, he said, will sing this to your mountains. Only Arcadians are skilled in singing. Oh how softly would my bones rest then, if only your pipe would sing my loves!']

Meanwhile, the end of our passage echoes Colin's final stanza in *June*, where, in the revelation of Rosalind's desertion of him *for another lover*, he was at his closest to the despairing Gallus who haunts all his appearances in the *Calender*:

> Ye gentle shepheards, which your flocks do feede,
> Whether on hylls, on dales, or other where,
> *Beare witnesse* all of thys so wicked deede:
> And tell the lasse, whose flowre is woxe a weede,
> And faultlesse fayth, is turned to faithlesse fere,
> That she the truest shepheards hart made bleede,
> That lyues on earth, and loued her most dere.
>
> (*June* 106–12, with my italics)

The echo contained in that 'witnesse', occurring in the same position in the line, but audible only because of the prominent shared intertext, points (like the evasive comments about his rhetorical treatment of Cynthia at 624–7) to an alternative reality underlying his panegyric. The 'bounty' Cynthia has bestowed on Colin could be perceived – and, as we are about to see, *is* perceived by one of his interlocutors – as placing him under an obligation to repay her with this sort of immortalizing praise. If so regarded, it puts him in the same position of dependency which, in the *Calender*, resulted in his deadly despair when Elizabeth failed to fulfil the promise of her own idealizing depiction, and her 'flowre ... woxe a weede'. It is this obligation and dependency itself which is intolerable, whether the bounty continues to flow or not, and this is why Colin has left Cynthia's court.

Colin's paean to the God of Love, by contrast, is as we have seen eagerly accepted and praised as evidence of Colin's divine inspiration, and Colin accepts the tribute: 'Indeed (said *Colin*)' (837). Nevertheless, it is the prelude to a final disagreement among the shepherds. At the end of his climactic hymn to Cupid, Melissa reiterates the praise of his deep divining and 'wondrous skill', concluding (899–902):

> To thee are all true louers greatly bound,
> That doest their cause so mightily defend:
> But most, all wemen are thy debtors found,
> That doest their bountie still so much commend.

Her trope of bounty and debt is applied in a general and moral sense, evoking the bonds of friendship which bind the pastoral community and their gratitude to Colin as prophet and teacher. (Melissa has already shown herself appreciative of Colin's love-lore, when she praised, in high terms, his expression of devotion to his private love in the central lines of the poem, at 480-4.) But the trope reminds Hobbinol of the unhappy negotiations of the *Calender*, and he interrupts the scene of contentment with an angry reminder of the earlier work, bearing witness to Rosalind's wicked deed (903-6):

> That ill (said *Hobbinol*) they him requite,
> For hauing loued euer one most deare:
> He is repayd with scorne and foule despite,
> That yrkes each gentle heart which it doth heare.

The allusion to this unhappy love as a tiding widely heard subtly but clearly marks it as a reference to one of Spenser's former poems – and clearly not the *Amoretti and Epithalamium*, which is most remarkable for its generically revolutionary culmination in marriage. Elizabeth Boyle did not repay Spenser with 'scorne and foule despite'. Lucid counters with a rebuke, which makes it clear that the *Calender* is the text Hobbinol has in mind (907-26):

> Indeed (said *Lucid*) I haue often heard
> Faire *Rosalind* of diuers fowly blamed:
> For being to that swaine too cruell hard,
> That her bright glorie else hath much defamed.
> But who can tell what cause had that faire Mayd
> To vse him so that vsed her so well:
> Or who with blame can iustly her vpbrayd,
> For louing not? for who can loue compell.
> And sooth to say, it is foolhardie thing,
> Rashly to wyten creatures so diuine,
> For demigods they be, and first did spring
> From heauen, though graft in frailnesse feminine.
> And well I wote, that oft I heard it spoken,
> How one that fairest *Helene* did reuile:
> Through iudgement of the Gods to been ywroken
> Lost both his eyes and so remaynd long while,
> Till he recanted had his wicked rimes,
> And made amends to her with treble praise:
> Beware therefore, ye groomes, I read betimes,
> How rashly blame of *Rosalind* ye raise.

At the beginning of her speech, Lucid confirms that the satirical portrait of Elizabeth as Rosalind in the *Calender* has had its desired effect, tarnishing her public image – and thus reminds readers, and Elizabeth herself, of the potency of the threat which formed one side of Spenser's negotiating strategy in the earlier volume. The ensuing lines, while they seem to criticize this public response, in fact merely repeat the *Calender*'s own prominent warnings about the dangers of criticizing the powerful, its insistent foregrounding of the risks run by its own satire. The poet punished with blindness for reviling Helen is the Stesichorus discussed in E.K.'s gloss to line 26 in the *Aprill* eclogue (the riddling gloss on the identity of Rosalind), where he is said 'so much to haue doted' on his beloved mistress,

> that in regard of her excellencie, he scorned and wrote against the beauty of Helena. For which his praesumptuous and vnheedie hardinesse, he is sayde by vengeaunce of the Gods, thereat being offended, to haue lost both his eyes.

It is for fear of such punishment by angry potentates that Lucid counsels the shepherds to 'Beware' of rash and foolhardy criticism of Rosalind, before it is too late. It is in this sense of possessing the power and will to harm that Rosalind is a 'demigod'. The allusion to *Aprill*'s paratext confirms that the Rosalind of this passage and the Rosalind of the *Calender* are one and the same, and, simultaneously, the application to Rosalind here of the same deifying rhetoric which Cuddy criticized in Colin's earlier description of Cynthia re-emphasizes the reason for its necessity there – the need for flattery when dealing with the powerful.

At the same time, and probably inadvertently on Lucid's part, the reminiscence of *Aprill* also reminds us why it is, in the strongest sense, wrong – actually sacrilegious – to worship Rosalind/Cynthia/Elizabeth as a god, for E.K.'s mention of Stesichorus forms part of *Aprill*'s warning against idolatry. He offends the gods with praise of his mistress which makes of her 'hys Idole', and E.K. compares the way in which Rosalind is 'commended to immortalitie' by Colin. Therefore his punishment looks forward to the punishment of the self-deifying queen Niobe in the lay, and Colin's reluctance to incur such punishment by comparing Elisa to the gods. There is a choice to be made, the allusion to *Aprill* reminds us, between worshipping queens and worshipping the true God, just as the present poem foregrounds the tension between praise of Cupid and praise of Cynthia. Whether she realizes it or not, Lucid's speech indicates to the reader which interpretation of Colin's praise of Cynthia is right and Christian, even as she cautions us to be careful about speaking it aloud.

Lucid was always by nature particularly lucid about the real-world conditions governing Spenser's pastoral, and resistant to his attempt to escape the dependency of his position in the *Calender* into an imaginary autonomy.[78] We might almost say that she does not fully believe in the pastoral domain of Spenser's creation in which she lives. Her earlier intervention comes at the end of Colin's catalogue of the poets at Cynthia's court. Animated by an awareness of the obligations conferred by patronage strongly reminiscent of the *Calender*, she has been following Colin's tale with a book-keeper's eye, and sharply warns him that so far he is found wanting (457–63):

> Shepheard, enough of shepheards thou hast told,
> Which fauour thee, and honour *Cynthia*:
> But of so many Nymphs which she doth hold
> In her retinew, thou hast nothing sayd;
> That seems with none of them thou fauor foundest,
> Or art ingratefull to each gentle mayd,
> That none of all their due deserts resoundest.

He has paid 'enough' to the male courtiers, but is open to the charge of ingratitude to the ladies if he doesn't pay up quickly. Interestingly, Lucid's admonition does not succeed, or at least not immediately. Almost as though putting off the disbursement of praise she calls for, or downplaying the obligation, Colin's immediate response is the speech about his mistress which occupies the centre of the poem. It takes Melissa's repetition of Lucid's request finally to elicit the desired catalogue of court-ladies, and she does so by first praising Colin's expression of private love in the highest possible terms, claiming that Colin has made 'woods, and hills, and valleyes ... / Her name to eccho vnto heauen hie' (482–3) – that image of music making the landscape echo which is so important in both Virgil's and Spenser's pastorals, and which carries Orphic undertones (as we shall see later). Only by thus accepting Colin's prioritization of his private love can Melissa persuade him to praise the court ladies.

That prioritization of his private love also creates the underlying tension in this closing exchange on Rosalind. Hobbinol's reference to

---

78 While we must not exaggerate the extent to which Spenser imagines Colin's interlocutors as characters in this poem, nevertheless it would be foolish to ignore the discernible hints of character and continuity which Spenser does give us. For other examples, see my observation on Melissa's consistently high valuation of Colin's praise of love, and consider also the limited perspective of Thestylis: he criticizes Colin sharply for his anti-court satire, which he sees as motivated by 'spight' (676); earlier he failed to appreciate the artificiality of Colin's praise of the court, asking him, bewildered, why he left (654); and before that he responded with superficial naivety to the tale of Bregog and Mulla, which he saw as merely a 'mery lay' (157), and desired to hear the Shepherd of the Ocean's song because of his country bumpkin's interest in 'forreine thing' (162).

Colin's 'hauing loued euer one most deare' compels the reader to set this passage beside the poem's exact centre (477–9),

> And I hers euer onely, euer one:
> One euer I all vowed hers to bee,
> One euer I, and others neuer none.

The very emphasis on the exclusivity of the love described in these central lines foregrounds the untenability of his supposed continuing devotion to Rosalind. The love of his new wife, Elizabeth Boyle, evoked in the central passage, with its imagery of day and night (472–3) recalling the temporal structure of the *Epithalamium*, is wholly in harmony with the eclogue's celebration of Bregog's faithful married love and its hymn to the God of Love. We are shown the incompatibility of the two 'loves', compelling us to choose between this life-affirming celebration of procreative marriage, on the one hand, and deadly devotion to Rosalind on the other, and to see through the latter as merely rhetorical. Once again, Colin's stance of continued devotion to Rosalind is marked as necessary to evade punishment (927–9):

> Ah shepheards (then said *Colin*) ye ne weet
> How great a guilt vpon your heads ye draw:
> To make so bold a doome with words vnmeet …

What they risk bringing down on their heads, in this physical image, by criticizing Rosalind, is not so much actual guilt as 'huge mightie stones' like those hurled by the angry Mole (150), or Homer's or Ovid's Polyphemus. That the 'love' thus feigned is deadly is evidenced by Colin's closing words (947–51):

> And ye my fellow shepheards which do see
> And heare the langours of my too long dying,
> Vnto the world for euer witnesse bee,
> That hers I die, nought to the world denying,
> This simple trophe of her great conquest.

This is of course a final resumption of the stance of Virgil's Gallus from Eclogue 10, dying for love, and hoping that the Arcadian herdsmen will sing of his loves after his death.

After this, the eclogue ends with the departure of the shepherds as night falls (952–5):

> So hauing ended, he from ground did rise,
> And after him vprose eke all the rest:
> All loth to part, but that the glooming skies,
> Warnd them to draw their bleating flocks to rest.

The ending appropriately recalls the *surgamus* ('let us rise', 10.75) as night falls at the close of Eclogue 10, which has been such an important intertext of Spenser's poem. But where Virgil willingly leaves the *umbra* ('shade', 75) of pastoral to ascend figuratively to higher genres, Spenser's shepherds are 'loth to part'. Thus they recall the other eclogue which ends this way in Virgil's book, Eclogue 6, the poem which contains the scene of Gallus' initiation (84–6):

> ille canit: pulsae referunt ad sidera valles;
> cogere donec ovis stabulis numerumque referri
> iussit, et invito processit Vesper Olympo.

['[All these songs] he [Silenus] sang: the resounding valleys carry them to the stars; until Vesper gave the command to gather the sheep in the fold and to count their number [or: 'to recite their verse'], and proceeded across an unwilling sky.']

The sky (in Virgil's metonymy, Olympus) is loth that the song of the wood-god Silenus should end, because it has listened to it with such delight. There is no suggestion of putting an inferior (or even harmful) genre behind him in this close. The song of Silenus is admittedly a strange kind of pastoral, a neoteric assemblage of amatory and etiological myths, anticipating what Ovid would do on a larger scale in his counter-epic *Metamorphoses*, and also chiming suggestively with Spenser's amatory etiological fable of Bregog and Mulla.[79] But it is nevertheless a kind of pastoral, and has shown that pastoral can be divine (Silenus is after all a god), and that it can reach the heavens to which epic and panegyric also aspire. The *ad sidera* of line 84 resonates with 9.29, Menalcas' unfulfilled promise to lift Varus' name *ad sidera*: the phrase occurs in the same line position. The praise of Varus will never materialize (and the *recusatio* which

---

79 The 1595 volume as a whole suggests a similar mingling, as if on equal terms, of pastoral and epic. For instance, Bryskett's 'The Mourning Muse of Thestylis', first of the elegies by other hands which follow Spenser's 'Astrophel', combines passages imitating pastoral elegy (including the mourning Venus and Cupid of Bion's *Lament for Adonis* at ll. 128–42, and the '*Siluan* Gods' (39) of Idyll 1 and eclogues 5 and 10) with imitations of several passages of the *Aeneid* (for instance the death of Euryalus at ll. 74–5, and the storm of *Aeneid* 1 at ll. 152–6), within a 'brief epic' treatment in alexandrines, clearly intended to evoke Latin hexameters. At 195 lines, it comes closest of the other elegies to the length of Spenser's (and its elaborate and freely varied rhyme scheme is also reminiscent of 'Colin Clouts Come Home Againe'). Spenser's two eclogues, in their unusual length and their extended narratives, also resemble a pastoral version of 'brief epic' or epyllion. The form was a favourite of the Callimachean poets of the Hellenistic period (there are mythological epyllia among Theocritus' non-bucolic poems), and Silenus' song is itself often described as a neoteric exercise in the genre.

opens Virgil's sixth eclogue offers Silenus' song precisely instead of an epic about this same Varus: 6.6–8), but this apolitical pastoral song reaches the stars Varus will never reach. The close of 'Colin Clouts Come Home Againe' thus evokes the two similar but contrasting endings of Virgil's two eclogues on Gallus, but from the meditation on and revision of Virgilian values in the body of the poem, it is clear that Spenser ends his eclogue not in the renunciatory mood of the tenth (we are after all about to go on to another eclogue in 'Astrophel') but with the lingering wonder of the sixth.

In the love for Rosalind which he reiterates perforce at the end of the poem, then, Colin is residually the Gallus of Eclogue 10, as he was in the *Calender*. But in this poem this stance is thrust to the margins, and hedged about with acknowledgements that it is to be understood as merely rhetorical, and only the Shepherd of the Ocean remains hopelessly caught in Gallus' deadly position of amatory servitude. Meanwhile, in his celebration of married love and the divine inspiration of his hymn to Cupid, Colin resembles the Gallus of Eclogue 6, who, in an imitation of Hesiod's encounter with the Muses at the beginning of the *Theogony*, receives Hesiod's pipes and Orphic powers from the hands of the Muses themselves. It chimes with the vision atop Mount Acidale which forms the pastoral climax of Book VI of Spenser's epic. I have written elsewhere of how this scene, where Colin summons a vision of dancing Graces, imitates the opening of the *Theogony*.[80] What I did not mention is that Hesiod is there remembered in conjunction with Virgil's scene of Gallus' initiation. An oddity about Virgil's passage is that Hesiod should have pipes at all. In the *Theogony* the Muses give him a staff as a symbol of his newfound ability to sing cosmogonic epic. (This is remembered in classical bucolic when Theocritus' Lycidas gives a staff to Simichidas in Idyll 7, and Virgil's Mopsus gives a staff to Menalcas at the end of Eclogue 5.) Hesiod has been a real shepherd (as opposed to a pastoral poet) before this encounter, but is now moving on to a new career as a singer. Another oddity of Virgil's passage is that Orphic powers to move the trees should be attributed to Hesiod: there is no hint of this in the *Theogony*. In the context of Virgil's eclogue-book, the passage is (thanks to these peculiarities) an almost comic, but nevertheless moving, fantasy of a specifically pastoral but supremely powerful and divine poetry. Colin on top of Acidale is of course playing on his pastoral pipe, exercising just such

80 Pugh, 'Spenser and Classical Literature', pp. 503–19.

a specifically pastoral but divine poetic power. And at the centre of the divine vision he has summoned we find, once again, as 'another grace', Elizabeth Boyle. The scene alludes to the vision of the graces dancing around Elisa as 'a fourth grace' in the *Aprill* lay (113), and Spenser underlines the displacement of the Queen by Colin's private love with his direct address to Gloriana, asking pardon for his making 'one minime of thy poore handmayd' (VI.x.28.6), among the many lays he has already sung of his queen. Where Virgil predicates Gallus' poetic vocation on the renunciation of love and generic ascent to Hesiodic poetry (anticipating his own *Georgics*), Spenser's claim to divine inspiration is centred on his personal experience and poetic treatment of love, and located firmly within the pastoral genre, now viewed as a height to which his epic aspires and which it fleetingly achieves at the climax of its final book.

Sit Tityrus Orpheus, Orpheus in Silvis[81]

Orphic powers such as those which are half-jokingly ascribed to Hesiod in the oddly pastoralized reworking of the *Theogony*'s opening are a subcurrent running through Virgil's eclogue-book. Spenser responds to this current, with its riddling, ambivalent thoughts about the potential of the 'humble' genre, exploiting and transforming them into a boldly imagined claim for the vatic status of his pastoral. The legendary archetypal poet, son of the Muse Calliope, whose song embodies the combination of (magical) 'spell' and 'song' in the Latin *carmen* in its power not only to charm wild beasts but to move stones and trees, and whose seven-stringed lyre gifted by the gods traditionally symbolizes the harmony of the seven spheres, might seem at first blush as far as could be imagined from the humble herdsmen of bucolic poetry with their rudely fashioned pipes. This is the thrust of the lines from Damon's song in Eclogue 8, which provide the heading for this section. Damon is calling for an upheaval of nature, a reversal of all order, to reflect his wild grief at his mistress' infidelity. (The passage imitates the closing words of Daphnis' lament in Theocritus' first idyll, the idyll which forms the chief model for Damon's song as for Eclogue 10.) Servius explains the intended absurdity: *vilissimus rusticus Orpheus putetur* ('Let the most worthless peasant be considered an Orpheus'). The irony is that the prologue to his song has already attributed Orphic powers to the herdsman Damon himself (8.1–5):

---

81 'Let Tityrus be an Orpheus, an Orpheus in the woods', Eclogue 8.55–6.

> Pastorum Musam Damonis et Alphesiboei,
> immemor herbarum quos est mirata iuvenca
> certantis, quorum stupefactae carmine lynces,
> et mutata suos requierunt flumina cursus,
> Damonis Musam dicemus et Alphesiboei.

['We will sing the pastoral muse of Damon and Alphesiboeus, at whose contest the heifer stood amazed, forgetting her grass, at whose song the lynxes were struck dumb, and the rivers, changed, stopped their currents; the Muse of Damon and Alphesiboeus we will sing.']

The amazement (*mirata*) of the animals recalls the wonder (*miratur*) of the mountains Rhodope and Ismarus at Orpheus' song, remembered (and outdone by Silenus' song) in Eclogue 6 (30); the feat of stopping rivers in their course is attributed to Orpheus by Horace at *Carmina* I.12.9–10. But Damon's song itself ties these supernatural suggestions to a more natural physical phenomenon. The refrain of Damon's song calls it 'a song of Maenalus', suggesting 'an Arcadian song', as though he, like the singers of the preceding eclogue, is an Arcadian. Its first tercet (8.22–4) describes how

> Maenalus argutumque nemus pinosque loquentis
> semper habet; semper pastorum ille audit amores,
> Panaque, qui primus calamos non passus inertis.

['Maenalus always has the ringing grove and speaking pines; always he listens to the loves of herdsmen, and to Pan, the first who would not allow the reeds to be idle.']

The listening of the mountain is associated with its 'ringing' groves, which will echo the song back to the singer; thus it is as if the 'song of Maenalus' is jointly produced by singer and mountain. Making a landscape echo with song is blurred into a kind of animation of the landscape, producing the very trope of personification Virgil is employing here.

Now, this motif of the echoing landscape is a favourite of Spenser's, to which he returns repeatedly. Thomas Cain's instinct was good when he claimed that it 'always recalls the effect of Orpheus' music'.[82] But the connotation is confirmed, and fully intelligible, only when

---

82 Thomas H. Cain, 'Spenser and the Renaissance Orpheus', *University of Toronto Quarterly* 41 (1971), 24–47, at 28. My chief disagreement with Cain's otherwise perceptive article is his insistent identification of Orphic song with political praise poetry, which seems odd, and for which he provides no explanation. Patrick Cheney's idea of the 'Orphic career' as one which culminates in hymn is much closer to what Orpheus would seem to signify to Spenser. (See *Spenser's Famous Flight*.)

we understand how it arises from the interplay of echo and the figure of Orpheus in Virgil's *Eclogues*. Echoes haunt Virgil's book, and the opening image of the book is a programmatic example (1.4–5):

> tu, Tityre, lentus in umbra
> formosam resonare doces Amaryllida silvas.

['you, Tityrus, at ease in the shade, teach the woods to echo "Beautiful Amaryllis".]

Meliboeus' phrase is striking, not initially for its reference to echoing, but rather for the idea that Tityrus is *teaching* the woods. Suggesting, of course, a personified or animated landscape, it also looks forward to the end of Eclogue 6, where Silenus is said to have sung (82–3)

> omnia, quae Phoebo quondam meditante, beatus
> audiit Eurotas, iussitque ediscere laurus

['all those songs which fortunate Eurotas once heard Phoebus performing, and ordered his laurels to learn by heart'.][83]

Tityrus' 'teaching' the woods in Eclogue 1 is thus aligned with the song of Phoebus himself (the same unusual verb, *meditaris/meditante* is also used to describe the singing of both), and specifically Orphic powers lurk beneath both passages.[84] The echoing valleys carry Silenus' song itself to the stars, as we have seen. Earlier in the poem, his singing is said to outgo both Phoebus and Orpheus (6.29–30):

> nec tantum Phoebo gaudet Parnasia rupes,
> nec tantum Rhodope miratur et Ismarus Orphea.

['not so much does the Parnassian cliff rejoice in Phoebus, nor does Rhodope or Ismarus wonder so much at Orpheus'.]

Virgil may look forward, in the *recusatio* at the end of Eclogue 4, to a heroic song which would outvie Orpheus, or Linus or Pan himself (4.55–9), but in the song of the wood god Silenus he apparently

---

83 Servius Danielis glosses the mention of Eurotas *hunc fluvium Hyacinthi causa Apollo dicitur amasse* ('Apollo is said to have loved this river for the sake of Hyacinthus'), suggesting (as Coleman notes) that 'the reference then is to the god consoling himself in song for the death of his beloved, just like Orpheus in Ovid, *Metamorphoses* 10.143ff., whose recital actually includes the tale of Apollo and Hyacinthus' (Coleman, *Eclogues, ad* 6.82–3). Like the epyllion-like Orpheus episodes of the fourth *Georgic* and the *Metamorphoses*, the song is effectively a neoteric epyllion: in its Callimachean poetics and its concern with love, it pulls against the impulse which propels the 'Book of Virgil' away from *Amor* and towards *Roma*.

84 Ross, *Backgrounds to Augustan Poetry*, sees Orpheus as the 'focus' of Eclogue 6 (p. 25).

achieves it within the bucolic genre, and the opening image of Eclogue 1 even hints that Tityrus, *vilissimus rusticus*, achieves it too. The idea that Tityrus might be considered an Orpheus in the woods no longer seems so palpably absurd.

Virgil's use of echo to suggest the supernatural is best explained as a response to Lucretius. Across his works, Virgil frequently imitates lines and phrases from his great predecessor's *De Rerum Natura* ('On the Nature of Things'), a long didactic poem in hexameters preaching the materialist doctrine of the Greek philosopher Epicurus. Purporting to contain the sum of scientific understanding amassed by humankind, its chief object is to release humanity from enslavement to foolish terrors by crushing superstition (*religio*) underfoot, and showing that Nature, *libera ... dominis privata superbis / ipsa sua per se sponte omnia dis agere expers* ('at liberty, relieved of her proud masters, herself does all things of her own accord, free from the gods', *De Rerum Natura*, 2.1091–2). The gods may exist in their own realm, but do not concern themselves with the earth. Two passages have a particular bearing on bucolic as a genre, and Virgil returns to them repeatedly in his eclogue-book. The first of these explains how belief in rural deities arose from a misunderstanding of the phenomenon of echo:

> haec loca capripedes satyros nymphasque tenere
> finitimi fingunt et faunos esse locuntur,
> quorum noctivago strepitu ludoque iocanti
> adfirmant volgo taciturna silentia rumpi;
> chordarumque sonos fieri dulcisque querellas,
> tibia quas fundit digitis pulsata canentum;
> et genus agricolum late sentiscere, cum Pan
> pinea semiferi capitis velamina quassans
> unco saepe labro calamos percurrit hiantis,
> fistula silvestrem ne cesset fundere musam.
>   (*De Rerum Natura*, 4.580–9)

['People living nearby imagine these places hold goat-footed satyrs and nymphs, and fauns are said to be there, by whose night-wandering uproar and merry play, they affirm to the world, the silent stillness is broken; they say there are sounds of lyre-strings and sweet laments, which the flute pours out, touched by the fingers of musicians; and that the country folk have caught the sound far and wide, when Pan, waving the covering of pine-branches on his half-brutish head, runs his curved lip repeatedly across the open-mouthed reeds, so that the pipe does not cease to pour out the sylvan music.']

So much for Pan, the god who, according to myth and to Virgil's Corydon, *primum calamos cera coniungere pluris / instituit* and *curat ovis oviumque magistros* ('first discovered how to join many reeds with wax; Pan cares for the sheep and for the masters of sheep', *Ecl.* 2.32–3). In Book 5, Lucretius has a more quotidian explanation for the invention of the panpipes, instrument of bucolic music (5.1379–98):

> at liquidas avium voces imitarier ore
> ante fuit multo quam levia carmina cantu
> concelebrare homines possent aurisque iuvare.
> et zephyri cava per calamorum sibila primum
> agrestis docuere cavas inflare cicutas.
> inde minutatim dulcis didicere querellas,
> tibia quas fundit digitis pulsata canentum,
> avia per nemora ac silvas saltusque reperta,
> per loca pastorum deserta atque otia dia ...
> haec animos ollis mulcebant atque iuvabant
> cum satiate cibi; nam tum sunt omnia cordi.
> saepe itaque inter se prostrati in gramine molli
> propter aquae rivum sub ramis arboris altae.
> non magis opibus iucunde corpora habebant,
> praesertim cum tempestas ridebat et anni
> tempora pingebant viridantis floribus herbas.
> tum ioca, tum sermo, tum dulces esse cachinni
> consuerant; agrestis enim tum musa vigebat.

['But imitating the clear voices of birds with their mouths came long before men could perform polished music by singing. And the whispering of the breeze through the hollows of the reeds first taught the country folk to blow into hollow straws. Then little by little they learned the sweet plaints which the pipe pours out when touched by the fingers of the musician, discovered in the remote forests or woods and mountain passes, in the deserted places and sunlit leisure of the shepherds ... With these they charmed and delighted their minds when they were full with food; for then all things please the heart. Often therefore they would recline together on the soft grass beside a stream of water under the branches of a tall tree. With not much expense they kept their bodies pleasurably, especially when the weather smiled and the season of the verdant year painted the grass with flowers. That is the customary time for jokes and conversation and delightful boisterous laughter; and then flourished the rustic muse.']

The first thing to notice is Virgil's emphatic reversal of Lucretius' images of teaching and learning at the beginning of the second passage. Where in Lucretius men learn to imitate the birds and are taught (*docuere*) by the breeze to blow into reed pipes, Tityrus himself *teaches* the woods,[85] and the laurels of Eurotas are commanded by the indwelling deity of the river to *learn* the songs which emanate from Phoebus, the supreme god of song. Virgil presents the phenomenon of echo as a *result* and sign of this supernaturally animate quality of the landscape, not as the cause of false and superstitious belief in it. Tityrus teaches the woods *to echo* his song; the resounding valleys actively carry Silenus' song to the stars. Lucretius' vignette of the shepherds reclining beside a stream in the shade of a tree to make their music – already a *locus amoenus* reminiscent of Theocritus (e.g. the opening of Idyll 1 and the final scene of Idyll 7) – becomes the setting of Tityrus' playing at the beginning of Eclogue 1, and of the music contests of eclogues 3 and 7 (3.55–7, 7.10–13). In Eclogue 1, Tityrus meditates the *silvestrem Musam* ('the sylvan muse', 1.2), the music which flows from the pipe of Lucretius' fictitious Pan at 4.589 of *De Rerum Natura*; at the beginning of Eclogue 6, under the direction of Apollo, he meditates the *agrestem Musam* ('rustic muse', 6.8), which flourishes in the pleasant but ordinary scene of pastoral merrymaking in Lucretius' fifth book (5.1398).[86] The echoing and animate landscape of Eclogue 10 conjures a procession of gods to sympathize with Gallus: Apollo, Pan (*quem vidimus ipsi*, 'whom we saw ourselves' (10.26) – tangibly present to the poet in a defiant denial of Lucretius' materialism) and Silvanus, whose description is conspicuously modelled on Lucretius' vivid depiction of his non-existent Pan (10.24–5):

> venit et agresti capitis Silvanus honore,
> florentis ferulas et grandia lilia quassans

['Silvanus also came, with the mark of rustic honour on his head, waving flowering branches and tall lilies']

At the most defiantly anti-Lucretian point of Virgil's book, where he is inventing a new god in the apotheosis of Daphnis, the animate woods and mountains of Menalcas' hymn, replete with Pan and dryads, *laetitia voces ad sidera iactant* ('fling their joyful voices to the stars', 5.62). The words clearly describe the phenomenon of echo: in fact they are based on another Lucretian description of echo in Book 2, *clamoreque montes / icti reiectant voces ad sidera mundi* ('the

---

85 Virgil is also remembering how Bion is said to have taught the birds their song in the *Lament for Bion*.
86 Noted Clausen, *Eclogues*, ad 1.2, 6.8.

mountains, struck with the clamour, fling back the voices to the stars in the heavens', *De Rerum Natura*, 2.327–8), and anticipate the valleys echoing Silenus' song *ad sidera* at 6.84.[87] But there is no explicit reference to echo: the groves *sonant*, rather than *resonant*. Material causes are thoroughly submerged in the religious vision Lucretius abhorred. Another significant echo of Lucretius in the opening of Menalcas' hymn underlines Virgil's triumph over his predecessor (5.56–9):

> Candidus insuetum miratur limen Olympi,
> sub pedibusque videt nubes et sidera Daphnis.
> ergo alacris silvas et cetera rura voluptas
> ... tenet ...

['Radiant Daphnis marvels at the unfamiliar threshold of Olympus, and beneath his feet sees clouds and stars. Therefore eager delight seizes the woods and the rest of the countryside ...']

The lines recall the beginning of Book 3 of *De Rerum Natura*, where Lucretius describes his wonder as all things are laid open to his sight by the divine mind of Epicurus, from the dwelling of the gods to the earth and what lies below it (3.26–30):

> nec tellus obstat quin omnia dispiciantur,
> sub pedibus quaecumque infra per inane geruntur.
> his ibi me rebus quaedam divina voluptas
> percipit atque horror, quod sic natura tua vi
> tam manifesta patens ex omni parte retecta est.

['Nor does the ground get in the way and prevent all things from being perceived, which carry on beneath our feet in the void below. Thereupon a certain divine pleasure and awe at these things takes hold of me, because nature, thus opening up to plain sight by your power, is laid bare on every side.'][88]

The verbal echo is in the line-opening *sub pedibus* (10.57) and the line-ending *voluptas* (10.58), but there is also an obvious transposition of mood and theme. And the cry of the landscape, *deus, deus ille, Menalca!* ('He is a god – a god, Menalcas!' 5.64) itself echoes Lucretius' grandest rhetorical tribute to Epicurus in the Proem to Book 5: *deus ille fuit, deus, inclute Memmi!* (*De Rerum Natura* 5.8).[89] But if Lucretius was willing to resort to such metaphysical language, superficially in tension with his materialist doctrines, to praise his

---

87 Noted Clausen, *Eclogues, ad* 5.62.
88 Noted Clausen, *Eclogues, ad* 5.56.
89 Noted Clausen, *Eclogues, ad* 5.64.

master Epicurus' illumination of humankind, in Virgil there are hints that his triumphal, and anti-Lucretian, reanimation of the landscape similarly bewrays his own quasi-divine powers as much as those of any external gods.[90] Menalcas' praise of Mopsus' song a few lines earlier subtly reinforces this sense, and again it does so with an evocation of Lucretius (5.45–7):

> Tale tuum carmen nobis, divine poeta,
> quale sopor fessis in gramine, quale per aestum
> dulcis aquae saliente sitim restinguere rivo.

['Your song, divine poet, is to me like sleep on the grass to the weary, like quenching my thirst in the summer's heat with a gushing stream of sweet water.']

With its *in gramine* and *aquae rivo*, the imaginary scene conjured by the simile echoes the bucolic *locus amoenus* of Lucretius fifth book:[91] the archetypal landscape of bucolic which Virgil has so successfuly reanimated exists in and depends on the song of the (Orpheus-like) 'divine poet'.

Where Lucretius sought to strip the landscape of its numinous presences and the universe of its comfortingly benevolent Providence, Virgil offers his sophisticated audience, in troubled times, a pleasurably nostalgic vision of that landscape reanimated, and he does so by artfully stealing Lucretius' lines and phrases and using their *enargeia* (vividness) and aesthetic force against him. And in the Caesarean eclogues 4 and 5 he shows his audience how this vision can be more than nostalgia for the simpler beliefs of a primitive age, and can be applied to their own lives and current events. Whether by mere happy coincidence or not, the ruler who was on his way to becoming emperor had similar ideas about reviving religion in Rome, manipulating it and harnessing it to his own political programme, and so Virgil's bucolic negotiation was successful, at least in a personal sense, to the extent that it gained him patronage under which to compose his *Georgics* and *Aeneid*.

90 Compare Virgil's prayer to the Muses at *Georgics* 2.475–502, where he hopes for the 'blessed' (*felix*, 2.490) condition of the man who knows the causes of things (Lucretius' Epicurus?) and has placed fear and fate and greedy Acheron beneath his feet (*subiecit pedibus*, 2.492 – reminiscent of Daphnis as well as Lucretius, of course). The lines immediately following suggest Virgil's pastoral correction of Lucretius: he who knows the rustic gods, Pan, Silvanus and the nymphs is also 'fortunate' (*fortunatus*, 493–4) – though the difference between *felix* and *fortunatus* should be registered, and note that a few lines earlier Virgil has presented pastoral poetry as a humbler alternative to the knowledge of the heavens he implores the Muses to grant him.
91 Noted Clausen, *Eclogues*, ad 5.46–7.

Spenser is happy to draw on Virgil's imagery of a landscape magically animated by the powers of the Orphic poet in his own self-presentation – though his sympathies in some important respects lie rather with Lucretius than with Virgil.[92] In *June*, Hobbinol alludes to the opening of Eclogue 1 in his praise of Colin's music,

> Whose Echo made the neyghbour groues to ring,
> And taught the byrds, which in the lower spring
> Did shroude in shady leaues from sonny rayes,
> Frame to thy songe their cherefull cheriping.
>
> (*June* 52–5)

The lines combine allusion to Virgil's first eclogue with allusion to the *Lament for Bion* (44–5), where Bion is said to have taught the birds to sing. The stanza attributes to Colin something akin to Orphic powers, as his song apparently transforms the 'wastfull hylls' (50) into a *locus amoenus*. But within a few stanzas Colin, picking up from the overtones of bucolic lament in the echo of pseudo-Moschus, gives Hobbinol's imagery a turn towards the related pastoral trope of the grieving landscape, from the lament for Daphnis in Theocritus' seventh idyll and Virgil's imitation in Eclogue 10, and does so in the context of an elegiac stanza remembering the dead 'Tityrus':

> I soone would learne these woods, to wayle my woe,
> And teache the trees, their trickling teares to shedde.
>
> (*June* 95–6)

This way of animating the landscape is also related to the figure of Orpheus in ancient bucolic: the *Lament for Bion* has the landscape grieve for the dead Bion, imitating Theocritus' seventh idyll, and ends with the hope that Bion's music will charm Persephone into releasing him from the Underworld just as Orpheus' once charmed her into releasing Eurydice.[93] In *October*, Piers will attribute Orphic powers to Cuddie (whom we are invited by E.K. to see as another persona for Spenser) by allusion to this part of the Orpheus story:

---

92 On Spenser and Lucretius, see Edwin Greenlaw, 'Spenser and Lucretius', *Studies in Philology* 17 (1920), 439–64; Anthony M. Esolen, 'Spenserian Chaos: Lucretius in *The Faerie Queene*', *Spenser Studies* 11 (1990), 31–51; Jonathan Goldberg, *Seeds of Things: Theorizing Sexuality and Materiality in Renaissance Representations* (Bronx, NY: Fordham University Press, 2009), pp. 105–116.
93 Compare also the grieving Orpheus of the fourth *Georgic*, whose laments affect the oaks, and whose dying cry of 'Eurydice', uttered by his severed head as the Hebrus bears it away, is re-echoed by the river's banks (*Eurydicen toto referebant flumine ripae*, *Georgics* 4.527).

> Soone as thou gynst to sette thy notes in frame,
> O how the rurall routes to thee doe cleaue:
> Seemeth thou dost their soule of sence bereaue,
> All as the shepheard, that did fetch his dame
> From *Plutoes* balefull bowre withouten leaue:
> His musicks might the hellish hound did tame.
>
> (*October* 25–30)

The audience bereaved of sense, meanwhile, recalls the cattle and lynxes *stupefactae* ('stupefied', 8.3) by the songs of Damon and Alphesiboeus in Eclogue 8.[94] But such Orphic music-making is a thing of the past for both Cuddie and Colin, and in the present, adverse political circumstances, both can only produce complaint. In effectively singing a veiled dirge for himself by alluding to the laments in Theocritus and pseudo-Moschus in *June*, Colin is striking the pose of the 'dying' Gallus in Eclogue 10, and of the suicidal lover of Damon's song in Eclogue 8. It is this elegiac mood which governs the sestina of *August*, whose dominant trope is that of the echoing woods.

In *Epithalamium*, however, the figure of echo returns in a positive key, and once more it is linked firmly to the notion of Orphic song. Spenser sings 'my owne loues prayses' (14) as 'Orpheus did for his owne bride' (16), and in the recurring refrain the woods 'answer' and echo back the music he elicits from the Muses (1), nymphs (37, 56), birds (78), the Hours (98), the Graces (103) and from the community of the town (129, 133, 137, 143, 167), climaxing in the music of the organ and choristers within the church as the ceremony begins (218, 221), and the singing of the Angels themselves as they are wed (240). The summoning of Muses, nymphs and Graces recalls the *Aprill* lay and the *Nouember* dirge, while reversing *Nouember*'s call for a turn from joyous song to lament at 12–14 and its imagery of faded or discarded garlands at 40–7, until the refrain changes at nightfall (in the seventeenth stanza, reflecting the time of sunset on Spenser's wedding-day) to the cessation of noise and of echo, calling for the peace and quiet appropriate to the privacy of the couple's night of procreative love-making.[95] Many have been struck by the oddity of alluding to Orpheus' wedding in the context of an epithalamic song: Richard McCabe thinks that it 'insinuates [a] more sombre element' by reminding the reader of Orpheus' ultimate failure to bring Eurydice back from the Underworld. More optimistically,

---

94 This is the line which prompts E.K.'s gloss on the power of 'harmonie and musicall nombers' over the mind (see Chapter 3).
95 A. Kent Hieatt, *Short Time's Endless Monument*.

Hieatt sees 'the quality of blessed love here being celebrated over against the doomed and distraught love of the less fortunate poet'.[96] Both McCabe and Hieatt are working here against the background of Virgil's version of the myth in the fourth *Georgic*, with its tragic ending. If we are to think with that version, Spenser in *Epithalamium* could be said to outdo Orpheus himself, as Virgil anticipates doing himself at the end of Eclogue 4 – but once again, where Virgil hopes to do this through an ascent to heroic epic, Spenser does it through the celebration of true love.[97] However, though Virgil's tragic ending quickly became canonical (being taken up, particularly influentially, by Ovid in the *Metamorphoses*, as well as by others), it appears to have been Virgil's invention. In all earlier accounts (including the *Lament for Bion*), Orpheus succeeds in restoring Eurydice to life.[98] Outside his translation of the pseudo-Virgilian *Culex*, which repeats the tragic version of the *Georgics*, Spenser's allusions to this part of the Orpheus myth consistently assume Orpheus' success as in the pre-Virgilian tradition.[99] Virgil's tragic narrative in the fourth *Georgic* strongly implies a rejection of the passionate love and uncontrolled *furor poeticus*, which Orpheus there embodies, in favour of the values of *labor*, *pietas* and social order, and the didactic poetics of social utility, which are reflected in the character of Orpheus' antagonist, the bee-keeper Aristaeus. The episode obliquely reflects the direction of Virgil's evolving *cursus* towards increasing complexity with Augustan order, with Orpheus here associated no longer with ascent to heroic epic (as in the fourth eclogue) but rather with the self-

---

96 A. Kent Hieatt, 'The Daughters of Horus: Order in the Stanzas of *Epithalamion*', in William Nelson (ed.), *Form and Convention in the Poetry of Edmund Spenser* (New York: Columbia University Press, 1961), pp. 103–21, at 114. Loewenstein, 'Echo's Ring', builds a darkly sceptical reading on the assumption of Orpheus' failure as described in the *Georgics*.

97 Virgil's treatment of the Orpheus myth in the fourth *Georgic* contains reminiscences of Eclogue 10, linking Orpheus' love and despair to Gallus (cp. particularly *Geo.* 4.508–9 and *Ecl.* 10.14–15, and see Putnam, *Virgil's Pastoral Art*, p. 351, n. 14). The backward-looking (literally, in his fatal glance over his shoulder, as well as metaphorically), mourning Orpheus is there counterpointed with the forward-looking, practical Aristaeus, in a way which suggests the division of Virgil's loyalties between an Orphic poetry of love, nostalgia and Greek artistry and an Italian poetry of commitment to Augustan politics on the other. The triumph of Aristaeus thus anticipates and figures the direction taken by his own career, and the values it enshrines, similar to the effect achieved by the fate of Gallus at the end of the eclogue-book. See Monica Gale, 'Poetry and the Backward Glance in Virgil's *Georgics* and *Aeneid*', *TAPA* 133 (2003), 323–52.

98 See Segal, *Orpheus*, pp. 1–10; Lee, *Virgil as Orpheus*, pp. 1–13.

99 The relevant passages are *October* 28–30, with E.K.'s gloss; *Ruines of Time* 390–2; *The Faerie Queene* IV.x.58.4–5. See Introduction above.

absorption and amatory obsession of bucolic song: his portrayal, like that of Gallus in Eclogue 10 (which it echoes conspicuously), is subjective and sympathetic, but nevertheless presents him as a negative model of a poetics which must be relinquished.[100] Just as, in the context of his pastoral poetry, we have seen Spenser recalibrating various aspects of the literary tradition to their pre-Virgilian state, so too his refusal to follow Virgil's tragic version of Orpheus' katabasis across his works should be seen as a deliberate undoing of Virgil's innovation and rejection of its ideological freight.

This self-confident Orphic power is Colin's from the very beginning of 'Colin Clouts Come Againe' and of the volume (1–9).

> The shepheards boy (best knowen by that name)
> That after *Tityrus* first sung his lay,
> Laies of sweet loue, without rebuke or blame,
> Sate (as his custome was) vpon a day,
> Charming his oaten pipe vnto his peres,
> The shepheard swaines, that did about him play:
> Who all the while with greedie listfull eares,
> Did stand astonisht at his curious skill,
> Like hartlesse deare, dismayed with thunders sound.

The suggestion of inferiority implied in his belatedness in relation to Virgil ('after *Tityrus*'), is balanced by the boast of innovation in '*first* sung his lay', recalling Virgil's and Horace's vaunts that they were the 'first' to bring Greek forms to Italy (*primus*, *Georgics* 3.10; *princeps*, Horace, *Carmina* 3.30.13). But more than this, the ostensible humility of the 'shepheard boy' persona is quite cancelled by the Orphic overtones of his music. 'Charming his oaten pipe' yokes together the Tityrean *avena*, humblest of all pastoral pipes, with the magical 'charm', drawing on the identification of magic and song in the Latin *carmen* (as exploited for instance in Alphesiboeus' song – which is literally a spell – in Eclogue 8 (69–71)), while the satirical sections of the poem may remind us of the potential for the poet

---

100 For suggestive parallels between the Aristaeus/Orpheus section of the fourth *Georgic* and the eclogues in which Gallus appears (6 and 10), see Howard Jacobson, 'Aristaeus, Orpheus, and the *Laudes Galli*', *AJP* 105 (1984), 271–300. Defending Servius' claim that part of the treatment of Orpheus in the *Georgics* was written to replace an earlier passage praising Gallus after his disgrace and death, Jacobson argues that 'the original ... contained a successful recovery of Eurydice' (295), while the revision introduced the innovative tragic ending 'so as to be able to concretely find expression for his deep grief' over 'the fate of his own Orphic poet-lover', Gallus (291).

to use these 'charms' agressively against political power, as Moeris does in Eclogue 9.[101] The effect he has on his audience, 'astonisht ... Like hartlesse deare', recalls Cuddie's audience bereaved of sense at *October* 27, and behind them the stupefied cattle and lynxes at the opening of Eclogue 8. In the story of Bregog and Mulla, Colin uses his powers to animate the landscape, literally, through mythopoeia and prosopopoeia. And at the centre of the poem he devotes them to praise of his beloved, as Melissa appreciates (480–3):

> Then thus *Melissa* said; Thrice happie Mayd,
> Whom thou doest so enforce to deify:
> That woods, and hills, and valleyes thou hast made
> Her name to eccho vnto heauen hie.

Evoking the echo figure of Virgil's *Eclogues*, with its claims for the poet's power over the landscape and its supernatural connotations, the lines particularly recall the apotheosis of Daphnis in Eclogue 5. As on Mount Acidale, the political ruler is replaced as the object of the poet's praise by his private love. But the lines differ from Menalcas' hymn in another important regard. They do not completely submerge the material phenomenon of echo, and they say only that her *name* has been thus lifted to heaven. Mopsus' lament in the first half of Eclogue 5 ends with the inscription on Daphnis' tomb, which boasts Daphnis' name as 'known from here to the stars' (*hinc usque ad sidera notus*, 43), but Menalcas promises that he, by contrast, will raise Daphnis *himself* to the stars (*Daphnim ad astra feremus*, 52). The pointed departure tells us that Colin is not engaging here in the idolatry he will later associate with the corrupt court, though he is making a rhetorical gesture in that direction ('*enforce* to deify' = 'strive to deify'). When Colin later applies the rhetoric of 'Angels and ... skie' (619) to his own ruler, it is as we have seen hedged about with warnings that he speaks under duress, and when the motif of the echoing landscape returns in connection with Cynthia at 635–6, it is in altogether more muted terms:

---

101 On the relation of magic to ideas of poetic praxis, emphasizing the political efficacy of song, see Genevieve Guenther, 'Spenser's Magic, or Instrumental Aesthetics in the 1590 *Faerie Queene*', *ELR* (2006), 194–226. Given the Irish setting of Spenser's late pastoral, and its gestures towards drawing on a native culture as an alternative to the classical inheritance, Sidney's reference at the end of the *Apologie for Poesy* to the tradition that Irish bards can 'rhyme to death' those who fail to patronize them seems also relevant. (See Highley, *Shakespeare, Spenser, and the Crisis in Ireland*, p. 30, also calling Colin 'an Irish Orpheus'.)

> The speaking woods and murmuring waters fall,
> Her name Ile teach in knowen termes to frame,

recalling rather the complaining Gallus, evoked so strongly by the immediate context of the lines (with its tree-carving and its anticipation of shepherds singing after Colin's death). Meanwhile, Colin comes closest to the figure of the *divinus poeta* in his inspired hymn to Love, the truly heavenly body of the poem.

The devotion of Spenser's Orphic powers to the celebration of love puts him at odds with Virgil, but aligns him interestingly with Virgil's antagonist in the *Eclogues*, Lucretius. *De Rerum Natura* opens with what seems on the surface to be the single exception to his doctrine that the gods do not interfere with earthly affairs, the great invocation to Venus, asking her to inspire his work (1.1–5, 19–25, 29–37):

> Aeneadum genetrix, hominum divumque voluptas,
> alma Venus, caeli subter labentia signa
> quae mare navigerum, quae terras frugiferentis
> concelebras, per te quoniam genus omne animantum
> concipitur visitque exortum lumina solis ...
> omnibus incutiens blandum per pectora amorem
> efficis ut cupide generatim saecla propagent.
> quae quoniam rerum naturam sola gubernas
> nec sine te quicquam dias in luminis oras
> exoritur neque fit laetum neque amabile quicquam,
> te sociam studeo scribendis versibus esse
> quos ego de rerum natura pangere conor ...
> effice ut interea fera moenera militiai
> per maria ac terras omnis sopita quiescant.
> nam tu sola potes tranquilla pace iuvare
> mortalis, quoniam belli fera moenera Mavors
> armipotens regit, in gremium qui saepe tuum se
> reicit aeterno devictus vulnere amoris,
> atque ita suspiciens tereti cervice reposta
> pascit amore avidos inhians in te, dea, visus,
> eque tuo pendet resupini spiritus ore.

['Mother of the race of Aeneas, delight of men and gods, nurturing Venus, who, gliding beneath the heavenly constellations, fill the ship-bearing sea and the fruitful lands; since through you every kind of creature is conceived and coming forth sees the light of the sun ... Striking alluring love into all breasts, you make them eagerly increase their generations after their kind. And since you alone govern the nature of things, and without you nothing comes forth on to the brightly lit shores of day or becomes glad or lovely, I am eager that you should be my companion in writing these verses, which I am trying to compose, on the nature of things ... Meanwhile, cause the savage works of warfare to subside into calm sleep through all the seas and lands. For you alone can aid mankind with tranquil peace, since Mars, mighty in arms, rules the wild works of war – Mars, who often flings himself down in your lap, conquered by the eternal wound of love, and thus, resting his smooth neck and looking up, he feeds his greedy eyes on you, goddess, gazing avidly, and as he reclines his breath hangs on your lips.']

In fact this Venus is not so much an exception to his Epicureanism as a personification trope, part of the 'sweet honey of the Muses' (1.947) with which he coats his medicinal teachings to make it palatable. She represents the regenerative power of Nature (often personified – without being deified – in Lucretius' poem), who inspires his wonder throughout the work, expressed here in procreative love, and seen as ethically opposite to the impulse to violence and war figured in Mars, which is the object of Lucretius' abhorrence throughout the work. The influence of Lucretius' opening invocation can be felt in the Proem to Book I of *The Faerie Queene*, with its invocation of Venus and the disarmed Mars. The vision of the perpetuity through change of material nature and the various species in the Garden of Adonis, dwelling place of 'great mother *Venus*' (III.vi.40.3), is strongly reminiscent of Lucretius 1.248–64, and the imagery of creatures planted in the garden is indebted to Lucretius' translation of Epicurus' *atomoi* as *semina*, 'seeds' (as for instance at 1.614: *natura reservans semina rebus*, 'Nature keeping safe the seeds of things'). This Lucretian theme of perpetuity is reprised in the *Mutabilitie Cantos*, where the vision of Nature in particular seems marked by the sense of wonder with which Lucretius regards nature's workings as revealed by Epicurus throughout his poem.[102] Most tangibly of all, the prayer to Venus at IV.x.44–7 closely paraphrases Lucretius' opening invocation. The hymn to Cupid in 'Colin Clouts Come Home Againe' is recognizably another version of this. But another point of contact between the eclogue and Lucretius' poem is in the opposition of its two types of love. For in the fourth book Lucretius returns to the subject of sexual desire, and presents it as a wound, a disease, and delusion – an unalloyed evil resulting in waste and suffering for the sake of ephemeral

---

102 Spenser's Lucretius is Christianized, of course; in this he draws on a tradition of accommodating Lucretius to Christian doctrine going back to the early Christian apologist Lactantius, who draws heavily on Lucretius' denunciation of Greek and Roman myth and religion, while appealing to his descriptions of Nature to support a monotheistic vision of Providence.

pleasures (4.1037–287). His treatment here reflects the language and tropes of contemporary love poets like Catullus, and may have influenced the ironic self-presentation of later Roman elegists from Gallus onwards.[103] Indeed, Virgil's depiction of Gallus in Eclogue 10 may draw on it.[104] It is clearly the sterility and selfishness of this kind of desire which repels Lucretius – 'their pleasure is not pure', he says (*non est pura voluptas*), for underlying it is always a desire to hurt (*laedere*) its object (4.1081–3). Meanwhile, he treats the unselfish domestic love of wife and children with poignant sympathy (3.894–6). Where Virgil's tenth eclogue could provide Spenser only with a critique of the amatory madness embodied in a particular genre of love poetry, Lucretius provided both this critique and a balancing vision of procreative love as a beneficent principle helping to order the cosmos. It seems likely that, in defining his Orphic social role in his mature pastorals, Spenser was thinking at least in part of the figure of Epicurus as presented in Lucretius' poem.[105]

But the poem's most pointed recollection of the revival of the landscape in Virgil's fifth eclogue is of course in Hobbinol's opening speech (22–31):

> Whilest thou wast hence, all dead in dole did lye:
> The woods were heard to waile full many a sythe,
> And all their birds with silence to complaine:
> The fields with faded flowers did seem to mourne,
> And all their flocks from feeding to refraine:
> The running waters wept for thy returne,
> And all their fish with langour did lament:

103 To take only the most obvious example, compare 4.1160–9 with Ovid, *Ars amatoria* 2.657ff.
104 For instance: with Virgil's *sollicitos amores* (10.6) compare Lucretius' *sollicitatur semen* (4.1037–8); with Virgil's *fluctus* (10.4), with the erotic overtones I have been arguing, Lucretius' *fluctuat ardor amantum* (4.1077); Virgil's use of the *militia amoris* trope at 10.44–5 with Lucretius' military simile at 4.1049–51; Gallus' plan to roam with nymphs over Maenalus (10.55), hoping it will be medicine for his madness (10.60), with Lucretius' advice that one cure the wounds of love by wandering after some wide-ranging (promiscuous) Venus (4.1070–1); and with Pan's comparison of remorseless Love to meadows never sated by the streams, Lucretius' analogy with unquenchable thirst in dreams (4.1097–100).
105 It should also be noted that, in Lucretius' account of the birth of pastoral music in Book 5, the idyllically happy scene of rural festivity leads on to a diatribe against our sophisticated modern taste for wealth and luxury, concluding *idque minutatim vitam provexit in altum / et belli magnos commovit funditus aestus* (5.1434–5), a combination of seafaring and war recalling those symptoms of Hesiod's declining ages (*Works and Days* 106–201) which we have seen invoked in Virgil's fourth eclogue and in 'Colin Clouts Come Home Againe', and strongly suggesting the association of Lucretius' primitive country folk with the Golden Age.

> But now both woods and fields, and floods reuiue,
> Sith thou art come, their cause of meriment,
> That vs late dead, hast made againe aliue ...

The hints, already in Virgil, that the deification accorded Daphnis is at least as much a revelation of the poet's quasi-divine powers are amplified to become the whole tenor of the passage, as Colin's absence and return produces the effects of Daphnis' death and apotheosis (simultaneously recalling the effects of Tityrus' absence and return in Eclogue 1, but writ large). Eclogue 5 has a wider relevance in 'Colin Clouts Come Home Againe', and here it will be useful to recall the two competing allegorizations of the fifth eclogue discussed in Chapters 1 and 2 – Vives' identification of Daphnis as Christ and Servius' identification of Daphnis as Julius Caesar. In his hymn to the newly deified Daphnis, Virgil's Menalcas institutes a cult, teaching his community how to worship the new god. (More than half of his song (ll. 65–80) is devoted to the altars he will set up and the annual feasts he will institute in Daphnis' honour.) In this he resembles Colin, especially when viewed through the lens of Vives' Christian interpretation, by which Daphnis is in fact the same god represented by Colin's Cupid under a different allegorical veil. Read as a political allegory, however (as by Servius), Menalcas' worship of Julius Caesar, father of Octavian, obviously resembles Colin's rhetorical praise of Cynthia. But the emphasis in Spenser's eclogue on the poet's vatic powers as independent of, rather than subserving, political power, and directed instead towards the religious (and specifically Christian) guidance of his community, makes it clear that Spenser is imitating the former conception of Menalcas, and distancing himself from the latter. The dynamic recalls that of *Nouember*, where as we have seen Spenser also weighed the competing allegorizations of the fifth eclogue against one another in the service of a similar political and religious critique of Virgil. But here there is an additional overtone, whereby Colin as poet takes the place of the deified Daphnis himself. It is his Orphic poetic skill which figuratively reanimates the landscape, and in the rest of the poem we see him deploying this skill in the service of his community, just as the deified Daphnis, Menalcas hopes, will be *bonus o felixque tuis* ('good and auspicious to your people', 5.65), a hope fleshed out in Eclogue 9's lines on Ceasar's star ensuring the crops. The ruler of Virgil's political apotheosis is displaced by Spenser himself as the conduit of divine power and benign providence. As at the end of Eclogue 6, with its echo of the unfinished panegyric recited in Eclogue 9, it is the song, not the political potentate, who is raised *ad sidera* ('to the stars', 6.84, 9.29).[106]

Now, Virgil's fifth eclogue forms a kind of diptych. Mopsus' lament on Daphnis' death and Menalcas' hymn on his apotheosis are of exactly equal length (twenty-five lines each). It also draws attention to the two halves of Virgil's book, since it shares the same primary model with Eclogue 10, in Theocritus' first idyll. These two eclogues are the ones, it will be remembered from Chapter 3, which stand outside the concentric ring structure organizing the book: Eclogue 5 is the triumphal centre around which the pairs 1/9, 2/8, 3/7 and 4/6 are organized; Eclogue 10 is a coda after the pattern has been completed. Thus 5 and 10 also form a kind of pair, bridging the second half of the book, in which the first four eclogues find their answering terms. In Eclogue 5 viewed as a diptych in itself, we go from literal death to triumphant assertion of immortality; in the pair of 5 and 10 we go from Daphnis' immortality to Gallus' metaphorical (literary) death. By prominent allusion to Eclogue 5 near the beginning of 'Colin Clouts Come Home Againe', Spenser draws attention to the structure of his own volume, which Patrick Cheney has aptly described as a 'poetic diptych'. The second half of this 'diptych' (comprising 'Astrophel' and the elegies by other hands, and preceded by the separate title page before 'Astrophel') is most clearly in the tradition of Eclogue 10, as lament for a fellow poet, while 'Colin Clouts Come Home Againe', with its scene of literal song exchange (the Shepherd of the Ocean's song in a dejected mood like Mopsus', and Colin's lay of Bregog and Mulla literally animating the landscape through personification, like Menalcas') and with its inclusion of hymn, resembles Eclogue 5. Thus we proceed from a kind of apotheosis (but with an emphasis on the divine inspiration and Orphic power of the poet himself) in

---

106 The remarkable passage at the end of the second *Georgic*, where Virgil speaks of himself as priest of the Muses (475–502), is also relevant. Virgil's praise here for the 'blessed' (*felix*) man who has attained knowledge of the causes of things, and placed beneath his feet (*subiecit pedibus*) fear of Acheron and all regard for public honours, 'the Roman state and kingdoms which will fall' (*res Romanae perituraque regna*, 2.498), is strongly reminiscent of Lucretius on Epicurus, and strikingly in tension with the worship of Caesar in the proem to Book 3 immediately following. Spenser may be thinking of the Muses' instruction at *Georgics* 2.477–82 at *December* 83–6. But the important thing to note here is that the passage in the second *Georgic* envisions pastoral as a second-best alternative to the inspired, Orphic knowledge of the heavens Virgil implores the Muses to grant him: he will subside into it if his 'cold blood' prevents him from attaining such heights. Spenser, by contrast, is confident that the poet can be an Orpheus without leaving the woods of pastoral.

the first half of the volume to lament in the second, reversing the direction of Eclogue 5, and following the direction of the Virgilian pair 5 and 10 (while literalizing the death treated in the latter). As Cheney puts it, the first half of the volume 'celebrat[es] the national authority of a living poet, Spenser', while the second forms 'a collective pastoral monument to a dead poet, Sidney'.[107] But as we have seen, Colin's/Spenser's Daphnis-like immortality is equally a theme in 'Astrophel', and Eclogue 10, with its metaphorical death brought on by *indignus amor*, is at least equally important in 'Colin Clouts Come Home Againe'. The contrast between, on the one hand, deadly forms of love and love poetry, reflecting particular ways of relating to the centre of political power, and, on the other, the immortality of divinely inspired and socially beneficent song is the continuous theme uniting the volume (or Spenser's part in it). As a whole work, it presents a large-scale revision of Virgil's triumphal central eclogue, conducted through a continued, meticulous and profound engagement with its companion piece, Eclogue 10, and rewriting Virgil's vision of the poet's role in relation to political rulers and to religion.[108]

Conclusion: reshaping the 'Virgilian career'

In Virgil's final eclogue, Gallus fantasizes about escaping into pastoral, but cannot. In 'Colin Clouts Come Home Againe', Colin is a Gallus who does manage this 'escape'. Reminding us of the Gallus-like stance he had adopted in the *Calender*, he here relinquishes it in favour of an altogether different stance of confident vatic authority in his reimagined version of Virgil's Arcadia, while leaving only Ralegh and Cynthia's other courtiers to languish in the deadly amatory servitude which is Gallus' in Eclogue 10. But the pastoral figured in Spenser's new Arcadia is not escapist, despite its claim to imaginative freedom. It is located recognizably within real geography as well as in fictional space, and maintains its dedication to serving a community of readers in the real world, and to dealing with the realities of contemporary politics. As Virgil's Arcadia was never more than a space for imaginative retreat from the pressure of those realities, so pastoral turned out to be for him only a humble prelude to serving Rome in

107 Cheney, '*Colin Clouts Come Home Againe, Astrophel,* and *The Doleful Lay of Clorinda*', p. 238.
108 On a smaller scale, the 'Pastorall Aeglogue upon the death of Sir Phillip Sidney Knight &c.' (the dialogue between 'Lycon' and 'Colin' in which Spenser may have had a hand), later in the volume, is strongly marked by combined imitation of the same pair of Virgilian eclogues.

'higher' genres – those genres anticipated in the initiation of Gallus by the Muses in the sixth eclogue – which he would do under the sign of divine inspiration, in the invocations at the beginning of the *Georgics* and the *Aeneid*. And thus the tenth eclogue would be Virgil's last, as the poet himself 'arises' and departs at its end. ('Tomorrow to fresh fields and pastures new', as Milton puts it at the end of *Lycidas*.) The pastoral of 'Colin Clouts Come Home Againe', by contrast, is not a prelude to vatic poetry but rather embodies it. As he abandons the political dependency figured in the stance of the dying Gallus he adopted in the *Calender*, Colin becomes the divinely inspired Gallus of the sixth eclogue. But where Virgil identified fidelity to that vocation with ascent to 'higher' genres, in which his dependency on and service to Augustus would become more pronounced, Colin fulfils his vocation and achieves his vatic status precisely by returning from epic to pastoral, and claims the freedom to satirize the court from within this domain, just as Colin rejects courtly values in favour of the virtues of his community at 'home'.

Virgil's abandonment of bucolics in favour of higher genres is intimately bound up with his denigration of sexual love. In the tenth eclogue, it is Gallus' passion which derails the career foreseen for him in Eclogue 6. The final book of the *Georgics* revisits the theme, with its contrast between the sterile and self-destructive passion of Orpheus and the piety of Aristaeus which ensures the continued life of his bees: while sympathy is shown towards Orpheus, as towards Gallus in Eclogue 10, it is Aristaeus, as *cultor nemorum* ('husbandman of the forests', *Georgics* 1.14), who is invoked as a god among gods in the proem to the work. In the *Aeneid*, Aeneas' abandonment of Dido for the sake of Rome's Augustan destiny, in obedience to the gods, exemplifies the poem's systematic subordination of *amor* to *Roma*, of individual love to public duty. Spenser overturns this hierarchy of values, identifying faithful married love with a religious ideal higher than the courtly and political imperatives of epic. The movement can already be seen in some parts of *The Faerie Queene*, particularly the Garden of Adonis and the vision on Mount Acidale, but it is in his second pastoral volume that it is stated most clearly. On this basis he builds his claim for a more authoritative and vatic status than was Virgil's, as pastoral poetry – reimagined, and independent of political power – is revealed to be the fit conduit for a Christian prophecy truer than the dynastic prophecies of Virgilian epic.

Before Virgil, bucolic and epic were conceived as rather akin than separate, both belonging to the genre of hexameter *epos*, and distinguished chiefly by their different subject matter. The generic kinship or even identity is what makes it possible for the *Lament for Bion* to draw its analogy between Bion and Homer (70–84):

> τοῦτό τοι ὦ ποταμῶν λιγυρώτατε δεύτερον ἄλγος,
> τοῦτο, Μέλη, νέον ἄλγος. ἀπώλετο πρᾶν τοι Ὅμηρος,
> τῆνο τὸ Καλλιόπας γλυκερὸν στόμα, καί σε λέγοντι
> μύρασθαι καλὸν υἷα πολυκλαύτοισι ῥεέθροις,
> πᾶσαν δ' ἔπλησας φωνᾶς ἅλα· νῦν πάλιν ἄλλον
> υἱέα δακρύεις, καινῷ δ' ἐπὶ πένθεϊ τάκῃ.
> ἀμφότεροι παγαῖς πεφιλημένοι, ὃς μὲν ἔπινε
> Παγασίδος κράνας, ὃ δ' ἔχεν πόμα τᾶς Ἀρεθοίσας.
> χὢ μὲν Τυνδαρέοιο καλὰν ἄεισε θύγατρα
> καὶ Θέτιδος μέγαν υἷα καὶ Ἀτρείδαν Μενέλαον·
> τῆνος δ' οὐ πολέμους, οὐ δάκρυα, Πᾶνα δ' ἔμελπε,
> καὶ βούτας ἐλίγαινε καὶ ἀείδων ἐνόμευε,
> καὶ σύριγγας ἔτευχε καὶ ἁδέα πόρτιν ἄμελγε,
> καὶ παίδων ἐδίδασκε φιλήματα, καὶ τὸν Ἔρωτα
> ἔτρεφεν ἐν κόλποισι καὶ ἤρεθε τὰν Ἀφροδίταν.

['O tunefullest of rivers, this makes thee a second grief; this, good Meles, comes to thee a new woe. One melodious mouthpiece of Calliope is long dead, and that is Homer; that lovely son of thine was mourned, 'tis said, of thy tearful flood, and all the sea was filled with the voice of thy lamentation: and lo! now thou weepest for another son, and a new sorrow melteth thee away. Both were beloved of a water-spring, for the one drank at Pegasus' fountain and the other got him drink of Arethusa; and the one sang of the lovely daughter of Tyndareus, and the great son of Thetis, and of Atreid Menelaus; but this other's singing was neither of wars nor tears but of Pan; as a herdsman he chanted and kept his cattle with a song; ... he taught the lore of kisses, he made a fosterling of Love, he roused and stirred the passion of Aphrodite.']

From this shared and equal origin, Virgil creates a hierarchy of genres, keyed into the hierarchy of values in his own ethical system, and to the social hierarchy and political values of Rome. Love remains the principal subject of pastoral, as in the *Lament for Bion*, but at best it is associated with *otium* (a concept which, for all the pleasant aura which surrounds it in the *Eclogues*, was for Virgil's contemporary audience fraught with connotations of culpable idleness and effeminacy), and at worst it is presented as a form of insanity leading to neglect of duties (2.69–72) and to death (2.7; 8.20, 41, 60; 10.10, 33). Looking back to the *Eclogues* from the end of the *Georgics*, Virgil characterizes his pastoral poetry as the 'play' of 'presumptuous youth' in 'ignoble ease' (*illo Vergilium me tempore ... studiis florentem ignobilis oti, / carmina qui lusi pastorum audaxque iuventa*, Georgics 4.563–5). The heroic song of 'kings and battles' (*reges et proelia*, *Ecl.* 6.3), which would ultimately take shape in the *Aeneid*, is even in *recusatios* of the *Eclogues* imagined as a higher genre. It is with a heroic song that Virgil predicts, at the end of Eclogue 4, he will surpass Orpheus, Linus and Pan. At the beginning of the same eclogue he justifies his stretching of the bounds of pastoral to something 'a little *greater*' (*paulo maiora*) with the argument that *humiles myricae* ('*humble* tamarisks') are not *consule dignae* ('worthy of a consul', 4.1–3), mapping genre on to social status. Bucolic and heroic *epos* are more sharply contrasted, and even opposed, in Virgil's metapoetic reflections across his works than they had been before his time, and the ingrained hierarchy of genres which he bequeathed to his successors in the very shape of his career recognizably reflects the values and the strongly hierarchical structure of the emerging imperial state.

By returning from epic to pastoral in *Colin Clouts Come Home Againe*, Spenser departs pointedly from the shape of Virgil's career, which had become such an influential model for Renaissance poets. It is by no means the only publication in which he fails to follow the path beaten by Virgil, but it is an especially *pointed* departure precisely because it is conducted in Virgilian terms, reversing the direction of Virgil's *cursus* by a recourse specifically to pastoral, and conducting a sustained intertextual engagement with Virgil's *Eclogues* – most particularly with the eclogue which marked Virgil's final farewell to the pastoral genre. The volume is *about* the Virgilian *cursus*. To see Spenser's return to pastoral as a retreat or a decline, as it has often been seen, is to cling to the assumptions inherent in the generic hierarchy constructed by Virgil, but it is precisely this hierarchy and its implied values which Spenser's volume pointedly rejects. Pastoral *otium* is not the idle play of irresponsible youth, the volume claims, but the setting of a *vita contemplativa* more truly beneficial to society than military or official activity in the service of political potentates. As a channel for teaching the moral, political and religious wisdom gained by such contemplation, pastoral is worthier than epic, conceived as praise of such potentates, can be.[109]

---

109 Of course, Spenser's epic is a great deal more than a panegyric for Elizabeth, and indeed the *Aeneid*, too, contains much which does not easily cohere with the notion of epic as praise of the ruler, as it is characterized in the *Eclogues*. But nevertheless the 'Augustan voice' is the loudest of the *Aeneid's* voices, and the pressure of expectation of such political panegyric is strongly felt in *The Faerie Queene*.

And love, the archetypal subject of pastoral, is not a base impulse opposed to the higher values of piety and public duty, but rather the highest ethical and religious ideal, which should underpin any truly worthy political and social organization – while the destructive perversions which mask themselves under the name of love are inextricably linked with the pernicious power-relations of a corrupt hierarchical society. Spenser is not an English Virgil in any simple sense. His pointed departure from the Virgilian *cursus* in his return to pastoral in 1595 is the most telling evidence of this, but the departure can be properly understood only in relation to the *cursus* it so deliberately and meaningfully reshapes. Spenser would make less sense if we read him without Virgil. His conception of his own role and purpose as a poet, across his career, is articulated very largely in relation to his great Roman predecessor, and only careful attention to his intertextual engagement with that predecessor's works can enable us to appreciate that conception and its implications fully.

Bibliography

Primary

Anon. *This boke treateth of the lyfe of Virgil, and of his death, and many other marvayles that he did in his lyfe tyme by witchecrafte and nygromancy, through the develles of hell* (London, 1550 (?))

Appian. *The Civil Wars*, tr. Horace White (Cambridge, MA: Harvard University Press, 1913)

Bacon, Francis. *The wisdome of the ancients written in Latine by the Right Honourable Sir Francis Bacon ... done into English by Sir Arthur Gorges, Knight* (London, 1619)

Bathurst, Theodore. *Calendarium Pastorale* (London, 1653)

Bion. *Moschi Syracusii, et Bionis Smyrnaei idyllia* (Antwerp: Plantin, 1584)

———. *The Greek Bucolic Poets*, tr. J. M. Edmonds (Cambridge, MA: Harvard University Press, 1912)

———. *Bucolici Graeci*, ed. A. S. F. Gow (Oxford: Clarendon Press, 1952)

———. *Bion of Smyrna: The Fragments and the Adonis*, ed. J. D. Reed (Cambridge: Cambridge University Press, 1997)

Callimachus, *Callimachi Cyrenaei hymni, epigrammata et fragmenta, quae extant* (Antwerp: Plantin, 1584)

Ciris: A Poem Atrributed to Vergil, ed. R. O. A. M. Lyne, Cambridge Classical Texts and Commentaries 20 (Cambridge: Cambridge University Press, 2004)

Elyot, Thomas. *The boke named the Gouernour* ([London]: Thomas Berthelet, 1537)

Fragments of Roman Poetry c. 60 BC–AD 20, ed. and tr. A. S. Hollis (Oxford: Oxford University Press, 2007)

Lucretius, *Titi Lucreti Cari De Rerum Natura Libri Sex*, ed. Cyril Bailey, 3 vols (Oxford: Clarendon Press, 1947)

Moschus. *Moschi Syracusii, et Bionis Smyrnaei idyllia* (Antwerp: Plantin, 1584)

———. *The Greek Bucolic Poets*, tr. J. M. Edmonds (Cambridge, MA: Harvard University Press, 1912)

———. *Bucolici Graeci*, ed. A. S. F. Gow (Oxford: Clarendon Press, 1952)
[Mulcaster, Richard]. *The passage of our most drad Soueraigne Lady Quene Elyzabeth through the citie of London to westminster the daye before her coronacion Anno 1558* (London, 1558 [=1559])
Pausanias. *Description of Greece*, tr. W. H. S. Jones and H. A. Ormerod, 5 vols (Cambridge, MA: Harvard University Press); 1918.
Poetae Principes Heroici Carminis et alii nonnulli (Geneva: Stephanus, 1577)
Puttenham, George. *The Art of English Poesy by George Puttenham: A Critical Edition*, ed. Frank Whigham and Wayne A. Rebhorn (Ithaca: Cornell University Press, 2007)
Quintilian, *Institutio oratoria*, ed. Michael Winterbottom (Oxford: Clarendon Press, 1970)
Sannazaro, Jacopo. *De partu virginis libri tres. Lamentatio de morte Christi. Piscatoria* (Paris: Robert Stephanus, 1527)
Sandys, George. *Ovid's Metamorphosis: Englished, Mythologiz'd, and Represented in Figures* (Oxford, 1632)
Servius. *Servii Grammatici qui feruntur in Vergilii carmina commentarii*, ed. Georg Thilo and Hermann Hagen, 3 vols. (Leipzig, 1878–87)
Sidney, Philip. *The Prose Works of Sir Philip Sidney*, ed. Albert Feuillerat (Cambridge: Cambridge University Press, 1968)
———. *Apology for Poetry*, 2nd ed., ed. R. W. Maslen (Manchester: Manchester University Press, 1989)
Spenser, Edmund. *Edmund Spenser: The Shorter Poems*, ed. Richard McCabe (Harmondsworth: Penguin, 1999)
———. *The Shorter Poems*, ed. William Oram *et al.* (New Haven: Yale University Press, 1989)
———. *Edmund Spenser: Selected Shorter Poems*, ed. Douglas Brooks-Davies (New York: Longman, 1995)
———. *The Faerie Queene*, ed. A. Hamilton (London: Longman, 1977)
Theocritus. *Theocriti Syracusani Eidyllia triginta sex ... Latino carmine reddita*, ed. Eobanus Hessus and Joachim Camerarius (Basel, 1531)
———. *Theocriti Aliorumque Poetarum Idyllia ... Omnia cum interpretatione Latina. In Virgilianas et Nas[onianas] imitationes Theocriti, Observationes H. Stephani* (Paris, 1579)
———. *Theocritus*, edited with a translation and commentary by A. S. F. Gow, 2 vols (Cambridge: Cambridge University Press, 1950)
Virgil. *In P. Vergilii Maronis Bucolica*, ed. Eobanus Hessus (Strasbourg, 1540)
———. *In publii Vergilii Maronis Bucolica interpretatio, potissimum allegorica*, ed. Ludovico Vives (Antwerp, 1543)
———. *P. Virgilii Maronis Opera ... cum ... commentariis Servii, Donati, Probi, Mancinelli* (Venice, 1544)
———. *Opera P. Virgilii Maronis, Pauli Manutii annotationes brevissimae in margine adscriptae* (Antwerp, 1572)

——. *P. Virgilii Maronis Bucolica, P. Rami, professoris regii praelectionibus exposita* (Paris, 1572)
——. *Vergil: Eclogues*, ed. Robert Coleman (Cambridge: Cambridge University Press, 1977)
——. *A Commentary on Virgil Eclogues*, ed. Wendell Clausen (Oxford: Clarendon Press, 1994)
——. *P. Vergilius Maronis: Aeneidos Liber Tertius*, ed. D. Williams (Oxford: Clarendon Press, 1962)
——. *Aeneidos liber quartus*, ed. A. S. Pease (Cambridge, MA: Harvard University Press, 1935)

Secondary

Adkins, David. 'Spenser's Humanist Virgil: The Recovery of Alexandrian Poetics in Sixteenth-Century Poetry and Philology' (Ph.D. thesis in progress, University of Toronto)
Alexander, Gavin. *Writing After Sidney: The Literary Response to Sir Philip Sidney 1586–1640* (Oxford: Oxford University Press, 2006)
Alexiou, Margaret. *Ritual Lament in Greek Tradition* (Cambridge: Cambridge University Press, 1974)
Alpers, Paul. *The Singer of the Eclogues* (Berkeley: University of California Press, 1979)
——. 'Pastoral and the Domain of Lyric in Spenser's *Shepheardes Calender*', *Representations* 12 (1985), 83–100
——. *What Is Pastoral?* (Chicago: University of Chicago Press, 1996)
Armitage, Christopher M. (ed.). *Literary and Visual Ralegh* (Manchester: Manchester University Press, 2013)
Arnold, Janet. 'The "Coronation" Portrait of Queen Elizabeth I', *The Burlington Magazine* 120 (1978), 726–41
Austin, Roland G. '*Ille ego qui quondam* ...', *Classical Quarterly* 18 (1968), 107–15
Baldwin, T. W. *William Shakespere's Small Latine and Lesse Greeke*, 2 vols (Urbana: University of Illinois Press, 1944)
Balot, Ryan Krieger. 'Pindar, Virgil, and the Proem to Georgic 3', *Phoenix* 52 (1998), 83–94
Barchiesi, Alessandro. *The Poet and the Prince: Ovid and Augustan Discourse* (Berkeley: University of California Press, 1997)
——. 'Lane-switching and Jughandles in Contemporary Interpretations of Roman Poetry', *TAPA* 135 (2005), 135–62
Bates, Catherine. *The Rhetoric of Courtship in Elizabethan Language and Literature* (Cambridge: Cambridge University Press, 1992)
Bednarz, James P. 'The Collaborator as Thief: Ralegh's (Re)Vision of *The Faerie Queene*', *ELH* 63 (1996), 279–307

Benko, Stephen. 'Virgil's Fourth Eclogue in Christian Interpretation', *Aufstieg und Niedergang der römischen Welt* II.31.1 (1980), 646–705

Berger, Harry. 'Mode and Diction in the *Shepheardes Calender*', *MP* 67 (1969), 140–9

———. *Revisionary Play: Studies in the Spenserian Dynamics* (Berkeley: University of California Press, 1988)

Bernard, John D. *Ceremonies of Innocence: Pastoralism in the Poetry of Edmund Spenser* (Cambridge: Cambridge University Press, 1989)

Bloom, Harold. *The Anxiety of Influence: A Theory of Poetry* (Oxford: Oxford University Press, 1973)

Bonner, Stanley F. *Education in Ancient Rome: From the Elder Cato to the Younger Pliny* (Abingdon: Routledge, 2012)

Boyle, A. J. *The Chaonian Dove: Studies in the Eclogues, Georgics, and Aeneid of Virgil* (Leiden: Brill, 1986)

Breed, Brian W. 'The Pseudo-Vergilian *Dirae* and the Earliest Responses to Vergilian Pastoral', *Trends in Classics* 4 (2012), 3–28

Brennan, Michael. *The Sidneys of Penshurst and the Monarchy, 1500–1700* (Aldershot: Ashgate, 2006)

Briggs, W. W. Jr. 'A Bibliography of Virgil's *Eclogues* (1927–1977)', *Aufstieg und Niedergang der römischen Welt* II.31.2 (1981), 1265–357

Brown, Georgia. *Redefining Elizabethan Literature* (Cambridge: Cambridge University Press, 2004)

Burchmore, David W. 'The Image of the Centre in "Colin Clouts come home againe"', *RES* 28 (1977), 393–406

Burrow, Colin. 'English Renaissance Readers and the *Appendix Vergiliana*', *Proceedings of the Virgil Society* 26 (2008), 1–16

Cain, Thomas H. 'The Strategy of Praise in Spenser's "Aprill"', *SEL* 8 (1968), 45–58

———. 'Spenser and the Renaissance Orpheus', *University of Toronto Quarterly* 41 (1971), 24–47

Cairns, Francis. *Generic Composition in Greek and Latin Poetry* (Edinburgh: Edinburgh University Press, 1972)

Chaghafi, Elizabeth. 'Spenser and Book History', in P. J. Hecht and J. B. Lethbridge (eds), *Spenser in the Moment* (Teaneck, NJ: Fairleigh Dickinson University Press, 2015), pp. 67–99

Chapman, Alison. 'The Politics of Time in Edmund Spenser's English Calendar', *SEL* 42 (2002), 1–24

Chaudhuri, Sukanta. *Renaissance Pastoral and Its English Developments* (Oxford: Clarendon Press, 1989)

Cheney, Patrick. 'The Laureate Choir: The Dove as a Vocational Sign in Spenser's Allegory of Ralegh and Elizabeth', *Huntington Library Quarterly* 53 (1990), 257–80

———. *Spenser's Famous Flight: A Renaissance Idea of a Literary Career*

(Toronto: University of Toronto Press, 1997)
——. 'Spenser's Pastorals', in Andrew Hadfield (ed.), *The Cambridge Companion to Spenser* (Cambridge: Cambridge University Press, 2001), pp. 79–105
——. '*Colin Clouts Come Home Againe*, *Astrophel*, and *The Doleful Lay of Clorinda*', in Richard McCabe (ed.), *The Oxford Handbook of Edmund Spenser* (Oxford: Oxford Univerity Press, 2010), pp. 237–55
——. 'Introduction: "Jog On, Jog On": European Career Paths', in Patrick Cheney and Frederick A. De Armas (eds), *European Literary Careers: The Author from Antiquity to the Renaissance* (Toronto: University of Toronto Press, 2002), pp. 3–23
—— and Frederick A. De Armas (eds). *European Literary Careers: The Author from Antiquity to the Renaissance* (Toronto: University of Toronto Press, 2002)
Clausen, Wendell. 'Callimachus and Roman Poetry', *Greek, Roman, and Byzantine Studies* 5 (1964), 181–96
Connolly, Joy. 'Border Wars: Literature, Politics, and the Public', *TAPA* 135 (2005), 103–34
Conte, Gian Bagio. *The Rhetoric of Imitation: Genre and Poetic Memory in Virgil and Other Latin Poets*, tr. Charles Segal (Ithaca: Cornell University Press, 1986)
——. *The Poetry of Pathos: Studies in Virgilian Epic*, ed. S. J. Harrison (Oxford: Oxford University Press, 2007)
Cooper, Helen. *Pastoral: Medieval into Renaissance* (Ipswich: D. S. Brewer, 1977)
Craik, Katherine A. 'Spenser's *Complaints* and the New Poet', *Huntington Library Quarterly* 64 (2001), 63–79
Cullen, Patrick. *Spenser, Marvell, and Renaissance Pastoral* (Cambridge, MA: Harvard University Press, 1970)
Cummings, R. M. *Spenser: The Critical Heritage* (London: Routledge & Kegan Paul, 1971)
Dasenbrock, Reed Way. 'The Petrarchan Context of Spenser's *Amoretti*', *PMLA* 100 (1985), 38–50
DeNeef, Alexander Leigh. *Spenser and the Motives of Metaphor* (Durham, NC: Duke University Press, 1982)
Donnelly, Michael L. 'The Life of Vergil and the Aspirations of the "New Poet"', *Spenser Studies* 17 (2003), 1–35
Dunlop, A. 'The Unity of Spenser's *Amoretti*', in A. D. S. Fowler (ed.), *Silent Poetry: Essays in Numerological Analysis* (London: Routledge & Kegan Paul, 1970), pp. 153–69
Durr, R. A. 'Spenser's Calendar of Christian Time', *ELH* 24 (1957), 269–95
Du Quesnay, I. M. Le M. 'Vergil's Fourth Eclogue', *Papers of the Liverpool Latin Seminar* 1 (1976), 25–99

Elder, J. P. 'Non iniussa cano: Virgil's Sixth Eclogue', *Harvard Studies in Classical Philology* 65 (1961), 109–25
Ellrodt, Robert. *Neoplatonism in the Poetry of Edmund Spenser* (Geneva: E. Droz, 1960)
Enterline, Lynn. *Shakespeare's Schoolroom: Rhetoric, Discipline, Emotion* (Philadelphia: University of Pennsylvania Press, 2011)
———. 'Drama, Pedagogy, and the Female Complaint: or, What's Troy Got to Do with It?', *Swiss Papers in English Language and Literature*, vol. 31, ed. Elizabeth Dutton and James McBain (Tübingen: Gunter Narr Verlag, forthcoming).
Erickson, Wayne. 'Spenser Reads Ralegh's Poetry in (to) the 1590 *Faerie Queene*', *Spenser Studies* 15 (2001), 175–84
———. (ed.), *Literary and Visual Ralegh* (Manchester: Manchester: University Press, 2013).
Esolen, Anthony M. 'The Disingenuous Poet Laureate: Spenser's Adoption of Chaucer', *Studies in Philology* 87 (1990), 285–311
———. 'Spenserian Chaos: Lucretius in *The Faerie Queene*', *Spenser Studies* 11 (1990), 31–51
Falco, Raphael. 'Spenser's "Astrophel" and the Formation of Elizabethan Literary Genealogy', *Modern Philology* 91 (1993), 1–25
———. *Conceived Presences: Literary Genealogy in Renaissance England* (Amherst, MA: University of Massachusetts Press, 1994)
Fantham, Elaine. 'Liberty and the People in Republican Rome', *TAPA* 135 (2005), 209–29
Fantuzzi, Marco. 'Theocritus and the Bucolic Genre', in Marco Fantuzzi and Richard Hunter, *Tradition and Innovation in Hellenistic Poetry* (Cambridge University Press, 2004), pp. 133–90
———. 'The Style of Hellenistic Epic', in Marco Fantuzzi and Richard Hunter, *Tradition and Innovation in Hellenistic Poetry* (Cambridge: Cambridge University Press, 2004), pp. 255–66
Fantuzzi, Marco and Richard Hunter, *Tradition and Innovation in Hellenistic Poetry* (Cambridge: Cambridge University Press, 2004)
Farrell, Joseph. 'Dialogue of Genres in Ovid's "Lovesong of Polyphemus" (*Metamorphoses* 13.719-897),' *AJP* 113 (1992), 235–68
———. 'Greek Lives and Roman Careers in the Classical Vita Tradition', in Patrick Cheney and Frederick A. De Armas (eds), *European Literary Careers: The Author from Antiquity to the Renaissance* (Toronto: University of Toronto Press, 2002), pp. 24–46
———. 'Ovid's Virgilian Career', *Materiali e discussioni per l'analisi dei testi classici* 52 (2004), 41–55
Feldherr, Andrew and Paula James. 'Making the Most of Marsyas', *Arethusa* 37 (2004), 75–103
Fishwick, Duncan. *The Imperial Cult in the Latin West: Studies in the Ruler*

Cult of the Western Provinces of the Roman Empire, 3 vols (Leiden: Brill, 1987, 1991, 2004)
Forster, Leonard. *The Icy Fire: Five Studies in European Petrarchism* (Cambridge: Cambridge University Press, 1969)
Fowler, Alastair. *Spenser and the Numbers of Time* (London: Routledge & Kegan Paul, 1964)
——. *Triumphal Forms: Structural Patterns in Elizabethan Poetry* (Cambridge: Cambridge University Press, 1970)
Gaisser, Julia Haig. 'A Structural Analysis of the Digressions in the *Iliad* and the *Odyssey*', *Harvard Studies in Classical Philology* 73 (1969), 1–44
Gale, Monica R. 'Poetry and the Backward Glance in Virgil's *Georgics* and *Aeneid*', *TAPA* 133 (2003), 323–52.
Giamatti, A. Bartlett. *The Play of Double Senses: Spenser's* Faerie Queene (Englewood Cliffs, NJ: Prentice-Hall, 1975)
Goldberg, Jonathan. *Seeds of Things: Theorizing Sexuality and Materiality in Renaissance Representations* (Bronx, NY: Fordham University Press, 2009)
Greenlaw, Edwin. 'Spenser and Lucretius', *Studies in Philology* 17 (1920), 439–64
Greg, W. W. *Pastoral Poetry and Pastoral Drama* (London: Bullen, 1906)
Guenther, Genevieve. 'Spenser's Magic, or Instrumental Aesthetics in the 1590 *Faerie Queene*', *ELR* 36 (2006), 194–226
Gutzwiller, Kathryn. *Theocritus' Pastoral Analogies: The Formation of a Genre* (Madison: University of Wisconsin Press, 1991)
Haber, Judith. *Pastoral and the Poetics of Self-Contradiction: Theocritus to Marvell* (Cambridge: Cambridge University Press, 2006)
Hadfield, Andrew. 'Spenser's Rosalind', *MLR* 104 (2009), 935–46
——. *Edmund Spenser: A Life* (Oxford: Oxford University Press, 2014)
Halperin, Nicholas. *Before Pastoral: Theocritus and the Ancient Tradition of Bucolic Poetry* (New Haven: Yale University Press, 1983)
Hamilton, A. C., et al. (eds). *The Spenser Encyclopedia* (Toronto: University of Toronto Press, 1990)
Hansen, Peter Allan. '*Ille ego qui quondam* ... Once Again', *Classical Quarterly* 22 (1972), 139–49
Hardie, A. 'The *Georgics*, the Mysteries and the Muses at Rome', *PCPS* 48 (2002), 165–208
Hardie, Colin G. 'The Tenth Eclogue', *PVS* 6 (1967), 1–11
Hardie, Philip. *Virgil's Aeneid: Cosmos and Imperium* (Oxford: Clarendon Press, 1986)
——. *The Epic Successors of Virgil: A Study in the Dynamics of a Tradition* (Cambridge: Cambridge University Press, 1993)
——. *Ovid's Poetics of Illusion* (Cambridge: Cambridge University Press, 2002)
——. 'The Self-Divisions of Scylla', *Trends in Classics* 1 (2009), 118–47

———. 'Ovid and Virgil at the North Pole: Marvell's "A Letter to Doctor Ingelo", in Jennifer Ingleheart (ed.), *Two Thousand Years of Solitude: Exile After Ovid* (oOxford: Oxford University Press, 2011), pp. 135–51

———. *Rumour and Renown: Representations of Fama in Western Literature* (Cambridge: Cambridge University Press, 2012)

Hardie, Philip and Helen Moore (eds), *Classical Literary Careers and Their Reception* (Cambridge: Cambridge University Press, 2010)

Harrison, S. J. *Generic Enrichment in Vergil and Horace* (Oxford: Oxford University Press, 2007)

Harrison, T. P. Jr. 'Spenser, Ronsard, and Bion', *MLN* 49 (1934), 139–45

Hecht, Paul J. and J. B. Lethbridge (eds). *Spenser in the Moment* (Teaneck, NJ: Fairleigh Dickinson University Press, 2015)

Helfer, Rebecca. *Spenser's Ruins and the Art of Recollection* (Toronto: University of Toronto Press, 2012)

Helgerson, Richard. *The Elizabethan Prodigals* (Berkeley: University of California Press, 1976)

———. 'The New Poet Presents Himself: Spenser and the Idea of a Literary Career', *PMLA* 93 (1978), 893–911

———. *Self-Crowned Laureates: Jonson, Spenser, Milton* (Berkeley: University of California Press, 1983)

Herron, Thomas. 'Love's "emperye": Ralegh's "Ocean to Scinthia", Spenser's "Colin Clouts Come Home Againe" and *The Faerie Queene* IV.vii in colonial context', in Christopher M. Armitage (ed.), *Literary and Visual Ralegh* (Manchester: Manchester University Press, 2013)

Hieatt, A. Kent. *Short Time's Endless Monument: The Symbolism of Numbers in Edmund Spenser's 'Epithalamion'* (New York: Columbia University Press, 1960)

———. 'The Daughters of Horus: Order in the Stanzas of *Epithalamion*', in William Nelson (ed.), *Form and Convention in the Poetry of Edmund Spenser* (New York: Columbia University Press, 1961), pp. 103–21

Higham, T. F. and C. M. Bowra (eds). *The Oxford Book of Greek Verse in Translation* (Oxford: Clarendon Press, 1942)

Highley, Christopher. *Shakespeare, Spenser, and the Crisis in Ireland* (Cambridge: Cambridge University Press, 1997)

Hinds, Stephen. *Allusion and Intertext: Dynamics of Appropriation in Roman Poetry* (Cambridge: Cambridge University Press, 1998)

Hoffman, Nancy Jo. *Spenser's Pastorals: The Shepheardes Calender and 'Colin Clout'* (Baltimore: Johns Hopkins University Press, 1977)

Holzberg, Niklas. *Ovid: The Poet and His Work*, tr. G. M. Goshgarian (Ithaca: Cornell University Press, 2002)

Hopper, Vincent Foster. *Medieval Number Symbolism: Its Sources, Meaning and Influence on Thought and Expression* (New York: Columbia University Press, 1938)

Horsfall, N. M. 'Virgil's Impact at Rome: The Non-Literary Evidence', in N. M. Horsfall (ed.), *A Companion to the Study of Virgil* (Leiden: Brill, 1995), pp. 249–56

——(ed.). *A Companion to the Study of Virgil* (Leiden: Brill, 1995)

Hubbard, Thomas K. *The Pipes of Pan: Intertextuality and Literary Filiation in the Pastoral Tradition from Theocritus to Milton* (Ann Arbor: University of Michigan Press, 1998)

Hughes, Merritt Y. 'Spenser and the Greek Pastoral Triad', *Studies in Philology* 20.2 (1923), 184–215

——. *Virgil and Spenser* (Berkeley: University of California Press, 1929)

Hulls, Jean-Michel. 'Recasting the Master: Further Faces of Virgil in Imperial Rome', *Proceedings of the Virgil Society* 27 (2011), 156–84

Hume, Anthea. *Edmund Spenser, Protestant Poet* (Cambridge: Cambridge University Press, 1984)

Hunter, Richard. 'The Aetiology of Callimachus' *Aitia*', in Marco Fantuzzi and Richard Hunter, *Tradition and Innovation in Hellenistic Poetry* (Cambridge: Cambridge University Press, 2004), pp. 42–88

——. 'Epic in a Minor Key', in Marco Fantuzzi and Richard Hunter, *Tradition and Innovation in Hellenistic Poetry* (Cambridge: Cambridge University Press, 2004), pp. 201–10

Jacobson, Howard. 'Aristaeus, Orpheus, and the *Laudes Galli*', *AJP* 105 (1984), 271–300

Jenkyns, Richard. *The Legacy of Rome: A New Appraisal* (Oxford: Oxford University Press, 1992)

Johnson, Lynn Staley. *The Shepheardes Calender: An Introduction* (Philadelphia: Pennsylvania State University Press, 1990)

Johnson, W. C. 'Gender Fashioning and the Dynamics of Mutuality in Spenser's *Amoretti*', *English Studies* 74 (1993), 503–19

Johnson, W. Ralph. *Darkness Visible: A Study of Vergil's* Aeneid (Berkeley: University of California Press, 1976)

Jones, Ann Rosalind and Peter Stallybrass. 'The Politics of *Astrophil and Stella*', *SEL* 24.1 (1984), 53–68

Kallendorf, Craig. *In Praise of Aeneas: Virgil and Epideictic Rhetoric in the Early Italian Renaissance* (Hanover, NH: University Press of New England, 1989)

Kelsey, Lynn. 'Spenser, Ralegh, and the Language of Allegory', *Spenser Studies* 17 (2003), 183–213

Kennedy, Duncan. 'Arcades ambo: Virgil, Gallus and Arcadia', *Hermathena* 143 (1987), 47–59

Klein, J. L. '"Let us love, dear love, lyke as we ought": Protestant Marriage and the Revision of Petrarchan Loving in Spenser's *Amoretti*', *Spenser Studies* 10 (1992), 109–38

Kolb, Robert. *For All the Saints: Changing Perceptions of Sainthood and*

Martyrdom in the Lutheran Reformation (Macon, GA: Mercer University Press, 1987)

Koller, Katherine. 'Spenser and Ralegh', *ELH* 1 (1934), 37–60

Kyriakidis, S. '*Georgics* 4.559–566: The Vergilian Sphragis', *Kleos* 6 (2000), 535–47

Lane, Robert. *Shepheards Devises: Edmund Spenser's Shepheardes Calender and the Institutions of Elizabethan Society* (Athens: University of Georgia Press, 1993)

Leach, Eleanor Windsor. *Vergil's Eclogues: Landscapes of Experience* (Ithaca: Cornell University Press, 1974)

Leahy, William. *Elizabethan Triumphal Processions* (Aldershot: Ashgate, 2005)

Lee, M. O. *Virgil as Orpheus: A Study of the Georgics* (Albany: State University of New York Press, 1996)

Levin, Carole. *The Heart and Stomach of a King: Elizabeth I and the Politics of Sex and Power* (Philadelphia: University of Pennsylvania Press, 2013)

Lindheim, Nancy. 'The Virgilian Design of *The Shepheardes Calender*', *Spenser Studies* 13 (1999), 1–21

Loewenstein, Joseph. 'Echo's Ring: Orpheus and Spenser's Career', *ELR* 16 (1986), 287–302

Lord, Mary Louise. 'Dido as an Example of Chastity: The Influence of Example Literature', *Harvard Library Bulletin* 17 (1969), 22–44, 216–32

Low, Anthony. *The Georgic Revolution* (Princeton: Princeton University Press, 1985)

Luborsky, Ruth Samson. 'The Allusive Presentation of *The Shepheardes Calender*', *Spenser Studies* 1 (1980), 29–67

———. 'The Illustrations to *The Shepheardes Calender*', *Spenser Studies* 2 (1981), 3–53

———. 'The Illustrations to *The Shepheardes Calender*, II', *Spenser Studies* 9 (1988), 249–53

Lyne, R. O. A. M. *Further Voices in Virgil's Aeneid* (Oxford: Clarendon Press, 1992)

MacCaffrey, Isabel. 'Allegory and Pastoral in *The Shepheardes Calender*', *ELH* 36 (1969), 88–109

Maley, Willy. *Salvaging Spenser: Colonialism, Culture and Identity* (New York: St Martin's, 1997)

Mallette, Richard. 'Spenser's Portrait of the Artist', *SEL* 19 (1979), 19–41

Marotti, A. F. '"Love Is Not Love": Elizabethan Sonnet Sequences and the Social Order', *ELH* 49 (1982), 396–428

Marshall, Peter K. *Servius and Commentary on Virgil*, Center for Medieval & Renaissance Studies, Occasional Papers 5 (Asheville, NC: Pegasus, 1997)

Martindale, Charles (ed.). *Cambridge Companion to Virgil* (Cambridge: Cambridge University Press, 1997)

Maury, Paul. 'Le secret de Virgile et l'architecture des Bucoliques', *Lettres d'Humanité* 3 (1944), 71–147

McCabe, Richard. '"Little booke: thy selfe present": The Politics of Presentation in The Shepheardes Calender', in Howard Erskine-Hill and Richard McCabe (eds), *Presenting Poetry* (Cambridge: Cambridge University Press, 1995), pp. 15–40

——. 'Annotating Anonymity, or Putting a Gloss on *The Shepheardes Calender*', in Joe Bray, Miriam Handley, and Anne C. Henry (eds), *Ma(r)king the Text: The Presentation of Meaning on the Literary Page* (Aldershot: Ashgate, 2000), pp. 35–54

——. *Spenser's Monstrous Regiment: Elizabethan Ireland and the Poetics of Difference* (Oxford: Oxford University Press, 2005)

——. 'Authorial Self-Presentation', in Richard McCabe (ed.), *The Oxford Handbook of Edmund Spenser* (Oxford: Oxford University Press, 2010), pp. 462–82

—— (ed.). *The Oxford Handbook of Edmund Spenser* (Oxford: Oxford University Press, 2010)

McCarthy, Penny. 'E.K. was Only the Postman', *N&Q* 47 (2000), 28–31

McFaul, Tom. *Poetry and Paternity in Renaissance England: Sidney, Spenser, Shakespeare, Donne and Jonson* (Cambridge: Cambridge University Press, 2010)

McLane, Paul. *Spenser's* Shepheardes Calender: *A Study in Elizabethan Allegory* (Notre Dame: University of Notre Dame Press, 1961)

Miles, G. B. *Virgil's* Georgics: *A New Interpretation* (Berkeley: University of California Press, 1980)

Miles, Geoffrey. *Classical Mythology in English Literature: A Critical Anthology* (London: Routledge, 1999)

Miller, David Lee. 'Authorship, Anonymity, and *The Shepheardes Calender*', *MLQ* (1979), 219–36

——. 'Abandoning the Quest', *ELH* 46 (1979), 173–92

——. 'Spenser's Vocation, Spenser's Career', *ELH* 50 (1983), 197–231

Montrose, Louis Adrian. '"The Perfecte Paterne of a Poete": The Poetics of Courtship in *The Shepheardes Calender*', *Texas Studies in Literature and Language* 21 (1979), 34–67

——. 'Gifts and Reasons: The Contexts of Peele's Araygnment of Paris', *ELH* 47 (1980), 433–61

——. '"Eliza, Queene of shepheardes," and the Pastoral of Power', *ELR* 10 (1980), 153–82

——. 'Spenser's Domestic Domain: Poetry, Property, and the Early Modern Subject', in Margreta de Grazia, Maureen Quilligan and Peter Stallybrass (eds), *Subject and Object in Renaissance Culture* (Cambridge: Cambridge University Press, 1996)

Most, G. 'The Virgilian *Culex*', in Michael Whitby, Philip Hardie and Mary

Whitby (eds), *Homo Viator: Classical Essays for John Bramble* (Bristol: Bristol Classical Press, 1987), pp. 199–209

Mustard, W. P. 'Lodowick Bryskett and Bernardo Tasso', *AJP* 35 (1914), 192–9

Nagle, Betty Rose. *The Poetics of Exile: Program and Polemic in the* Tristia *and* Epistulae ex Ponto *of Ovid* (Brussels: Latomus, 1980)

Neuse, Richard. 'Milton and Spenser: The Virgilian Triad Revisited', *ELH* 45 (1978), 606–39

Nohrnberg, James. 'Ralegh in Ruins, Ralegh on the Rocks: Sir Wa'ter's Two Books of Mutabilitie and Their Subject's Allegorical Presence in Select Spenserean Narratives and Complaints', in Christopher M. Armitage (ed.), *Literary and Visual Ralegh* (Manchester: Manchester University Press, 2013).

O'Connell, Michael. '*Astrophel*: Spenser's Double Elegy', *SEL* 11 (1971), 27–35

——. *Mirror and Veil: The Historical Dimension of Spenser's Faerie Queene* (Chapel Hill: University of North Carolina Press, 1977)

Ogilvie, Robert M. 'The Song of Thyrsis', *JHS* 82 (1962), 106–10

Oram, William. 'Spenser's Raleghs', *Studies in Philology* 87 (1990), 341–62

——. 'What Did Spenser Really Think of Sir Walter Ralegh When He Published the First Installment of *The Faerie Queene*?', *Spenser Studies* 15 (2001), 165–74

Otis, Brooks. *Vergil: A Study in Civilized Poetry* (Oxford: Clarendon Press, 1963)

Papanghelis, T. D. *Propertius: A Hellenistic Poet on Love and Death* (Cambridge: Cambridge University Press, 1987)

Parmenter, Mary. 'Spenser's "Twelve Aeglogves Proportionable to the Twelve Monethes"', *ELH* 3 (1936), 190–217

Parry, Adam. 'The Two Voices of Virgil's Aeneid', *Arion: A Journal of Humanities and the Classics* 2 (1963), 66–80

Patterson, Annabel. *Pastoral and Ideology: Virgil to Valéry* (Oxford: Clarendon Press, 1988)

——. *Fables of Power: Aesopian Writing and Political History* (Durham, NC, and London: Duke University Press, 1991)

Pauly-Wissowa, *Real-Encyclopädie der klassischen Altertumswissenschaft* (Stuttgart, 1894)

Perkell, Christine. *The Poet's Truth: A Study of the Poet in Virgil's* Georgics (Berkeley: University of California Press, 1989)

——. 'The "Dying Gallus" and the Design of Eclogue 10', *CP* 91 (1996), 128–40

Peterson, Richard S. 'Laurel Crown and Ape's Tail: New Light on Spenser's Career from Sir Thomas Gresham', *Spenser Studies* 12 (1998), 1–35

Pigman, G. W. *Grief and English Renaissance Elegy* (Cambridge: Cambridge University Press, 1985)

Poggioli, Renato. *The Oaten Flute: Essays on Pastoral Poetry and the Pastoral Ideal* (Cambridge, MA: Harvard University Press, 1975)

Powell, Anton. *Virgil the Partisan: A Study in the Re-Integration of Classics* (Swansea: Classical Press of Wales, 2008)

Prescott, Anne Lake. 'The Thirsty Deer and the Lord of Life: Some Contexts for *Amoretti* 67-70', *Spenser Studies* 6 (1985), 33-76

Prescott, H. W. 'A Study of the Daphnis-Myth', *Harvard Studies in Classical Philology* 10 (1899), 121-40

Pugh, Syrithe. *Spenser and Ovid* (Aldershot: Ashgate, 2005)

——. 'Spenser and Classical Literature', in Richard McCabe (ed.), *The Oxford Handbook of Edmund Spenser* (Oxford University Press, 2010), pp. 503-19

——. 'Supping With Ghosts: Imitation and Immortality in Herrick', in Ruth Connolly and Tom Cain (eds), *'Lords of Wine and Oile': Community and Conviviality in the Poetry of Robert Herrick* (Oxford: Oxford University Press, 2011), pp. 220-49

——. 'Reinventing the Wheel: Spenser's "Virgilian Career"', in *Spenser in the Moment*, ed. Paul J. Hecht and J. B. Lethbridge (Teaneck, NJ: Fairleigh Dickinson University University Press, 2013), pp. 1-31

——. 'Jonson and the Cavalier Poets', in Cathy Bates (ed.), *Blackwell Companion to Renaissance Poetry* (Oxford: Blackwell, forthcoming)

——. 'Adonis and Literary Immortality in Pastoral Elegy', in Syrithe Pugh (ed.), *Conversations: Classical and Renaissance Intertextuality* (Aberdeen: Aberdeen University Press, forthcoming)

Putnam, Michael C. J. *The Poetry of the Aeneid: Four Studies in Imaginative Unity and Design* (Cambridge, MA: Harvard University Press, 1965)

——. *Virgil's Pastoral Art: Studies in the Eclogues* (Princeton: Princeton University Press, 1970)

——. 'Some Virgilian Unities', in Philip Hardie and Helen Moore (eds), *Classical Literary Careers and Their Reception* (Cambridge: Cambridge University Press, 2010), pp. 17-38

Quint, David. 'Archimago and Amoret: The Poem and Its Doubles', in Patrick Cheney and Lauren Silberman (eds), *Worldmaking Spenser* (Lexington: University Press of Kentucky, 2000), pp. 32-42

Rambuss, Richard. *Spenser's Secret Career* (Cambridge: Cambridge University Press, 1993)

Reed, Joseph D. 'Ovid's Elegy on Tibullus and Its Models', *Classical Philology* 92 (1997), 260-9

Richardson, J. M. *Astrological Symbolism in Spenser's* The Shepheardes Calender: *The Cultural Background of a Literary Text* (Lewiston, NY: E. Mellen Press, 1989)

Roche, Thomas P. Jr. 'Astrophil and Stella: A Radical Reading', *Spenser Studies* 3 (1982), 139-91; repr. in Dennis Kay (ed.), *Sir Philip Sidney: An Anthology of Modern Criticism* (Oxford: Clarendon Press, 1987), pp. 185-226

Rosenberg, Donald Maurice. *Oaten Reeds and Trumpets: Pastoral and Epic in Virgil, Spenser, and Milton* (Lewisburg: Bucknell University Press, 1981)

Rosenmeyer, Thomas G. *The Green Cabinet: Theocritus and the European Pastoral Lyric* (1969; repr. London: Bristol Classical Press, 2004)

Ross, D. O. *Backgrounds to Augustan Poetry* (Cambridge: Cambridge University Press, 1975)

Røstvig, Maren-Sofie. 'The Shepheardes Calender – A Structural Analysis', *Renaissance and Modern Studies* 13 (1969), 49–79

Rüpke, Jörg. *The Roman Calendar from Numa to Constantine: Time, History, and the Fasti*, tr. David M. B. Richardson (Oxford: Blackwell, 2011)

Schleiner, Louise. 'Spenser's "E. K." as Edmund Kent (Kenned / of Kent): Kyth (Couth), Kissed, and Kunning-Conning', *ELR* 20 (1990), 374–407

Schmidt, Ernst A. 'Arcadia: Modern Occident and Classical Antiquity', in Katherina Volk (ed.), *Oxford Readings in Classical Studies: Vergil's Eclogues* (Oxford: Oxford University Press, 2008), pp. 16–47

Sedgwick, Eve Kosofsky. *Between Men: English Literature and Male Homosocial Desire* (New York: Columbia University Press, 1985)

Segal, Charles. '*Tamen Cantabitis, Arcades*: Exile and Arcadia in Eclogues One and Nine', *Arion* 4 (1965), 237–66

——. *Orpheus: The Myth of the Poet* (Baltimore: Johns Hopkins University Press, 1989)

Shafer, Robert. 'Spenser's Astrophel', *Modern Language Notes* 28 (1913), 224–6

Shore, David. 'Colin and Rosalind: Love and Poetry in the Shepheardes Calender', *Studies in Philology* 73 (1976), 176–88

——. *Spenser and the Poetics of Pastoral: A Study in the World of Colin Clout* (Montreal: McGill-Queen's University Press, 1985)

Sinfield, A. 'Astrophil's Self-Deception', *Essays in Criticism* 28 (1978), 3–17

Sirago, V. A. 'Cesare', in *Enciclopedia Virgiliana* 1 (1985), 753–56

Skutsch, F. *Aus Vergils Frühzeit* (Leipzig: Teubner, 1901)

Skutsch, O. 'Symmetry and Sense in the Eclogues', *Harvard Studies in Classical Philology* 73 (1969), 153–69

Smith, Peter L. '"Lentus in Umbra": A Symbolic Pattern in Vergil's *Eclogues*', *Phoenix* 19 (1965), 298–304

Snell, Bruno. 'Arcadia: The Discovery of a Spiritual Landscape', in *The Discovery of the Mind* (Oxford: Blackwell, 1953), pp. 281–309

Spargo, J. W. *Virgil the Necromancer: Studies in Virgilian Legends* (Cambridge, MA: Harvard University Press, 1934)

Strong, Roy C. *The Cult of Elizabeth: Elizabethan Portraiture and Pageantry* (Berkeley: University of California Press, 1977)

Syme, Ronald. *The Roman Revolution* (Oxford: Oxford University Press, 1963 [1939])

Tarrant, R. J. 'Aspects of Virgil's Reception in Antiquity', in Charles Martindale (ed.), *Cambridge Companion to Virgil* (Cambridge: Cambridge University Press, 1997), pp. 56–72

Tennenhouse, Leonard. 'Sir Walter Ralegh and the Literature of Clientage', in Guy Fitch Lytle and Stephen Orgel (eds), *Patronage in the Renaissance* (Princeton: Princeton University Press, 1981), pp. 235–58

Theodorakopoulos, Elena. 'Closure: The Book of Virgil', in Charles Martindale (ed.), *The Cambridge Companion to Virgil* (Cambridge: Cambridge University Press, 1997), pp. 155–65

Thomas, R. F. 'From *recusatio* to Commitment', *Papers of the Liverpool Latin Seminar* 5 (1985), 61–71

——. *Reading Virgil and His Texts: Studies in Intertextuality* (Ann Arbor: University of Michigan Press, 1999)

——. *Virgil and the Augustan Reception* (Cambridge: Cambridge University Press, 2001)

Tromly, F. B. 'Lodowick Bryskett's Elegies on Sidney in Spenser's *Astrophel* Volume', *RES* 37 (1986), 384–8

Tudeau-Clayton, Margaret. *Jonson, Shakespeare and Early Modern Virgil* (Cambridge: Cambridge University Press, 1998)

Tufte, Virginia. *The Poetry of Marriage: The Epithalamium in Europe and Its Development in England* (Los Angeles: Tinnon-Brown, 1970)

Tylus, Jane. 'Spenser, Virgil, and the Politics of Poetic Labour', *ELH* 55 (1988), 53–77

Van Sickle, John B. 'Epic and Bucolic (Theocritus, Id. VII; Virgil, Ecl. 1)', *Quaderni Urbinati di cultura classica* 19 (1975), 45–72

——. 'Theocritus and the Development of the Conception of Bucolic Genre', *Ramus* 5 (1976), 18–44

——. *The Design of Virgil's Bucolics* (Rome: Edizioni dell'Ateneo & Bizzarri, 1978)

——. 'Staging Vergil's Future and Past', *Classical Journal* 93 (1998), 213–14

——. 'Virgil *vs* Cicero, Lucretius, Theocritus, Plato, & Homer: Two Programmatic Plots in the First Bucolic', *Vergilius* 46 (2000), 21–58

——. 'Virgil Bucolics 1.1-2 and Interpretive Tradition: A Latin (Roman) Program for a Greek Genre', *Classical Philology* 99 (2004), 336–53

——. *Virgil's Book of Bucolics, the Ten Eclogues Translated into English Verse, Framed by Cues for Reading Aloud and Clues for Threading Texts and Themes* (Baltimore: Johns Hopkins University Press, 2011)

Volk, Katherina (ed.). *Oxford Readings in Classical Studies: Vergil's Eclogues* (Oxford: Oxford University Press, 2008)

Waldman, Louis. 'Spenser's Pseudonym "E.K." and Humanist Self-Naming', *Spenser Studies* 9 (1988), 21–31

Walker, S. F. 'Poetry Is/Is Not a Cure for Love: The Conflict of Theocritean and Petrarchan *Topoi* in *The Shepheardes Calender*', *Studies in Philology* 76 (1979), 353–65

Wallace, Andrew. *The Poetics of Pedagogy in Renaissance England* (Oxford: Oxford University Press, 2010)

Whitby, Michael, Philip Hardie and Mary Whitby (eds). *Homo Viator: Classical Essays for John Bramble* (Bristol: Bristol Classical Press, 1987)

Whitman, Cedric. *Homer and the Heroic Tradition* (Cambridge, MA: Harvard University Press, 1958)

Williams, Gordon. *Tradition and Originality in Roman Poetry* (Oxford: Clarendon Press, 1968)

Williams, Mary Frances. 'The *Sidus Iulium*, the Divinity of Men, and the Golden Age in Virgil's *Aeneid*', *Leeds International Classical Studies* 2 (2003), 1–29

Williamson, Colin. 'Structure and Syntax in *Astrophil and Stella*', *RES* 31 (1980), 271–84

Wilson, E. C. *England's Eliza* (Cambridge, MA: Harvard University Press, 1939)

Wilson-Okamura, David Scott. *Virgil in the Renaissance* (Cambridge: Cambridge University Press, 2010)

——. 'Problems in the Virgilian Career', *Spenser Studies* 26 (2011), 1–30

——. *Spenser's International Style* (Cambridge: Cambridge University Press, 2013)

Worden, Blair. *The Sound of Virtue: Philip Sidney's* Arcadia *and Elizabethan Politics* (New Haven: Yale University Press, 1996)

Yates, Frances. *Astraea: The Imperial Theme in the Sixteenth Century* (London: Routledge & Kegan Paul, 1975)

Zanker, Paul. *The Power of Images in the Age of Augustus* (Ann Arbor: University of Michigan Press, 1988)

Index of works and passages

Note: Numbers in brackets denote sections or line numbers in within works.

Anacreontea (33) 24
Apollonius of Rhodes, *Argonautica* 37
Appian, *Civil Wars* (5.27) 41n2

Bacon, Sir Francis, *De Sapientia Veterum* 48n18
Bathurst, Theodore, *Calendarium Pastorale* 88n11, 127n76
Bion, *Lament for Adonis* 22, 27, 70, 107, 184–5, 213–14
    fr. 13 ('Love and the Birdcatcher') 29
[Bryskett, Lodowick], 'The Mourning Muse of Thestylis' 27, 207, 277n79

Callimachus, *Aitia* 12, 19
    'Hymn to Apollo' (105-12) 12n33, 19, 20
    Epigram (2) 209

Elyot, Sir Thomas, *The Boke Named the Gouernour* 4

Hesiod
    Theogony (1-34) 13, 200, 278
    Works and Days 13, 200
Homer
    Iliad
        (2.488-90) 249n44
        (7.299-305) 58
        (18.483-607) 18
    Odyssey 19
        (6.149-52) 125
        (9.231-542) 249, 250–1
        (11) 30
Horace, *Carmina*
    (1.12.9-10) 280
    (3.5.1-4) 178
    (3.30.10-16) 240, 290

Lodge, Thomas *Scyllaes Metamorphosis* 28, 252n52
Lucretius, *De rerum natura*
    (1.1-37) 292–3
    (1.248-64) 293
    (2.327-8) 284–5
    (3.26-30) 285
    (3.894-6) 294
    (4.580-9) 282–4
    (4.1037-287) 293–4
    (5.8) 285
    (5.1379-98) 283–4, 286
Lyfe of Virgil (London, 1550) 61n39

Index of works and passages

Minturno, Antonio *De poeta* 18
Moschus, 'Love the Runaway' 23, 29
    fr. 3 ('Alpheus') 239, 241
[Moschus], *Lament for Bion* 22, 107, 287, 184–5, 213–17
    (1) 241–2
    (44–5) 100n28, 284n85, 287
    (53–4) 209, 216
    (70–84) 21, 201, 239–40, 299
    (93–7) 215
    (99–104) 139n86
    (123–4) 287, 289
Mulcaster, Richard, *The passage of our most drad Soueraigne* 116–23, 128, 130, 142

Orosius, *Seven Books of Histories Against the Pagans*
    (6.1) 73
Ovid
  Amores
    (1.15) 209
    (3.9) 209, 214–15
  Ars amatoria (1.518) 249
  Fasti (1.27–44) 147n98
    (4.865–70) 130–1
    (6.703–8) 104
  Heroides 27
  Metamorphoses 29, 277
    (1.94–6) 249
    (1.131–4) 259
    (5.346–53) 250
    (5.638) 249
    (6.148–312) 125–6
    (6.383–400) 104
    (10.1–78) 35
    (10.708–39) 27, 216
    (11.132–5) 259
    (11.146–7) 259
    (11.153–71) 103–4, 258–9
    (11.172–9) 258
    (13.723–7) 252
    (13.730–4) 252
    (13.738–14.74) 28, 252
    (13.742–5) 249
    (13.759–60) 250
    (13.764–5) 249
    (13.780–8) 249, 250, 253–5
    (13.810–30) 251
    (13.865–6) 248–9
    (13.867–9) 250
    (13.882–97) 248
    (14.75–7) 253
    (15.843–8) 71n49

Pausanias, *Description of Greece*
    (5.7.2–3) 239n22
    (6.22.9) 248n41
    (10.26.1) 35n81
Petrarch, *Rime sparse* 192
    (60.3–4) 179–80
Plato, *Phaedrus* (245a) 34n80
Pliny, *Natural History* (2.93–4) 69, 152
Puttenham, George, *Art of Poesy*
    (1.18) 9
    (3.5–6) 6
    (3.18) 233
    (3.25) 233

Ralegh, Walter, *Ocean to Cynthia* 227–8, 232
    'Our passions are most like to Floods and streames' 245

Sannazaro, *De Partu Virginis*
    (3.196–236) 72
Servius, on
  Aen. (1.287) 72n53
  Aen. (3.20) 104
  Aen. (3.424) 252n53
  Aen. (3.661) 254
  Aen. (4.58) 104

Aen. (6.790) 72n53
Aen. (8.861) 72n53
Eclogues 42
Ecl. (1.27) 49
Ecl. (1.29) 48, 50
Ecl. (2.6) 22–3, 43, 55, 65, 75n59, 98, 173
Ecl. (2.73) 43, 57–8, 93, 98
Ecl. (3.20) 42
Ecl. (3.71) 56, 77, 89, 98
Ecl. (4.1) 115
Ecl. (4.10) 69
Ecl. (4.12) 148
Ecl. (5.20) 70
Ecl. (5.29) 71
Ecl. (5.65) 144–5
Ecl. (8.6) 13n36
Ecl. (8.55) 279
Ecl. (9.5) 58–60
Ecl. (9.23) 75
Ecl. (9.48) 148–9
Ecl. (9.50) 76
Ecl. (10.1) 91, 111, 185, 236, 239
Ecl. (10.4) 239
Ecl. (10.9) 198–9
Ecl. (10.10) 236
Ecl. (10.28) 91, 257n63
Ecl. (10.44) 264
Ecl. (10.45) 263
Ecl. (10.46) 91–2, 109, 185, 204, 214, 242
Ecl. (10.71) 13
Georgics 20
Shakespeare, William, *Venus and Adonis* 27, 216
Sidney, Philip
  Apology for Poetry 80, 196
  Arcadia 187
  Astrophil and Stella 187, 192–5, 208, 210n32, 214
    (Song 1) 192n12
    (Song 2) 192
    (sonnet 24) 195
    (sonnet 25) 192
    (sonnet 35) 195
    (sonnet 52) 192
    (sonnet 62) 210
    (sonnet 69) 210
    (sonnet 74) 194
    (sonnet 81) 194
Spenser, Edmund
  Amoretti and Epithalamion 23–4, 192–3, 218–19, 221, 244
  Amoretti
    (65) 218
    (68) 218
    (75) 127n75
  Anacreontics (4) 24, 29
  Epithalamion 169, 288
    (16) 35–6, 288–9
    (417–23) 218–19
  'Astrophel' 24, 27, 39, 183–220, 222–3, 226, 230–1, 236
    prologue 203, 265
    (1–6) 187, 200
    (9–12) 193
    (25–30) 188, 208
    (31–4) 184, 189–90, 201
    (37–42) 189–90, 201
    (43–8) 189–90, 201
    (49–54) 190–2
    (61–6) 191, 195
    (67–72) 195, 238
    (73–8) 196
    (79–80) 193
    (86–8) 196
    (91) 196
    (101) 193
    (111–12) 196
    (127–32) 197
    (149–50) 184
    (205–6) 204
  'Lay of Clorinda'
    (1–6) 203–4, 219
    (7–8) 204

Index of works and passages

(13–15) 204
(19–25) 204, 206
(25–30) 205, 223
(37–42) 207
(43–8) 208–9, 210, 217
(67–88) 210–13, 216
(89) 207
(92–4) 219
(96) 207
(105–6) 204
'Colin Clouts Come Home
    Againe' 24, 27, 31, 39,
    183–4, 222–301
  dedication to Ralegh 197,
    224–6, 265
  (1–9) 223, 290
  (13) 228
  (22–31) 220, 223, 294–6
  (33–5) 223
  (40–7) 224, 235
  (58–9) 227–8
  (62–3) 227
  (72–9) 227–8, 267
  (80–7) 268–9
  (88–95) 231, 244, 247, 248
  (96–9) 268–9
  (112–15) 261–2
  (116–19) 238, 242–3, 247
  (120–9) 243, 251
  (135–45) 238, 247
  (149–55) 246–7, 248, 251,
    276
  (157) 238
  (164–7) 227–8
  (180–3) 232, 264
  (209–11) 259, 260n68
  (290–1) 269
  (304–7) 269
  (308–26) 264
  (312–19) 224
  (332–455) 264
  (360–7) 230, 270
  (457–63) 275

(472–9) 191, 244, 276
(480–4) 273, 275, 291
(485–615) 264
(604) 235
(612–15) 235
(616–19) 268, 274, 291
(620–7) 270, 272
(628–47) 271–2, 291–2
(654) 193
(665–6) 193
(690–8) 188, 234
(699–702) 233, 236
(703–30) 264
(707–10) 269
(726–8) 188, 243
(736) 142
(762–3) 188
(776–92) 194, 233
(789–90) 188, 195, 233
(799–804) 212, 237
(823–38) 212, 237, 269, 272
(839–42) 218, 237
(863–72) 237
(870–1) 218
(888) 218
(891–4) 232, 233, 264
(899–902) 272
(903–6) 232, 273
(907–26) 273–4
(927–9) 276
(947–51) 276
(952–5) 276–7
'Mother Hubberds Tale' 30,
    31–3, 243
'Muiopotmos' 29, 30
'Ruines of Time'
  (4–7) 262
  (332–6) 201
  (390–2) 35
The Faerie Queene
  (I.Pr.1) 10, 16, 23, 182
  (I.Pr.3) 293
  (I.i.23) 30n73

(I.i.35) 234
(I.ii) 23
(I.viii) 208
(II.vii.29) 235–6
(II.vii.44–50) 234–6
(III) 244
(III.Pr.4) 228
(III.i.25) 243
(III.ii) 29
(III.v.42–7) 228, 245
(III.vi.11–23) 29
(III.vi.29–50) 23, 245, 293
(III.vi.30–3) 211, 213
(III.vi.34) 218
(III.vi.41–2) 211
(III.vi.47) 216
(III.vi.48) 211–12
(IV.ii.1) 37
(IV.vii.35–viii.17) 228–9, 245
(IV.x.44–7) 293
(IV.x.58) 35–6
(V.Pr.5–6) 151–2
(V.ix.25–6) 33, 247
(VI) 25
(VI.ix.24–5) 224
(VI.x.10–28) 278–9
(VII) 29
(VII.vi.38–55) 29, 33, 248n41
Dedicatory Sonnet 14 (to Walter Ralegh) 230–1
The Shepheardes Calender
  'Epistle to Harvey' 8–9, 16, 37, 149, 181
  'Generall argument' 147, 156, 162
  Januarye 84–93, 128, 134, 160, 163, 166, 170, 174
    Argument 85, 165
    (5–6) 85
    (13–18) 90–1
    (19–20) 94
    (39–40) 88, 142, 165
    (43–8) 85
    (49–54) 86, 129, 223
    (55–60) 88, 143–4, 192
    (63–6) 89, 104
    (67–72) 90, 140
    emblem 93, 106
    (1 gloss) 9
    (57 gloss) 88
    (59 gloss) 88–9
    (60 gloss) 86, 126
    emblem gloss 106
  Februarie 163, 170–1
  March 29, 163, 167, 168, 173
    (40–2) 163
    (100) 163
  Aprill 38, 114–35, 136, 160, 163, 166–7, 170, 235–6
    Argument 98, 114, 129, 141
    (9–12) 129
    (13–16) 128–9
    (25) 232
    (37–41) 97, 130
    (43–4) 111
    (48) 111, 116, 130, 139
    (50–1) 97, 121
    (55–63) 116, 120, 130, 164
    (64–5) 97, 130
    (73–8) 156
    (82–5) 97, 130
    (86–90) 125–6, 274
    (91–4) 97, 121
    (95–9) 124, 127, 143
    (100–3) 97, 100
    (104) 116, 139
    (109–17) 97, 127
    (122–6) 116, 139
    (127–35) 130, 131, 140
    (136–44) 116, 120, 131, 139, 164, 189–90
    (147–53) 127–8, 129, 144
    (154–7) 131, 232

(158–61) 108, 132, 232
emblems 125, 130
(26 gloss) 126–7, 129, 140, 274
(50 gloss) 121, 134, 141, 155
(68 gloss) 121
(86–7 gloss) 125
Maye 163–4, 166
(14) 164
June 93–114, 160, 163, 164, 167–8, 170, 174–6, 231
(1–8) 94, 99
(9–13) 95, 98, 111
(14–16) 96, 113
(17–24) 96, 99
(25–32) 96, 100
(33–8) 97, 98
(41–6) 97–9, 140, 143, 189–90
(49–56) 99–100, 109, 140, 189–90, 287
(57–64) 100–2, 189–90
(65–72) 102–5, 141, 259n66
(73–80) 103, 141
(81–2) 105
(91–6) 107, 287
(100–4) 108, 110, 113, 156, 158
(106–12) 110, 111, 129, 131, 156, 272
(113–20) 111, 174
emblem 106
(25 gloss) 157–8
(43 gloss) 98
(81 gloss) 105
(97 gloss) 108
(102 gloss) 108
Julye 164, 166
August 160, 163, 164, 166–7, 168, 170
(101) 163

(145–6) 173
(151–89) 204, 288
(190–3) 174, 201
(131 gloss) 173
September 164, 166
(91) 243–4
(136–9) 67
(177) 174
(254–7) 67
October 39, 163, 164, 168, 171–3
Argument 176, 179, 270
(25–30) 287–8, 291
(37–40) 9, 16, 35
(55–66) 172–3, 177
(83–4) 177, 232n13
(93–4) 179, 270
(96–8) 179
(109–18) 172
(1 gloss) 9, 173–4
(21 gloss) 176
(27 gloss) 165–6, 177, 288
(28 gloss) 35, 37
(65 gloss) 176–7
(93 gloss) 179–80
(113 gloss) 172
Nouember 38, 114, 135–58, 160, 164–6, 167, 168, 170, 183, 202, 222, 295
Argument 138, 140
(7–8) 136
(9–17) 136–7, 150–2, 157, 165
(30) 201
(31–2) 137
(43–4) 141
(50–1) 141
(67–8) 137, 156
(71) 189–90
(75–6) 139, 206
(77–9) 140, 208–9
(83–9) 139, 206
(93–102) 143–5

324 Index of works and passages

(108–9) 139, 140, 165, 207
(113–22) 141–2, 189–90
(124–9) 137
(133–5) 137
(136–7) 154
(143–7) 138, 207
(153–7) 142–3
(166–9) 153
(171–2) 140
(175–6) 153–6
(178–82) 153, 155, 158
(185–8) 154
(191) 154–5, 158
(193–9) 154
(16 gloss) 141, 150
(38 gloss) 138, 140–1
December 147, 160, 163, 164–5, 166, 170, 182
(45–6) 201
(91) 174
(143–4) 157
Viewe of the Present State of Ireland 266
'Virgils Gnat' 30–1, 35, 289

Theocritus, Idylls 17
(1) 22, 104, 135, 161, 165, 166, 184–5
(1.1–14) 284
(1.15–18) 136
(1.20) 18
(1.29–55) 18–19
(1.66–9) 197
(1.81–7) 190
(1.117) 201, 239
(1.140) 197–8
(1.141) 105
(2) 59, 60n35
(3) 18, 22, 52, 88
(3.1–7) 45–6, 53, 75, 133
(3.10–11) 54, 55
(3.22–3) 54
(3.25–6) 46
(3.34–6) 53
(3.52) 90
(5) 18
(7) 22, 73
(7.21–22) 55
(7.36) 18
(7.43–4) 278
(7.47–9) 18, 19
(7.71–8) 45, 106–7, 185, 205
(7.87–9) 52
(7.96–7) 126
(7.133–47) 51–2, 284
(11) 47–8, 53, 57, 75, 88, 90, 134, 249, 251, 253–4
(11.1–4) 22
(11.50–3) 250
(13) 18, 19
(15) 18, 213
(16) 18
(17) 18, 41n1
(17.1–4) 177–8, 232n13
(24) 18, 19
[Theocritus] (19) 24, 29

Virgil, Aeneid
(1.1a–d) (disputed Ille ego opening) 10, 182
(1.1) 23
(1.1–7) 96, 113
(1.201–2) 252
(1.328) 125
(2.199–227) 30
(2.740–95) 33–4
(3.420–8) 252
(3.559) 253
(3.565) 260n68
(3.570–82) 250, 251–2
(3.614–15) 257n64
(3.619–20) 251
(3.632) 251
(3.655–61) 252, 254–5
(3.664) 251

Index of works and passages 325

(3.678) 251
(3.670–4) 251, 254, 255–6
(3.683–5) 253
(3.690–1) 252
(3.694–6) 239–40, 253
(4) 23, 32, 146
(6) 23, 30
(6.472–4) 158
(6.748–51) 213
(6.847–53) 35
(8) 25
(12.952) 25

Eclogues
  (1) 16, 26, 41, 43, 79, 84–8,
      105, 134, 161, 170
  (1.1–5) 15, 25, 45–6, 52, 64,
      66, 74, 94, 95, 99–100,
      108–9, 112, 180, 228,
      281, 284, 287
  (1.6–8) 15, 27, 41n1, 71, 124,
      235
  (1.9–10) 95, 127
  (1.12–13) 85
  (1.16–17) 66
  (1.27–39) 46–50
  (1.31–5) 87–8, 93, 106
  (1.36–9) 220, 223
  (1.42) 161
  (1.45) 48
  (1.46–50) 95
  (1.51–8) 94–5
  (1.59–63) 62–4, 72, 224, 235,
      247n40
  (1.64–6) 95–6
  (1.67–9) 62
  (1.70–2) 61
  (1.73) 49, 76, 147
  (1.74–8) 62, 90
  (1.79–84) 25, 67
  (2) 22, 43, 75, 88, 133–4, 161,
      170–1
  (2.2) 89
  (2.5) 65
  (2.6–7) 22–3, 53, 59, 89
  (2.8–11) 54, 59n35
  (2.12–13) 54
  (2.14–15) 54
  (2.32–3) 91, 283
  (2.36–7) 167n10, 249
  (2.40–4) 53, 56–7, 88
  (2.45–50) 54, 56n31, 143
  (2.51–2) 54, 88, 98
  (2.56) 88, 142
  (2.69–73) 57, 88–9, 93, 174,
      242
  (3) 161, 173
  (3.33–4) 163
  (3.55–7) 284
  (3.60) 177
  (3.70–71) 54, 55, 77, 90
  (3.94–7) 74
  (3.109) 173
  (3.110) 241
  (4) 26, 38, 43, 77, 79, 114, 122,
      128, 130, 161, 166, 175
  (4.1–3) 11, 12–13, 15, 102–3,
      115, 269, 300
  (4.6) 69, 123–4
  (4.10) 69
  (4.17) 69
  (4.31–9) 260
  (4.53–9) 11, 26, 27, 33, 101,
      200, 201, 215, 262, 281,
      300
  (5) 11, 26, 38, 43, 79, 104, 114,
      135, 146–9, 152–3, 184,
      202, 222, 296–7
  structural centre of
    Eclogues 161, 163–5, 296
  (5.10–15) 136, 229
  (5.16–18) 137
  (5.20–3) 70, 74, 76, 223
  (5.24–8) 137, 223
  (5.34–9) 137, 205, 223
  (5.38–9) 74
  (5.40–1) 74

(5.43) 70, 291
(5.45–7) 286
(5.51–2) 70, 75, 135, 291
(5.56–80) 134, 155
(5.56–8) 285
(5.62–4) 33, 70, 72, 73, 205, 221, 223, 284–5
(5.65–73) 144, 147, 149, 154, 295
(5.76–80) 72, 73
(5.86–7) 73, 75
(5.88–90) 278
(6) 161, 174–5
(6.1–2) 17, 112, 240n25
(6.3–5) 11–12, 15, 16, 112–13, 124, 268
(6.6–8) 112, 278, 284
(6.29–30) 280, 281
(6.64–73) 13, 33, 39, 187–8, 199–201, 205, 215, 231, 278
(6.84–6) 175–6n20, 277, 284, 285, 295–6
(7) 161, 173
(7.1–13) 187, 262, 284
(7.53–60) 220
(7.70) 174
(8) 22, 26, 133–4, 161
(8.1–5) 13, 33, 279–80, 288, 291
(8.6–13) 13, 26, 27, 112, 171–2, 177, 232n13
(8.22–4) 280
(8.33) 89
(8.52–56) 33, 63, 279
(8.58–60) 63, 198
(8.69–71) 59, 290
(8.95–99) 59–60
(8.109) 59
(9) 16, 26, 27, 38, 41, 43, 73–7, 105–6, 135–6, 146–7, 161, 170
(9.2–3) 62

(9.5–6) 58–60
(9.7–13) 33, 63–4, 105–6, 132
(9.11–13) 33, 132
(9.14–16) 106
(9.19–20) 74
(9.23–5) 74–5, 133
(9.26–9) 26, 56, 75, 101, 134, 146, 153, 178, 277–8, 295–6
(9.39–43) 75
(9.46–50) 76, 134, 146–7, 153–5
(9.51–4) 77, 133
(9.67) 77
(10) 22, 24, 26, 34, 39, 104, 147, 164–5, 182–7, 221, 222, 228, 231, 236, 296–7
(10.1–3) 109–11, 186, 198, 200, 204, 225, 230, 238, 245
(10.4–6) 238–42, 245–6
(10.8) 109, 204
(10.9–12) 197–202
(10.13–15) 107, 205
(10.17–18) 214
(10.22–3) 108
(10.24–6) 284
(10.28–30) 90
(10.31–4) 110, 185–6, 204, 208, 271
(10.44–8) 263–4
(10.50–4) 186, 200, 228, 229, 271
(10.60–3) 90, 186, 200
(10.70–2) 13, 182, 201, 215, 225, 242
(10.73–4) 186, 228, 229
(10.75–6) 13, 15, 16, 180, 182, 265, 277
(10.77) 111, 182
Georgics 200
(3.8–9) 14, 15, 16

(3.10–17) 240, 290
(3.266–83) 34n80
(3.291–3) 34n80
(4) 33–6
(4.171–3) 256n62
(4.315–558) 33–4, 389–90
(4.433–6) 176n20
(4.559–62) 14
(4.563–6) 15, 16, 34,
    299–300

[Virgil]
  Ciris 29
  Culex 7, 30, 31, 35, 289
  Dirae 26, 48n19, 60–8, 178, 265
    (4–8) 62–5
    (18–19) 65
    (26–36) 61, 65–7
    (48–62) 63
    (80–3) 61–2
    (86–94) 62
    (98–101) 62

General index

Note: 'n' after a page reference indicates the number of a note on that page.

Achilles 14, 18, 21
Adkins 20n50, 254n56
Adonis 211–21, 222–3, 245
Aeneas 3, 14, 23, 25, 28, 30, 34–5, 70, 72n50, 96, 113–14, 125, 130, 158, 239–40, 251–7, 258n65, 260n68, 298
Aesop 31, 165
Alençon, François, Duc d' 9, 22, 38, 83, 108, 114, 135, 142, 145–6, 149–52, 158–9, 181, 207, 236n20
Alexander, Gavin 219n47
Alexiou, Margaret 213n36
Alexis 22, 43, 53–7, 59, 88–90, 91, 93, 98, 143
allegory
  avoiding censorship 9, 16, 30, 141, 233, 243–4
  Christianizing 72–3, 114–15, 134–5, 156, 295
  political suit as wooing 22–3, 38, 42–57, 61, 63, 65, 83–4, 87, 92–3, 98–9, 108, 133, 166, 171, 173, 178, 198, 229
  use of persona *see* Colin Clout; Cuddie; Menalcas (in Virgil); Tityrus (in Virgil)

Alpers, Paul 78n66, 94n21, 109n44, 111n47, 114n51, 137n84, 187n6
Alphesiboeus 13, 33, 59n35, 60n36, 64n40, 112, 171, 173, 280, 288, 290
Alpheus 238–53 *passim*
Amor (god) 19, 21, 24, 91, 212, 216, 218, 221, 232, 233, 236, 237, 241, 242, 244, 246, 257n63, 265, 269, 272, 274, 276, 277n79, 278, 292, 293, 294n104, 295, 299
Amoret 245
Anchises 35, 213, 253
Antony, Mark 102n30, 111, 236
Aphrodite *see* Venus
Apollo 12–13, 69, 70, 101, 103–4, 112, 124, 125, 169, 170, 190, 199–200, 214, 258–9, 268, 281n83, 284
Appian 41n2
Arcadia 26, 39, 168–9, 176, 185–7, 222, 239–40, 248n41, 257n63, 261–5, 297
Arethusa 238–48, 249, 261
Ariosto 23, 29
Aristaeus 33–5, 289, 298
Arnold, Janet 116n54

General index

ascent into heavens
  of Christian soul 152–8, 209–11
  of name 26, 56, 70, 75, 76–7, 146, 291
  of poet 8, 14, 15, 16, 37, 177–9, 181
  of potentate 14, 69–71, 75–7, 135, 146–7, 152–3, 178–9, 291
  of song 277, 296
  see also deification; hierarchy of genres; Virgilian career
Astraea 123
Augustus *see* Octavian
Austin, Roland G. 10n28
authority, poetic *see* poetic authority
authority, political *see* monarchy

Badius Ascensius 60n36
Baldwin, T. W. 2n5, 4n10
Balot, Ryan Krieger 240n25
Barchiesi, Alessandro 152n106, 169
Bates, Catherine 232n15
Bednarz, James P. 226n4, 230n10, 231n12
Benko, Stephen 72n54
Berger, Harry 98n25, 112n48
Bernard, John D. 24n60, 111
Bion of Smyrna 19, 21, 23, 24, 28, 100n28, 209, 213–17, 237n21, 239, 242, 277n79, 284n85, 287, 299
  see also Index of words and passages
Bloom, Harold 185n4, 215
Boccaccio 158n112
Bonfont 33, 247
Bonner, Stanley 2n4
Boyle, A. J. 68n44, 80n68
Breed, Brian 60n37
Bregog and Mulla 27n64, 29n72, 36, 39, 230, 238, 242–8, 251, 252n52, 257–8, 261, 275n78, 276, 277, 291, 296
Brennan, Michael 142n90
Brown, Georgia 28n69
Bryskett, Lodowick 27, 207, 267, 277n79
Burchmore, David W. 191, 244n35
Burghley, William Cecil, Lord 25, 31–2, 208, 243, 244, 246, 251, 258, 265
Burrow, Colin 8n22

Cain, Thomas H. 101, 120–1, 280
Cairns, Francis 48n17
calendar 147–9, 152–3, 155–7
Callimachean poetics 11–13, 19–20, 26–9, 103n33, 112, 240n25, 268, 277n79
Callimachus 11, 12, 19, 37, 200, 209
Calliope 21, 97, 100–3, 189, 279, 299
Calvus 28
Catullus 11, 12n33, 28, 29n72, 294
censorship 9, 16, 30–1, 33, 65, 67, 83, 270, 274
Chaghafi, Elizabeth 183n2
Chapman, Alison 152n105, 155n108
Chaucer 105, 158n112, 165
Chaudhuri, Sukantra 42nn5–6
Cheney, Patrick 2n2, 7n20, 8n23, 14n37, 103n34, 112n49, 183, 227n5, 229n7, 230, 252n52, 266nn74–5, 280n82, 296–7
Christ 72, 134–5, 156–7, 237, 295
Churchyard, Thomas 165
Cicero 49n21, 67n43, 71n51, 236
civil wars
  in England 121, 146, 155, 157
  in Rome 41, 49, 60, 145, 256n62
Clausen, Wendell 11n30, 13n36, 49, 91n15, 92n17, 109n44, 214n38, 241n29, 262n70, 284n86, 285nn87–9, 286n91

Coleman, Robert 58n34, 71n50, 100, 281n83
Colin Clout 9, 10, 25, 27n64, 36–40, 159, 166–8, 189–92, 201–3
  Orphic power 100, 179, 181, 223, 287, 290–2, 295–6
  as prophet 24, 237–8, 297–8
  and Virgil's Alexis 88–9
  and Virgil's Corydon 88–93, 108, 109n43, 170–1, 174
  and Virgil's Gallus 90–3, 108–11, 232, 238, 271–2, 276, 278–9, 288, 292
  and Virgil's Meliboeus 85–6, 87, 90, 92–3, 94–6, 111, 114, 170–1
  and Virgil's Menalcas 106, 132, 135–6, 291, 295
  and Virgil's Tityrus 85–8, 92, 97, 105, 170
Connolly, Joy 50n24
Conte, G. B. 34n78, 35n82
Cooper, Helen 42n6
Corydon 9, 22, 43, 53–7, 59, 63, 65, 75, 88–93, 98, 133, 142–3, 167n10, 187, 242, 249, 256–7, 262, 283
  see also Colin Clout; Cuddie
Craik, Katherine A. 7n21
Creusa 34–5
Cuddie 9, 35, 36, 37, 159, 162n9, 163, 164, 165, 171–4, 175, 177–81, 268–70, 287–8, 291
  as Spenser's *persona* 174
  and Virgil's Corydon 171–4
Cullen, Patrick 103n34, 131n81, 157n111
Cupid *see* Amor (god)
curse 26, 58–68, 80
cursus honorum see Rome
Cynthia (character in Spenser) 24, 37, 39, 40, 194, 202, 207, 218, 224–97 *passim*, 232–7, 268–72

Damon 13, 33, 63, 89, 90n13, 109n43, 112, 133, 134, 171, 173, 198, 232n13, 257, 279–80, 288
Daphnis (in Theocritus) 22, 70, 91, 104–7, 109n43, 165–6, 184–6, 190, 197, 201, 239, 279, 287
Daphnis (in Virgil) 70–6, 105–6, 135–8, 144–7, 152–4, 160–1, 165–6, 170, 184, 202, 205–6, 211, 220–3, 229, 284–5, 286n90, 291, 295–7
Dasenbrock, Reed Way 24n58, 193n14
decorum 5, 115–16, 124, 188, 255, 268–70
deification 14, 27, 56, 69–72, 75–7, 124–7, 129, 134–5, 144, 152–5, 177–8, 205, 223, 235–6, 265, 269–70, 274, 291, 295
Dekker, Thomas 120
DeNeef, Alexander Leigh 112n48
Devereux, Penelope, Lady Rich 195
Diana (goddess) 97, 125, 130, 169, 248n41
Dido (in Spenser) 114, 135, 137–46, 150, 152, 154–6, 158, 165, 189, 190, 205, 206, 209, 211, 217
  identity of 137–41
Dido (in Virgil) 3, 23, 146, 158, 242n32, 253, 257, 258n65, 298
Donatus 42n4, 70n47, 260
Donnelly, Michael L. 2n2
Dudley, Robert, Earl of Leicester 30, 142, 196
Dunlop, A. 162n7
DuQuesnay, I. M. 70n46
Durr, R. A. 157nn110–11

echo 99, 109–10, 186–7, 204–6, 228, 275

General index

and animation of landscape 280–5, 287–8, 291
Elder, J. P. 199n24
elegy, amatory 22, 39, 50, 91, 110, 231, 242, 246, 249–50, 258, 264, 294
elegy, funerary 39, 104–7, 109–10, 135–58, 165, 183–221, 222, 296
Ellrodt, Robert 244
E. K. 159–60, 246
   and Servius 82–3, 86, 141
   see also Index of words and passages
Elisa 97–8, 100–1, 114–35 *passim*, 138–9, 141, 143–4, 161, 206, 208, 257n64, 274, 279
Elizabeth I 1, 9, 22, 31–2, 37–8, 84, 87, 98, 101, 111–12, 114–15, 129, 138, 141, 179, 244, 266, 279
   censorship 83
   coronation 116–23, 128n77, 130, 135, 139, 207
   court 115, 188, 193–6, 201–2, 207–8, 224, 232–7, 243–4, 247, 251, 266–7, 275, 291, 298
   marriage plans 83, 93, 108, 114, 135, 142, 145–6, 149–59, 170, 181, 207
   patronage 224, 226, 230
   Petrarchism and 87, 99, 180, 226n3, 228n6, 231–7, 244–6, 261
   see also Cynthia; Dido (in Spenser); Elisa; monarchy; Ralegh; Rosalind; Spenser
Elyot, Sir Thomas 4, 5
Ennius 14, 17
Enterline, Lynn 3, 6n17, 28–9, 252n52
epic, heroic 1, 4, 8, 11–14, 17–22, 24, 26, 30, 37, 39, 41, 77n63, 178, 212, 221, 231, 248–60, 277n79, 298–9
epos, bucolic as variety of 17–22, 25, 37, 249, 298–300
epyllion 6n17, 7, 19–20, 27–33, 183, 216, 241, 252n52, 277n79
Erickson, Wayne 226n2, 227n5
Eros *see* Amor (god)
Errour 30n73
Esolen, Anthony 287n92
Estienne, Henri (Henricus Stephanus) 241n28
etiology 13, 200, 243, 277
Eurydice 33–6, 287–90
Evander 25, 240
exile 48–9, 58–60, 64, 77, 96, 113–14, 231–2, 257n64, 266

Falco, Raphael 183n2, 187, 191n10, 195n16, 196n18, 202, 211n32, 215, 216n42
Fantham, Elaine 104n37
Fantuzzi, Marco 18n41, 19n43, 19n45, 22n53, 28n66, 237n21
Farrell, Joseph 16–17, 20, 28n67, 249nn43–45, 250, 251, 254n55, 255, 256
Faunus 29, 33, 248n41
Feldherr, Andrew 104n39
Fishwick, D. 71nn51–52
Forster, Leonard 232n15
Fowler, Alistair 161, 162n7
freedom of speech 65–6, 104
   see also censorship; Marsyas
friendship 37, 109, 184–7, 205, 221, 227, 236, 266

Gaisser, Julia Haig 160n1
Galatea (in Ovid) 248–50, 252n52, 253, 255n57, 257–8
Galatea (in Spenser) 249n42

General index

Galatea (in Theocritus) 47–8, 75, 249, 256
Galatea (in Virgil) 29n72, 46–8, 50, 55, 60n35, 75, 87–8, 93, 99
Gale, Monica 34n77, 34n79, 35n83, 289n97
Gallus 13, 33–4, 39, 90–3, 108–11, 185–8, 197–202, 204–8 *passim*, 214–17 *passim*, 225, 228–32, 236, 238, 242, 246, 263–4, 276–9, 284, 289n97, 290n100, 296–8
  see also Colin Clout and Virgil's Gallus; elegy, amatory
Gascoigne, George 83
generic mixing 27, 36, 186–7, 242, 245–6, 248–60, 277
genre *see* hierarchy of genres; *epos*, bucolic; epic, heroic; generic mixing
Giamatti, A. Bartlett 234n18
gifts 58, 117–23, 145
  see also pastoral offerings
Goldberg, Jonathan 287n92
Golden Age 69–70, 72n53, 77, 101, 114, 115, 122–4, 135, 148, 259–60, 294n105
Greek bucolic tradition 3, 17–22, 37, 240–1, 256–7, 298–9
Greenlaw, Edwin 287n92
Graces 127
Greg, W. W. 42n6
Guenther, Genevieve 291n101
Gutzwiller, Kathryn 47n17

Haber, Judith 79n66
Hades 23, 30, 158, 260n68, 287–9
Hadfield, Andrew 86n7, 226n2
Halperin, Nicholas 18n40, 19, 20
Hamilton, A. C. 36
Hansen, Peter Allan 10n28
Hardie, A. 240n25
Hardie, Colin 187n7, 198n22

Hardie, Philip 14n37, 50n23, 85n5, 250n48, 258n65
Harrison, S. 187n7, 241n30, 242, 264n72
Harrison, T. P., Jr. 23n55, 185n3
Harvey, Gabriel 267
Helen of Troy 21, 126, 273–4
Helfer, Rebecca 7n20
Helgerson, Richard 2n2, 7n21, 24n60, 103n31, 103n34, 112n48, 195
Hercules 102n30
Herron, Tom 227n5
Hesiod 13, 20, 33, 200, 205, 278–9, 294n105
  see also Index of works and passages
Hessus, Eobanus 46n15, 53nn27–8, 54n29, 73n57, 177n21, 256n61
Hieatt, A. Kent 162n7, 169n16
hierarchy of genres 13, 17, 20, 24, 30–2, 36–7, 102–5, 113–14, 182, 187, 200, 221, 248, 256–60, 277, 279, 298–300
hierarchy, social 1, 5–6, 15, 24, 31, 37, 104, 113, 190, 225, 227, 232–7, 243, 250–1, 257n64, 261, 266, 299–300
hierarchy of styles 5–6, 30
Highley, Christopher 261n69, 267n76, 291n101
Hinds, Stephen 46n14
Hippocrene 21, 239, 299
Hobbinol 88–9, 94–111 *passim*, 125, 128–32, 220, 223, 267, 273
  and Virgil's Corydon 88
  and Virgil's Tityrus 94–6, 111
Hoffman, Nancy Jo 97n24
Holzberg, Niklas 50n23
Homer 4, 17–22, 44
  see also Index of works and passages

hope 93, 106, 114, 118–20, 128, 130–2, 134, 139, 143–7, 153, 155, 170
Hopper, V. F. 169n17
Horace 11, 12n33, 169
  see also Index of works and passages
Horsfall, N. M. 2n4, 42n4
Hubbard, T. K. 47, 96, 112n49, 172n18
Hughes, Merritt Y. 23n55, 139n86, 185n3
Hulls, Jean-Michel 2n4
Hume, Anthea 131n81
Hunter, Richard 13n35, 19n43, 20n49
hymn 36, 70, 72, 75–6, 97, 144, 165, 177–9, 212, 238, 278, 280n82, 291–2

imitation
  and friendship 185–7, 228, 230
  and immortality 217
immortality 39, 126, 129, 135, 208–9
Ireland 26, 36, 40, 224–6, 229, 232, 249n42, 257, 260–67, 291n101

Jacobson, Howard 290n100
James, Paula 104n39
Jenkyns, Richard 42n4
Johnson, Lynn Staley 86n7, 157n111
Johnson, W. C. 193n14
Johnson, W. Ralph 80n68
Jones, A. R. 87n9
Jonson, Ben 120
Julius Caesar 69–72, 75–7, 105, 135, 138, 145–55 *passim*, 160–5 *passim*, 170, 211, 221, 223, 229 256n62, 295
  and Roman calendar 147–9
Jupiter 32, 60, 66, 72n53, 250

Kallendorf, Craig 158n112
Kelsey, Lynn 208n28, 243, 246
Kennedy, Duncan 242n31
Klein, J. L. 24n58, 193n14
Kolb, J. L. 155n108
Koller, Katherine 226n2
Kyriakidis, S. 35n83

land-confiscations *see* Octavian
Lane, Robert 103, 126n74, 152n105
Leach, Eleanor Windsor 12n34
Leahy, William 120n68, 128n77
Lee, M. O. 34n79, 289n98
Leicester, Earl of *see* Dudley, Robert
Libertas
  personification in *Eclogues* 47, 127
  political slogan 49–50
  republican ideal 49, 67, 104
  see also freedom of speech; political independence; Tityrus (in Virgil's *Eclogues*), slave-status
Lindheim, Nancy 147–8
literary career, idea of 16–17
locus amoenus 50–2, 55, 94–7, 284, 287
Lodge 27, 252n52
Loewenstein, Joseph 36n84, 289n96
Lord, M. L. 158n112
love
  anti-eroticism in Virgil 3, 22, 221, 241, 246, 256–7, 298–9
  as bucolic subject 3, 18, 21–4, 41, 43, 256–7, 299
  celebrated by Spenser 23–4, 36–7, 39, 191–3, 213, 218, 221, 237–8, 242–6, 275–9, 298, 301
  neoplatonic 179–80, 192, 210
  as pathology 22, 36, 52, 185–7, 293–4, 299
  veil for social ambition 194–5,

199, 233, 243–6
  see also allegory; Amor (god); elegy, amatory; Petrarchism
Low, Anthony 7n19
Luborsky, R. S. 82nn1–2, 84
Lucid 268, 273–5
Lucretius
  on love 292–4
  on pastoral music 282–3
  and religion 282–6
Lyne, R. O. A. M. 80n68, 253n53

McCabe, Richard 36, 82n2, 85n5, 93n20, 107n41, 114n51, 116, 130nn, 146n94, 179, 261n69, 288–9
MacCaffrey, Isabel 157n111
McCarthy, Penny 82n2
McFaul, Tom 218n45, 219n46
McLane, Paul 86, 108, 114n52, 138n85, 145–6, 149–51
Macrobius 147n98, 258n65
Maley, Willy 86n7
Mallette, Richard 112n48, 157n111
Mancinelli, Antonio 46n12
Mantuan, Baptista Spagnuoli 4, 31, 165
Manutius, Paulus 55n30, 69
Marlowe, Christopher 27
Marot, Clément 137–8, 139n86
Marotti, A. F. 87n9, 98, 232n15
Marshall, Peter K. 42n5
Marsyas 104, 190
Maury, Paul 160, 168n11
Melibee 224
Meliboeus 25, 27, 46–68 *passim*, 84, 105, 112, 113, 147, 159, 174, 176, 223, 224, 226, 256n62, 265, 281
  see also Colin Clout and Virgil's Meliboeus
Melissa 272–3
Menalcas (in Spenser) 108

Menalcas (in Virgil) 26, 70–7 *passim*, 98, 106, 132, 147, 284–6, 295
  see also Colin Clout and Virgil's Menalcas
Mercury 32–3
Midas 104, 258–9
Miles, G. B. 34n78
Miles, Geoffrey 214n37
Miller, David Lee 2n2, 24n60
Milton, John 37, 240–1, 298
Minturno, Antonio 18
Moeris 27, 33, 50n22, 58–60, 62, 63–4, 68, 73–7, 106, 132–3, 147, 159, 256n62, 291
Mole 238–58 *passim*
monarchy
  contractual 80–1, 84, 122, 134–5, 145–6
  divine 31, 70, 73, 81, 84, 120, 122, 126
  duties of monarch 117–20, 122, 128, 132, 134, 142
  Roman attitude to 69–70, 71
Montaigne 169
Montrose, Louis Adrian 2n2, 87n8, 97, 114n51, 120, 128, 225
Moore, Helen 14n37
More, Thomas 83
Moschus (and pseudo-Moschus) 19, 24, 28
  see also Index of works and passages
Most, Glenn 7n22
Mulcaster, Richard 116–24
Mulla *see* Bregog and Mulla
Muses 12, 13, 35, 39, 97, 100–5, 111, 116, 120, 130, 138, 139, 163, 187, 198, 200–2, 205, 206, 215, 221, 222, 225, 231, 238–40, 242, 264n72, 278, 286n90, 288, 296n106, 298
Mustard, W. P. 27n65

Nagle, Betty Rose 50n23
Nashe, Thomas 27
neoteric poetry 11, 12, 13, 20, 28, 29, 44
Neuse, Richard 2n2, 7n18
Niobe 125–6, 236
Nohrnberg, James 227n5
number 39, 147–9, 166–70, 175

O'Connell, Michael 23n55, 185n3, 187, 235n19, 245
Octavian 1, 3, 6, 13, 43, 56–7, 58, 60, 65, 67, 92, 102n30, 148, 152, 169, 173, 177, 180, 198
   and divinity 14, 27, 56, 69–72, 77, 178, 101–2, 122, 177–8, 265
   emphasis on religion 286
   land-confiscations 16, 22–3, 26, 30, 41, 43, 48–50, 55, 56, 60–8, 73–7, 93, 105–6, 114, 132–3
   see also civil wars in Rome; Virgil and Octavian
Oram, William 226n2, 227n5, 230, 231n11, 232n14, 233n16, 244–5
Orpheus 11, 33–7, 40, 63, 101, 199n24, 200–1, 205–6, 220, 223, 275, 278–82, 286–92, 295–6, 298, 300
   sacrificed to Augustan values in Georgics 33–5, 289–90
   successful katabasis in Spenser 35–6, 289–90
Otis, Brooks 78n64, 160n1, 161, 175n19
otium 15, 50–3, 65–7, 97, 99, 127, 224, 299–300
Ovid 12n33, 27–30, 36, 39, 50, 183, 185, 239, 248–59 passim, 260n68, 265n73
   see also Index of works and passages

Pan 11, 21, 90, 91, 97, 101, 103–4, 115, 120–1, 134, 136, 141, 185, 190, 201, 209, 216, 258–9, 262, 280–4 passim, 286n90, 299, 300
Parmenter, Mary 142n89, 149n101
Parry, Adam 25n63
'pastoral' and 'bucolic' (terminology) 17–21
pastoral and Golden Age 259–60, 294n105
pastoral as political negotiation 26–27, 38, 56–60, 61, 75–81, 84, 93, 98, 105–6, 134, 177–9, 181, 224, 265, 273
   see also hope; pastoral offerings; political critique; political praise; power of song, polemical
pastoral community 109–12, 143, 202–3, 219–21, 222–4, 228, 295, 298
   egalitarianism 37, 39, 236, 266–8
   piety 235, 265–7
   respect for poet 265–8, 272–3
   vulnerability 41, 48–50, 68, 132–4, 154–8, 224, 250, 258
   see also friendship; poet, social role of
pastoral offerings 80–1, 84, 189–91, 224
   conditional 56–7, 59, 84, 93, 118–20
   extorted by force 49n21, 59, 77, 80
   funeral offerings 84, 138–40, 145, 206–7
   market produce 47, 87
   poems as gifts 43, 48, 55, 56, 59, 77, 80–1, 89, 97, 105, 139–40, 145–6, 186–7, 224–5
   sacrifice 55, 59, 80, 84, 124, 126, 127, 135, 144, 225

symbols of political contract 38
tributes to potentates 43, 48, 55, 58, 84, 105, 116, 139, 206–7, 225
wooing-gifts 38, 43, 53–5, 80–1, 84, 87, 98, 105, 140, 143–4
see also gifts; hope; pastoral as political negotiation
pastoral settings 24, 26, 36, 39–40, 60, 62, 66–7, 74, 187–8, 249n42, 226–7, 248, 261–8
see also Arcadia; Ireland; *locus amoenus*; Sicily
patronage 10, 39, 56, 94, 97–8, 112, 143–5, 172–3, 177, 180–1, 224–6, 235, 265, 272, 275
see also Elizabeth I, patronage; Spenser, Edmund, patronage by Elizabeth I
Patterson, Annabel 31n74, 42n5, 85n4
payment 47, 48, 127–8, 131–2, 143–4, 275
see also gifts; pastoral offerings
Pease, A. S. 158n112
Perkell, Christine 35n83, 92n17, 110n46
Peterson, Richard S. 33n76
Petrarch 1n1, 42, 87, 92, 126, 158n112, 179–80, 192, 218, 235
Petrarchism 24, 39, 87, 88, 89, 92, 127, 129, 187, 192–3, 218, 221, 226n3, 231–3, 236–8, 244–6, 261
see also Elizabeth I, Petrarchism and
Philotime 235–6
Pigman, G. W. 139n86
Poggioli, Renato 263n71
Platonic *furor poeticus* 34, 36, 176, 179
poet, divinely inspired 12, 24, 34, 36, 177–9, 181, 200–2, 210–13, 215–16, 220–1, 231, 237–8, 268, 272, 278–9, 298
see also prophetic pastoral
poetic authority 1–2, 15, 24, 27, 32–3, 37, 84, 181, 183, 203, 223, 267–8, 297
poetry as recreation 195, 197, 208, 222, 238, 265
poet, social role of 8, 24, 29, 31, 34, 36, 39–40, 166, 196–7, 202, 220–1, 222, 297
see also pastoral as political negotiation; prophetic pastoral
political critique and satire 30–2, 38, 39, 65–8, 93, 110–13, 156–8, 164–6, 175–6, 181, 183, 208, 232–7, 243–7, 265–6, 268, 272–4, 298
in Virgil's *Eclogues* 9, 16, 22, 26, 43, 48–50, 53n26, 59, 61, 65, 68, 73–8, 83–4
political independence 24–6, 27, 35, 40, 224, 261, 265
political praise and propaganda 1, 14, 16, 24, 26, 38, 39, 56–7, 65, 67, 68–81, 84, 93, 98, 101–2, 112, 114–15, 122, 134–5, 146, 156, 161, 168–9, 175, 177–9, 224, 268–72, 275, 300
Pollio, Asinius 6, 13n36, 43, 69, 101, 102, 269
Polyphemus
in Homer 249, 250, 251n51, 276
in Ovid 248–58, 276
in Theocritus 47–8, 57, 249, 250, 251, 256, 257
in Virgil 251–8, 260n68
Pompeius, Sextus 49, 57n33, 256n62, 262
Powell, Anton 57n33, 79–80, 102n30, 256n62

power of song
  emotive 166, 203
  magical 59–60, 290–1
  polemical 57, 60, 77, 79, 84, 111, 273, 290–1
  therapeutic 57
  see also authority, poetic; curse; Orpheus
Prescott, Anne Lake 24n58
Prescott, H. W. 104n38
Probus 73–4
Propertius 11, 12n33, 91n16, 240n25
prophecy, Virgilian 11, 23, 32, 40, 69, 123, 298
  see also allegory, Christianizing
prophetic pastoral 24, 37, 39–40, 181, 272, 298
prosopopoeia 33, 36, 250, 291
  see also echo and animation of landscape
Protestantism 6n17, 24, 38, 83, 108, 130, 145, 155–9, 164, 196, 207
Ptolemy II 41n1, 177
Pugh, Syrithe 7n20, 23n56, 104n35, 208n29, 209n31, 278n80
Putnam, Michael 25n61, 68n44, 80n68, 289n97
Puttenham, George 5–6, 9, 11, 17, 43, 44, 233n17

Ralegh, Walter 39, 184, 197, 224–32, 236–7, 246, 257n64, 260, 267, 297
  marriage 228–9, 230, 244–5
Rambuss, Richard 7n21
Ramus, Petrus 46n12
recusatio 11–13, 33, 38, 101–5, 112–13, 171–81, 277–8, 300
Redcrosse 23, 30n73
Reed, J. D. 22n53, 23n55, 214
Republic of Letters 40, 265

Richardson, J. M. 150–1
Roche, T. P. 192nn12–13
Rome 1, 3, 113–14, 265
  cursus honorum 14–15, 17, 26, 31, 37
  and Greek culture 14, 240–1
  pedagogy 2, 12, 15
  republicanism 49, 67, 70
  see also civil wars in Rome
Rosalind 38, 86–9, 93, 110–11, 126–7, 140–1, 189–90, 204, 231–2, 268, 272–8
Rosenberg, D. M. 94n21, 103n32, 147n96
Rosenmeyer, Thomas G. 42n6, 263n70
Ross, David 11n30, 13n35, 28n66, 92n17, 109n44, 199n24, 281n84
Røstvig, Maren-Sofie 162n7
round-trip journeys 46–50, 73–4, 86, 87, 223–4, 232, 246, 260

satire *see* political critique and satire
Schmidt, Ernst 18n39
Scylla 28, 29n72, 252–3, 258n65
Shafer, Robert 213n35
Segal, Charles 34n79, 78n66, 289n98
Servius 16, 18, 20, 38, 41–4, 61, 63, 67–8, 74, 141
  see also Index of Works and Passages
Servius Danielis 13n36, 16, 41n3, 70n48, 76n61, 169
Shore, David 87n8, 96n22, 139n86
Sicily 36, 42n6, 53n26, 57n33, 238–9, 242, 248–57, 261, 262, 265
Sidney, Mary 202
Sidney, Philip 17, 39, 42–3, 68, 80, 83, 93, 145–6, 155, 183–223

passim, 230, 233, 234, 264, 267, 291n101, 297
Silenus 33, 175, 199, 277–8, 280–1, 284–5
Sinfield, Alan 192n13
Singleton, Hugh 83
Skutsch, F. 110n35, 185n5
Skutsch, O. 160n1, 168n11, 169n13
Smith, Peter L. 67n43
Snell, Bruno 263n71
Spargo, J. W. 61n39
Spenser, Edmund
  censorship of *Complaints* 33
  collaborative authorship of *Colin Clouts Come Home Againe* volume 184, 267
  education 5, 44, 117
  friendship with Ralegh 224–5, 230
  illustrations to *Shepheardes Calender* 82, 84–5, 115–16, 150, 153, 164
  in Ireland 225–6, 265–6
  marriage to Elizabeth Boyle 191, 244–5, 276
  patronage by Elizabeth I 180, 230
  print readership 183, 203, 265
  structure of *Shepheardes Calender* 38–9, 147, 159–81
  unity and structure of *Colin Clouts Come Home Againe* volume 183–4, 296–7
Statius 2n4
Stesichorus 126–7, 274
Strong, Roy 152n106
Stubbes, John 83, 155
Suetonius 71n51
Syme, Ronald 49n20

Tarrant, R. J. 2n3
Tasso, Bernardo 27n65

Tennenhouse, Leonard 226n3
Theocritus 17–22, 28, 36–7, 38, 41, 42, 44–57 *passim*, 70, 73–5, 81, 240, 248, 262, 265
  see also Index of Works and Passages
Theodorakopoulos, Elena 11n29, 25
Thomas, R. F. 2n3, 11n31, 141n87, 255–6
Tityrus (in Spenser) 9, 105–7, 223
Tityrus (in Theocritus) 45, 47, 53
Tityrus (in Virgil) 25, 41, 62–8, 112
  loves of 43, 46–50, 52, 54, 55
  lowliness 12, 33, 279
  otium 25, 43, 50–3, 65–7
  ruler-worship 27, 41n1, 55, 56, 59, 65, 68, 71, 97, 112–13, 124–9 *passim*, 176
  slave-status 47–50, 65, 89, 98–9, 127, 265
  as Virgil's persona 9, 15, 49, 73, 106, 223
  see also Colin Clout and Virgil's Tityrus
Tromly, F. B. 267n77
Tudeau-Clayton, Margaret 2n5, 3, 5–6, 61n39
Tufte, Virginia 108n42
Tylus, Jane 7n19

Una 23, 234
Underworld *see* Hades

Van der Noodt, Jan 123
Van Sickle, John 17n39, 64–5, 113n50, 160n1, 161n5, 162n8, 167n10, 168–9, 175n19, 239n23, 240n26
Varus 26, 56, 70n47, 75, 76, 77, 101, 112, 113, 146, 153, 178, 277–8
Venus 19, 21, 22, 70, 211–12, 213, 237, 277n79, 292–3, 299

Virgil
  Callimachean poetics in *Eclogues* 11–13, 20, 26, 112, 175, 199n24, 200, 268, 281n83
  career as 'the Book of Virgil' 10–16, 25–7
  commentary tradition 22–3, 38, 42–4, 69, 82–3, 92, 198–9, 236
    see also Servius in Index of Works and Passages
  escapism and nostalgia in 25–7, 175–6, 262–3, 265, 297
  and Octavian 1, 14–16, 22–3, 26, 35, 56–60, 79, 93, 98, 180, 265, 286, 289–90, 298, 300n109
  in pedagogy 2–6, 15–16, 24, 28, 44
  structure of *Eclogues* book 39, 148, 160–2, 296
Virgilian career 1, 3, 6, 7, 10–16, 31, 37, 39, 177–8, 181, 182, 187, 200, 221, 248, 265, 277, 279, 289–90, 297–8
  ideological implications 3, 7, 9, 22, 24, 25, 28–9, 40, 183, 289–90, 299–300
  Spenser's revision of 7–10, 24, 29, 33, 40, 181, 221, 260, 261, 300–1
  see also hierarchy of genres; hierarchy of styles
vita activa 3–5, 24, 28, 29, 31, 35, 67, 195–6, 198, 226, 265, 300
  see also Elizabeth I, court; Rome, *cursus honorum*; Spenser, in Ireland
vita contemplativa 24, 35, 39, 198, 225–6, 257, 265, 300
  see also poet, social role of
Vives, Ludovico 50n24, 56n31, 70n47, 71, 87n10, 92, 156, 198–9, 202, 236, 264n72, 295
Volk, Katherina 78n65

Walker, S. F. 87n8
Wallace, Andrew 3n5
Williams, Gordon 79n66
Williams, Mary Frances 72n53
Williams, R. D. 252n53, 255n57, 255n59, 256n60, 256n62
Williamson, Colin 187n9
Wilson-Okamura, David Scott 2n2, 42n5, 213n35
Worden, Blair 31nn74–5

Yates, Frances 123n73

Zanker, Paul 68n44

EU authorised representative for GPSR:
Easy Access System Europe, Mustamäe tee 50,
10621 Tallinn, Estonia
gpsr.requests@easproject.com

www.ingramcontent.com/pod-product-compliance
Lightning Source LLC
Chambersburg PA
CBHW030316240426
43673CB00040B/1181